Pottery and People

D1567610

Foundations of Archaeological Inquiry

Pottery and People
A Dynamic Interaction

Edited by

James M. Skibo and Gary M. Feinman

THE UNIVERSITY OF UTAH PRESS
SALT LAKE CITY

Foundations of Archaeological Inquiry
James M. Skibo, editor

Library of Congress Cataloguing-in-Publication Data

Pottery and people : a dynamic interaction / edited by James M. Skibo
    and Gary M. Feinman.
        p.   cm. — (Foundations of archaeological inquiry)
    Includes bibliographical references (p.   ) and index.
    ISBN 0-87480-576-7 (cloth : acid-free paper). —
    ISBN 0-87480-577-5 (paper : acid-free paper)
    1. Pottery—Themes, motives.   2. Pottery—Analysis.   3. Indian
pottery.   4. Pottery, Ancient.   I. Skibo, James M.   II. Feinman,
Gary M.   III. Series.
GN433.P68   1998   98-38075
306.4'7—dc21

Contents

Figures

List of Tables

Acknowledgments

The chapters of this book were first presented as papers at the "Pottery and People Conference" held at Illinois State University, October 19–22, 1996. Everyone except Michael Schiffer and Barbara Stark participated in the conference, which involved short presentations followed by lively discussion. The original idea for the conference is shared by a number of people, including Dean Arnold, Philip Arnold, James Brown, Gary Feinman, and James Stoltman, who believed that we should take advantage of the relatively large number of prestigious archaeological pottery specialists who reside at Midwestern universities. I was invited to present a paper at Northwestern University's monthly colloquia where James Brown and I discussed the need to have a conference to take advantage of this happy coincidence of pottery specialists in the Midwest. After subsequent communications with other participants, I wrote a proposal to hold the conference on the campus of Illinois State University.

This volume was made possible through both the hard work and generous financial support of many people. First, I would to thank Gary Feinman for his fine work as a co-editor. The high quality of this volume's finished product has a lot to do with Gary's skills as an editor. Jeff Grathwohl, director of the University of Utah Press, had the foresight to understand the importance of the volume and he generously provided partial funding for the conference. His guidance and well-placed advice also contributed to a rapid turnaround from manuscript to published book. Financial support was also provided by several Illinois State University departments and programs. Robert Young, director of the University Research Office, Paul Schollart, dean of the College of Arts and Sciences, and Robert Walsh and Nicholas Maroules, former and present chair of the Department of Sociology and Anthropology, provided funds to support the conference. Conference volunteer help was provided by the Society for Student Anthropologists at Illinois State University, and Rodney Donaldson, an anthropology student assistant, needs to be especially commended for his work before and during the conference. Robert Dirks, Anthropology Program coordinator, Charles Orser and other members of the anthropology program also provided help and support. Ann Cohen, associate dean of the College of Arts and Sciences, Mickey McCombs, administrative assistant for the Department of Sociology and Anthropology, and the rest of the college and departmental staff provided invaluable assistance during the conference preparation. Finally, I would like to thank the participants who not only met deadlines with minimal prodding but also worked hard to make the conference and volume a success.

Pottery and People

James M. Skibo

A nonarchaeologist would probably be astounded to learn the amount of time and effort prehistorians spend on the study of broken pieces of pottery. We analyze individual sherds even to the molecular level and fill out page after page with measurements of minutia that would appear to most people as unimportant and certainly uninteresting. But what outsiders do not immediately understand is that archaeologists discovered long ago that these details collected on each piece of fired clay are our window into the lives of those who made and used these vessels. What did they eat? How many people lived in a house? How did they organize themselves? Who were their trading partners? These are just some of the questions that have been addressed through detailed analysis of prehistoric pottery.

But the elevated status of ceramics in archaeology cannot be transferred to their prehistoric makers and users. It is likely that prehistoric people would also be surprised by our focus on pottery, which is just one of the many types of material culture that is part of the lives of traditional people. In many societies, past and present, pottery is rather insignificant, a regular and often quite invisible part of everyday life (Trostel 1994). What is more, potters are often of low status and attempt to eke out a life by making pottery when other opportunities are not available (Foster 1965; Kramer 1985:80; Longacre, this volume, Chapter 4; Rice 1987: 172; Si-

nopoli, this volume, Chapter 8). But because pottery is often regular and common, it is a link to the lives of everyday people—the focus of much archaeological research. Moreover, pottery, once it appears prehistorically, becomes one of the most frequently recovered artifacts, and it has remarkable preservation once broken into sherds.

Pottery, then, is both a unique and ideal artifact. Pottery is made frequently, broken often, has excellent preservation, and it can be made into endless varieties to meet various social or economic needs. But has pottery been overstudied? One need only read Rice's (1996a, 1996b) reviews of ceramic analysis to understand the explosion of pottery studies in archaeology. Thus, has everything interesting now been discovered? Certainly not. Remarkably, more is being learned everyday about the relationship between pottery and people. Although Rice makes clear the many advances in ceramic analysis, she also demonstrates that there are unresolved and understudied questions as well. Her review concludes with the statement, "More research is needed" (Rice 1996b:191).

Pottery, like any piece of material culture, is woven into the complex tapestry of people's lives. People make pottery vessels and then distribute, use, break, and discard them in the archaeological record all in the context of their everyday life. The contributors to this volume probe deeply into the relationship between pottery and people, and not only make new discoveries through traditional lines of inquiry, but in some cases provide methodological breakthroughs and expose innovative new areas for research.

POTTERY AND PEOPLE

Humans are unique in that we cannot be considered apart from our material culture. Our work, our pleasure, and all behaviors between, both past and present, are accomplished with our artifacts. The term "material culture" is a revealing way to refer to pottery and all other artifacts because it highlights a unique dual existence. Artifacts have both a physical (material) and metaphysical (cultural) existence and, consequently, have been studied from wide-ranging perspectives in both the hard and soft sciences. Archaeology, a discipline that focuses on the relationship between artifacts and people, is, by necessity, interdisciplinary; it is considered within the social sciences, humanities, physical sciences, and natural sciences (Hodder 1992:11; Kingery 1996a). This schizophrenic existence is especially visible in pottery studies in which the pottery analyst must often lead a dual personality. To measure the formal variability of pottery, chemically source the clay, or perform residue analysis, we must call to the fore our hard science background, whereas to explain and interpret our data we may resort to our second personality as social and behavioral scientist. This can be a real problem, however, because archaeologists are pressured early in their careers to be more hard- or soft-science oriented and there is often a lack of communication between specialties (Feinman 1989). Although this struggle between "objectivism" and "relativism" is not new to archaeology (Wylie 1993), our discipline is becoming increasingly dominated by factions of researchers and often a good deal of "cross-disciplinary friction" (De Atley and Bishop 1991:361). Scholars in each faction have their own journals, national meetings, and increasingly find it difficult to communicate to archaeologists outside their own group. Prown (1996) has referred to this problem as the age-old dispute between the "cowman and farmer," with the farmer being the hard scientist and the cowman the soft scientist. Prown (1996:26) argues both groups must come to a mutual understanding that reality probably lies somewhere in the middle. Clearly, pottery analysts, and all archaeologists, cannot escape the fact that we will always need to straddle the ever-widening divide between the hard and soft sciences. Since we cannot cure our schizophrenia, it is wise to learn to live with it.

One way to integrate the various disciplines in the study of pottery is by employing a life-history approach (see Schiffer 1995a: 55–66; Walker and LaMotta 1995). Pottery life-history consists of three primary stages: manufacture and distribution, use, and discard (a more complete life history would include secondary reuse, like storing grain in an old cooking pot, and recycling a vessel or sherds for various uses). In each of these three stages a researcher often employs various hard and soft science techniques to find the people behind the pots. The following chapters are also organized according to these vessel life-history categories.

MANUFACTURE AND DISTRIBUTION

The organization of ceramic production is a particularly useful index into prehistoric economies because it can be made along a wide manufacturing continuum from the household to full-time craft industries (Mills and Crown 1995:1–16; Rice 1987:176–191). Archaeologists, therefore, strive to learn where the pottery was made, how it was made, and who it was made for. But as Sinopoli (Chapter 8) clearly demonstrates, finding production locations is often quite difficult. Others (e.g., Stark 1985; Sullivan 1988) have found it equally frustrating to locate household pottery-making locations, so archaeologists are often left to infer the level of production from the composition of the vessels themselves.

Compositional Studies.

At the core of compositional studies is the assumption that local or nonlocal pottery manufacture is an index of the level of ceramic production (i.e., from household production to full-time craft specialization) or the nature of pottery distribution (see Rice 1996b:166–173 for a review). Archaeologists are quick to embrace new techniques but experience has taught us that mistakes are common in the initial applications (Plog and Upham 1989). When problems do arise it often can be traced back to the fact that either the non-archaeologist performing the analysis does not understand archaeological data, or the prehistorian treats the analytical technique as a mysterious black box (see also De Atley and Bishop 1991; van Zelst 1991). The most successful applications occur when the prehistorian either makes a serious attempt to understand the details of a particular technique and perform the analysis themselves (e.g., Abbott and Walsh-Anduze 1995; Bishop et al. 1988) or finds a collaborator who understands archaeological data (e.g., Zedeño 1994).

There is also a growing consensus that "low-tech" methods like petrography often are sufficient to answer many questions about production location, and that a good analytical strategy is to first examine ceramics petrographically before employing more costly techniques (Tite 1995:171). Stoltman (Chapter 2; 1989, 1991) has played an important role in resurrecting petrography, which is a technique first introduced to archaeology by Anna Shepard (1956). In Chapter 2, Stoltman demonstrates the power of petrography by analyzing thin sections, actually prepared by Anna Shepard, from Chaco Canyon vessels. Chaco Canyon, located in northwestern New Mexico, was the center of an important series of large sites that reached their height of power between A.D. 900 and 1140. Scholars have long debated this anomalous aggregation of people, and pottery analysis has played an important role in the various economic and social models. Based on a preliminary analysis, Shepard found that the temper from many Chaco vessels comes from the Chuska Mountains located 70–80 km to the west. One unanswered question, however, was whether the finished pots or the temper were being transported to Chaco Canyon. To address this question,

Stoltman examined the minerals in the clay fraction of the vessels with Chuskan temper. He is able to provide more data to support Shepard's hypothesis that whole vessels were being made in the Chuska Mountains and then transported to Chaco Great Houses, possibly as part of periodic public ceremonies.

Pottery Learning.
The American Southwest and pottery analysis took center stage in the late 1960s and early 1970s in the first case studies of the "New Archaeology." Sometimes referred to as "ceramic sociology" (Hill 1970; Longacre 1970), these analyses, inspired by the teachings of Lewis Binford (1962) are best known for ushering in a new era in American archaeology (Longacre and Skibo 1994). But what is important in the context of this volume is that these researchers, in their attempt to make archaeology more anthropological, inferred more about the people who were making and using the vessels. Longacre (1970) and Hill (1970), for example, attempted to discover, through an analysis of pottery designs, marital residence rules in twelfth-century northeastern Arizona. At the core of their argument were two important assumptions related to ceramic production; they assumed that women were the potters and that mothers taught daughters how to make vessel designs. Although the studies by Longacre and Hill inspired a great deal of debate and reanalysis (e.g., Lischka 1975; Schiffer 1989; Skibo et al. 1989a), one topic that was rarely discussed again in the Southwest was how individuals learned pottery-making. Patricia Crown in Chapter 3 revisits this issue with an innovative investigation of the age at which children were taught pottery manufacture and decoration. She devises a method, which assesses motor skills and cognitive ability, to determine the age of learning among the makers of Mimbres Black-on-white, Salado Polychrome, and Hohokam Red-on-buff. Although it is well known that pottery-making is often learned by children and that they also can play a large role (e.g., gathering clay, helping in firing) in household pottery manu-

facture (Kramer 1985:79), Crown points out that "children are among the most ignored individuals in our reconstructions of the prehistoric Southwest." Crown presents a method, which can and should be more widely applied, to get a glimpse at prehistoric child socialization and the organization of ceramic production.

Production, Specialization, and Standardization.

Three contributors to this volume (D. Arnold, Feinman, and Longacre) explore the important issue of pottery production and specialization. The topic of specialization has received so much attention, both prehistorically and ethnoarchaeologically, because it is a core concept for understanding the rise of more complex forms of political and social organization (Rice 1996b). In a recent review article, Rice (1991) assesses the state of pottery specialization studies since she proposed a model for the evolution of specialized production (i.e., Rice 1981). She concludes that archaeologists have moved forward in their ability to infer production organization from pottery, "but not far" (Rice 1991:279). One reason for the lack of real progress is that sometimes it is a long leap to go from measurements of metrical properties analyzed with various statistical tests of diversity or standardization of the product, to inferences of the level of production organization. But the three papers in this volume make great strides toward better understanding this connection.

Ethnoarchaeology has the greatest potential to enable us to understand ceramic production organization and other relationships between pottery and people because of its ability to observe both the behaviors and the material consequences. No two individuals have contributed more to our understanding of the relationship between pottery and people from an ethnographic perspective than William Longacre and Dean Arnold. In this volume, using data from regions where they have had ongoing research for over a quarter of a century, both Longacre and Arnold examine issues related to production

organization and specialization. Based on fieldwork among a group of specialized potters from the Philippine Island of Luzon, Longacre (Chapter 4) explores the issue of potter's skill for understanding vessel standardization, which is an important and often-used index of specialization. He does find that the skill of the potter (i.e., older and more experienced versus younger and less experienced) does significantly affect vessel standardization.

On the other side of the globe, D. Arnold (Chapter 5) explores production organization in Ticul, Mexico. His conclusions, made possible only because he has focused on the same group of potters for over 30 years, also have to do with the topic of "skill" but from a very different perspective. He explores both the reasons the potters adopt the vertical-half molding technique and the effects it has on the organization of the craft. One of his findings is that mold-made pottery generally takes less skill and that between 1965 (when hand-made pottery was most common) and 1994 there was a net reduction in the average individual potters' skill despite the fact that extremely standardized products are produced (Chapter 5). Although the level of production organization is more developed in 1994, the skill of the individual forming the vessel has been reduced because of the segmentation of tasks and the appearance of the vertical-half mold.

Feinman (Chapter 6) explores the issue of specialization from the archaeological perspective with his excavations of Classic period craft-producing households from Ejutla, Oaxaca. He finds that there is an extremely high density of craft waste (shell and ceramic) produced within a completely domestic context. He argues that if one used traditional models of production organization, this type of craft debris could easily be assigned, incorrectly, to nondomestic workshops. Feinman suggests that the situation found at Ejutla may be more common than previously thought and we need to rethink the common association between full-time craft specialization in workshops and ancient states and empires.

POTTERY USE

Pots are indeed tools (Braun 1983; Reid 1989) but they can also be signs and symbols (Kingery 1996b:3). Thus, the study of pottery use requires a mix of soft- and hard-science techniques. A very profitable area of research has been to apply a materials science–like approach to understand the relationship between ceramic manufacture and use (Bronitsky 1989; Rice 1996a:138–148). This research focuses on understanding how potters designed their vessels to meet the performance characteristics associated with cooking, storing water, transport, and other functions related to the use of pottery as a tool. Critics have charged (e.g., Gosselain and Smith 1995:157–158), incorrectly, that this focus on the technical attributes related to design and functional performance privileges the utilitarian explanations for pottery design and change at the expense of nonutilitarian, symbolic, or cultural performance characteristics. The focus on what has been referred to as techno-function, however, came about because of unsatisfactory explanations for pottery design variability (Schiffer and Skibo 1987). One objective of the research I have conducted, for example, was to determine how a particular temper or surface treatment related to a vessel's performance in cooking (Schiffer et al. 1994; Skibo et al. 1989b). Previous to these experiments little was known about the relationship between pottery design and use. To explain ceramic variation, investigators either offered untested utilitarian connections or simplistic "cultural" explanations. It is only after a long series of experiments that we can now begin explanations of ceramic variability and change with a core set of principles about the relationship between technical attributes and performance. But this does not imply that all pottery design can be explained solely by techno-functional performance. Although the focus on much of the early work was on techno-functional performance, it has never been suggested that all design variability should focus in these aspects alone (see Schiffer and Skibo 1987, 1997). However, explanations for ceramic design that privilege the social, cultural, or symbolic and do not consider techno-functional performance *at all* are immediately suspect. The technical properties are not just a trivial "side effect," as proposed by Gosselain and Smith (1995: 158), nor can they be considered as the end products of people making engineer-like decisions (O'Brien et al. 1994) somehow removed from their cultural and social milieu (Rice 1996b:185–186). In this volume, the issue of pottery use is explored in the American Southwest, Mesoamerica, India, and Greece.

Pottery Consumption.

In the Southwestern United States, archaeologists have often noted the increase in vessel size through time and have used a number of explanations, from changes in food preparation to an increase in feasting, to account for this change. Mills (Chapter 7) addresses this question directly by looking at food preparation and consumption patterns from the Mesa Verde and Tusayan areas. Mills considers each of the likely causes for the increase in vessel size and favors a social explanation. She argues that the increase in vessel size is the result of a trend through time toward larger extended households and an increased participation in suprahousehold ritual feasting.

The issue of pottery consumption and use is also taken up by Sinopoli (Chapter 8) using data from the remarkable site of Vijayanagara in southern India. This imperial capital, with up to a quarter of a million people, was composed of dozens of different castes and at least three different languages. Using a combination of written documents and ceramic data, Sinopoli describes the various social, ideological, and economic factors that impact pottery variability and use. One interesting aspect of Hindu society is that there are no elite wares or high-status pottery because it is thought to be vulnerable to the absorption of impurities and thus it is avoided by the higher castes. Nonetheless, Sinopoli found evidence for widespread use of pottery and was able to, among other things, examine the different functional classes of vessels present in different parts of the city. For example, some areas had a full range of functional types and were likely residential compounds but others had restricted numbers of types suggesting that these areas were administrative centers or areas where low-status servants lived in the elite district. Moreover, she finds that in the "Islamic Quarter," where there would not be restrictions regarding eating food prepared or served in pottery, there are higher frequencies of bowls used in food consumption.

In contrast to the high castes of Vijayanagara, the elites from the Gulf lowlands of Mesoamerica used and distributed elaborately decorated pottery. Stark (Chapter 9) considers the symbolic roles that fine ceramics played during the Preclassic, Classic, and Postclassic periods. Using data from Mextequilla, Stark explores whether elaborately made ceramics adhere to the patterns suggested by Helms (1993) for crafts imbued with sacred cosmology and social power. Stark finds some support for this model during the Early Classic period as fine ceramics seem to have a restricted distribution and are dominated by the ritual forms of Teotihuacan. But during other periods in the Gulf lowlands, the fine serving wares are present in sufficient quantities to suggest to Stark that they do not match the model proposed by Helms (1993).

Origins.

Several contributors also consider the origins of pottery as a container, which is a topic that inevitably comes back to vessel use. The key to understanding the appearance of pottery is to determine how the vessels were used, and research into this question suggests that there is no single use nor single answer for pottery origins (Barnett and Hoopes 1995; Rice n.d.). Pottery can have many uses that may include cooking, storage, serving, or ritual, and any of these reasons and more could have been the original impetus to make ceramic containers. Three contributors offer explanations for the first pottery during the Early Mesoamerican Formative period from Mesoamerica, Basketmaker II of the Colorado Plateau, and the Greek Neolithic. One

interesting coincidence is that both P. Arnold (Chapter 10) and Skibo and Blinman (Chapter 11) focus on the same type of vessel form, the spherical neckless jar, which is referred to as a *tecomate* in Mesoamerica and a seed jar in the American Southwest. In both of these chapters the authors reach similar conclusions regarding the design of the vessels; the spherical neckless jar has a design that would permit it to function adequately in a number of uses. It is the quintessential multifunctional pot. P. Arnold goes on to suggest that the *tecomate* was part of the tool kit for highly mobile groups. What is more, he argues that during the Early Formative period in Coastal Lowland Mesoamerica, people maintained a high degree of residential mobility.

The first pottery in the northern Southwest was also made and used by groups who cultivated corn and possibly other domesticates but relied heavily on hunting and gathering and still maintained a high level of residential mobility. Skibo and Blinman focus on early brown ware that is dominated by the seed jar shapes. An analysis of use-alteration traces reveals that many of the vessels were used for cooking but others were not. On the Colorado Plateau corn appears much earlier than pottery, so they also explore why these people begin to regularly make pottery by about A.D. 200. Skibo and Blinman suggest that it may be to cook items, like beans, that require long-term boiling, which is a process that is not easily accomplished with stone-boiling in baskets or skins.

The earliest Greek pottery, in contrast, shows no evidence of being used over a fire. What is more, Vitelli (Chapter 12) finds no evidence that the vessels served any function related to subsistence. It is not until later in the Neolithic sequence that one finds the more typical cooking and storage pots. Vitelli suggests that these infrequently found vessels, without any evidence for utilitarian use, had an important ritual function, and the first potters, she argues, may have been female shaman. During the middle and late Neolithic period the number of vessels produced increases as does the range of functions.

Vitelli argues that this pottery was first invented for ritualist needs but then the clay was rapidly made into new shapes and sizes as utilitarian functions of ceramic vessels were discovered.

Meaning.

Thus far it has been shown how archaeologists who study ceramics in their quest to investigate the people behind the pot must employ both hard- and soft-science techniques. Nonetheless, there still is one area of ceramic studies where many researchers still draw the line—artifact meaning. Some archaeologists believe that it is the most important aspect of pottery while others think that it is the one area of pottery studies that may be out-of-bounds using prehistoric data. Several of the contributors to this volume, however, broach the issue of ceramic meaning. For example, Sinopoli (Chapter 8), with the aid of ethnohistoric documentation, is able discuss the meaning of pottery in Hindu and Islamic society; Stark (Chapter 9) is able to at least begin to explore what elaborately painted designs may have meant in Mesoamerican society; and Vitelli (Chapter 12) considers the possible use and meaning of early Neolithic pottery after exhausting other utilitarian possibilities. Schiffer (Chapter 13) argues, however, that our interpretations of artifact meaning are forever doomed in archaeology if we rely on a humanistic framework. He proposes an artifact-based theory of communication that uses the activity as the basic unit of analysis. Because activities in a communication process can be inferred from the archaeological record, Schiffer's behavioral theory provides archaeologists with the ability to infer artifact meaning without resorting to hermeneutics or other various interpretive archaeologies. By tackling artifact meaning and communication, Schiffer probes into perhaps the most elusive relationship between pottery and people.

POTTERY DISCARD

This issue directly impacts all archaeologists because the data are created through various discard behaviors. Pottery can enter the ar-chaeological context at any point in their life history. Some vessels break at their point of manufacture just minutes after being fired while others may be passed down as heirlooms or ritual containers and last for generations. Because pots are rarely deposited at the exact point they were made and used, the strength of our inferences is dependent upon our ability to understand how our deposits were formed. Both Sinopoli (Chapter 8) and Feinman (Chapter 6) confront directly the formation processes responsible for the visibility of pottery-making locations. After over a decade of doing an intensive survey at the site of Vijayanagara, Sinopoli and her team have been unable to find a single pottery-making location. Other craft workshops, like stone or iron working, have been located, but the estimated 100 to 200 pottery shops are invisible to the archaeologist. One important reason for this problem, according to Sinopoli, was the practice of using household and industrial waste as fertilizer in agricultural fields. One often used clue to pottery-making workshops is the high density of sherds (wasters) that result from breakage during firing. But Sinopoli argues that these wasters are redeposited along with the other household waste and results in the low density of ceramics scattered across the metropolitan area.

Feinman is confronted with the opposite depositional problem—he finds massive quantities of craft debris that he believes are created entirely by household-level manufacture. The question of whether crafts were produced at the household or nonresidential workshop is extremely important to Mesoamerican archaeologists because it is at the heart of inferences about production organization. As Feinman notes, others have suggested that pottery-making was being conducted in nondomestic contexts. Obviously, this difference can only be resolved with studies that focus on pottery depositional behaviors and the other formation processes associated with discriminating residential and nonresidential workshops.

Understanding how and when vessels entered archaeological context is especially important as archaeologists continue to ask ever-more specific questions about the people who made and used the pottery. Nowhere is this more important than in the investigation of ritual objects. Two chapters in this volume (Stark and Vitelli) discuss pottery vessels as ceremonial objects. But if we are to develop further the innovative work of these contributors, archaeologists must be aware of the different depositional behaviors associated with ritual objects. Walker (1995, 1996; Walker and LaMotta 1995) demonstrates that ritual objects often have special life histories and are deposited differently than the more common everyday items. Inferring the life history of "ceremonial trash" is the key to understanding ritualistic pottery use in prehistory (Walker 1995).

The importance of discard behaviors is equally evident in the study of "children's" vessels. Crown (Chapter 3) introduces a new and exciting area of ceramic research in her investigation of vessel designs made by children who are just beginning to learn the craft, but with most innovations in archaeology there is often a lag in the method and theory. When archaeologists have found inferiorly painted vessels of the type that Crown attributes to children, they are most often treated as curiosities and considered no further. But

prehistorians should now take greater care to understand the discard behaviors of these vessels and begin to ask relevant life-history questions. Were they ever used? Were many made but never fired? Where were they deposited? Should they be considered ritual objects?

Some might argue that we may now be asking too much of our archaeological data and that the type of analyses suggested by the above contributors is beyond the reach of the prehistorian. It is easy for many to see that we must understand discard behaviors and that vessels pass through life histories, but it is more difficult for the prehistorian to understand how they can begin to make some of these inferences from their pile of sherds. It is possible, however, to reconstruct a vessel's life history if one considers both the context of use and use-alteration traces (Skibo 1992).

The relationship between pottery and people is not simple, nor is it easily understood. It requires that the archaeologists understand the life history of the vessels and combine a series of both hard- and soft-science techniques in their investigation. The papers in this volume illustrate the state-of-the-art method and theory for inferring the makers and users of prehistoric pottery.

2

The Chaco-Chuska Connection: In Defense of Anna Shepard

James B. Stoltman

The hypothesis of the importation into Chaco Canyon of significant quantities of pottery vessels manufactured 70–80 km west in the Chuska Mountain region was "stumbled upon accidentally" by Anna Shepard (1963:22) during her technological analysis of ceramics excavated by Earl Morris in the La Plata Valley (Shepard 1939). In 1936, while in the midst of this analysis, Shepard was sent by Neil Judd what he felt was "a trustworthy cross section of local ceramic history" from his excavations in Chaco Canyon in hopes that she could one day embark upon a "thorough inquiry into the makeup of Pueblo Bonito pottery" (Judd 1954:235). Unfortunately, this never happened. But, to assist in assessing the apparent Chaco affinities of some of the La Plata Valley ceramics (especially from Sites 39 and 41), Shepard had thin sections prepared for at least 59 Chaco vessels of various types. In addition, using a binocular microscope, she analyzed 1,682 sherds from two different excavated, stratified contexts at Pueblo Bonito—Test II beneath the West Court and Test IV in the West Mound (Shepard 1939: 280; Judd 1954:235). It was in the process of analyzing these data that she first recognized a unique igneous rock temper in the Pueblo Bonito ceramics that she suspected could not possibly be obtained locally in Chaco Canyon.

She referred to this distinctive rock—a combination of pyroxene, magnetite, and biotite occurring as poikilitic (i.e., small, randomly oriented) inclusions within an unlikely matrix of sanidine—as "sanidine basalt" (Shepard 1939:279). It was through conversations with Earl Morris, with his extensive knowledge of the Four Corners area, that she identified the Chuska Mountains as the likely source of this material (Shepard 1939:279, 1963:22). Because this rock type occurs both as bedrock outcrops and as the predominant temper in the local ceramics in the Chuska region, while only sedimentary rocks outcrop in Chaco Canyon, Shepard (1954:236, 1963:22) proposed that trade was the most logical explanation for the occurrence of these pottery containers in Chaco Canyon. Although she recorded sanidine basalt temper in some of the black-and-white vessels from Pueblo Bonito, she also made the interesting observation that this temper occurred more commonly in corrugated vessels, commenting that "it is perhaps the large percentage of corrugated ware with sanidine basalt temper which makes the trade theory difficult to accept" (Shepard 1954:237).

Because of its unusual combination of minerals, which defies easy assignment to any of the major igneous rock types commonly recognized by geologists, subsequent authors have been prone to refer to "sanidine basalt" by different terms. The most common designation for it in the recent archaeological literature is trachyte (e.g., Garrett and Franklin

1983; Toll 1981; Warren 1967; Windes 1984b), while terms like trachybasalt (e.g., Williams et al. 1954:58) or melatrachyte (e.g., Loose 1977:568) seem to have more currency in geological circles. Because no consensus has yet emerged over the proper designation for this rock, and in deference to Shepard's original recognition of its archaeological significance, it shall be referred to as sanidine basalt in this paper. Although Shepard's name for this rock has not been universally adopted, her belief that its ultimate geological derivation must be the Chuska Mountains has never been seriously challenged. Instead, the main issue became whether it had been traded from the Chuskas as a raw material for use as temper in vessels manufactured in Chaco Canyon or, as Shepard postulated, whole ceramic vessels, especially corrugated ware, had been manufactured in the Chuskas and then traded into Chaco Canyon.

This issue was clearly set forth by Neil Judd in his 1954 monograph on Pueblo Bonito material culture. He and Shepard had corresponded about the topic over the years. As a prelude to an excerpt of a letter from Shepard that Judd published in his 1954 report—a letter that he termed a "rebuttal" to his own views (Judd 1954:236)—he states that, as far as he was concerned, the pots-versus-temper importation issue "still hangs in midair" (Judd 1954:235). It is this very issue that the present paper addresses.

For unknown reasons, Shepard never wrote a formal report devoted purely to her Chaco observations. As a result, her ideas on this issue lie obscurely embedded in reports whose titles or listed authors give no overt clues as to their presence. The hypothesis first appeared in her appendix, entitled "Technology of La Plata Pottery," to Morris's La Plata Valley monograph (Shepard 1939:279–281). Later, it was presented in the excerpt from the letter to Judd discussed above, but, except for Judd's prefatory remarks, one would have no clue to its presence buried deeply within the volume (Shepard 1954). Much later, Shepard mentioned the hypothesis again, but only in-

cidentally within a paper devoted primarily to ceramic production in Oaxaca, Mexico (Shepard 1963). In retrospect, however, it seems clear that, despite her inherently cautious nature, she never wavered from her view that the common occurrence of Chuska-derived temper in Chaco Canyon ceramics constituted a likely example "of specialization that led to extensive trade" (Shepard 1963:21).

As Cordell (1991:132) has aptly noted in reference to the reception that Shepard's ideas received from Southwestern archaeologists, "many of her discoveries—and most importantly, the implications of her work— were largely ignored in her lifetime." Current thinking on this problem has changed significantly since the inauguration of intensive research into what has come to be known as "the Chaco phenomenon" conducted by the Chaco Center on behalf of the National Park Service during the 1970s (e.g., Judge and Schelberg 1984; Vivian 1990: 69–78). In the interregnum between the primary period of Shepard's research and the establishment of the Chaco Center in 1971, archaeology in the Southwest, as in the rest of North America, had undergone a profound transformation. Deep in the throes of the processual "revolution," Southwestern archaeologists of the 1970s were bombarded with literature and rhetoric utilizing or championing cross-cultural comparison of culture change within the neo-evolutionary framework of bands, tribes, chiefdoms, and states (e.g., Service 1971), the relationship between environment, resources, and population, and the virtues of adopting a regional as opposed to a site-specific perspective in conducting field research. Thus, it is not surprising to see participants in the Chaco Center program largely sympathetic to the idea that specialized ceramic production and redistribution had occurred within the Chaco regional system (e.g., Toll et al. 1980).

Typical of Shepard, ever the cautious scholar, she regarded her temper observations as "only circumstantial evidence, not proof" of specialized ceramic production and trade

(Shepard 1954:236). To test this hypothesis she suggested a more comprehensive analysis should be conducted of sanidine-tempered pottery from Pueblo Bonito and the Chuskas that "compares features such as finish, *type of clay,* and particularly painted design" (emphasis added) under the supposition that "If systematic comparison should prove that the two are identical in these respects, the trade theory would seem the most logical explanation of the Chaco occurrences" (Shepard 1954:237).

No such comprehensive comparative analysis has yet been conducted, but cumulative research over the years has added much relevant new evidence. For example, research in the Chuskas has provided strong confirmation that not only does sanidine basalt outcrop there, but that this material was the preferred temper for locally manufactured gray and white wares after ca. A.D. 800 (Peckham and Wilson 1965; Warren 1967). Meanwhile, the huge new ceramic data base generated by the Chaco Center project—approximately one quarter million potsherds (Toll et al. 1980:95)—has largely confirmed Shepard's initial insights, namely, that sanidine basalt occurs in great abundance in Chaco Canyon ceramics, especially in corrugated wares, during the primary episodes of canyon occupation between A.D. 920 and A.D. 1220. Add to these new data (1) the recent documentation of the major system of roadways radiating out from Chaco Canyon and its positive implications for long-distance trade (Vivian 1990: 318–328), (2) recent archaeological evidence suggesting that ceramic production and exchange had occurred in volume in other parts of the Anasazi region in prehistory (e.g., Plog 1980), (3) a more sympathetic reading of the ethnographic literature supporting the possibility of suprahousehold ceramic production in the Southwest (e.g., Ford 1972:38–39; Toll 1981:87–88), and (4) recent ethnoarchaeological evidence to the effect that potters rarely procure their raw materials beyond a radius of about 7 km (e.g., D. Arnold 1980: 149; Toll 1981: 91–92), and it is not surprising to see a greater

readiness to accept the idea that ceramic products of the Chuskas were imported in volume into Chaco Canyon (e.g., Toll 1981, 1984, 1991; Toll et al. 1980; Vivian 1990; Windes 1977).

Shepard no doubt would be pleased at this shift in thinking about the Chuska-Chaco ceramic connection, but it is likely that she would still consider the evidence circumstantial in light of the absence of the kind of comparative ceramic analysis that she had suggested. This study, while not fully what Shepard advocated, is nonetheless intended to be a step in that direction. Of the three domains that she singled out for comparative analysis—finish, type of clay, and painted designs (Shepard 1954:237)—the focus of this paper is on one of them, type of clay.

Shepard's own observations on Chacoan ceramics, which she probably would have considered preliminary, perhaps even cursory, had focused primarily upon temper, thus had nothing to say about clays. More recently, refiring of sherds has been employed as a rough indicator of the chemical content of clays used in ceramic vessels from both the Chaco and Chuska regions (e.g., Toll et al. 1980; Vivian and Mathews 1965: 69; Windes 1977). The results of this research suggest that Chaco clays are generally poorer in iron than those of the Chuska region, the former tending to refire to a buff color in contrast to a redder color for the latter (Toll et al. 1980; Vivian and Mathews 1965; Windes 1977). Unfortunately, however, these differences are not absolute, but appear only to be tendencies, which means that refiring tests are not conclusive indicators of the source of individual vessels.

As documented below, this study confirms Shepard's hypothesis of the importation of substantial numbers of Chuska Gray Ware vessels into Chaco Canyon during the Bonito phase. In deference both to Shepard's insight and Cordell's observation concerning the general failure of archaeologists to consider seriously the implications of her work, the final section of this paper examines those implications at some length. Based upon these considerations, a revised model of the Chaco political economy is proposed, one in which a corporately organized leadership (e.g., Blanton et al. 1996) sponsored periodic "Rites of Intensification" (Chapell and Coon 1942) that, rather than an organized procurement system, markets or chiefly redistribution, served as the preeminent integrative device helping to maintain the integrity of the Chaco system.

METHODOLOGY AND DATA

Using a petrographic microscope and the point counting approach outlined in Stoltman (1989, 1991), 85 thin sections made from 63 ceramic vessels and three clay samples from Chaco Canyon and 19 vessels from the Two Gray Hills site in the Chuska Valley were analyzed. The goal is to provide data pertinent to the issue of whether temper or whole ceramic vessels had been imported into Chaco Canyon from the Chuskas during the Bonito phase. This study is intended to complement Shepard's temper-oriented observations by providing quantitative as well a qualitative data on the natural inclusions in the silt and sand size ranges that occur in the clays from which various local and presumably nonlocal vessels recovered in Chaco Canyon were manufactured. As advocated by Shepard, this analysis focuses especially upon the clay-rich sediments from which the vessels were made and is comparative in approach. This comparative analysis purports to test Shepard's hypothesis of the nonlocal manufacture of sanidine basalt-tempered gray wares recovered in Chaco Canyon under the supposition that the clays from which they were made should be discernibly different from those of the locally made white wares (i.e., those that are grog tempered) while at the same time closely resembling the pastes of Chuska-area ceramics (i.e., the 19 vessels from Two Gray Hills). At the same time, clays used in the manufacture of local vessels should resemble local Chaco Canyon clays, while the presumed imported vessels should be different. Unfortunately, no soil samples from the Chuskas are available for this study, so the only direct evidence of the physical character of Chuska clays for this study comes from paste observations on the 19 thin-sectioned vessels from Two Gray Hills that were in the Shepard collections.

The physical properties of this sample of ceramic vessels and clays will be presented in terms of three indices: paste, body, and sand-temper sizes (Stoltman 1991). *Paste,* the primary focus of this study, is defined as the naturally occurring, clay-rich sediments, exclusive of any intentional human additives, that were used in the manufacture of ceramic vessels. Paste as thus conceived is expressed as an index consisting of the percentages of three main naturally occurring ingredients: (1) clay (matrix), (2) silt (naturally occurring mineral inclusions larger than .002 mm but smaller than .0625 mm in diameter in all dimensions), and (3) sand (mineral inclusions whose maximum diameter exceeds .0625 mm). Any grains in excess of 2.00 mm in maximum diameter, technically gravel, will simply be included in the "sand" category. Paste is an index whose job is to identify, if possible, the sources of clayey sediments used in ceramic manufacture.

Body, by contrast, is paste combined with any intentional human additives, i.e., temper. Body as an index thus reflects the bulk composition of a ceramic vessel and is expressed as an index composed of three ingredients: (1) matrix, i.e., clay and silt combined, (2) naturally occurring sand, and (3) temper, i.e., all human additives (for a discussion of ways to distinguish naturally occurring sand from temper, see Stoltman 1991:110–111). Body, then, is an index that is hopefully sensitive to "engineering" considerations of the ceramic manufacturers, presumably reflecting functional or other cultural considerations that influence ceramic production.

The intentional addition of sand as temper presents a special problem because it makes the objective distinction of naturally occurring sand inclusions from "temper" virtually impossible. In such cases the paste-body distinction becomes untenable. Instead of two separate indices, a single combined index—*bulk composition* (comprised of matrix, silt, and all sand)—may be substituted, but its comparative value is limited, i.e., it can be used reliably only versus other sand-tempered vessels. Since the primary focus of this study is to assess the potentially exotic character of sanidine basalt-tempered gray wares, the few sand-tempered sherds encountered will be excluded.

The third basic index used to characterize the physical properties of vessels is a size index, applied separately to temper and to naturally occurring sand, that is, two separate indices are recorded for each vessel. These indices are expressed as a value between 1.00 and 5.00 based upon the measurement of all sand-size (or larger) mineral inclusions encountered during point counting, each of which is then assigned to the appropriate weighted size class within the following ordinal scale:

1.00   .0625–.249 mm (fine)
2.00   .25–.499 mm (medium)
3.00   .50–.99 mm (coarse)
4.00   1.0–1.99 mm (very coarse)
5.00   > 2.0 mm (gravel)

The calculation of temper and sand size indices for each vessel involves multiplying the sum of all grains per class X the weighted value for that class, then summing these totals and dividing by the number of grains counted for all classes combined.

In making the basic microscopic observations upon which these indices are based, precautionary measures were taken to ensure, insofar as was possible, that each thin section was treated as an independent entity. Thus during the point counting, only the thin section number, but not the vessel type, was recorded, and the calculations of the indices for each thin section were deferred so that the findings (e.g., the amount of silt or sand size) for one thin section could not influence the findings for another. A minimum of 100 points, not counting voids, was recorded for each thin section. The interval between points was 1 mm (See Stoltman 1989: 148–149), and when the thin section was too small to produce the target minimum of 100 points exclusive of voids, the thin section was reversed and counted a second time. When a thin section was counted twice—over half of

those in the current sample—the second count was always conducted "blind" with respect to the earlier count.

The thin sections to which these observations were applied were initially selected from among those in the Shepard collection curated at the University of Colorado Museum. Fifty-nine thin sections—all having CU Museum numbers between 1607 and 1690—were made from Pueblo Bonito sherds apparently forwarded to Shepard by Neil Judd in 1936. The nineteen thin sections from Two Gray Hills in the Chuska Valley bore the CU Museum numbers 2336 to 2354. In many, but not all of these cases, the actual sherds from which the thin sections were made were also present so that the ceramic type could be confirmed. Twenty-one of these thin sections—13 red ware, 6 polished black, and 2 polychrome—were immediately excluded from this study on typological grounds because they are most probably of nonlocal and non-Chuska derivation. Following initial screening under the petrographic microscope, 17 other thin sections were later also excluded on various grounds—one was a poor thin section, 11 were sand tempered (which prevented reliable paste identification necessary for the comparative analysis), and five had andesite or diorite temper indicative of a northern (probably La Plata Valley) derivation. This left a remainder of 61 thin sections that formed the core of the initial analysis: 41 Cibola White Ware vessels (with grog-tempered pastes) that were presumably of local, Chacoan manufacture, a single sanidine basalt-tempered, corrugated vessel of presumed Chuskan origin, 14 Chuska White Ware vessels from Two Gray Hills (with a mix of grog and sanidine basalt temper), and 5 Chuska Gray Ware vessels (with sanidine basalt temper) from Two Gray Hills.

This sample seemed large enough to provide a reasonably reliable physical characterization of the ceramic pastes for both Chaco Canyon (at least for Pueblo Bonito) and for the Chuskas (at least for Two Gray Hills), but a single sanidine basalt-tempered vessel was obviously an inadequate basis for characterizing the postulated Chuska imports in

TABLE 2.1.
Body and Paste Values for Local White Ware Vessels by Type

BODY*					
Type	N	% Matrix	% Sand	% Temper	Temper Size Index
Kana'a Black-on-white	1	83	4	13	2.31
Red Mesa Black-on-white	17	85.6 ± 4.3	5.7 ± 2.3	8.7 ± 3.9	2.49 ± .37
Puerco Black-on-white	5	87.4 ± 5.6	3.0 ± 0.7	9.6 ± 6.1	2.71 ± .58
Gallup Black-on-white	5	87.6 ± 5.1	4.2 ± 2.6	8.2 ± 5.4	2.49 ± .58
Chaco Black-on-white	8	91.1 ± 2.7	4.4 ± 2.3	4.5 ± 2.3	2.45 ± .65
Chaco-McElmo Black-on-white	10	87.3 ± 4.0	5.4 ± 2.8	7.3 ± 4.6	2.42 ± .33
Mesa Verde Black-on-white	1	82	4	14	3.39
TOTAL	47	87.2 ± 4.5	4.9 ± 2.4	7.9 ± 4.5	2.50 ± .47

PASTE					
	N	% Matrix	% Silt	% Sand	Sand Size Index
Kana'a Black-on-white	1	93	2	5	1.60
Red Mesa Black-on-white	17	88.8 ± 2.8	5.1 ± 2.0	6.1 ± 2.4	1.53 ± .33
Puerco Black-on-white	5	88.2 ± 3.4	8.6 ± 4.0	3.2 ± 0.8	1.27 ± .28
Gallup Black-on-white	5	88.2 ± 4.0	7.6 ± 2.2	4.2 ± 2.6	1.45 ± .45
Chaco Black-on-white	8	89.2 ± 3.2	6.2 ± 2.1	4.5 ± 2.3	1.44 ± .26
Chaco-McElmo Black-on-white	10	88.2 ± 3.4	5.7 ± 3.1	6.1 ± 2.5	1.32 ± .30
Mesa Verde Black-on-white	1	90	5	5	1.00
TOTAL	47	88.7 ± 3.1	6.0 ± 2.7	5.3 ± 2.4	1.42 ± .32

*Grog is the dominant temper in all types

Chaco Canyon. Through the kindness of a number of people, the sample of sanidine basalt-tempered gray ware vessels that had been recovered in Chaco Canyon was increased from the initial single vessel to a total of 16, while 6 additional Cibola White Ware vessels from site 29SJ626 were also later added to the sample. The sherds for the additional thin sections were derived primarily from two sources: (1) the general collections at the University of Colorado Museum and (2) the National Park Service collections from site 29SJ626. Thomas Windes of the National Park Service also provided the three soil samples, also from site 29SJ626, that are used in this study to characterize local Chacoan clays. The net result is a sample of 85 thin sections that were used specifically for this study: 47 of these are derived from presumably local Cibola White Ware vessels, 16 are from presumably imported Chuska Gray Ware vessels, 3 are from 29SJ626 soil samples, while 19 (14 white ware and 5 gray ware) pertain to Chuska Valley vessels. The basic data derived from the petrographic observations of this sample of 85 thin sections—the body, paste, and size indices—are recorded by type or class in Tables 2.1, 2.2, and 2.3 and are portrayed graphically in Figures 2.1 and 2.2.

RESULTS

As can be seen from Table 2.1, the sample of 47 Cibola White Ware vessels is represented by types derived from all pottery-making stages of occupation of Chaco Canyon from Pueblo I to Pueblo III times. The vast majority—46 (i.e., all except the Kana'a-like Black-on-white vessel)—is comprised of types that derive from the Early, Classic, and Late Bonito phases, dating from ca. A.D. 920 to A.D. 1220 (e.g., Vivian 1990; Windes 1984a). All 47 vessels are grog tempered. It should be noted that this sample does not represent the full range of variation present in local Chacoan white wares because those with sand temper (five were encountered that almost certainly can be considered local manufactures) were excluded from the analysis because their pastes could not be compared

TABLE 2.2.

Body and Paste Values for Vessels with Sanidine Basalt Temper from Chaco Canyon and from
Two Gray Hills in the Chuska Valley

BODY					
Type	N	% Matrix	% Sand	% Temper	Temper Size Index
Chaco: Corrugated	16	69.6 ± 5.8	1.3 ± 0.9	29.1 ± 5.0	2.48 ± .38
Two Gray Hills					
Black-on-white (organic paint)	6	76.3 ± 4.5	2.3 ± 0.8	21.3 ± 4.0	1.94 ± .57
Black-on-white (mineral paint)	8	82.6 ± 4.0	2.5 ± 1.1	14.9 ± 3.8	1.21 ± .15
Corrugated	5	72.0 ± 5.9	1.4 ± 0.9	26.6 ± 5.9	2.11 ± .42

PASTE					
Type	N	% Matrix	% Silt	% Sand	Sand Size Index
Chaco: Corrugated	16	93.7 ± 3.6	4.4 ± 2.2	1.9 ± 2.0	1.18 ± .24
Two Gray Hills					
Black-on-white (organic paint)	6	93.2 ± 3.7	3.8 ± 2.7	3.0 ± 1.4	1.20 ± .17
Black-on-white (mineral paint)	8	93.0 ± 3.5	4.2 ± 3.2	2.8 ± 1.4	1.09 ± .13
Corrugated	5	95.4 ± 1.3	2.6 ± 0.9	2.0 ± 1.2	1.13 ± .18
MEAN	19	93.7 ± 3.2	3.7 ± 2.6	2.6 ± 1.3	1.14 ± .16

objectively with the grog and sanidine basalt–tempered vessels that were the primary focus of this study.

A perusal of Table 2.1 reveals a surprising uniformity in both body and paste properties of local white wares throughout the Chaco sequence. These data show no discernible changes, no clear-cut temporal trends in the "ceramic engineering" practices of Chaco potters throughout the duration of the main occupation of the canyon.

There are two possible exceptions to this generalization. The first pertains to the earliest appearance (in this sample) of sanidine basalt as a minor constituent of the body in vessels of the type Gallup Black-on-white. Thereafter, its presence was also observed in vessels of the Chaco, Chaco-McElmo, and Mesa Verde Black-on-white types—it occurs in 15 of the 24 vessels of these 4 types in amounts ranging from just a trace up to 8 percent. Because of the generally low frequencies and fine sizes of the sanidine basalt inclusions and their recurrent presence within grog grains in most vessels, the appearance of this rock type in Cibola White Wares is presumed to reflect the use of sanidine basalt–tempered gray ware sherds as temper. None of the vessels in the current sample was tempered solely with sanidine

basalt. The second exception is the one Mesa Verde Black-on-white vessel whose paste appears to be entirely local, but whose body is notably different from most other vessels in the sample—its combination of abundant (14 percent) and coarse (size index = 3.39) grog is unusual. These differences may reflect new vessel-forming practices perhaps associated with the construction of thicker vessel walls, which are a hallmark of this type; however, the representativeness of this single vessel is obviously suspect. Thin sections from two other Mesa Verde Black-on-white vessels in the Shepard collection from Chaco Canyon were observed, both of which had andesite temper and La Plata Valley–like pastes so were excluded from further consideration in this study.

It is also noteworthy that ten vessels of the carbon-painted type Chaco-McElmo Black-on-white differ in no discernible way either in body or in paste from the remainder of the Cibola White Ware vessels observed in this study (most of which were decorated with mineral paint), although one such vessel with diorite temper and a La Plata Valley–like paste was excluded from further consideration because of its clear exotic origin. These data strongly support the expressed views of Vivian and Mathews (1965:83) and Windes

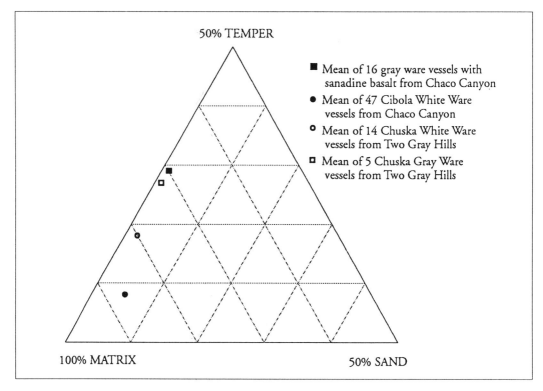

Fig. 2.1. Mean body values for the ceramic vessels analyzed in this study by site and by ware.

(1985) that this carbon-painted type was locally produced in Chaco Canyon.

Turning now to the results of the comparative analysis, as can be seen from Tables 2.1 and 2.2 and Figure 2.1, the bodies of the 47 local white ware vessels differ significantly from those of the 16 presumed Chuska Gray Ware vessels: the former has far less temper on the average than the latter (8 percent versus 29 percent), and yet the mean temper size indices are virtually identical (2.50 versus 2.48). Because the Cibola White Wares are grog-tempered in contrast to the grit-(i.e., sanidine basalt) tempered gray wares, these differences could be related to functional considerations of the potters rather than solely to cultural differences. That is to say, it is difficult to infer from these body differences alone that the two pottery classes were made in different places, but at the very least, these new quantitative data, when considered in the context of the unambiguously exotic derivation of the sanidine basalt, are

fully consistent with the hypothesis of a nonlocal origin for these gray ware vessels. Further support for this hypothesis is provided by comparing the body values of these presumably intrusive gray ware vessels to those of the five Chuska Gray Ware vessels recovered from the Two Gray Hills site. As can be seen from Figure 2.1 and Table 2.2, the two are closely similar.

The more compelling evidence for evaluating the hypothesis of the nonlocal derivation of the sanidine basalt–tempered gray ware vessels found in Chaco Canyon comes from the paste indices (see Tables 2.1, 2.2, and 2.3 and Fig. 2.2). Before considering these quantitative data, however, mention must be made of a potentially significant qualitative feature that characterizes the Chacoan pastes.

A seemingly invariant qualitative feature of the Cibola White Ware pastes is the occurrence of fragments of microcline and chalcedony in the silt and sand fractions. Neither is ever abundant. Indeed, they rarely turn up

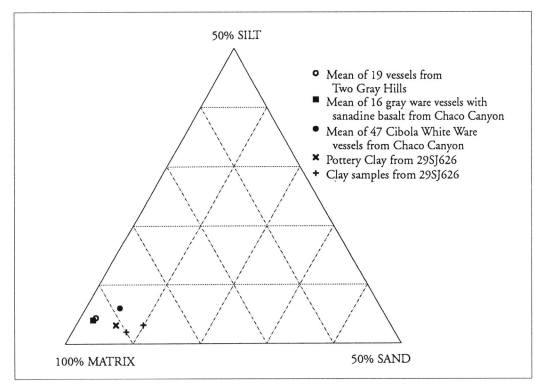

50% SILT

o Mean of 19 vessels from
   Two Gray Hills
■ Mean of 16 gray ware vessels with
   sanadine basalt from Chaco Canyon
● Mean of 47 Cibola White Ware
   vessels from Chaco Canyon
✖ Pottery Clay from 29SJ626
+ Clay samples from 29SJ626

100% MATRIX   50% SAND

Fig. 2.2. Mean paste values for the ceramic vessels and soils analyzed in this study by site.

TABLE 2.3.
Paste Values for Three Soil Samples from 29SJ626

Type	N	PASTE			
		% Matrix	% Silt	% Sand	Sand Size Index
"Pottery Clay"	1	91	3	6	1.22
"Clay"	1	90	2	8	1.42
"Clay"	1	87	3	10	1.46
MEAN	3	89.3 ± 2.1	2.7 ± .6	8.0 ± 2.0	1.37 ± .13

in the point counts, so they normally constitute less than 1 percent of the paste by volume. But, their invariant presence in minor amounts appears to be a ubiquitous feature of Chaco Canyon clays, an observation confirmed by the presence of both minerals in the three clay samples from 29SJ626. By contrast, these minerals appear more sporadically, often not at all, in both the sanidine basalt–tempered gray wares recovered in Chaco Canyon and in the 19 vessels from Two Gray Hills. In the future, by using a finer point counting interval than 1 mm, it should

be possible to gain a more precise estimate of the relative quantities of these minerals, which could then be used to distinguish Chacoan clays objectively. Meanwhile, it should also be noted that the identification of these minerals within the paste of a vessel would be virtually impossible in hand specimens because of their relative scarcity and generally small size.

As can be seen from Tables 2.1 and 2.2 and Figure 2.2, the Cibola White Ware vessels tend to have a greater incidence of both sand and silt in their pastes and the sand grains are generally larger. But, unlike the body indices, which are dramatically different (see Fig. 2.1), the paste differences between the Cibola White Wares and the presumed Chuska Gray Wares are not so pronounced (compare Figs. 2.1 and 2.2). Accordingly, to assist in evaluating the significance of these observed differences in sample means, four t-tests were calculated comparing the matrix, silt, sand, and sand size values for each of the two ceramic classes. The results of these t-tests are recorded under "Problem 1" in Table 2.4.

If the gray wares were imported from outside Chaco Canyon, their pastes should show discernible differences from the pastes of the local Cibola White Wares. As can be seen from Table 2.4, the t-test values for all four components of the paste indices are significant at the .05 probability level, fully consistent with the expectations of the nonlocal production of these vessels.

A further test of the hypothesis of a nonlocal derivation of the sanidine basalt–tempered gray wares is to compare the pastes of both the local and the presumed nonlocal ceramics with local clays. Ideally, clay samples from both the Chaco and Chuska regions should be used, but, unfortunately, only three clay samples from site 29SJ626 in Chaco Canyon are available for the present analysis. One of these samples was derived from a coil, hence is believed to be "pottery clay," while the other two soil samples were derived from floors (i.e., appear to be structural clays). All three soil samples were excavated from Pitstructure 1 in an Early Bonito phase context dating ca. A.D. 920–1020. All were unfired. The paste values of these clays are recorded in Table 2.3 and shown graphically in Figure 2.2.

In a similar vein to the t-tests comparing the paste values of the white wares and gray wares, two series of t-tests were computed that compared each of the ware classes with the mean paste values of the three 29SJ626 soil samples. The null hypothesis here is that there should be no significant differences between the wares and the clay samples if all shared a common, local derivation. The results of these t-tests are recorded under Problems 2 and 3 in Table 2.4.

While not as dramatic as those comparing the two ware classes, and mindful of the small samples involved, the results of these tests nonetheless suggest that the Cibola White Ware pastes are more similar to the local soil samples than are the gray ware pastes. Of the four t-tests that comprise "Problem 2," three show no significant differences between the local white wares and the local clays. Only the silt mean percentage differences are significant at the .05 level (but just barely: .05< p >.04). By contrast, gray ware paste indices (Problem 3 in Table 2.4) generally display greater differences from the Chacoan clays, although only the sand percentage difference exceeds the .05 level of significance (but note that it does so in dramatic fashion: p < .001).

A final test of this hypothesis involves the comparison of paste values from the 19 Chuska Valley vessels with those of the various ceramic and clay classes from Chaco Canyon. As can be seen from Table 2.2, the paste values for the three ceramic classes from Two Gray Hills—6 white ware vessels with organic paint, 8 white ware vessels with mineral paint, and 5 gray ware vessels—are indistinguishable from one another in all dimensions. This indicates that, unlike Chaco Canyon, both the white wares and the gray wares at this Chuska Valley site were made from the same clays. Accordingly, the mean paste indices for these 19 vessels will be used as the best available indicators for characterizing Chuska-area clays.

The most dramatic result of this comparison of Two Gray Hills pastes with those of vessels from Chaco Canyon is that the mean values are identical (when rounded off to the nearest whole number) for the 19 Two Gray Hills vessels and the 16 sanidine basalt–tempered gray ware vessels recovered in Chaco Canyon (Table 2.2 and Fig. 2.2). Considering the virtual identity of body as well as paste values for these two ceramic classes, and the fact that they have identical tempers, the evidence appears to be compelling that the sanidine basalt-tempered gray wares recov-

TABLE 2.4.
Summary of t-Test Results

Problem 1: Cibola White Wares (N=47) versus Gray Wares with Sanidine Basalt (N=16)

	White Wares	Gray Wares	Degrees of Freedom	t	p
Matrix Mean	88.7 ± 3.1	93.7 ± 3.6	61	5.35*	< .001*
Silt Mean	6.0 ± 2.7	4.4 ± 2.2	61	2.14*	< .03*
Sand Mean	5.3 ± 2.4	1.9 ± 2.0	61	5.09*	< .001*
Sd Size Mean	1.42 ± .32	1.18 ± .24	61	2.77*	< .01*

Problem 2: Cibola White Wares (N=47) versus Local Chaco Clays (N=3)

	White Wares	Clays	Degrees of Freedom	t	p
Matrix Mean	88.7 ± 3.1	89.3 ± 2.1	48	.33	>.7
Silt Mean	6.0 ± 2.7	2.6 ± 0.6	48	2.09*	<.05*
Sand Mean	5.3 ± 2.4	8.0 ± 2.0	48	1.90	>.05
Sd Size Mean	1.42 ± .32	1.37 ± .13	48	.26	> .8

Problem 3: Gray Wares with Sanidine Basalt (N=16) versus Local Chaco Clays (N=3)

	Gray Wares	Clays	Degrees of Freedom	t	p
Matrix Mean	93.7 ± 3.6	89.3 ± 2.1	17	2.02	>.05
Silt Mean	4.4 ± 2.2	2.7 ± 0.6	17	1.30	>.2
Sand Mean	1.9 ± 2.0	8.0 ± 2.0	17	4.85*	< .001*
Sd Size Mean	1.18 ± .24	1.37 ± .13	17	1.30	> .2

*Denotes t-test values significant at the .05 level of probability

ered in Chaco Canyon were imported from production centers in the Chuska region.

Accepting that the Chaco white ware and gray ware pastes are different, couldn't this be due to the use of different *local* clays by Chacoan potters consonant with the performance differences expected of the two wares? As discussed above, the data from Two Gray Hills show conclusively that the same clays were used in the manufacture of both gray wares and white wares in the Chuskas. This, of course, does not prove that the Chaco potters did the same, but, considering the totality of the evidence—that the sanidine basalt–tempered gray wares recovered in Chaco Canyon differ in body and paste characteristics from the local white wares (and from local Chaco clays) while simultaneously closely matching those of the Chuska region—the most parsimonious explanation is that the sanidine basalt–tempered gray wares recovered from Chaco Canyon were imported from the Chuska region.

In sum, this study has provided a series of new data characterizing San Juan Basin ceramics that are relevant to the issue of the importation of Chuska Gray Wares into Chaco Canyon during the Bonito phase. First, through an analysis of the body and paste properties of 47 white ware vessels, it provides a baseline for identifying and characterizing locally manufactured white ware ceramic vessels within Chaco Canyon. Cibola White Ware, as these ceramics are generally designated (e.g., Windes 1984a), has a grog-tempered body with only moderate amounts of temper, averaging only about 8 percent by volume in generally moderate sizes, and a mean temper size index of about 2.50. The pastes from which these ceramics were manufactured contain roughly equal proportions of silt and sand inclusions in moderate amounts, each averaging 5–6 percent by volume, while minor amounts of naturally occurring microcline and chalcedony are invariably present. These body and paste properties appear to endure in a surprisingly uniform fashion throughout the duration of the Early, Classic, and Late Bonito phases.

Besides the grog-tempered white ware, both gray wares and white wares with sand-tempered pastes (some with a minor admixture of grog) were probably manufactured locally. Eleven such vessels—six gray ware and five white ware—were encountered during the course of this study. Each possessed 12 to 26 percent sand by volume and had sand size indices ranging from 2.00 to 3.78, both values significantly greater than any of the grog-tempered Cibola White Ware vessels. The pastes of all eleven of these vessels contained grains of both microcline and chalcedony, further support for the view that they were locally manufactured. As noted previously, however, these vessels were excluded from the comparative analysis because of the inability to discriminate between natural sand and sand added as temper. The above characterization of Cibola White Wares must thus be viewed as pertaining to some, although not all, of the ceramics locally produced in Chaco Canyon.

The 16 probable Chuska Gray Ware vessels stand out in stark contrast to the Cibola White Ware sample. All paste parameters—percent matrix, percent silt, percent sand, and sand size index—differ significantly from comparable values for the Cibola White Wares (Table 2.4), and the occurrences of microcline and chalcedony are rare to absent. The comparative body values also differ profoundly—nearly 30 percent temper on the average in the gray ware versus only about 8 percent in the Cibola White Ware (Fig. 2.2). While both the paste and body values of the Cibola White Ware and the suspected Chuska Gray Ware imports are significantly different as expected if the nonlocal derivation of the latter is to be postulated, the virtual identity of all paste and body parameters of the suspected imports and the Two Gray Hills vessel sample adds considerable force to the import hypothesis. These data, combined with the greater disparity in paste values in contrast to the Chacoan clays currently available (Table 2.3), argue strongly that the sanidine basalt–tempered gray wares recovered in Chaco Canyon were imported from the Chuska region as finished vessels as originally hypothesized by Shepard.

IMPLICATIONS

In concluding this paper let us turn now to a consideration of the implications of accepting Shepard's hypothesis that corrugated vessels manufactured in the Chuska region had been imported in significant quantities into Chaco Canyon during the heyday of the Chaco phenomenon. It is these very implications that Cordell (1991:132) noted "were largely ignored during her [i.e., Shepard's] lifetime." In order to place this issue in proper perspective at least four factors must be stressed: (1) the particular ceramics postulated to have been produced by specialists and exchanged over a distance of some 70 km, Chuska Gray Wares, are generally regarded as "utility" or "culinary" wares used for such everyday tasks as cooking and storage (e.g., Shepard 1939:281; Toll 1984:121; Vivian 1990:315) and this view is supported by the high incidence of sooting on the exteriors of these vessels and their abundant occurrence in everyday refuse in Chaco Canyon (Toll 1984); (2) the number of such vessels imported into Chaco Canyon was substantial, steadily increasing over time within the Bonito phase until they constituted as much as 60 percent of the gray wares in use by the end of the Classic Bonito phase (Toll 1984: 115, 125); indeed, one estimate would place up to 49,000 imported gray ware vessels at Pueblo Alto alone during the 60-year Gallup period of trash mound accumulation at that site (Toll 1991: 96); (3) the imported gray wares occur both in the large towns and in the smaller sites within Chaco Canyon, but they are relatively more abundant at the former (Toll 1984:121, 124–125); and (4) the imported gray wares are abundant only at sites in the Chuska region and in Chaco Canyon within the Chaco system (Powers et al. 1983:334–35; Toll 1984:130, 1991:96).

Any discussion of the implications of these findings for better understanding the Chaco system must begin with a consideration of whether it was the vessels themselves, or their contents, that were the primary commodities being exchanged. Dry foods, such as maize, beans, pinyon nuts, etc., are the most likely candidates for commodities that could have been transported in gray ware vessels from the Chuska region to Chaco Canyon. Toll (1991:101–102) has considered this possibility and concluded that "such movements [of foodstuffs] should not be ruled out on present evidence." Since the exchange of perishables like foodstuffs is inherently difficult to evaluate through archaeological testing, this alternative can never be entirely discounted. But, in this case it seems particularly implausible because of the substantial distances involved, the bulkiness and fragility of the pottery vessels, even when empty (e.g., Wilson and Blinman 1995:65), and the ready availability of textile containers, which would have been far superior for the task of long-distance pedestrian transport of dry foodstuffs.

Germane to this issue are two oft-cited studies that attempt to determine the maximum distances that foodstuffs (in this case, mainly maize) could be effectively delivered to a region considering the relative energy costs and gains involved in pedestrian transport (Drennan 1984; Lightfoot 1979). Unfortunately, the findings of these two studies are contradictory—50 km being suggested by Lightfoot (1979) versus 275 km by Drennan (1984). Depending upon which authority one prefers, the Chuskas may be considered beyond or within effective provisioning distance for Chaco Canyon. Pending resolution of these contradictory findings, this approach to the food-versus-containers problem must be considered inconclusive.

Regardless of whether or not foodstuffs were actually transported in the gray ware vessels, the use of these containers for food preparation in communal ceremonies is an alternative that deserves further consideration. It is certainly reasonable to suggest that the plazas of Chacoan Great Houses like Pueblo Alto were the scenes of recurrent ceremonial gatherings (Toll 1984:132) and that the leaders or organizers of such gatherings owed

much of their influence or authority to their religious knowledge (Sebastian 1992: 25). Judge (1984:8–9) has advocated a somewhat more extreme version of this view in postulating a "ritual pilgrimage hypothesis" in which "the canyon served mainly as a ritual locus." This latter view arose in part to accommodate lower total population estimates being proposed for the canyon—from ten or more thousand to only a few thousand—by adopting the view that a high percentage of the Great House rooms were not used as permanent residences but only for intermittent or seasonal visitors (Windes 1984b).

In contrast to this periodically vacant-center hypothesis, an alternative postulating periodic population increases due not to fluctuations in the numbers of permanently resident people (whatever that may have been! See Schelberg 1992:62–64 for a recent reconsideration of the population issue), but to periodic influxes of outsiders attending major ceremonies, is offered below. Let us presume, for the sake of argument, that periodically, say once or twice a year, one or more of the Great Houses like Pueblo Alto sponsored a ceremony that was open to all within the Chaco system. Not everyone could attend, for space and resources were limited. But, nonetheless, large numbers of people, perhaps designated representatives, perhaps only those who could afford to attend, came from all corners of the Chaco system. While in session, the ceremonies no doubt would have involved a mixture of religious, social, and economic activities, and of course the people in attendance brought food that was used for feasting (Ford 1983:716) and "for feeding the supernaturals" (Lamphere 1979: 758). The unusually large numbers of food-preparation vessels (Toll 1984) and deer bones (Akins 1984) recovered from the Pueblo Alto trash mound are consistent with this view, as is: "The commingling of ceramics in great quantity from a number of sources at sites like Pueblo Alto . . . [showing] . . . evidence for broad geographical interaction" (Toll 1984:132).

From an anthropological perspective, such

gatherings clearly would have had the beneficial, indeed, indispensable, effect of allowing members to reaffirm their common bonds and corporate interests as members of a far-flung, multicommunity system. With such varied activities as praying, dancing, socializing, gift-giving, and bartering surely involved, terms like "feast" (e.g., Hayden 1995b) or "fair" (e.g., Ford 1972) seem inadequate to convey the complexity that must have characterized such multidimensional gatherings. A more appropriate designation would perhaps be that of Chappel and Coon (1942:507–528), who refer to such ceremonial gatherings as "Rites of Intensification," examples being harvest rites or planting ceremonies:

> The principal characteristics of these ceremonies is that they accompany a change in the interaction rate within an institution or group of institutions, and provide a dramatic representation of the habitual relationships of the individuals in the sets of which the system is composed. . . . This acting out of the ordered interaction of the members has the effect of reinforcing or intensifying their habitual relations. . . . (Chappel and Coon 1942:507)

It is impossible to know whether or not religious or social sanctions might also have been employed to encourage attendance at such Rites of Intensification, but it is easy to imagine numerous positive inducements— for example, direct participation in the important ceremonies that influenced the gods, the chance to obtain exotic commodities, the chance to make new friends—for people from far and wide to attend without formal coercion. And for the people who came, was there a "price of admission"? It would be reasonable to assume so: perhaps a bag of maize or a cut of venison for the communal meals, a jar to be used for cooking, a bowl for serving the food. And while there, why not bring along some handicrafts for exchange? This, too, would obviously be beneficial because it would further promote system solidarity. As Sahlins (1965:140) expresses it, "the material flow [of goods] underwrites or initiates social relations."

It is suggested that the above scenario offers a realistic and plausible framework within which the major features of the archaeological record of Chaco Canyon can be most parsimoniously understood. In particular it accounts for the large numbers of imported gray ware vessels from the Chuskas that were clearly "consumed" in the Canyon, i.e., used for food preparation (over 50 percent from Pueblo Alto show exterior sooting; Toll 1984:127) and then discarded in local refuse deposits in "almost unbelievable quantities" (Toll 1991:93) without having to invoke such agencies as formal procurement systems, redistribution, markets, chiefdoms, or centralized coercive power.

This is not to assert that there was no central leadership associated with the Chaco system. It is difficult to imagine the existence of such a large, complex, and obviously interactive entity without some sort of central planning and control, but the central leadership need not have taken the form of the traditional chiefdom as defined by Service (1971) and popularly attributed to the Chaco system (e.g., Schelberg 1992). An alternate model, that of the corporate, as opposed to the network, mode of leadership seems to fit this situation admirably (Blanton et al. 1996; Feinman 1995). Unlike the network-based system in which leaders are aggressively self-aggrandizing and actively involved in wealth-based, prestige-goods exchanges with outsiders, the corporate-based system involves group-oriented leaders whose personal status is downplayed and whose activities as representatives of the leadership group, like organizing feasts and rituals, are what is aggressively pursued. In both systems effective central leadership exists, but in the latter the trappings of elite status, like personal badges of office or "royal tombs," are much less prominent or even lacking.

Accepting that people traveled substantial distances from throughout the Chaco system to attend periodic Rites of Intensification held at various of the Great Houses within Chaco Canyon, it still seems fair to ask why such bulky items as gray ware pottery vessels were brought along in volume. One answer, that they contained foodstuffs, has been dismissed as implausible. A more likely explanation concerns the scarcity of suitable fuels for the local manufacture (i.e., firing) of pottery vessels that must have become increasingly acute through time in the immediate vicinity of Chaco Canyon.

As all who have visited the region are aware, trees of any kind are nonexistent in and around Chaco Canyon today, a condition that almost certainly had developed progressively during the Bonito phase as populations grew and the use of wood for building materials and fuel for cooking, heating, and ceramic firing was more and more intensively harvested. While pinyon and juniper were perhaps never entirely extirpated in the immediate vicinity of Chaco Canyon (e.g., Windes and Ford 1996), there are clear indications that they were becoming short in supply. Thus, as noted by Dean (1992:39), pinyon disappeared as a building material in Chaco Canyon after A.D. 1000, while Hall (1988:588) reports that the main fuels burned in hearths in canyon sites were saltbush and greasewood. Master ceramic craftsman Clint Swink, who has devoted countless hours to replicating Anasazi ceramics, has found that the successful firing of 30 white ware vessels in a 1-by-2-m pit kiln like those known to have been used in the Four Corners region in prehistory requires at least one mature pinyon or juniper tree (Swink, pers. comm.). Because gray ware vessels are normally well over twice the size of white ware bowls, the same size pit kiln could be expected to hold no more than half as many gray ware vessels. A realistic minimal estimate of the fuel cost to fire gray ware vessels, then, can be suggested to be one pinyon or juniper tree per 15 vessels. If the estimate of 49,000 gray ware vessels contained in the Pueblo Alto trash mound alone is at all accurate (Toll 1991:96), it can be readily appreciated why the ceramic needs of the residents of Chaco Canyon would have impelled them to take fuel conservation measures. One such conservation measure would have been to turn over the manufacture of large, utilitar-

ian ceramic vessels to neighbors residing in fuel-rich regions such as the Chuska Mountains. Viewed in this context, there appears to be great force to Toll's observation that fuel scarcity "is likely to have limited local production and created a need . . . to import ceramics" (Toll 1981:93). As the overall system population grew through the Bonito phase and the costs of sponsoring the postulated Rites of Intensification grew, perhaps geometrically, it is easy to imagine that the production of pottery vessels would have been increasingly turned over to others who had easier access to the essential fuels. Whether these vessels were actively "procured" by the canyon populace through a formal exchange-redistribution system as has sometimes been suggested or simply arrived more informally with the guests as part of the "price of admission" to periodic ceremonies (with some extras also brought along for gifts and exchange) is perhaps a moot point. The latter alternative is simpler and in this sense is preferable.

SUMMARY AND CONCLUSIONS

The goal of this study was to test Anna Shepard's hypothesis that gray ware ceramics had been manufactured in the Chuska region and subsequently imported in substantial numbers into Chaco Canyon during the heyday of the Chaco system, especially ca. A.D. 900–1140. Using quantitative as well as qualitative observations on thin sections made from 63 Chaco Canyon ceramic vessels, 3 local Chaco soil samples, and 19 ceramic vessels from Two Gray Hills in the Chuska Valley, new data were produced that amplify Shepard's temper-only observations. By demonstrating that the clay-rich fraction of the suspected Chuskan imported vessels recovered in Chaco Canyon is unlike that of local Chacoan vessels while simultaneously being virtually identical to that of demonstrable Chuskan ceramics, these new data strongly support Shepard's hypothesis of the Chuskan manufacture of the sanidine basalt–tempered gray wares recovered in Chaco Canyon.

The implications of these findings to furthering our understanding of the Chaco system were then explicitly considered and a revised model of the Chaco political economy was proposed. This model postulates that a major mechanism contributing to the operation and maintenance of the Chaco regional system was the periodic staging of public ceremonies, "Rites of Intensification," at the Chaco Great Houses that were multidimensional in character, no doubt involving religious ceremonies, feasting, bartering, gift giving, and socializing. Exactly how these ceremonies were apportioned among the various Great Houses to minimize intercommunity competition and to maximize intrasystem solidarity, remains an unsolved problem, but presumably some form of central leadership, organized in the corporate as opposed to the network mode, was operative. As this system of recurrent ceremonial enactment matured, and no doubt increased in scale along with the entire Chaco phenomenon, the costs of staging these rites must have become increasingly burdensome on the populace of Chaco Canyon. One of the critical local resources that was likely to have been subject to overexploitation was wood needed for fuel. Meal preparation and heating were two essential uses of wood fuels that could not easily be transferred nor eliminated, but the use of wood for the firing of ceramic vessels was one wasteful activity for which there was a possible solution: allow residents of those portions of the regional system where firewood was more plentiful, say the Chuska Mountain region, to produce a substantial portion of the pottery. Periodic ceremonies then served the invaluable function of providing a forum within which various regional specialty products could not simply be consumed, but also exchanged to residents of the canyon while at the same time serving to promote social integration.

3

Socialization in American Southwest Pottery Decoration

Patricia L. Crown

This paper begins an exploration of the relationship between socialization in pottery production and the organization of production among prehistoric groups occupying the Greater American Southwest. I report a pilot study that tests a method for assessing the age at which children began learning to decorate pottery. Using small samples of Hohokam, Mimbres, and Salado vessels with poorly executed designs, I evaluate chronological age of the artists through a series of attributes related to cognitive maturity and motorcoordination. Cross-cultural and ethnographic data provide expectations concerning age at socialization in pottery decoration. I conclude that there were differences in the motor skills and cognitive ability of children painting poorly executed pottery of the three wares, but that most children probably began painting their first pots around the ages of 9 to 12. Although I examine only pottery from the American Southwest, the methods employed are applicable to other regions.

THEORETICAL BACKGROUND

Studies in psychology and education reveal that drawing ability is related to motor coordination, cognitive maturity, and previous experience (Biber 1962; Cox 1993; Deregowski 1980; Goodnow 1977; Krampen 1991). Cross-cultural studies indicate some regularities in the general ages at which children are able to draw certain forms and in their ability to render them in an accurate manner. The major changes in drawing content, motor skills, and cognitive maturity relative to age are outlined in Table 3.1. Children with access to drawing materials will begin using them as early as the age of 1. Below age 2, drawing materials are viewed as toys for manipulation. By the age of 4, most children with continued practice in drawing will hold drawing tools in the adult manner (Biber 1962). Control in linework increases after this age. Children's expanding intelligence and conceptual maturity lead to changes in the subject matter and ability to copy designs. By age 7, children can copy basic geometric shapes correctly (Goodnow 1977; Krampen 1991). Between ages 7 and 9, children in different cultures have developed distinct, culturally specific styles for the same subject matter (Dennis 1942:347; Wilson and Ligtvoet 1992; Wilson and Wilson 1984). Children are able to render some symmetrical motifs by the age of 4 (although they rarely do). Their ability to manipulate symmetry patterns apparently follows a sequence from simple repetition, to rotation around a point, to reflection across a vertical or horizontal line, to reflection across a diagonal line (Drora Booth described in Goodnow 1977:40–41). Between the ages of 8 and 12, children generally attain the ability to produce realistic drawings with perspective and proportion (Krampen 1991).

While this discussion and Table 3.1 indicate general ages at which specific drawing

TABLE 3.1.
Relationship of Age, Motor Skills, Cognitive Maturity, Subject Matter, and Drawing Ability

Age	Drawing Stage	Subject Matter	Motor Skills	Cognitive Ability
< 2	scribbling	lines	large arm motion	materials are toys 100%
2–2.5	greater control	circles/spirals, whole sheet used	tool held overhand, can stop muscles	materials are toys 50%
2.5–3	technique mastery	single lines drawn	index finger guides tool	materials are tools, names drawing
3–4	design	paper as field, elaborate designs	tool held as by adult, has preferred hand	shapes juxtaposed, bounded, each has own space
4–5		symmetry possible		
5–8/9	intellectual realism	draw everything they know is there, no perspective, proportion-threaded/ contoured drawings	controlled	show all even if not actually possible to see "transparent" drawings
7/9	style mastered	can copy basic shapes		distinct styles in different cultures for same subjects
8–12	visual realism	perspective, proportion mastered, show what is actually there, profile drawings		

Based on the work of Biber (1962), Goodnow (1977), Krampen (1991), Wilson and Ligtvoet (1992).

accomplishments are attained, intracultural and cross-cultural studies also confirm significant differences in the drawing ability of children and in the content of drawings of children within a single age cohort. Thus, most researchers agree that the actual production of children's drawings is influenced by their environment and previous experience. Children raised in settings where artistic achievement leads to higher status, or where adults often engage in drawing, tend to develop drawing abilities at an earlier age than children raised in settings without these advantages (Cox 1993:102). Children with access to drawing materials who practice drawing from an early age progress in their drawing ability faster than children without such experience (Biber 1962). Furthermore, the subject matter and motifs used in children's drawings are significantly influenced by the visual stimuli in their immediate environment (Thomas 1995:116). For instance, illiterate adults from rural Turkish villages, who rarely practiced drawing and had little access to illustrations, drew human figures in the same manner as 3–5-year-old children from Turkish cities and Britain (Cox 1993: 103). However, in all studies of such artistic "deprivation," the subjects' drawing ability rapidly advanced to their appropriate age level once they had access to drawing materials. In contrast, a type of IQ test using drawings of humans administered to 6- to 11-year-old children from six different Native American groups (including Hopi, Zuni, Navajo, and Tohono O'odham children) revealed significantly higher scores than equivalently aged Caucasian Americans, apparently because drawing was highly regarded and often practiced among the Native American groups (Havighurst et al. 1946). Even an individual child may show significant differences in drawing ability from one rendering to the next. Such differences make it hazardous to assign a specific age to any single drawing.

Additional influences make cross-cultural evaluations of an artist's age difficult. For instance, subject matter differs considerably in cultures. In Western cultures, children often draw humans and buildings. Adults encourage children to draw such "pictures," in contrast to strictly geometric "patterns" or "designs," which subsequently are not as highly valued or as often rendered after an early age (Goodnow 1977:42). This stands in marked contrast to many other cultures, where other representational subject matter or pure designs dominate children's drawings (Cox 1993: 106–107).

Differences in subject matter often have a gendered basis as well. In Western societies, boys tend to show human figures in action, while girls tend to render humans with greater attention to detail and decoration (Cox 1993:91). In contrast, on the island of Alor, Du Bois (1944) found that girls drew tools four times more frequently than boys, while boys drew decorative and detailed drawings, and particularly drawings of animals, more often than girls. In eliciting drawings for the "Draw-a-man" test among 5- to 10-year-old Zuni children, Russell reported that the younger children were reluctant to draw human figures because of cultural taboos.

> Until they have started their period of initiation into the tribe, young boys are not expected to draw men or attempt to represent any of the Zuni dancers. Girls are never expected to draw dancers and usually confine their efforts to pottery designs. These points cannot be over-emphasized since they indicate that practice in drawing human figures. . . . was held at a minimum if not entirely absent due to cultural taboos. (Russell 1943:12)

Cultural conventions may make it difficult to estimate the age of an artist as well. For instance, among the Walbiri in Australia, adult women and children render humans as a single "U," representations that are so distinct from Western drawings as to be unrecognizable without an interpreter (Munn 1973). Children in Africa and India often render humans in "chain" drawings, with bodily features (including facial features) drawn in a list-like manner along a vertical axis from head to toe, with, for instance, the nose, eyes, and mouth drawn outside of the head (Paget 1932; see also Fortes [1940] on African "pin-head" human depictions).

Changes in artistic media may also influence the visual "maturity" of a child's drawing. Human figures drawn by Bushmen children in sand are much simpler in detail than the same subject matter drawn with pencil and paper (Deregowski 1980:181). Furthermore, figures rendered in sand on the ground were viewed as "lying down," while figures rendered on an upright medium (such as paper on an easel) were viewed as "standing up," with subsequent differences in the shape of the figures (Deregowski 1980:183).

The stages in drawing ability listed in Table 3.1 thus represent a general sequence that can be considered applicable to cultures where children draw using a pencil and paper (or similar medium) and where artistic endeavor is valued in roughly the same manner as it is in Western culture. Specific ages are more difficult to assign, particularly to individual renderings. Assignment of age based on motor skill and cognitive ability is likely to be more accurate than assignment of age based on subject matter or detail.

PREHISTORIC AND ETHNOGRAPHIC POTTERY PRODUCTION IN THE AMERICAN SOUTHWEST

In this section, I briefly review aspects of prehistoric pottery production that provide evidence for its place in Southwestern society. I then discuss the scant ethnographic literature on socialization in pottery production in the Southwest. Finally, I present expectations based on the prehistoric and ethnographic data.

Virtually all sedentary populations living in the American Southwest after A.D. 500

used pottery with painted decorations on a daily basis. Studies indicate that nonspecialist potters produced most of Southwestern pottery for household use, although specialized production of pottery occurred at specific times and places as well (Mills and Crown 1995). Females were probably responsible for forming and firing the vessels, and in most areas for decorating them as well. Researchers infer this using crosscultural analogy, historical data on Southwestern groups, as well as the incidence of potter's kits in prehistoric mortuary contexts (Mills and Crown 1995). Some scholars argue that men painted the representational drawings on Mimbres pottery, based on the subject matter (Brody 1977:116; Jett and Moyle 1986:716–717).

Certain expectations concerning the ability of prehistoric Southwestern children to render pottery designs can be based on what we know about the craft itself. Both the spatial ubiquity and sheer volume of decorated pottery in Southwestern sites attest to the high visibility of pottery designs within villages. Children were exposed to designs on pottery and other objects from birth. They routinely saw adults engaged in painting pottery in villages where the craft was practiced, in addition to other artistic endeavors. Adults expended time and effort in painting pottery, and the endless variety of designs suggest that value was placed on artistry, creativity, and innovation among Southwestern farming communities (Hagstrum 1995). Crossculturally, children in such settings are encouraged to develop their artistic ability. I expect that prehistoric Southwestern children learning pottery production had visual stimulus, encouragement, aspiration, and parental expectation equivalent to crosscultural situations where children exhibit maturity in artistic ability at a relatively early age.

Additional assumptions are derived from ethnographic analogy. There are surprisingly few descriptions of craft learning among children in Southwestern Native American groups. Results of the "Draw-a-man" test administered to Hopi children aged 6–11 revealed that boys performed better than girls,

and that girls on First Mesa performed better than girls from Oraibi (Havighurst et al. 1946). Asked to comment, anthropologist Laura Thompson responded that,

> The life which the boys lead, and especially their economic and ceremonial responsibilities, forces them to become more observant and to express themselves aesthetically more than does the life of the girls. . . . the Hopi culture offers the girls less rich mental and emotional development and less creative outlet at the aesthetic level. At Oraibi this is mainly in the form of plaque-making, in which the medium limits the design development more than is the case at First Mesa where painted pottery is the main medium of aesthetic expression. (Havighurst et al. 1946:58)

These results mirror those derived from an earlier test at Hopi, which the author also interpreted as due to gender differences in graphic expression and practice (Dennis 1942:347). Similar gender differences found at Zia led Florence Ellis to comment that boys were encouraged to draw from an early age because they had to be able to paint animals on house walls at Christmas and paint ceremonial paraphernalia, while girls "are expected to paint nothing but the conventionalized designs used on pottery" (Havighurst et al. 1946:59). As described above, similar differences exist in the subject matter of Zuni children's drawings. Such gender differences did not exist in the drawings by Tohono O'odham children, where one sex is not encouraged to draw more than the other (Havighurst et al. 1946:60). These data confirm that artistic endeavor is generally encouraged among Native American children in the Southwest (John-Steiner 1975:120), but that the subject matter rendered by children differs by sex, and that girls from villages where pottery decoration is practiced exhibit greater artistic maturity than girls from villages where pottery is not produced. While the IQ of girls was generally evaluated as lower than boys using human representation as the testing medium, the researchers would likely have obtained different results by evaluating strictly geometric designs. Gender differences in artistic subject matter apparently apply to a variety of media among the Pueblos (Underhill 1945:133).

Specific information on socialization in pottery production comes from ethnographies. I particularly sought monographs that reported information prior to extensive teaching of pottery production in the public school system. Pueblo girls learn to make pottery largely by observation and imitation of their mother, aunts, grandmothers, or other adult females in the village (Fowler 1977; Hill 1982:139; John-Steiner 1975). Formal direct instruction is apparently rare, although adults may correct children who are imitating them and give brief instructions (Fowler 1977:29; Hill 1982:139). Learning appears to follow a sequence that mirrors the production sequence, with forming of vessels at the youngest age, followed by decoration, and finally firing, with the progression largely driven by the child's interest and skill level. Specific ages are rarely given. But, while no ethnographies report children shaping pots prior to age 5, several cite age 5 as the youngest age when girls are expected to begin learning adult tasks (Dennis 1940:40; Hill 1982:139). At Hopi, groups of girls under age 12 sometimes make small pots and fire them outside (Dennis 1940:50). Lydia Wyckoff (1990:138–139) argues that Hopi children internalize appropriate concepts of design placement and space by age 9–10. Parsons (1991:94–95) reports that Zuni girls begin to coil, paint, and fire bowls after age 6–7. Hopi-Tewa potter Daisy Hooee Nampeyo learned pottery production from her grandmother Nampeyo, and apparently began painting small pots before 10 years of age (Fowler 1977:29). Fowler's description of this learning process provides the greatest detail,

> [Daisy] had difficulty painting the straight lines that encircled the round bowls. The paint had to be applied correctly the first time. . . . Nampeyo told her that she was not holding the yucca fiber brush correctly. She put the brush between Daisy's thumb and index finger

and anchored her last three fingers on the bowl. Then Nampeyo told Daisy to pull the brush over the bowl. That was all that Nampeyo ever taught Daisy about painting. (Fowler 1977:29)

In all of the pueblos with appropriate descriptions of socialization, girls were generally expected to remain at home working with the adult females in the household after age 12 and to have all of the knowledge to run their own home by age 15 (Dennis 1940: 40).

On the basis of this scant ethnographic information, I expect that girls informally observed adult women painting pottery throughout their childhood. They decided when they were interested in learning pottery production and began more formal observational learning from a skilled adult relative, probably between the ages of 5 and 12. By age 15, young women would have to be capable of making their own household pottery.

The information derived from cross-cultural studies of children's drawings (Table 3.1) indicate that by age 5, children would hold paint brushes in the correct manner. They would have gained some control over their linework, but they probably would not be able to imitate all of the basic motifs and symmetries present in Southwestern pottery designs. Girls would attain the motor control and cognitive maturity to replicate the decorative style of their culture, the symmetry functions, and the geometric shapes probably sometime between ages 9 and 12.

In one of the few ethnoarchaeological studies of how children learn to make art, Warren DeBoer (1990) examined geometric designs produced by children among the Shipibo-Conibo in Peru. He reports two common teaching practices for ceramic designs: having the child add secondary lines to a design begun by an adult, and having the child paint over lines faintly incised by an adult. These teaching practices differ from those reported among the historic groups in the American Southwest, but potters may have employed them during earlier time periods. DeBoer also found that learning Shipibo-Conibo art involved successive mastering of a few design elements and operations for their transformation into complex patterns. Children began the process at around age 5 and had mastered the full artistic repertoire by age 16. He particularly notes that cognitive maturity often outstrips artistic performance and motor skill (DeBoer 1990:88). It seems likely that children learning to decorate Southwestern pottery went through a similar process in gradually mastering the intricacies of producing appropriate designs.

METHOD OF ANALYSIS

In selecting the sample for analysis, I chose pots with poorly executed designs from large collections of whole vessels. In comparison to the "standard" vessels in these assemblages, the designs on my sample vessels display poor motor coordination and at best a rudimentary understanding of the "grammatical" rules for executing culturally appropriate designs. There are various possible explanations for this subset of poorly executed designs in these assemblages, all related to the lower motor skills and cognitive maturity evinced by these designs. The possibilities include that the artisan was under the influence of drugs or alcohol, had brain damage or other physical impairment, or was a child lacking the motor skills and cognitive maturity of adults. It is unlikely the drug or alcohol use would account for these designs however, because substance abuse may make artists clumsy, but does not mask their cognitive maturity (Carolyn Wix, associate professor of Art Education, University of New Mexico, pers. comm., 1996). Artisans "under the influence" often decorate using more elaborate designs, rather than childlike imagery. Although adults with physical or mental impairment may have painted the pottery, on strictly logical grounds it seems most likely that children painted these vessels because the incidence of children in villages is certain, while the incidence of the mentally or physically impaired is speculative. Two art educators viewed the vessel designs and confirmed that children likely painted them, although they could not rule out adults with the motor skills or cognitive ability of chil-

dren (Haine Crown and Caroline Wix, pers. comm., 1996).

The contexts of recovery lend support to my proposition that these vessels were painted by children. Twenty of the twenty-eight vessels used in the study come from burials (four come from rooms and four from unreported contexts). Age of the skeletal material is available for only six of these vessels; the other burials were either cremations, so that age could not be determined, or inhumations with no documentation of the skeletal evidence. The six vessels with aged burials all come from the Galaz Ruin, where a large sample of 995 burials was recovered, most (714) from the same time period as the poorly executed pots (Anyon and LeBlanc 1984). Among this large sample, 60 percent of all burials were adults or adolescents over the age of ten. Of the six vessels with poorly executed designs from burials at the site, five were recovered with burials of children and one with an adult. This small sample of pottery thus occurs more often than expected with child burials, suggesting a strong association with children.

While my ultimate sample sizes are small, the samples constitute the most poorly executed designs in these large assemblages. The first group of vessels comes from the Hohokam area of southern Arizona. The Hohokam occupied the Sonoran Desert of southern Arizona from about A.D. 1 to approximately A.D. 1450. Hohokam decorated pottery has distinctive red designs on a buff-colored paste, sometimes with a buff wash used to lighten the paste further. Artisans formed Hohokam vessels using paddle and anvil thinning. The Hohokam ceramics used in this study consist of ten Sacaton Red-on-buff (A.D. 900–1150) pots drawn from an assemblage of 1,324 vessels by Dr. Owen Lindauer (see Lindauer 1988). The sample includes four jars, five bowls, and one ladle recovered at three different sites (Snaketown, Gatlin, and an unnamed site). Eight of the vessels come from cremations and two from unknown contexts. Seven show little to no use wear, and three have use wear on the interior or exterior base.

The second group consists of nine Mimbres Black-on-white (A.D. 1000–1150) bowls drawn from published photographs of 821 vessels from the Galaz Ruin in southeastern New Mexico (Anyon and LeBlanc 1984). A branch of the Mogollon culture, the Mimbres area was occupied by pottery-producing farming groups from approximately A.D. 200 to 1450. Classic Mimbres Black-on-white vessels are among the most widely prized pottery among collectors, and hence pot hunting has devastated Mimbres sites. Made by coiling and thinned by scraping, and painted using black paint on a white slip, Mimbres vessels are primarily bowls and often recovered in burial contexts. Mimbres designs include both representational and geometric images. Six of the vessels with poorly painted designs come from inhumations (five children and one adult), one from a room, and two from unknown contexts. Only two of the vessels had "kill" holes, holes commonly knocked through the bottom of Mimbres bowls found in burials. Three vessels show little to no use wear, but the remaining six have moderate to heavy abrasion on the interior.

The final sample of ceramics consists of nine Salado polychrome bowls (A.D. 1300–1450) drawn from an assemblage of 778 vessels published by Crown (1994). Salado polychrome pottery is among the most widely produced ceramic wares in the prehistoric Southwest, distributed in most of Arizona, and portions of New Mexico, Chihuahua, and Sonora. Formed by coiling and thinned by scraping, the bowls used in this sample have black-on-white designs on the interior and red slip on the exterior. The nine vessels come from eight different sites. Six of the bowls were recovered from inhumations and the remaining three from rooms. Although ages are not available for the skeletal material in the burials, one of the vessels from Los Muertos comes from a burial pit that is child-sized (Haury 1945, fig. 17, Burial 81 in Room Q). Three bowls showed little to no use wear, while the other six had heavy wear. I recognize that the sample sizes are small, but consider this a pilot study.

Analytical techniques utilized the vast literature on children's art in the fields of psychology and education, extrapolating attributes closely tied to cognitive and motor development cross-culturally (Table 3.1). I included attributes employed in evaluating drawing tests administered for psychological and educational purposes (see particularly Goodnow 1977; John-Steiner 1975). I structured the coding format to avoid the ethnocentric biases present in many of the psychological tests that use drawings as measures of intelligence. In some cases, information from drawing studies indicated age-specific changes that are tied to the pencil and paper medium used in those tests. I avoided the use of these attributes as well, or modified them to fit renderings using paint and a brush. I recorded 18 attributes for each vessel (Table 3.2). The first 12 attributes are best characterized as reflecting cognitive development, including the ability to replicate geometric shapes, understand the grammatical structure of a design, and use symmetry functions. The second group of 6 attributes measure motor control in executing the designs. However, motor controls relate to chronological age as well as previous experience. An experienced 5-year-old may draw as well as an inexperienced 8-year-old. For this reason, assignment of an absolute chronological age was not possible. The value codes for each attribute increase with increasing complexity, and thus a higher number, both for individual attributes and total score, is assumed to reflect an older artist.

Slides or photographs of individual vessels were examined in detail, and codes and notes recorded. Totals for vessels and groups of vessels were tallied. Because of the small sample sizes, I did not attempt any further statistical manipulation of the data. Prior to reviewing the results of the study, I briefly provide the reasoning behind the attributes selected for study.

ATTRIBUTES FOR SOCIALIZATION STUDY

1. Number of motif units. The basis for this attribute derives from two aspects of children's drawings. First, children tend to be economical in their use of units in drawings,

TABLE 3.2.
Coding Format for Socialization Study

1. Number of motif units
2. Motif state
   1. empty
   2. solid
   3. hatched
3. Amount of field filled with design
   1. 25%
   2. 50%
   3. 75%
   4. 100%
4. Type of drawing:
   0. indescribable
   1. simple geometric
   2. complex geometric, e.g., interlocking
   3. representational
   4. both
5. Integration of motifs
   1. no integration of motifs
   2. integration of 2 motifs in drawing
   3. integration of 3 or more motifs in drawing
6. Grammatical structure
   1. no grammatical structure, doesn't follow cultural grammar in structure
   2. clear, but clumsy attempt at traditional structure
   3. clear, correct grammatical structure
7. Proportions of motifs
   1. same motifs of different sizes, do not fit design
   2. motifs of roughly equivalent sizes
   3. motifs of appropriate, equivalent sizes
8. Execution
   1. scribble shapes
   2. outline and fill in
   3. contour (threading) and fill in
9. Direction of spiral
   1. counterclockwise
   2. clockwise
10. Symmetry (highest level for any motifs)
    1. asymmetrical
    2. repetition
    3. rotation around point
    4. reflection across vertical/horizontal line
    5. reflection across diagonal line
11. Use of vessel as field
    1. no attempt to include vessel shape in field of painting
    2. clear, but failed attempt to use vessel shape
    3. uses vessel as field
12. Shapes
    1. lines
    2. plus circles, spirals
    3. plus other geometric shapes (squares, rectangles)

TABLE 3.2 Continued

13. Overlapping lines
    1. uncontrolled use of space
    2. each shape to own space
    3. appropriate overlapping linework/motifs

14. Number of clear errors in painting
    1. over 10
    2. 5–10
    3. 1–5
    4. none

15. Motor control/linework
    1. sloppy, overlapping, many liftings of brush
    2. fewer brush liftings, some overlaps
    3. fine, continuous linework

16. Linework/direction
    1. random
    2. inappropriate (bottom to top, right to left)
    3. appropriate (top to bottom, left to right)

17. Line width (finest)
    1. fat/variable
    2. medium/variable
    3. medium/controlled
    4. fine

18. Line control
    1. shaky
    2. better, but not parallel
    3. controlled, parallel lines

using the same motifs repeatedly rather than many different attributes (Goodnow 1977: 150). Elaboration increases with age. Second, Piaget has shown that children cannot copy a complete range of geometric shapes until they reach age 7 (Krampen 1991:37). Therefore, the number of different motifs used in a drawing may reflect the age of the artist.

2. Motif state. Young children tend to leave geometric shapes as open as possible, with each unit having its own boundary (Goodnow 1977:150). They also have problems staying within the lines in filling in larger geometric shapes. For these reasons, empty shapes are more likely to be the products of younger children, followed by solid shapes, and finally hatched shapes. Hatching requires both greater cognitive maturity and motor skills to achieve.

3. Amount of field filled with design. Young children tend to render drawings in only one corner of a sheet of paper (Biber 1962), with increasing use of the whole sheet of paper with increasing age (John-Steiner 1975:114–116). In evaluating this attribute, I did not consider the size of the design significant, if it was placed centrally within the vessel; that is, a design might occupy only 25 percent of the total vessel surface, but be given a rating of 100 percent if the design was centrally placed and appropriate within the particular culturally defined decorative repertoire.

4. Type of drawing. Young children tend to draw geometric designs with little recognizable pictorial content. The average age at which a child draws something recognizable to an adult is 3 years, 9 months (Biber 1962). It is assumed then that the youngest children would not even have the skill to draw a simple geometric drawing. With increasing age, children would master simple geometric designs, more complex geometric designs

(with interlocking motifs, for example), representational designs, and finally designs with both representational figures and geometric patterns integrated into a whole.

5. Integration of motifs. Children master increasing numbers of geometric figures with age, but they also are increasingly able to integrate these into a coordinated pattern (Biber 1962). Only older children could execute designs that incorporate interlocking or concentric motifs.

6. Grammatical structure. All cultures maintain a decorative style characterized by recognizable, repeatable grammatical rules. These include rules concerning proper design placement, relationships of motifs, design structure (layout), and use of symmetry functions. Understanding of the grammatical structure of a particular culturally defined decorative tradition is clearly present cross-culturally by ages 7 to 9 (Wilson and Ligtvoet 1992). Correct placement of motifs, embedding of smaller figures within larger motifs, and use of advanced symmetry functions all occur in chronological sequences that begin as early as age 4, but are not likely to be completely acquired until after age 7 (Krampen 1991:37–39).

7. Proportions of motifs. Southwestern pottery designs were rarely sketched on vessels prior to painting. Placement of equivalently-sized motifs in the design from one portion of the drawing to the next was a particularly difficult task, probably possible only with increasing ability to control proportions (Goodnow 1977:46; Krampen 1991:39) at about ages 7 to 9.

8. Execution. Linework using drawing materials follows a clear sequence from scribbling, to single lines, to contour or threaded lines used to outline an entire figure (Biber 1962; Goodnow 1977). Although contouring is considered a more advanced method for outlining motifs, use of paints would limit the amount of contouring possible because of the need to resupply the paint on the brush at intervals. Nevertheless, contoured outlines for motifs were given higher scores than motifs outlined with multiple short lines.

9. Direction of spiral. With increasing age,

children develop rules for drawing specific shapes. These include drawing circles and spirals in a clockwise fashion (Goodnow 1977:96). This particular rule is abandoned in Western cultures at school age, because teachers instruct children to make the letter "O" in a counterclockwise fashion.

10. Symmetry. The work of Drora Booth (described in Goodnow 1977:40–42) indicates a sequence for learning symmetry functions cross-culturally, from simple repetition (translation) to rotation around a point, to reflection across a vertical or horizontal line, to reflection across a diagonal line.

11. Use of vessel as field for decoration. Young children learn to use a sheet of paper as the field for a drawing by about the age of 3½ (Biber 1962). Designs that mold the motifs to the vessel shape are clearly more advanced than designs that ignore the shape of the vessel walls.

12. Shapes. Children learn motifs in a regular sequence, beginning with lines, followed by circles, spirals, dots, and then more complex geometric forms. Highly complex geometric forms are generally not possible before about age 7 (Krampen 1991:37–39).

13. Overlapping lines. Young children or children with little practice drawing are not able to control their muscles to prevent overlapping lines in drawing. With increasing age (up until about ages 4 to 7), children tend to prefer to keep motifs separate, with clear boundaries and no purposeful overlap. By age 7 and up, children are increasingly able to control their muscles to prevent overlapping lines and understand the appropriate use of motifs touching one another according to specific principles of design elaboration (Goodnow 1977:150).

14. Number of errors. There is good evidence that adult potters purposely incorporated some errors in some Southwestern pottery designs (Crown 1994; Lindauer 1988). The actual number of errors in pottery designs painted by adults tends to be low and to follow specific rules. For this reason, the rate of errors in these children's designs is believed to relate largely to their ability to execute a design correctly based on age and practice.

TABLE 3.3.
Means and Ranges for Scores for Total Drawing Ability, Motor Skills Attributes, and Cognitive
Maturity Attributes for Three Wares

Ware	Mean of Total Score	Range for Total Scores	Mean for Motor Skills	Range for Motor Skills	Mean for Cognitive Maturity	Range for Cognitive Maturity
Hohokam	.62	.46–.72	.5	.3–.7	.64	.46–.76
Mimbres	.63	.33–.82	.58	.3–.95	.62	.34–.8
Salado	.64	.52–.84	.64	.4–.85	.64	.46–.85
Possible Scores		.26–1.00		.3–1.00		.24–1.00

15. Motor control/linework. With increasing age and practice, children are increasingly able to limit the number of times they must lift the brush off a vessel to replace the paint, particularly within a single straight line.

16. Linework/direction. Goodnow (1977: 87–96) reviews a number of rules followed by children (and adults) cross-culturally in drawing designs. These include drawing horizontal lines left to right, vertical lines right to left, and contouring (threading) lines whenever possible. Such rules are strongly adhered to by age 7, and studies show that children will increasingly turn the paper around to follow the rules, rather than break them in tracing an oddly shaped form (Goodnow 1977: 102). To some extent, these rules are dictated by the medium used and handedness, because incorrect use of the rules might result in smearing of a line if the hand drags over the paint. In literate cultures, such rules may be altered with the introduction of writing. In evaluating use of such rules, I accounted for the use of paint as the medium.

17. Line width. With increasing motor coordination, children are increasingly able to control the width of their linework, so that individual lines do not vary in width and all lines are of equivalent width, where appropriate. Finer lines of equivalent width are assumed to be the work of older children, or children with more practice.

18. Line control. Line control is probably largely a function of practice in using paint brushes on vessels. Ethnographies describe techniques such as turning the vessel while holding the brush steady and pulling the

brush over the vessel (rather than pushing it) as important in mastering line control on pottery (Fowler 1977:29).

RESULTS

After examining and coding each vessel, I tallied the codes to derive a total score. A single attribute, spiral direction, could not be recorded for every vessel because spirals were not present on every vessel. Therefore, the total scores for each vessel were divided to normalize the scores by the highest possible score (61 or 63) depending on whether a spiral was present. These normalized total scores for vessels of each ware are presented in Figure 3.1, and means and ranges for each group of vessels are presented in Figure 3.2 and Table 3.3. In addition, I divided scores into their cognitive and motor components, with the normalized scores, means and ranges presented in Figures 3.3–3.5 and in Table 3.3 (here the "spiral" attribute was omitted). Finally, Figure 3.6 presents histograms of motor skill scores subtracted from cognitive maturity scores. Negative scores here indicate higher motor coordination than cognitive maturity, while positive scores indicate higher cognitive maturity than motor skills. In interpreting the results, I assume that the "motor skills" scores reflect a combination of age and previous experience, while the "cognitive maturity" scores are a stronger indicator of age alone. I also assume that the pots examined reflect an adequate range of children's products for that ware. Finally, I assume that, because these are the sloppiest vessels in each assemblage, they represent the earliest efforts of budding potters. It is

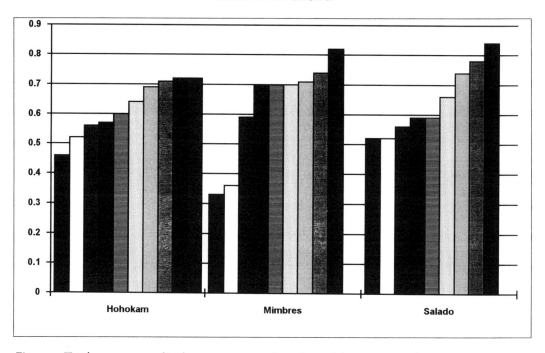

Fig. 3.1. Total scores normalized as percentages of total possible points (63) for eighteen attributes. Each bar represents a single vessel.

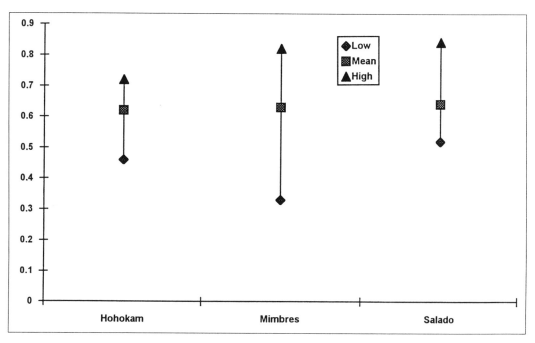

Fig. 3.2. Means and ranges for normalized scores.

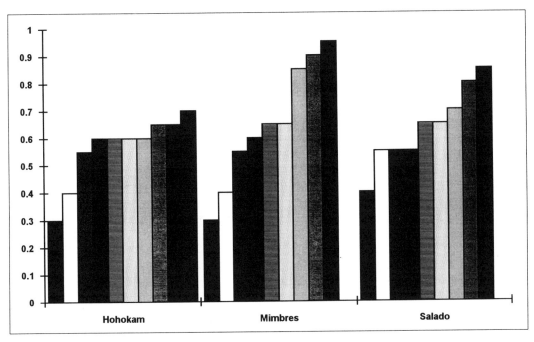

Fig. 3.3. Normalized scores for variables related to motor control for pottery decorations. Higher scores indicate greater motor coordination evident in designs, related to age and practice. Possible scores range from .3–1.00. Each bar represents a single vessel.

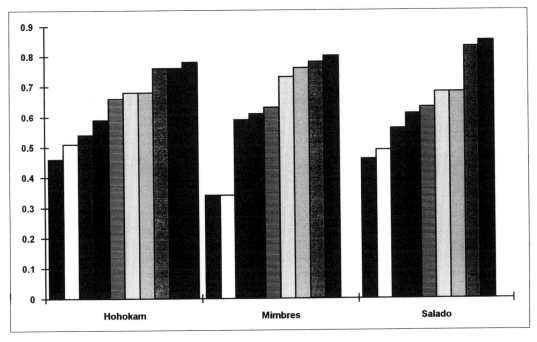

Fig. 3.4. Normalized scores for variable related to cognitive ability on pottery. Higher scores indicate greater cognitive ability related to age. Possible scores range from 10 up (because one variable, number of motif units, may have any number). Each bar represents a single vessel.

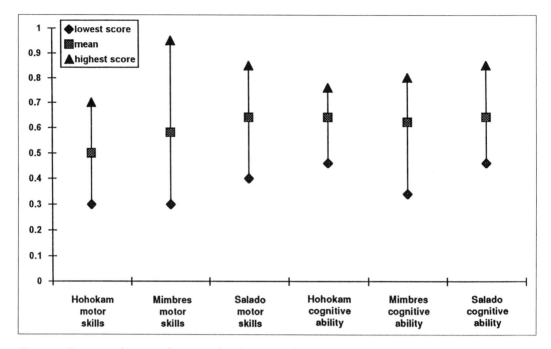

Fig. 3.5. Range and means for normalized scores related to motor skills and cognitive ability for three wares.

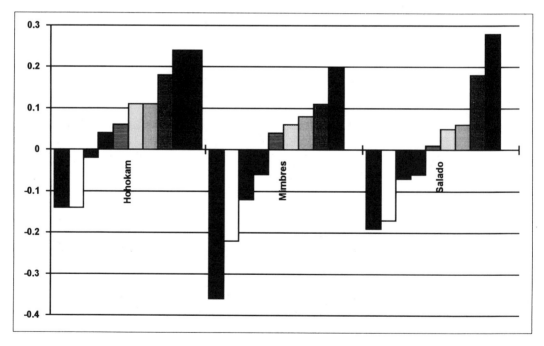

Fig. 3.6. Normalized cognitive maturity minus motor coordination scores for vessels. Negative scores indicate higher motor coordination than cognitive maturity, while positive scores indicate higher cognitive skills. Each bar represents a single vessel.

entirely possible however, that even earlier efforts were attempted, but not fired. The results demonstrate considerable uniformity in the mean total scores, although the ranges for each ware differ. I review the results for each of the different wares before returning to general conclusions.

The Hohokam sample exhibits the smallest range for total score, suggesting that Hohokam children painted these pots at roughly the same age and skill level. Interestingly, the Hohokam sample also exhibits the lowest mean score for motor skills, suggesting that the children were either younger or had less previous artistic practice than children painting the vessels in the other two samples. The fact that the scores for cognitive maturity are fairly high implies that the children lacked previous experience rather than that they were younger than the other groups. As shown in Figure 3.6, the Hohokam sample had the least number of vessels with negative scores, indicating that on most vessels the scores for cognitive maturity were higher than those for motor skills. Indeed, the combination of narrow ranges of scores and low mean score for motor skills suggests a possible cohort effect; that is, girls may have begun decorating pottery at roughly the same age. Either cultural taboos or the lack a suitable medium may have kept them from practicing drawing prior to that age. The results imply a more formal training of Hohokam girls in pottery decoration. This conclusion is borne out by the scores for the grammatical structure attribute. Eighty percent of the Hohokam vessels show that the painters had a clear understanding of how a "Hohokam" design should look, even though they could not reproduce one well (for example, Fig. 3.7b, c). This contrasts with the Mimbres and Salado samples, where only 67 percent and 44 percent respectively indicated a clear understanding of the correct structure of their design systems. Only two of the vessels have the uneven, asymmetrical shape that suggests they were formed by inexperienced children. Adults may have shaped the pots for these young artists to decorate, or children may

have honed their skills in forming pottery before they were allowed to paint the pots.

In contrast, the Mimbres pots show the greatest range of scores for all groups of attributes. Two vessels in particular are poorly executed, with single lines drawn with no apparent understanding of how designs on Mimbres Black-on-white pottery are typically structured (Fig. 3.7d, e). These poorly executed vessels suggest that Mimbres children were allowed to decorate pottery at an early age, perhaps gaining practice experience. This interpretation is borne out in Figure 3.6; Mimbres vessels show the greatest discrepancy between motor skills scores and cognitive maturity scores. I conclude from this that Mimbres children probably began decorating pottery when they decided they were ready, much as Hopi children did (Dennis 1940; Fowler 1977). Children probably formed four of the nine vessels, as well. Interestingly, the two vessels painted by the youngest artisans are too carefully, symmetrically formed to be the products of equivalently aged children; they almost certainly were formed by adults who allowed children to paint these well-made pots.

The Salado vessels had the highest overall scores, with ranges between the Hohokam and Mimbres samples. Although apparently older than the youngest Mimbres artists, there is no evidence of a "cohort effect" among the Salado sample. I have argued elsewhere that the Salado polychrome vessels were manufactured in a variety of different locales throughout the Southwest (Crown 1994). Unlike the other samples, the Salado bowls examined here may well have been decorated in several different villages by children raised in different "cultures" (they come from eight different sites stretching from Four Mile Ruin in northern Arizona to the Davis Ruin in southern Arizona). Interestingly, the two bowls from the Hohokam site of Los Muertos produced scores that fall within the ranges for Hohokam red-on-buff vessels. Seven of the nine Salado polychrome vessels appear to have been formed by children as well, suggesting that they parti-

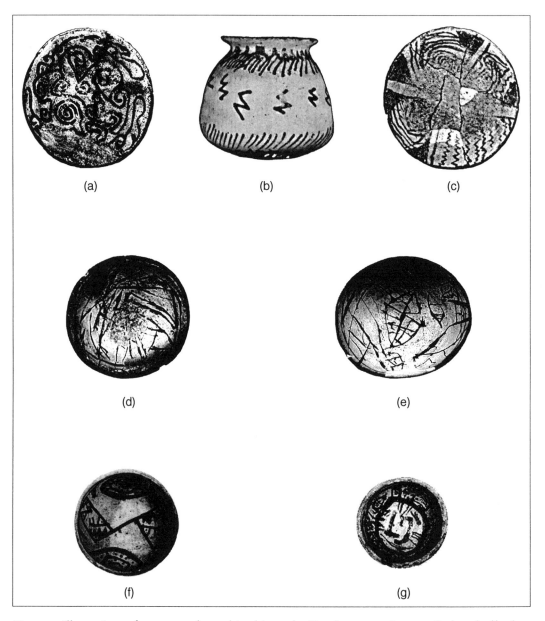

Fig. 3.7. Illustrations of some vessels used in this study. Vessels a–c are Sacaton Red-on-buff, photographs courtesy of Owen Lindauer (Arizona State Museum catalog numbers GP43340 [a], LP-4 [b], and GP43714 [c]). Vessels d–e are Mimbres Black-on-white vessels, photographs from the Mimbres Archive, University of New Mexico, Albuquerque, Maxwell Museum of Anthropology (Mimbres Archive catalog numbers 3104 [d] and 3366 [e]). Vessels f–g are Salado polychrome bowls, photographed by the author (Arizona State Museum catalog numbers GP12586 [f] and GP11245 [g]).

cipated in every aspect of the production process of most of these vessels.

Some additional patterning is worth noting. First, the most common motifs on the vessels, lines, spirals, squiggle lines, and circles, represent the earliest motifs drawn by children throughout the world, generally by age 3 (Krampen 1991:67). In his study of the Shipibo-Conibo, DeBoer (1990) notes that children begin their artistic careers by learning the most basic element, the cross, followed by increasingly complex operations for altering and filling it. It appears that children learning to paint Southwestern pottery may have begun with a fairly limited range of motifs as well, perhaps mastering the appropriate incorporation of these in designs before progressing to more complex decorative patterning. Only two vessels had representational drawings: one Mimbres bowl had a beetle and one Salado bowl depicts a flower. Second, virtually all of the designs reflect an understanding and use of the vessel shape as the field structuring the decoration. Despite this understanding, many of the budding artisans did not appear to understand how to turn the vessel while painting it; instead, they held the pot in a single orientation while painting the designs, resulting in portions of motifs that were well-executed and portions that were agonizingly distorted. Studies show that Western children increasingly rotate their drawings from ages 3 to 6 to maintain a consistent hand movement in producing geometric shapes (Goodnow 1977: 102), and that the rules for line orientation are assimilated by age 7. The fact that some designs demonstrate that these children had not yet learned to turn the pots suggests that the rules for hand motion were incompletely assimilated when the pots were decorated. Third, as shown in Figure 3.6, cognitive maturity and motor skills were clearly at odds on many of these vessels. Some exhibited complex designs clumsily executed, and others exhibited controlled brushwork with little understanding of appropriate design standards. Poor planning characterized virtually all of the designs, with motifs of radically different sizes squeezed to fit the space.

Figure 3.7 illustrates vessels with many of these problems. The linework in Vessel A (Fig. 3.7) shows considerable motor control over the brushwork, clear contouring of lines, with virtually no overlap of this intricate design. Such motor coordination suggests an older child painted the vessel. Surprisingly, however, the design does not fit the traditional stylistic parameters for Hohokam pottery, particularly with its asymmetrical

pattern and lack of focus. Although Hohokam pottery occasionally exhibits an asymmetrical design, the decoration usually has a clear central focus (and is often a large, single spiral). Vessel B reveals the problems that arise when young potters do not turn vessels. The parallel lines at the base of the jar are painted from top to bottom, as shown by the "blobs" of paint where the paintbrush first contacted the jar surface. These lines follow the rules for linework, painting vertical lines from top to bottom, and they are nicely executed. The lines at the top of the jar suggest that the artisan did not continue to paint from top to bottom. The clumsiness of these lines suggest that the child did not turn the vessel around and paint from top to bottom, but instead held the vessel in a constant position and painted from bottom to top. The blobs of paint are now at the bottom of the lines, rather than at the tops. Hence, the lines are not evenly spaced, but are slightly wavy and of uneven length. Yet here, the Hohokam child had a clear conception of the appropriate rules for painting a jar; only the execution suggests a lack of practice in the best way to paint vessels. A young artisan began painting Vessel C as a traditional Hohokam design, identical in layout to typical Sacaton Red-on-buff designs (Haury 1976, fig. 12.18). Their initial attempt to quarter the vessel created fairly unequal quarters. The squiggle-line hatchure in the lower left quarter and the spiral in the lower right quarter are appropriate fillers, although clumsily executed. Indeed the spiral seems to show the effects of a lack of vessel turning as well, so that the artisan had to lift the brush often to paint each small turn of the curves. The top two quadrants are not appropriate, they should match their opposites. Instead, yet another spiral was attempted where squiggle lines should have been in the upper right, and a combination of squiggles and spirals placed where one large spiral should be in the upper left. In both of the latter two examples, the Hohokam children were old enough to know how a vessel should look, but inexperienced in the mechanics of linework on a three-dimensional vessel.

The two Mimbres vessels illustrated in Figure 3.7 (d, e) were painted by children who lacked either the cognitive maturity to replicate traditional Mimbres designs or the motor coordination to control their linework. The motifs are unrecognizable and the linework reveals that the brush was lifted often to replenish paint.

A Salado polychrome bowl from Gila Pueblo (Fig. 3.7f) had one of the highest total scores of any vessel in the case study. The layout is appropriate for this ware, and in general the linework shows considerable control over the brushwork. The motifs reveal the relative inexperience of this potter, however. The two spirals are not appropriate motifs for Salado polychrome pottery. Instead, Salado potters often employed curvilinear scrolls in their designs and filled them with hatchure or solid black paint. This young potter apparently did not know how to make the scrolls, and made single spiral lines instead. She then began to fill the upper spiral with hatchure, before apparently recognizing that she had not executed a true scroll and abandoning the hatching for a series of dots, which are highly unusual motifs on this ware. The lower spiral is filled only with dots. The extreme variation in line width also suggests inexperience, as single lines waver from thick to thin. The small bowl in Figure 3.7g is from a burial at a site in the Tonto Basin. The initial layout of the design is appropriate, with thick lines bordering a band around the interior. The fillers are not traditional designs however, with an array of small dots and lines failing to form any recognizable or symmetrical pattern. The frequency of overlapping lines suggests a relative lack of motor coordination in brush control. The thicker lines on the vessels appear more controlled in execution, and may actually have been painted with the artisans fingers rather than a brush.

Pottery decoration constrained these young artisans. Paint had to be applied correctly the first time (Fowler 1977:29). Vessel shape distorted designs, and small vessel sizes made it difficult to fit hands and brushes inside the vessels. Many of the designs indicate a complex goal incompletely realized. While Native American girls today practice pottery designs on paper, prehistoric children had no comparable medium for practicing this craft before actually painting pots. They could etch on plaster walls or draw in the sand, but these are not directly equivalent to mastering the yucca brushes, dripping paint, and curving walls of ceramic vessel decoration. The only way to learn to paint a pot was to begin painting pots. The fact that most of these vessels have considerable use-wear indicates that they were considered appropriate vessels for incorporation into household or personal assemblages.

Assigning ages to the children who painted these prehistoric vessels is difficult. With the exception of the two most poorly executed Mimbres bowls, the linework, knowledge of how a design should look, adoption of the distinctive cultural styles, and ability to execute geometric shapes and basic symmetry relations suggests that these children were at least 7 years of age. The complexity of many of the designs suggests that most of the children were older than this, probably 9 to 12. The two Mimbres vessels with the lowest scores (Fig. 7d, e) could have been painted by children perhaps as young as 4 to 6. One of these bowls (Fig. 7e) accompanied the burial of a child, between 3 and 10 years of age (Anyon and LeBlanc 1984). The other bowl came from a room (Anyon and LeBlanc 1984).

SUMMARY AND CONCLUSIONS

This pilot study provides a method for assessing the general ages at which children were socialized in pottery decoration. The results using small samples confirm that differences exist in the ages at which children were first allowed to decorate pots among the different wares present in the Southwest. They suggest that Mimbres children began decorating pottery at an earlier age than children elsewhere. They also suggest that Hohokam girls were introduced to pottery decoration later than the other children, perhaps as a cohort. Finally, they reveal that most children were better able to visualize designs than execute them correctly, indicating greater cognitive maturity than practical skill in painting pottery. The proposed ages at learning pottery decoration largely agree with those documented in the Southwestern ethnographic record.

The vessels used in this study were derived from large assemblages. The fact that relatively few vessels fit the criteria of pots decorated by children suggests that children never painted large quantities of Southwestern pottery, or that if they did, only select practice vessels (such as the first attempt) were actually fired or kept. Expanding the samples for additional assessment of pottery socialization will require examining even larger assemblages in the future. Clear understanding of the painting process is best achieved through direct observation of the vessels rather than photographs. Use of collections from known proveniences with adequate documentation of associated skeletal material or accompanying artifactual remains is

also important. Examination of middens to determine the incidence of such vessels in trash is also important for understanding the relatively low frequency of whole vessels painted by children, and would particularly aid in resolving whether other products were disposed before or after firing, rather than incorporated into household assemblages.

The methods presented here have great potential to expand our understanding of family and community dynamics in the past. Children are among the most ignored individuals in our reconstructions of the prehistoric Southwest. In becoming productive adults, Southwestern children learned myriad skills. By evaluating when this socialization began, we will achieve a larger perspective on social organization, adult workloads, and the organization of production in the past. We will also take one additional step toward putting faces on the people that we study.

4

Standardization and Specialization: What's the Link?

William A. Longacre

For over twenty years, archaeologists have been concerned with the identification of the early appearance of specialized production and the implications of such a production mode for understanding the rise of complex forms of social and political organization. One vector to approach specialization has been to look at standardization, an expected correlate of increasing specialized production. At first, these arguments were based upon "common sense" notions and most focused upon pottery. One of the earliest of these statements is, not surprisingly, by Anna O. Shepard (1958:452) as noted by Rice (1991:258). Many examples of authors pointing to the expected relationship between specialization and product standardization can be listed (e.g., Benco 1988; Hagstrum 1985; Longacre et al. 1988; Rice 1981, 1987:201–204; 1991; Riley 1979; Rottlander 1966, 1967; Sinopoli 1988; Tosi 1984; van der Leeuw 1977), and this is not an exhaustive list!

More recent discussions have explored data from complex societies in Mesopotamia (Blackman et al. 1993; Stein and Blackman 1993) or from China (Underhill 1991) or from the Americas (D. Arnold and Nieves 1992; P. Arnold 1991; Costin and Hagstrum 1995; Crown 1995; Stark 1995). There is one recent example from ethnoarchaeology (London 1991). In both the earlier and recent discussions, product standardization is viewed usually as a by-product of specialization. It results from routine and repeated actions in the formation of ceramic products (see Sinopoli 1988:582). Routinization is responsible for decreased variability in the products produced, according to this view.

Greatly stimulated by the work of Rice over the years and especially by her comments in her recent review essay (1991) on these matters, I designed field work to explore these relationships. I was especially taken by her comments about the place of skill in our consideration of standardization (Rice 1991:268–273). Although Rice argues that we really do not have satisfactory definitions of what we mean by specialization (1991: 277), when I use the term, I am referring to what she has termed Producer Specialization (Rice 1991:263). I use it to refer to those individuals who carry out no additional economic pursuits except pottery making.

Ceramic ethnoarchaeology has a bias in that our focus is upon whole pots, not sherds. Standardization has been studied by assessing whole vessel morphological variation in such studies. Measuring pots and comparing such measurements through statistics such as the coefficient of variation has been the rule. Rice (1991:279) seems to hint that metrical variation might not be a suitable approach for studying product standardization. But it is such an obvious tactic for exploring variation in products that I continue to use such data as a means for assessing degree of standardization.

But is increasing standardization simply the brute result of routinization, of repetitious behaviors over time? Or does skill play a role? Indeed, is standardization a deliberate, sought after feature in container design? Blackman et al. (1993:75) argue that some of the differences in the ceramics they studied might reflect differences in the skills of the individual artisans who produced the pottery in their study. Dean Arnold in this volume (Chapter 5) also discusses the role of skill in pottery production. His conclusions are somewhat different from the ones drawn here.

What better place to explore the potential relationships between producer specialization and product standardization than in the modern world? We can do this through ethnoarchaeology, wherein the archaeologist takes her or his hypotheses to a living community to examine the linkage between material culture and human behavior and organization to improve archaeological inference. Our task is to document correlates that will permit the prehistorian to strengthen his interpretations.

Two published studies to date by me and my colleagues have explored the linkage between degree of producer specialization and degree of product standardization based upon ethnoarchaeological data (Longacre et al. 1988; Kvamme et al. 1996). In both studies, there does, indeed, seem to be a link. In this study, I report the results of an additional study, designed to explore the impact of skill, acquired through time as a result of practice, in the production of standardized products by producer specialists. This ethnoarchaeological project was initiated in the spring and summer of 1995 and continued during the summer of 1996 among a small group of specialized pottery producers in the town of San Nicolas in Ilocos Norte Province in the northwestern part of the island of Luzon in the northern Philippines (Fig. 4.1).

The field site is Barangay number six, San Juan Bautista, in San Nicolas. There are only eight houses that have potters active in the neighborhood; all together there are 20 potters working. Several of them only make flower pots with the rest making cooking pots of several sizes and water jars.

Imbedded in the larger project I am carrying out at San Nicolas is my plan to test the related hypotheses that skill does play an important role in producing product standardization and that increasing skill over time results in increased standardization of the product. The research design focuses upon only one vessel category, the regular size water jar (malabi). And I focus upon only four potters. Two of the potters are the most experienced and most expert (community consensus) of the active potters. The other two are younger and less experienced. The sole male potter in the community is only 18-years-old and only recently has learned to make the water jar. Crown (Chapter 3) explores the implications for very young potters learning the art of pottery making and their lack of skill in relation to the nature of the products produced.

If the hypotheses are supported, then we will expect that the water jars made by the two older, more experienced potters will exhibit less metrical variation, i.e., increased standardization when compared to the pots produced by the younger, less experienced potters. This will be expected if skill in pottery making is principally the result of experience. But there is one other consideration to explore in this study. This is the difference between standardization as a brute result of experience and that produced by deliberate effort by the potters.

Do the potters have in mind a specific metrical design for a water jar? How exacting are their designs? Is acquired skill an important predictor of achieving specific metrical dimensions of water jars (height, aperture, and maximum circumference)? As this pottery is produced by hand, using the paddle and anvil technique for forming, shaping, and thinning, along with the "slow wheel" or "tournette" or, as I prefer in this case, the turning platform, it does seem like an excellent place to explore these hypotheses.

All potters use the same clay and all have equal access to the clay deposit. There is no cost for the clay but it is located some dis-

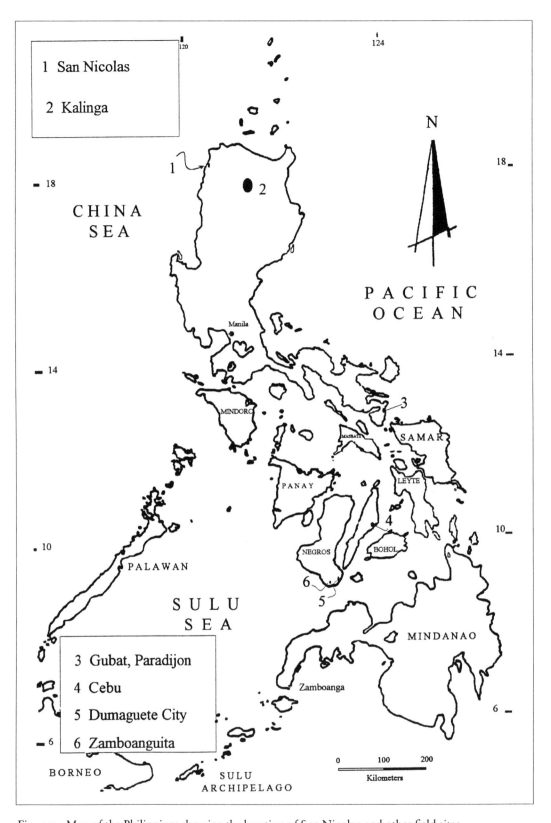

Fig. 4.1. Map of the Philippines showing the location of San Nicolas and other field sites.

tance from the community (some 5 km) and must be dug by hand during the dry season (March and April). To transport it to the potters' homes, a large cart pulled by a bullock is required. Many of the potters own such a cart and those that do not must hire one. The clay is tempered with river sand available less than 1 km away. They mix about three parts clay and one part sand for both cooking pots and water jars.

Men mine the clay and collect the sand at the river and they tend to be related to the potters (often their husbands or fathers). They also help to collect firewood along with the rice chaff from local rice mills for firing the pots.

The stages of manufacture for the water jars as defined by the potters are interesting in their direct reference to standardized sizes:

Ramas: mixing sand and clay

Tukel: making the desired rim size for the water jar

Agbibir: to make the mouth of the pot

Ibilag: to sun-dry

Bennagen: to form the sides ("shoulder") of the pot using the paddle *(pik-pik)*

Addukayen: making the water jar large enough

Banan: achieving the desired or proper size

Aquklios: making the surface finer (polished) using the paddle

Imlo: finishing touches on the water jar—last use of the paddle

Idi-iden: polishing after sun-drying with stone or piece of shell

Pula-an: making it red (applying ground hematite mixed with water, covering the entire vessel surface

Cebba-en: to "burn" the pot

When it is not raining, the potters can make hundreds of pots per week and easily earn 1,000 pesos per week for their effort. During the rainy season, their productivity plummets and they can only occasionally produce pots. The middleperson advances them money at no interest to help the potters get through this period of low production. That loan is paid off in pots at the beginning of the drier times. Almost all the potters sell their products to the middleperson with only one (Avelina)

making two trips a year to sell her pots in a distant town in another province for a much higher profit.

The annual income of a potter (less expenses) approaches that of a school teacher in the Philippines, about 30,000 pesos a year. But the social status of a potter is at the lowest level in San Nicolas society. Social status is not necessarily a product of income. Dean Arnold (1985:196–198) suggests that female potters enjoy relatively high status because they are successful in supplementing household income in agricultural societies. Here at San Nicolas this is not the case. Households depend on agricultural production for their main source of subsistence and income; potters supplement that through the sale of pots. But potters' status is low and most daughters of working potters in San Nicolas do not intend to become potters. Instead, most daughters want to become nurses or school teachers.

The data that form the basis for this small study come from two sources. There are interview data collected from the potters of San Nicolas and there are observations recorded visually and on film during the periods of field work. In addition, water jars were measured and the results analyzed at the University of Arizona. A substantial collection of the water jars used in this study are curated in the Anthropology Museum at the University of the Philippines, Diliman, Quezon City in the Philippines.

The two older, expert potters I will call Avelina and Estrella (Figs. 4.2–4.4). Together, they have about 100 years of experience in potting in this community. They are sisters who married cousins and so have the same last name. They live across from one another in the *barangay* and often make pots in the courtyard that separates their houses. They are each about 60-years-old and have been making pots since they were "little girls." Both learned from their mother (who died in 1996 while I was doing this field study).

The two younger potters chosen for this project I will call Salcedo and Dennis. Salcedo is younger than Avelina and Estrella,

Fig. 4.2. Estrella making a water jar.

Fig. 4.4. Avelina using a large paddle to shape a large water jar.

Fig. 4.3. Avelina and her son, Dennis, making pots.

about 45-years-old. She is the daughter of Estrella's sister-in law and is a widow. Dennis is the son of Avelina and is quite young, about 18 in 1996 (Fig. 4.3). Both learned to make pottery from their mothers. Salcedo has been potting for about 35 years and Dennis for about 10 years. He only knew how to make flower pots until 1996 when his mother be-

came proactive and insisted that he learn the skills involved in the making of water jars and cooking pots. This is so he has a trade for his future income according to Avelina.

During the fieldwork, I observed row upon row of water jars taken out of the stack immediately following firing. I jokingly referred to them as "Xerox copies" of one another (Figs. 4.5–4.7) and asked the potters how they could do that. I joked with them, telling them they must have rulers and templates that they hide when they see me coming! They laughed and told me that it is a matter of skill, of practice in learning how to achieve the standard size of the water jar. They did point out to me that, although the water jars do appear to be of the same size, there are subtle differences that allow them to identify the makers of pots. They claim they can identify the potter by examining the pot with 100 percent accuracy. At least one non-potter, the owner of a warehouse and middle person who buys many of the pots produced at San Nicolas, claims that she, too, can identify the potter by examining the pots. In several "blind" tests, both she and the potters agreed on the potter when shown a series of pots.

They told me that it is a matter of hands and eyes that allows them to produce such standardized pots. They learn "by feel" the correct amount of clay to start with, forming a cylinder of clay as the first step in making a water jar. Each cylinder is identical. They claim that beginners cannot make such standardized pots as they are not yet "expert." That, through time, beginners become increasingly expert and their water jars show decreased variation. Thus, the potters would seem to agree with conventional wisdom ("common sense") and the anthropologists. Are these notions backed by an analysis of the pots themselves? The potters claim that the driving force behind their attempt to produce standard sizes is customer demand. The expectations of the people who purchase the pots—that the pots will be of a certain metrical size and volume—seems to be the expectation that the potters are geared to meet.

The pots made by Dennis, the least "expert" of the potters are noticeably smaller than the water jars made by the other potters (see Table 4.9; Fig. 4.9a). The potters suggested that Dennis does not have the necessary skill yet to produce full-size *malabi*. Even if the pots made by Dennis reveal a degree of standardization, their smaller size points to a lack of skill and experience.

The statistical analyses of the metrical data reveal a number of patterns. Dennis's pots show the greatest coefficients of variation (C.V.) compared to those of Avelina and Estrella, but the differences are not great (Tables 4.1–4.10). Interestingly, the pots of Salcedo show even smaller C.V. scores for circumference but high scores for height and aperture (Table 4.11; Figs. 4.8e, 4.9e, 4.10e). Overall, the hypothesis that there should be a gradient or trajectory of increasing standardization from the pots of Dennis to the pots of Salcedo to those of Avelina and Estrella is supported, albeit not robustly. Sample size variation may play some role in explaining these results. Perhaps the strongest support

Fig. 4.5. Estrella removing water jars from the fire.

Fig. 4.6. Water jars drying on Estrella's porch.

Fig. 4.7. Water jars in use in Estrella's house.

TABLE 4.1.
F-ratio of Sample Variances for Experienced and Inexperienced Potters
Analysis of Variance (ANOVA)

	F-Ratio	Df	p
Ratio	2.60	141	.135
Circumference	41.659	141	.000
Height	6.749	141	.010
Aperture	21.678	141	.000

If p<.05 then reject the null hypothesis (i.e., no difference between experienced and inexperienced potters).

TABLE 4.2.
F-ratio of Sample Variances for Two Experienced Potters, Avelina and Estrella
Analysis of Variance (ANOVA)

	F-Ratio	Df	p
Ratio	.678	96	.412
Circumference	31.725	96	.000
Height	4.468	96	.037
Aperture	12.079	96	.001

TABLE 4.3.
F-ratio of Sample Variances for Two Inexperienced Potters, Dennis and Salcedo
Analysis of Variance (ANOVA)

	F-Ratio	Df	p
Ratio	13.860	43	.001
Circumference	30.924	43	.000
Height	.006	43	.941
Aperture	1.843	43	.182

TABLE 4.4.
Kruskal-Wallis Tests for Significant Differences in the Rank Distribution between Samples
One-way Analysis of Variance for 143 Cases

	Kt	Df	p
Ratio	15.773	3	.001
Circumference	60.889	3	.000
Height	8.220	3	.042
Aperture	24.490	3	.000

A probability (p) of <.05 suggests that there is a statistically significant difference between samples (i.e., between potter's vessels). Measurements of ratio, circumference, height, and aperture were compared between all four potters.

TABLE 4.5.
Pooled Statistics for All Potters: Avelina, Estrella, Salcedo, and Dennis
Total Observations: 143

	Aperture	Height	Circumference	Ratio
N of Cases	143	143	143	143
Minimum	18.000	23.000	94.000	3.728
Maximum	25.700	27.700	108.300	4.457
Mean	19.328	25.262	103.395	4.097
Variance	0.780	0.841	7.282	0.024
Standard d.v.	0.883	0.917	2.698	0.156
Skewness	2.732	0.255	−0.741	0.134
Kurtosis	17.168	0.029	0.985	−0.699
C.V.	0.046	0.036	0.026	0.038
Median	19.200	25.200	103.500	4.095

TABLE 4.6.
Pooled Statistics for Inexperienced Potters: Dennis and Salcedo
Total Observations: 45

	Aperture	Height	Circumference	Ratio
N of Cases	45	45	45	45
Minimum	18.000	23.000	94.000	3.778
Maximum	25.700	27.000	105.400	4.457
Mean	19.802	24.973	101.500	4.068
Variance	1.481	0.860	7.629	0.023
Standard D.V.	1.217	0.927	2.762	0.153
Skewness	2.382	0.069	−1.010	0.489
Kurtosis	10.281	−0.393	0.168	−0.220
C.V.	0.061	0.037	0.027	0.038
Median	19.800	25.000	102.000	4.071

TABLE 4.7.
Pooled Statistics for Experienced Potters: Avelina and Estrella
Total Observations: 98

	Aperture	Height	Circumference	Ratio
N of Cases	98	98	98	98
Minimum	18.000	23.000	99.000	3.728
Maximum	20.700	27.700	108.300	4.420
Mean	19.110	25.394	104.265	4.110
Variance	0.318	0.784	4.768	0.025
Standard D.V.	0.564	0.886	2.184	0.157
Skewness	0.195	0.430	−0.192	−0.024
Kurtosis	−0.098	0.035	−0.463	−0.765
C.V.	0.030	0.035	0.021	0.038
Median	19.000	25.200	104.350	4.116

TABLE 4.8.
Statistical Results for Avelina
Total Observations: 62

	Aperture	Height	Circumference	Ratio
N of Cases	62	62	62	62
Minimum	18.100	24.000	100.200	3.815
Maximum	20.700	27.700	108.300	4.413
Mean	19.253	25.535	105.090	4.120
Variance	0.328	0.816	3.339	0.025
Standard D.V.	0.573	0.904	1.827	0.159
Skewness	0.214	0.582	−0.019	−0.153
Kurtosis	−0.421	−0.591	−0.549	−1.041
C.V.	0.030	0.035	0.017	0.039
Median	19.200	25.300	105.000	4.140

TABLE 4.9.
Statistical Results for Dennis
Total Observations: 20

	Aperture	Height	Circumference	Ratio
N of Cases	20	20	20	20
Minimum	18.000	23.000	94.000	3.877
Maximum	25.700	26.600	103.800	4.087
Mean	20.075	24.985	99.525	3.985
Variance	2.245	0.848	8.485	0.005
Standard D.V.	1.498	0.921	2.913	0.072
Skewness	2.649	−0.284	−0.196	0.016
Kurtosis	8.263	−0.641	−1.233	−1.368
C.V.	0.075	0.037	0.029	0.018
Median	19.800	25.100	99.750	3.996

TABLE 4.10.
Statistical Results for Estrella
Total Observations: 36

	Aperture	Height	Circumference	Ratio
N of Cases	36	36	36	36
Minimum	18.000	23.000	99.000	3.728
Maximum	19.500	27.200	106.800	4.420
Mean	18.864	25.150	102.844	4.093
Variance	0.212	0.655	4.112	0.024
Standard D.V.	0.461	0.804	2.028	0.154
Skewness	−0.532	−0.067	−0.027	0.199
Kurtosis	−0.966	0.615	−1.043	−0.081
C.V.	0.024	0.032	0.020	0.038
Median	19.000	25.000	102.750	4.091

TABLE 4.11.
Statistical Results for Salcedo
Total Observations: 25

	Aperture	Height	Circumference	Ratio
N of Cases	25	25	25	25
Minimum	18.200	23.300	100.900	3.778
Maximum	21.000	27.000	105.400	4.457
Mean	19.584	24.964	103.080	4.135
Variance	0.826	0.906	1.418	0.028
Standard D.V.	0.909	0.952	1.191	0.168
Skewness	−0.018	0.323	0.322	−0.276
Kurtosis	−1.512	−0.205	−0.797	−0.337
C.V.	0.046	0.038	0.012	0.041
Median	19.800	24.900	103.000	4.148

of the hypothesis is seen in the pooled summary statistics for the inexperienced potters compared to the experienced potters (Tables 4.6 and 4.7).

I have adopted the C.V. as the tool for inferring degree of metrical standardization in this case study. It is a powerful tool for assessing such variability in a single field site or within the same cultural setting. The alternative measurement explored in a comparative study of several ceramic assemblages in the Philippines (Kvamme et al. 1996) is most useful in comparing multiple samples that crosscut cultural boundaries.

The metrical data presented in the tables and graphically presented in the plots (Figs. 4.8–4.12) show that there are, indeed, differences among the potters revealed in their pots. This would support interview data suggesting that such differences can be used to identify the products of individual potters. Notice that the pottery produced by Avelina consistently stands out in the measured dimensions (see Table 4.8). Pots produced by Avelina and Estrella only vary about 3 percent metrically whereas pots made by Dennis and Salcedo show greater variation (Tables 4.6–4.11). The pots made by Dennis are clearly smaller, especially in circumference, compared to the water jars made by the other potters.

Pooling the results of the metrical analysis for all the potters produces a view of the water jars that might be more comparable to what we might see in an archaeological sample (Table 4.5 and Fig. 4.12). Here we see the degree of standardization higher than that reported for Kalinga, Gubat (Paradijon), or Cebu (Kvamme et al. 1996; Longacre et al. 1988). The Kalinga pottery varied about 12 percent metrically whereas the pots from Gubat varied about 6 percent. Here at San Nicolas, the variation ranges between about 3 and 4 percent, making it one of the most standardized assemblages I have encountered to date.

Obviously, more data must be collected to arrive at a more secure or even robust conclusion. But these data do support the hypotheses that began this study. There is support for the suggestion that skill, developed as a result of experience, does accumulate through time. The amazing degree of standardization in the San Nicolas water jars also points to the success of the deliberate efforts of the potters to create pots that their consumers expect in terms of size and shape. The older, more experienced potters seem to be able to meet their customer's expectations with greater accuracy than the younger, less experienced ones.

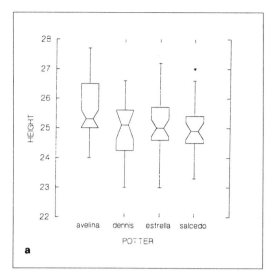

a

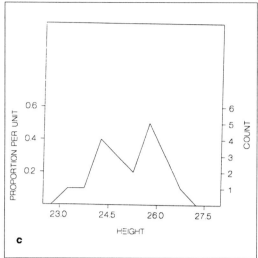

c

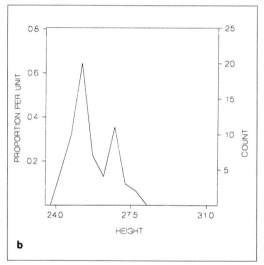

b

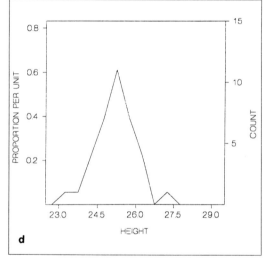

d

Fig. 4.8. Distribution of height; (a) height for all potters, (b) height against frequency for Avelina, (c) height against frequency for Dennis, (d) height against frequency for Estrella, (e) height against frequency for Salcedo.

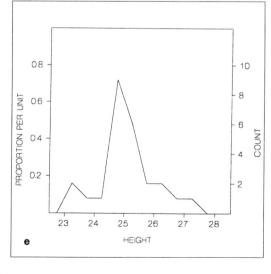

e

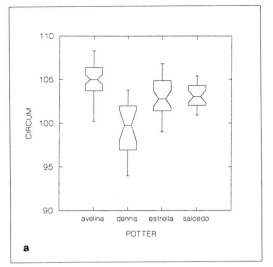

a

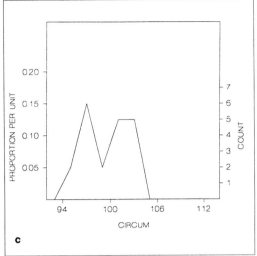

c

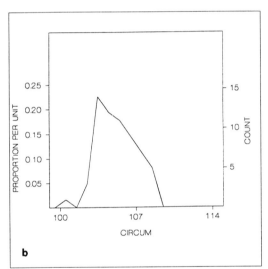

b

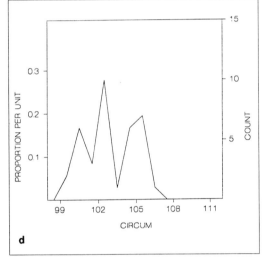

d

Fig. 4.9. Circumference values; (a) distribution of circumference values by potter. This graph depicts the distribution of circumference for all measured water vessels by potter. With the exception of Dennis, circumference revealed the greatest standardization based on the coefficient of variation, (b) circumference by frequency for Avelina, (c) circumference by frequency for Dennis, (d) circumference by frequency for Estrella, (e) circumference by frequency for Salcedo. Graphs b–e suggest that there might be several different vessel sizes and more uniformity in the products by these potters than is reflected statistically.

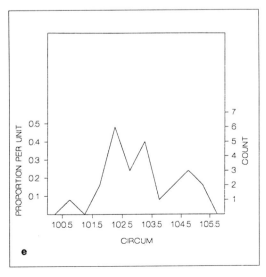

e

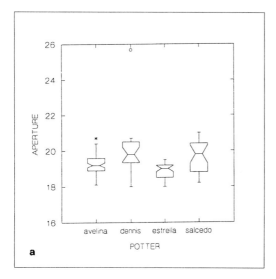

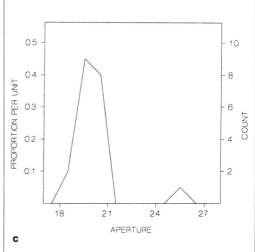

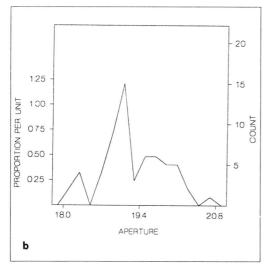

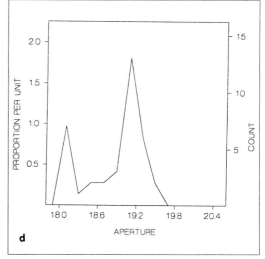

Fig. 4.10. Distribution of aperture; (a) aperture size by potter, (b) aperture by frequency for Avelina, (c) aperture by frequency for Dennis, (d) aperture by frequency for Estrella, (e) aperture by frequency for Salcedo.

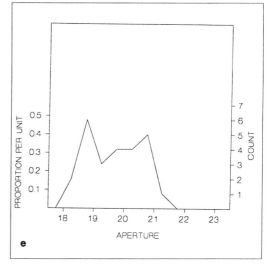

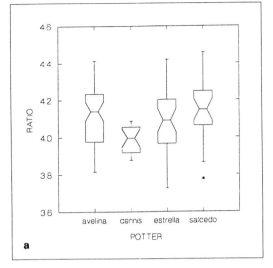

a

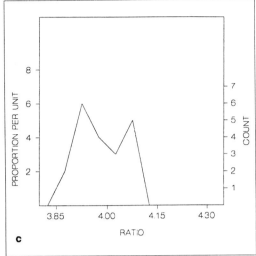

c

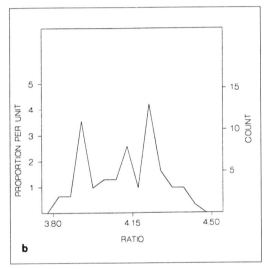

b

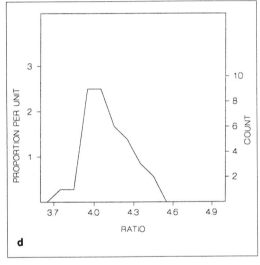

d

Fig. 4.11. Ratio between vessel circumference divided by height (ratio); (a) distribution of ratio values for all potters. Vessels by all potters are relatively standardized, but values for Dennis, an inexperienced potter, are surprisingly uniform. This may be due to the smaller sample size (n=20) for Dennis's assemblage, (b) plot of ratio for Avelina, (c) plot of ratio for Dennis, (d) plot of ratio for Estrella, (e) plot of ratio for Salcedo. Figures b–e check whether ratio is normally distributed. Multiple peaks may suggest that the potters were building more than one shape. In other words, vessels with a larger ratio value might be slightly more squat that vessels with a low ratio value.

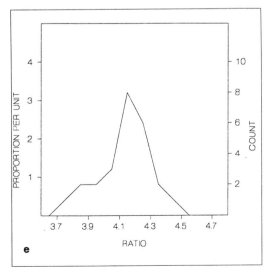

e

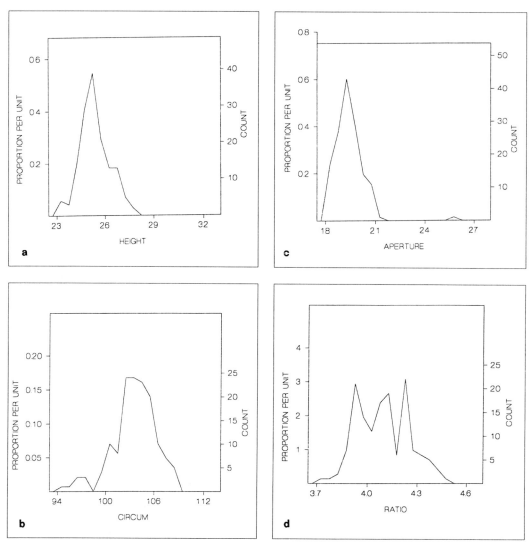

Fig. 4.12. Distribution of height, circumference, aperture, and ratio from the pooled values of all four potters; (a) pooled values for height, (b) pooled values for circumference, (c) pooled values for aperture, (d) pooled values for ratio.

5

Advantages and Disadvantages of Vertical-Half Molding Technology: Implications for Production Organization

DEAN E. ARNOLD

INTRODUCTION

One of the prevailing themes in the study of ceramic production is the organization of the potter's craft. Much of the recent research on this theme has focused on the conceptual refinement of that organization, its products, its evolution, and its identification in the archaeological record (Costin 1991; Mills and Crown 1995; Pool 1992; Rice 1981, 1991). While there has been an expansion of useful terminology, theoretical syntheses, and applications of these approaches to identify ancient production organization, there appears to be little ethnoarchaeological research that provides data to illuminate organizational explanations. Specifically, certain aspects of ceramic technology and their changes through time are viewed as consequences of evolving organizational forms. While caveats are provided about the feedback effect of environment and technology, changes in pottery and its technology are used as surrogate indices of changing types of production organization. Changes in uniformity and production technology thus are believed to reflect changing organizational "types" or forms, whether they are "context," "concentration," "scale," or "intensity," may be identified by "standardization," "efficiency," and "skill" (Costin 1991). Once a link between an aspect of ceramic technology and an organizational variable is proposed, ceramics are then used as a surrogate indicator to identify that organizational form in antiquity.

Studies that infer the organization of the potters' craft in the past thus have provided an exciting prospect for archaeologists who are anxious to reconstruct the intangible past from the tangible archaeological record. Ceramics, however, like all cultural phenomenon, have multiple causes, and technology *may itself* exert a causal influence on production organization and constrain or stimulate the evolution of that organization. Production organization, of course, does indeed affect technology, but the reverse is also true: technology can also exert a causal force on certain aspects of production organization. Technology is not just a dependent variable that is a consequence of production organization and its changes. Rather, the relationships between production organization and technology are complex and mutually causal.

The importance of technology as a causal force upon socio-economic organization is an old one in anthropology. It is found in Marvin Harris's cultural materialism (1979), Julian Steward's cultural ecology (1955), and, of course, Marx's seminal work of the effect of infrastructure on production organization. Critiques of modern cultural materialism have argued that it is too deterministic. While this may be true historically, any anthropologist who has done ethnography or thought seriously about the factors that affect cultural behavior recognizes that the causes of behavior are multiple and systemic. Some causes are ideological or cognitive (beliefs and values). Others are social structural (organizational) while still others are technological. In ceramic studies, organizational causes of (or linkages with) technological patterns are still hypothetical (what Rice [1991] called the "specialization hypothesis") and tend to emphasize role of production organization in ceramic variability rather than the role of the technology in that variability.

Materialistic, technological, and ecological (as opposed to organizational) approaches to ceramics, however, can uncover interpretive principles that have universal applicability. The technology of ceramic production around the world shares a relatively narrow range of common behavioral consequences because of the nature of clay minerals and the processes required to transform clays into a sturdy product (D. Arnold 1985). Once the relationship of these consequences with production organization are understood, the linkages can provide the basis for comparative inferences about production organization removed in space and time (see D. Arnold 1985, 1993 and also Pool 1992). The fragility of ceramic vessels before firing, for example, constrains the movement of potters (D. Arnold 1985). Areas with seasonal cold and rainfall limit production to warmer and dryer periods and favors household production combined with part-time agriculture (D. Arnold 1975a, 1975b, 1985, 1993:15–26). Furthermore, distances to ceramic resources are not totally elastic, but are almost always less than 7 km from a production location when human carriers are used for transport. Most such resources occur less than 3–4 km from production locations and 37–48 percent of them are less than 1 km away (D. Arnold 1985, 1993:200–204). Similarly, studies of ceramic use wear constrains inferences about vessel function (Skibo 1992; Skibo and Schiffer 1987).

One example of the tendency to assign the causal priority of organization over technology is the relationship between production organization and fabrication technology. While concepts like "efficiency," "skill," "scale," and "intensity" occur in the litera-

ture of production organization, treatments of the relationship of these notions to fabrication technology are often brief, superficial, and lack empirical support. The principal problem linking forming technology with organizational variables is the direction of the causation. Changing organizational forms is not the only cause for changes in forming technology. Rather, forming technology may also affect production organization. Indeed, the effects of the forming technology are multiple, interrelated and may stimulate or place constraints on the organization of the craft. Changes in such technology are not just the result of increasing "scale" mediated and identified by "standardization," "skill," or "efficiency," but rather technological changes may also affect the way in which the craft is organized—whether those changes relate to the scale of production, the use of space, or the kind and amount of skill involved. Most important, the relationship between these variables is not necessarily what one might predict from the current literature on the subject. Rather, the relationship between technology, in general, and production organization is mutually causal and multidimensional.

In this paper, I will develop two interrelated themes. The first will show that a fabrication technology may have a significant causal role in certain variables of the organization of ceramic production. In developing this theme, I will examine vertical-half molding technology and its relationship to production organization in Ticul, Yucatán where I have done field work 10 times during the last 32 years. In Ticul, I have seen ceramic production evolve from a household-based craft into several organizational types. At the end of the paper, I will explore the relationship of these data and recent changes in Ticul to the notions of "skill," "standardization," and "scale."

MOLD-MADE CERAMIC PRODUCTION
Ceramic production using molds is sometimes regarded as the result of a process in which efficiency has created a more uniform, standardized product (e.g., Rice 1981:223).

Molds are cited as an example of the result of a drive to increased efficiency (D. Arnold 1985:204) resulting from economies of scale (Rice 1981:223). These statements suggest that the use of molds would appear to be the result of a more complex level of production organization. This relationship, however, does not take into consideration the contextual aspects of the molding technology itself nor their effects upon craft organization.

To help remedy the lack of information about fabrication technologies, I want to explore the advantages and disadvantages of vertical-half molding in Ticul, Yucatán. The adoption of this technique is much more complicated than simply the result of increased efficiency, economies of increased scale, or the increased intensity of production. Rather, the adoption of a molding technology has important implications for the organization of the craft and exerts a feedback relationship with organizational variables such as "scale" and the amount of space devoted to production. These implications provide important insights for interpreting the archaeological record and understanding the evolution of ceramic production. Because these implications result from the nature of the technology of molding itself, rather than organizational or sociopolitical causation, it is hoped that these observations will contribute to formulating a middle range theory about how technology is causally related to aspects of production organization.

BACKGROUND

Forming pottery through the use of molds is a widespread phenomenon that exists with a number of variations throughout the world (summaries in D. Arnold 1985:202–208; Foster 1955, 1967; Rice 1987:125–128; and see Adan-Bayewitz 1995). In Mexico, Foster (1955, 1967) has classified pottery molding according to "convex" and "concave" types based on the morphology of the molds themselves, and Rice (1987:125–128) has continued using these same types in her review of fabrication techniques. These types, however, do not have much to do with the behavior of fabrication and its variability. Consequently,

Foster's types may obscure the implications for production organization that follow from using different molding technologies.

One of the many variations of molding technologies is a technique called "vertical-half molding" (Foster 1948, 1955:6, 1967:115). With vertical-half molding, the potter uses clay, cement, or plaster of paris to create two molds for each vessel. Each mold is created to form half of a vessel along a vertical axis. The clay is first forced into one vertical half of the mold and then into the other half. After a brief drying period, the two halves are joined, allowed to dry for a few minutes, and then removed (see Foster 1948:357, 1955:6, 1967:115; for molding in Yucatán, see Brainerd 1958:68). Although apparently simple, vertical-half molding actually consists of a total of thirteen distinct, sequential steps (Table 5.1; Figs. 5.1, 5.2). Every use of the terms "molding" or "molding technology" hereafter in this paper thus specifically refers to "vertical-half molding" rather than another molding technology.

The use of vertical-half molding originated in Ticul during the late 1940s when a workshop sponsored by the Mexican government tried to introduce this technique among the potters in the community. When Raymond Thompson studied pottery making in Ticul in 1951, the government workshop was still operating. The potter in charge (Juan Chab) was not from Ticul, but was from Campeche and knew

> ... the traditional methods of pottery making, but since learning wheel and mold techniques under a federal program to teach improved methods to Yucatecan potters, he considers the old way unnecessarily laborious and time consuming. (Thompson 1958:20)

Although Thompson illustrates one of Chab's vessels (Thompson 1958, fig. 48b, pp. 138–139), which was fired and painted by a Ticul potter, Chab's innovative fabrication techniques (vertical-half molding and the wheel) were not yet shared by other potters in the community. Potters at this time were household potters and, according to Brainerd, had no specialized structures (except the

TABLE 5.1.
The Principal Steps in Fabricating a Vessel Using a Vertical-Half Mold

1. Flatten a lump of clay with the hands
2. Dust the first half of the mold with *sah kab* temper* to keep the clay from sticking to the mold
3. Press the flattened clay in the first half of the mold
4. Set the mold and its contents aside to dry
5. Dust the second half of the mold with temper
6. Flatten a lump of clay with the hands
7. Press the flattened clay in the second half of the mold
8. Set the mold and its contents aside to dry
9. Combine the two halves of the mold
10. Set the two halves and their contents aside to dry
11. Remove the object from the mold
12. Set the object aside to dry
13. Obliterate the mold marks on the vessel by:
    a) cutting off the mold-marks with a knife or gourd scraper
    b) smoothing the joint with a hand dipped in water. (On vessels which are circular, but are made with vertical-half molds, the mold-marks may be smoothed and finished on the turntable or wheel.)

*This temper is a combination of the clay minerals attapulgite (palygorskite) and montmorillonite and the nonplastic minerals of calcite and dolomite (Arnold 1971). The clay minerals in the temper absorb water from the clay so that the clay releases easily from the mold keeping the clay from sticking to it.

Fig. 5.1. A girl making a vessel using a vertical-half mold (Step 3, Table 5.1). The box of temper used for dusting the mold prior to forming (Step 2 and 5, Table 5.1) lies at her feet. Completed vessels showing mold-marks lie in the lower portion of the photograph. A companion (left) is smoothing the vessels to obliterate the mold marks (Step 13b, Table 5.1).

kiln) devoted to pottery production (Brainerd 1958:69).

According to informants, three Ticul potters learned the molding technique and introduced it to other potters, but its diffusion was slow. From Thompson's few illustrations (Thompson 1958:138), the molding technique was only used for coin banks which were fabricated in the shapes of animals such as swans, ducks, pigs, and bulls and were similar to those shapes produced in Ticul in the late 1960s (Fig. 5.3). Initially, there was little demand for these vessels and shortly after Thompson's visit, the workshop closed. By the late 1960s, however, the use of molds had grown and were used exclusively for making coin banks. Occasionally, these banks were formed in the image of a saint, a cartoon character such as Mighty Mouse, or a barrel of *chile jabanero* (a very spicy variety of chili pepper). The banks were sold in the markets of the peninsula or were used as prizes in games of chance that potters took to fiestas in Yucatán and other parts of southeastern Mexico. Since the 1970s, however, inflation and the devaluation of the Mexican peso appear to have greatly diminished the

Fig. 5.2. Adolescent girl making a small flower pot using a vertical-half mold. She has just finished Step 7 (Table 5.1) of the process and is adding a small piece of clay that she is rolling in her hands to add to the clay in the mold. The piece of cloth between the lump of paste (left) and the girl is used as a surface for flattening the clay and for lifting the flattened clay off the floor. The cloth is peeled off before the clay pancake is pressed into the mold. The smaller vessels in the photograph are all mold-made and the two larger vessels behind the girl are fabricated on the turntable with modified (slab) coiling. Each of the larger vessels has a footprint equivalent to about four or five of the small vessels.

Fig. 5.3. A Ticul potter selling mold-made coin banks in the Ticul Market in 1984. The two water-carrying vessels on the left (*cantaros*, see Thompson 1958:36, 124–125), and the two water-storage vessels on the right (the *tinaja* [below] and *apaste* [above] see Thompson 1958: 40, 45, 116, 122) are made with modified coiling on the traditional turntable (the *kabal*, see Ralph and Arnold 1988; Thompson 1958: 76–81). The remainder of the vessels are mold-made and are similar to those produced in Ticul in the late 1960s.

demand for these banks and their production had declined relative to other vessels. In 1997, however, the banks appeared to be regaining some of their former popularity.

A workshop at a tourist hotel at the archaeological site of Uxmal (ca. 1959–1982) and another government-sponsored workshop in the mid-1970s reinforced the use of molding and taught potters how to fabricate a wider variety of vessels—mainly copies of archaeological objects (figurines, masks, and stelae). By 1984, molding was used to make copies of these objects and other small vessels that were painted with ancient Maya designs.

To my knowledge, vertical-molding has never been used successfully to fabricate traditional vessels except small food bowls. Traditional vessels are formed in several stages and were used for cooking, carrying and storing water, and to store, process and serve

food (see Thompson 1958). Mold-made production thus never replaced traditional fabrication technology, but only supplemented it to produce innovative vessel forms.

THE ADVANTAGES OF VERTICAL-HALF MOLDING

Fabricating pottery using vertical-half molding possesses several inherent advantages. First, it can be used to make objects that cannot be produced in other ways. Most of the coin banks and copies of ancient Maya figurines cannot be formed using the traditional forming technology of modified coiling. Such objects are usually noncircular vessels and cannot be formed on the traditional turntable. When a template for making a mold was not available, it was made using a modeling technique. Modeling, however, was very labor-intensive, required a great deal of skill, and created too much variability in form. As a result, it was never used to form an object (other than a mold template) which was larger than a small effigy whistle (e.g., similar to those illustrated in Thompson 1958:135).

A second advantage of vertical-half molding is that it requires much less skill than virtually any other type of forming technique. Most traditional forming techniques require a set of specific motor habit patterns that have been learned over an extended period of time (see D. Arnold 1985:205–207). In Ticul, potters require a period of at least one or two years to learn the patterns that are necessary to fabricate a vessel using the traditional technique of modified coiling. Potters must also learn about raw materials like clays, tempers and firewood, and how motor habits, measurements of vessel shapes, and firing techniques are combined to produce a wide range of vessels.

To avoid removing economically productive adults from subsistence activities during the learning process, the knowledge and skills required for making pottery are best learned during childhood (Fig. 5.4). Indeed, those who become potters as adults are seldom considered to be as skilled or as knowledgeable as those who have learned the craft as children.

The most effective context for learning the knowledge and skills of making pottery is the household. In the household, learners can be supported economically by others when production by neophytes may not be economically viable nor sufficient for sustenance. Children's residence in their natal household is long enough to learn all the aspects of the craft and to use that knowledge to produce a broad range of vessels. Given the lengthy process of learning motor habit patterns, and the knowledge and skills required for making pottery, the transmission of the craft from generation to generation coincides with the same rules that define household composition, location, and its perpetuation (Arnold 1989:175–181). In Ticul, these rules consist of patrilocal postnuptial residence, the patrilineal inheritance of household land, and

Fig. 5.4. A small boy making a vessel with vertical sides using modified coiling on the turntable. While this vessel is one of the easier vessels to fabricate using this technique, a minimum of one to two years is necessary to learn the knowledge and skills of traditional Maya pottery production.

their accepted variants (Arnold 1989). These variants may bring single females, widows, and unmarried or abandoned mothers into a household. Such individuals are almost always lineal or collateral relatives, but they never inherit household land. The composition of potters' households is thus never just the result of simple inheritance and residence rules.

Learning the craft does not itself obey these rules of household composition, locus, and perpetuation, but the rules merely provide the personnel for the social context of that learning. While the transmission of the craft to a new generation can be described by such rules, they do not explain the perpetuation of the craft nor do they insure that all household members will become potters. In reality, only a fraction of those who reside in the household and learn the craft in their youth actually become potters. Often unmarried females, widows, and unmarried or abandoned mothers find pottery making attractive after they return to their father's household because they have no other means of economic support.

In contrast to traditional fabricating patterns, vertical-half molding does not require motor habits that are the product of long periods of learning (see Arnold 1985:203–208). Vertical-half molding is easy to learn and requires much less skill compared to traditional techniques. Almost anyone can produce a molded object with little practice.

Although some skilled potters use molds, mold-made objects are usually produced by children (Figs. 5.1, 5.2) and other individuals who are not skilled in traditional potting techniques. Vertical-half molding is the first forming technique learned by children and those who learn the craft as adults. By making pottery using vertical-half molds, anyone can be economically productive in a relatively brief period of time. It is, in fact, so easy to learn this technique that potters proficient in traditional potting skills regard those who only use molds as not being potters at all. Experienced potters would repeatedly express this bias in conversations with me and in my surveys of the community. Knowing that an individual made pottery using molds, but was not mentioned by informants as a potter, would prompt me to ask:

"And, what about so-and-so *(fulano/a)?*"
"Is he/she a potter?"

"No", a potter would reply, "He/she is not a potter *(alfarero/a)*. He/she only knows how to make pottery with molds *(Solo sabe moldear)*."

My principal informant also expressed this bias in distinguishing between "old potters" (those who possessed traditional potting knowledge and skills) and "new potters" (who had only learned specialized aspects of the craft in workshops). "New potters" possessed a very narrow, limited range of pottery knowledge and skill, and often knew how to use vertical-half molds.

The lesser amount of skill required for making mold-made vessels means that unskilled individuals can be drawn into the craft quickly to increase production without going through a lengthy process of learning: (1) the muscular patterns required for modified coiling, (2) the shape categories, their subparts, their measurements, and (3) how to combine these components to produce a finished vessel. Production of mold-made objects can thus be increased quickly with an immediate infusion of unskilled labor and the potter can respond easily to an increase in demand without delay.

This short response time to an increase in demand can be illustrated by the food bowls produced annually prior to the Day of the Dead *(Día de los Difuntos)* rituals. These activities occur during the time when the Roman Catholic Church celebrates All Saints Day *(Todos los Santos)* on November 1. In Yucatán, however, the Day of the Dead rituals occur on October 31, November 1, and November 6. During the preceding months, potters produce thousands of small food bowls *(cajetes)* that are placed on household altars (see Arnold and Nieves 1992:97) to feed the spirits of the dead relatives who are believed to return to the homes of their earthly relatives. Usually, these bowls are formed by modified coiling on the traditional turntable, but in October of 1984, I noticed that one informant possessed a mold for such bowls, but had never used it. After asking him why, he responded that the molds had been used by his children when they were unskilled in making pots. The demand for food bowls prior to the Day of the Dead rituals is the most lucrative time of the year for potters, and in order to increase production, my informant had asked his children to use a mold to make the bowls. The children produced the bowls in the morning, and their father finished them on the turntable when he returned for lunch. By using a molding technology, unskilled children increased household production during times of peak seasonal demand.

The lack of elaborate motor skills required for using molds means that this technique is compatible with virtually any number of existing muscular patterns associated with traditional fabricating techniques. Molding can thus be easily integrated into existing working positions and can exist along with any number of traditional patterns. In Ticul, for example, molding is compatible with sitting on the floor, or on a low stool (the *k'an che*), which are the predominant positions for making pottery (Figs. 5.1, 5.2, 5.4), resting, or doing any number of other activities.

A third advantage of a molding technology is the ease of producing new vessels with minimum skill. When a potter sees a new object that he wants to produce, he can copy it by building a mold around it using plaster of paris. Producing molds requires much more skill than making pots from them, but still requires less skill than using traditional techniques for other vessels. While the traditional forming technology in Ticul requires different knowledge and skills for different vessels, molding technology requires the same skills and knowledge to fabricate different vessels.

Potters continually make new molds from vessels obtained in various ways. They may obtain mold templates from clients or from other potters. In 1966, one potter sold figurines to other potters solely to be used as templates for new molds. In 1984, one informant received vessels from a client to use as templates. If a potter is skilled in forming pottery, then he may make the mold template himself and build a mold around it.

A fourth advantage of a vertical-half molding technology is that it creates a uniform product. Figurines are the most likely objects made by molding because the integrity of the image can be insured, and maintaining this integrity may be the most important characteristic desired by the potter. Figurines can be hand modeled, but in the hands of unskilled producers, modeling may produce too much variability in form. Even in the hands of skilled potters, however, the variability created by modeling may be undesirable to consumers. If the figurine image has religious significance, a molding technology insures its iconographic uniformity in order to achieve a response that would prompt a consumer to acquire it.

Uniformity of size and shape of other vessels besides figurines may also be important to consumers. The chief impetus for such uniformity in recent years has been the demand for vessels that are small enough to fit into a tourist's suitcase. In fact, uniformity may be so important to potters' clients that vessels usually made with another technique also may be produced with a mold to meet the client's requests for a uniform product. If a client wants identical copies of a vessel that is usually fabricated by modified coiling, then the potter will make a mold of the vessel to assure that the finished products will be uniform in size. A small water-carrying vessel (cantaro) used as a tourist curio, for example, was usually fabricated with modified coiling, but it was made with a mold if a client wanted the vessels to be identical. When one client of my principal informant wanted 100 identical copies of two small vessels in 1984, the client provided two broken vessels as mold templates to assure uniformity of the finished product.

DISADVANTAGES OF USING VERTICAL-HALF MOLDS

Besides the advantages, there are also disadvantages of vertical-half molding. First, like other techniques, vertical-half molding is shape-, size- and resource-dependent for its success. Molding requires a clay plastic enough to be spread into a mold without cracking. Some highly plastic clays, however, cannot be used to form molded vessels because the clay body will sag after it is removed from the mold. Because the clay used by Ticul potters consists of randomly mixed layers of kaolinite and the highly plastic clay mineral montmorillonite (Schultz et al. 1971), only small vessels and those vessels that are totally enclosed (such as coin banks) can be made successfully with vertical-half molds. Larger and more open vessels are formed by modified coiling in separate stages that are interspersed with drying periods in order to prevent sagging.

One informant asserts that the largest vessels that can be made successfully with molds are cylindrical vessels (called vasos in Ticul) about 20 cm tall. Such vessels can be removed from the molds without sagging because they have straight sides that provide support for the clay above. In contrast, larger vessels that are completely enclosed can be made with molds because the curved walls provide strength and support. Indeed, the largest vessel that I have seen successfully produced with a mold was a coin bank in the form of large pig that had a body 31 cm long and 24 cm wide. No open vessels this large are fabricated with molds, but rather are made with modified coiling on a turntable.

Molds may be used for larger vessels. In the summer of 1997, I saw some large molds for objects that had a height of approximately 60 cm. Since my informant had told me in earlier years that mold-made vessels could not be made with a height greater than 20 cm, I asked him how vessels of such size could be made with molds. He replied that molds could be used for large objects, but they had to remain in the mold for a long time after forming.

A second disadvantage of vertical-half molding technology consists of its relative lack of efficiency compared to other techniques. If a vessel is small enough to be made with vertical-half molding and can be made with more than one fabricating technique, vertical-half molding is not the technique of choice. Food bowls *(cajetes)*, for example, can be made using modified coiling, vertical-half molding, or the wheel. Although the actual fabrication time of a mold-made vessel may be the same as that made with modified coiling on the turntable (Table 5.2), the total production time takes longer because the potters have to handle the mold-made vessel more often than one made with modified coiling.

This problem of handling results from the amount of time and energy required to execute all of the steps in the molding process (see Table 5.1). Between each of the fabrication steps (at Steps 4, 8, and 10), a period of drying is required when the vessel must be set aside, allowed to dry partially, and then picked up again for the next fabrication step. With modified coiling or the wheel, however, a potter can complete a vessel without this repeated handling. If the vessel is small and does not require multiple stages of fabrication, then it can be formed and finished in one operation using modified coiling or the wheel without handling it again and again. Fabrication times of mold-made vessels and those of

the turntable (Table 5.3) thus do not take into account the additional effort and handling time required to fabricate a mold-made vessel. With molds, production time is not just affected by the actual fabrication time, but also by the lengths of the combined segments of preparation, drying, and finishing (see Table 5.1).

The efficiency of vertical-half molding comes with larger vessels that require a lengthy fabrication process. Efficiencies with molding occur when forming time can be collapsed into two segments and the lengthy drying time between stages can be reduced into three brief periods: one after each half of the vessel is formed and the third after the two halves are combined. Thus, the use of two-piece vertical-half molds for large vessels *can* result in greater efficiency of production, and in some cases, it can be more cost-effective than any other technique except the wheel (D. Arnold 1985:203–208). But the clay must be suitable for making larger vessels. In Ticul, molding is not a viable choice for large vessels because they sag when removed from the molds. The presence of montmorillonite in the Ticul clay creates too much plasticity in the paste. The larger the vessel or object, the longer it must dry in the mold so that it retains its shape and does not sag when it is removed from the mold. If large objects are produced with molds, then those objects must remain in the molds for a long period and any efficiency in using molds for those vessels is lost.

The molding technology in Ticul thus works best with small objects. Molding, however, does not work well for small vessels that have a neck formed above a constriction in the vessel body. Such vessels will sag after removal from the mold because there is nothing to bear the weight of the clay above. If such vessels (such as the *tibor* shape) were entirely mold-made, removed immediately from the mold, and placed upright, then the body of the vessel would break open from the weight of the neck on the unsupported clay (Fig. 5.5). If the vessel was turned upside down to dry, then the weight of the base would distort the shape of the top of the ves-

TABLE 5.2.
Fabrication Time of Food Bowls *(Cajetes)*

Forming Technique	N	Mean (sec)	Range	Height[a] (cm)	Mouth[a] (cm)
Mold	3	211[b]	147–259	6.5	13.5
Turntable	5	231	181–278	–[c]	14.5

[a] Mouth and height diameters refer to modal measurements of the size of fired vessels except for the turntable vessels which are measurements of unfired vessels. Shrinkage of the green vessels from drying and firing would be expected to lose about 1 cm of width placing them within the 13–13.5 cm range of mouth diameters shown in this table.

[b] Mean values for each half of the forming process for the two piece molds for this vessel was: first half = 114 seconds, range 73–134; second half = 97 seconds, range = 74–125. Mean for forming the vessel combined the means forming times for both halves; the combined ranges consist of adding the ranges of the lowest values to those of the highest values.

[c] Although the height of these vessels was not measured, all *cajetes* of the same mouth diameter are roughly the same height.

TABLE 5.3.
Comparisons of Fabrication Times Combining Different Vessel Shapes According to Technique

Technique	N	Mean (sec)	Range (sec)	St. Dev. (sec)
Mold	15	311	147–654	139
Turntable *(bowl)*	5	231	181–278	36
Turntable *(risado)*	14	794	586–1033	166

sel. If a potter wants to make uniform vessels of this shape *(tibores)* using a mold, then he must allow each vessel to dry a long time in its mold, and many molds would be needed. In order to use only one mold, however, potters must remove the vessel from the mold immediately. So, in order to produce identical vessels using a single mold and still prevent sagging, the potter forms only the body of the vessel with the mold. Then, it is removed from the mold, dried partially, and then the neck and the rim are added using the kick wheel. By carefully measuring the neck and the mouth diameters on the wheel, the potter can insure that the dimensions of each vessel are identical. These combined techniques maximize production by minimizing capital investment in molds and yet still insure vessel uniformity.

After the mold-made vessels are fired, they are sanded before they are painted with an enamel oil-based paint. Because painting covers the entire vessel, mold-made figurines that have cracked during firing are repaired using plaster of paris before they are sanded and painted. Although repair salvages vessels that would otherwise be discarded, more time is invested in the vessels along with increased capital costs of plaster and sand paper. Repairing mold-made figurines allows lower levels of fabrication and firing skill because paint will completely cover both the repaired areas and the firing clouds. The repair of cracked mold-made objects thus increases their labor and capital costs and decreases the cost-effectiveness of using molds, but it allows those who lack skills in mixing clay, fabricating, and firing to produce a marketable object.

A third disadvantage of a molding technique concerns the complexity of using more than one mold to form a vessel. This limitation occurs mainly with the production of certain kinds of figurines. If a potter uses different molds for the parts of a figurine, then the fabrication time is greatly extended because of the time required to execute the sequence of 13 major steps (Table 5.1) for each set of molds used. As a result, using more than one two-piece mold to form a figurine

Fig. 5.5. Pile of discarded vertical-half molds in a potter's household in Ticul. The mold of the vessel with the tall neck in the center of the photograph is the mold of the *tibor*, which failed to produce a successful vessel because the weight of the neck caused the body to sag. With Ticul clay, the body of a vessel will support a constricted neck of clay only when the body has dried and remained in the mold for a lengthy period.

increases the number of steps by a factor of 13 for each two-piece mold used.

This disadvantage can be illustrated by the fabrication of a coin bank in the form of a large pig. The pig must be made with five sets of two-piece molds. First, the body is made using a two-piece mold. After the two halves have been joined and partially dried, each leg is fabricated with a two-piece mold, and then attached. Finally, the ears are modeled and attached. This means that even before the ears are added, each pig requires 65 distinct steps simply to form all of its mold-made parts. Thirteen steps are required for the body, and 13 steps are necessary for each of the four legs. Although this pig cannot be produced in any other way, there is no time advantage in producing vessels that require more than one two-piece mold because the sequence of using different molds for forming different parts of a vessel greatly extends fabrication time by increasing forming, handling, and drying time.

This disadvantage can also be illustrated with ancient mold-made figurines from coastal Ecuador (Cummins 1994) where molding took place in distinct stages using different molds for the parts of a figurine. If one uses different molds for the face, body, legs, and arms, then any efficiency in using molds is lost because of the time required to execute the sequence of construction and the amount of drying required at each step. The same pattern probably also occurred at Maymi on the south coast of Peru (Anders et al. 1994) where molds were found for fabricating different parts of a feline figurine. The molds were important to maintain the integrity of this figurine because the feline image was an important religious symbol in the ancient Andes. Molds thus did not increase the efficiency of fabrication in these cases, but actually decreased it by extending fabrication time. They did, however, maintain the integrity of the molded image.

Fourth, the production of mold-made pottery is limited by the number of molds available. Since each vessel must dry for a period of time in each half of the mold and then together when the molds are joined, production will be limited by the number of molds available for that vessel. In this case, the drying time, rather than the forming time, is the significant variable. This portion of the molding process is critical because highly plastic clays will sag if removed from molds too quickly. By extending drying time in a mold, the mold is unavailable for use by other potters.

This limitation has great implications for the organization of production. Using non-molding techniques, multiple potters can make many vessels of the same shape. With molding, however, each potter must have his own mold to produce a vessel. Multiple potters require multiple molds because a mold could only be used by one potter at a time. Increased production of a vessel shape means that one must increase the number of molds as well as the number of potters.

A fifth disadvantage of a vertical-half molding technology is that the use of molds requires increased capital in the form of increased overhead costs. In Ticul, mold-made production is constrained by the capital necessary to buy the materials to make the molds, and potters seldom, if ever, have more than one mold for each shape. Since the cost of a mold depends on the cost of the plaster of paris *(yeso)* used to make it, potters must have capital in order to buy it and then assess whether the returns from a mold-made vessel are worth the cost. In 1984, for example, the plaster required to produce a mold of a small replica of the vessel used to carry water cost 75 pesos (3 kg at 25 pesos/kg). With an order of 100 vessels, the cost of this mold would increase the overhead of each vessel by 1 peso. The increased cost of making this vessel, however, is counterbalanced by the use of unskilled labor to make it.

IMPLICATIONS FOR CRAFT ORGANIZATION: SPACE

The disadvantages of a molding technology create profound implications for the amount of space needed for ceramic production. Philip Arnold (1991) has shown that space is a significant constraining variable in the technology and scale of ceramic production and can significantly affect the visibility of that production in the archaeological record. In Ticul, mold-made production has a spatial "footprint" that is much larger than the traditional fabrication technology using modified coiling.

There are several reasons why molding technology affects the spatial requirements of ceramic production. First, because a molding technology can produce only small vessels successfully, potters can fabricate many more vessels per unit of clay. Large numbers of small vessels create more spatial demands on drying areas because smaller vessels take up more drying space than the larger vessels (Fig. 5.2). Ten small vessels have a larger footprint than one large vessel of equivalent weight because most of the clay in the large pot occurs in the vertical dimension of the vessel. In smaller vessels, however, the same amount of clay is spread out over a greater horizontal area because drying vessels should not touch one another until they are completely dry. Stacking drying vessels can cause them to deform and break. Drying racks and shelves can increase the space available for drying, however, but such innovations still increase the spatial "footprint" of small ves-

sels. *The drying "footprint" per unit of clay is thus larger for smaller vessels than it is for larger vessels.*

If production is household-based, drying areas will compete with living areas and be subject to the risks of playing children, indiscrete domestic animals, leaking roofs, and clumsy adults. Drying outside will, of course, alleviate this problem, but it creates others. Rains may destroy drying pots and the heat of the sun and the low humidity in the dry season may dry them too quickly causing them to crack and break (see D. Arnold 1985: 61–98). Moving the vessels outside the house and then inside again increases risk of damage from movement. Even with drying outside, however, pots eventually must be moved inside at night so that night rainfall and morning fog and dew will not damage the vessels. *The critical spatial context with the drying footprint of small vessels is thus the amount of interior space.*

Second, a molding technology requires more space to make pots than traditional techniques because the molds must be stored when they are not in use (Figs. 5.6, 5.7). Since molding is an inflexible fabricating technique, a different mold must be made for each size and shape produced. Furthermore, a mold can only be used by one potter at a time. So, if more people are drawn into the craft to make molded vessels, the number of molds available must be increased. As the number of molds increase, they must be stored to avoid breakage or damage. If styles change, vessels must change, and molds must change. If change occurs often, or, if the potter has many molds available, storage of molds can put demands on available space (Fig. 5.6). The more variability and innovation in shapes fabricated with a molding technology, the greater the need for more space for storing the molds (Fig. 5.7). *A molding technology thus also has a larger spatial footprint than traditional technology because of the area required for the storage of the molds.*

Third, as mold-made vessels (such as figurines) become more complex with several molded portions, the spatial requirements for production will also increase. With the in-

Fig. 5.7. A small structure in a potter's house lot built to protect a stack of unused molds from rainfall. This kind of a structure occurred in several potter's house lots, but did not exist in the late 1960s.

Fig. 5.6. A stack of unused molds stored in a potter's house in Ticul. Using molds to produce new sizes and shapes of vessels requires increased numbers of molds. This stack is stored in an unused portion of a small structure between an older traditional house (in the distance) and a newer house from which the photograph was taken.

creased steps required to make such complex vessels, the space needed for drying will increase as the potter requires space to dry one part of a vessel while he or she fabricates another part of that vessel.

The problem of limited space can be alleviated, of course, by increasing the interior areas used for ceramic production. Potters, for example, could expand the amount of space by adding extra-household structures or expanding existing households to accommodate the spatial requirements of mold-made production. Indeed, one of the significant changes in households that produced pottery between 1965 and 1984 was the increased amount of space set aside exclusively for the production of pottery (Fig. 5.7). There are, of course, other reasons for the increase in working space during this 20-year period, but the larger spatial footprint of a molding technology is one significant factor that has created spatial demands in households and is a significant factor in this expansion.

IMPLICATIONS FOR ANCIENT PRODUCTION ORGANIZATION

A vertical-half molding technology also has implications for the study of production organization in general. The first of those implications involves the social context of production: vertical-half molding requires very little social continuity for the learning and perpetuation of the technology. Most traditional forming techniques require certain culturally patterned muscular habits (see D. Arnold 1985:147–149). These motor habit patterns tend to be congruent with other activities in the culture, are learned unconsciously, and are reinforced by furniture (or the lack thereof). These patterns are probably the most difficult part of the pottery-making process to learn and they thus take the most time to acquire.

The motor habit requirements of ceramic production are most effectively learned in the household during enculturation. Households not only provide the setting to learn the culture, but they also provide the setting to learn the traditional motor habit patterns of ceramic production (and other aspects of the craft). As I have already mentioned, household learning of pottery making is important because the initial negative economic consequences of learning can be absorbed without adversely affecting the labor required for the sustenance of the household. When children learn the craft, for example, their skill may not be adequate enough to make a quality pot (Fig. 5.4). Their failures, however, can be tolerated because their value to the production unit is not just economic and a household could thus risk the children's temporary lack of productivity as the price of training. Unlike an extrahousehold workshop where effort must be compensated, the value of children extends beyond their ability to make an economic contribution to the household. At the same time, children can participate in other aspects of the craft that do not require much skill.

Although Ticul potters can learn some aspects of the craft quickly, mastering the motor habits of modified coiling for making large complicated traditional vessels requires the greatest amount of learning time. The most experienced potters have acquired this skill as residents of the household of their youth. Such traditional potters have broad knowledge of pottery making and distinguish themselves from "new potters" who only know very narrow specialized tasks and how to make pottery from molds.

Since traditional motor habits used for a forming technology are learned during childhood, are reinforced by tools, furniture, and other material culture, and take a long time to learn, such patterns are very resistant to change and tend to persist through time. This resistance to change in motor habits can be seen in North American culture with the muscles used for carrying loads. A modern backpack with the weight pulling on the straps between the shoulders utilizes the same muscles used in colonial America when a yoke was placed around the neck and shoulders to carry buckets of water. In spite of massive social and technological evolution in the last 250 years in North America, muscular patterns for carrying loads have remained the same. Different carrying patterns exist in the Mesoamerica and the central Andes where indigenous carrying patterns still persist even after 500 years of massive acculturation (see D. Arnold 1993:121–124, particularly figs. 6.1–6.3).

Change in motor habit patterns is difficult and can take a long time. Such change is most effective when new patterns are learned during enculturation as the individual is placed in a different material culture context that requires a different set of motor habit patterns. It is likely, then, that changes in the motor habit patterns required for pottery forming technologies may require at least a generation to change (see D. Arnold 1979, 1981: 37–38) and are disrupted only when pottery production moves out of the household, or when a population of potters is replaced with a new population that uses a new forming technology. In light of the North American example cited above, motor habits involved with work or burden-bearing in a continuing population may not change at all in spite of massive technological changes.

In contrast to traditional forming technologies, potters can change to a molding technology quickly because of the small amount of skill required. Such a technology can be adopted easily without a long period of learning because elaborate motor habits are not required. The potter can use the same few behavioral patterns for each shape made with a mold. Only the molds will change.

The limited skill required by mold-made production means that increased demand for mold-made objects can be met quickly by drawing unskilled workers into the craft. This expansion of labor can occur without a lengthy process of learning the specific motor habit patterns that are necessary for paddle and anvil, coiling, modified coiling, or modeling techniques.

These observations about a household-based craft help explain why traditional pottery-forming techniques in the New World have survived down to the present day even after 500 years of massive acculturation. While Precolombian state-organized ceramic technologies have disappeared, technologies transmitted by households have survived. In Ticul, the rules of household composition (inheritance of house lots and postnuptial residence) were still responsible for the persistence of the potter's craft between 1965 and 1994 (D. Arnold 1989) in spite of massive changes in production organization, vessel shapes, demand and the marketing of ceramic products (see D. Arnold 1987; Arnold and Nieves 1992).

In Ticul, the traditional household organization of production has evolved into new forms of organization outside of the household. These forms still utilize traditional technologies, but have added innovations that mitigate the limitations of a household-based craft. Production is now dominated by large entrepreneurial workshops that supply ceramics to the tourist and resort market in Mérida and Cancún. This type of organization still uses traditional Maya ceramic technology, but has grown out of a traditional household craft where women were potters and men made pottery only when they were not working in their fields. Such entrepreneurial workshops, however, do not invest the time to train their own personnel in more than a few specialized tasks unless they are household-based and use household members as laborers. Even then, household members spend years as understudies. Without household labor, such workshops are dependent upon recruiting personnel trained in pottery-making households where pottery-making skills are taught to the young. Such large-scale extrahousehold workshops could not survive using traditional technology without potters who were trained in household contexts.

A second archaeological implication of a mold-making technology involves the effect of changes in the locus of production. Once the craft moves outside of the household, and household production disappears, the learning of traditional motor habit patterns of vessel fabrication would be disrupted and could not be learned effectively. If the craft moved into nonhousehold workshops (or factories), such learning may be too time consuming, may not be perpetuated in the next generation, and would not be cost-effective unless the workshop was subsidized by elites or some entity like the state. Fabrication techniques would change and those techniques that required little skill and time for learning (like vertical-half molding) would have a selective advantage. Mold-made fig-

urines, for example, can be produced easily by any suprahousehold production organization without a lengthy process of skill development. Where elites control the production process in order to control distribution and consumption of elite high-status goods ("attached" workshops or "attached specialization," see Brumfiel and Earle 1987; Costin 1991:7–9), a low-skill technology such as vertical-half molding would have a strong selective advantage.

A third implication of a molding technology for the study of ancient production organization lies in the cause of uniformity of the molded vessels. In figurine production, uniformity of the visual image is essential for the assurance of consumer demand (whether by individuals or by the state). Such uniformity probably does not result from the standardization of the image simply caused by the development of sociocultural or sociopolitical complexity, the control of the flow of information, or an increase in production "intensity" or "scale." Rather, such uniformity comes from the demand for pottery (i.e., the market) and a desire to maintain the iconographic integrity of the image. Because religious symbols can evoke powerful responses that have economic consequences (they "buy" or acquire them in some way), maintaining "image integrity" is crucial for successful marketing of an image (Fig. 5.8). One modern example of such a powerful response would be the strong feelings evoked by the Virgin of Guadalupe among modern Mexicans. If potters faithfully copy the image of the Virgin to a clay mold, then they can create and maintain a market for their figurine production. Consumers would probably not tolerate much variability from that image and would prefer as much similarity as possible. Mold-made production thus assures that images will have iconographic integrity—particularly those figurines for which production is removed in space and time from the source of the original.

This same process occurs in modern society with images such as the Buddha, Barbie dolls, the Saints, the Christian Cross, and the Star Wars figures. Consumers' possession of

Fig. 5.8. An adolescent putting the finishing touches on a copy of an ancient mask made with a mold. The use of a mold insures the iconographic integrity of the image. Three vertical-half molds occur to the left of center (beneath the sandal).

such figures not only evokes responses of tranquility (the Buddha), pleasure (Barbie), penitence (the Cross), petition (the Saints), or adventure (GI Joe or Luke Skywalker), but also creates a large market for such objects—a relationship that is well-understood by manufacturers of modern toys and religious images. Iconographic integrity is so important in modern marketing that images (and their two-dimensional counterparts, trademarks) are protected by copyright laws. Indeed, several toy makers recently made competitive bids of up to a billion U.S. dollars to George Lucas for the rights to produce the Star Wars figures after the successful re-release of the Star Wars movie trilogy. It is not accidental that many three-dimensional images are also mold-made—not just because of the intensity and scale of production, but also to maintain the iconographic integrity of the image. If elites control iconographic symbols and if such symbols are expressed in three-dimensional forms, then molding has a strong selective advantage over other forming techniques.

Fourth, a molding technology creates greater space demands than traditional technologies. This problem, of course, can be alleviated by a change in the spatial organization of production where potters utilize structures outside of the household for storage of raw materials, unfired pottery, fired wares, and molds (Fig. 5.7). The size of the large ceramic workshop at the site of Cerro Mayal on the coast of Peru (Russell et al. 1994) is probably at least a partial consequence of the increased space required for the production of the mold-made Moche pottery. With high fabrication times resulting from increased steps in such production, the space needed for drying will increase dramatically as potters use the increased drying time for part of a vessel to fabricate another part of that vessel. Since this site also occurs in the seasonal fog zone of the coast of Peru (D. Arnold 1993:225–226), drying times of vessels made during humid and overcast weather would be extended and would put pressure on the amount of covered space required to dry vessels without breakage. Since the demand for drying space would put great strains on household space, production space would need to expand by adding extra-household structures. The spatial demands of a vertical-half molding technology thus produces an archaeologically more visible production location. The larger amount of space required for a molding technology means that its spatial requirement would be easier to recognize in the archaeological record than other kinds of traditional forming technologies.

A fifth implication of a molding technology is that the amount of material paraphernalia for vertical-half molding is larger in comparison to more traditional fabrication technologies. With turntable production in Ticul, for example, each potter has one turntable to produce all shapes and sizes. By way of contrast, mold-made production requires a different mold for every shape and size of vessel produced. Molds may break and a mold of an unpopular shape may be discarded (Fig. 5.9). If a mold is made for an innovative shape and the vessel cannot be made successfully because of the limits of the clay, the mold becomes part of the discarded material residue of the production area. In an ancient production context, one would thus expect to find mold fragments, rejected molds, and molds of shapes that were no longer made (see Fig. 5.9) even though potters may have long departed, taking some of their molds and other tools with them.

One potter stored his molds in distinct locations according to the frequency of their use. The molds currently being used occur within the production area. Those which are not used, but which still are perceived to have value, are stored outside the production area in a sheltered location to keep them dry. Those molds, which were abandoned with little or no prospect of future use, are not covered, but are simply stacked in a location that will not interfere with household activities. Finally, the broken, defective, and unusable molds are simply discarded in the garbage midden around the household.

A final archaeological implication of mold-made production relates to the notion of skill. Skill has been used as a concept to link attributes of ceramics to more evolved production organization (Costin 1991:39–40; Costin and Hagstrum 1995:623). "Skill" in pottery production relates most obviously to the forming technology. With vertical-half molding, molds substitute for fabrication skill. So, as molding becomes more common, molds become more abundant and potters' skill level is decreased. Rathje (1975:430) calls this increased use of molds "economies of skill" by which he characterizes mass-production systems that create products that "acquire at least certain aspects of technical superiority." These and his other subsequent characteristics, however, appear to be only partially valid for the evolution of production in Ticul. Vessels made with molds are not technically superior and still crack and break. But, unlike regular vessels, they can be repaired after firing with cement, and then can be sanded and painted showing no evidence of damage. In other words, vessels made with less skill in mixing raw materials, fabrication, and firing can still be marketed. Molds thus do not create vessels with "technical superiority" nor do they provide an efficiency of fabrication time. Minimizing risks and reduction of loss by technical error may appear to be an effect of a molding technology, but apart from vessels that cannot be

Fig. 5.9. A pile of discarded vertical-half molds in a potter's house lot in Ticul. When demand for shapes and sizes of vertical-half molds changes, potters are left with many such molds. Usually, potters store these molds in a covered area, and this places pressure on storage space. In this case, however, the potter has stored the molds outside, but this is rare in Ticul and may mean that the potter has no intention of using these particular molds again. The spherical object in the upper center is the tree gourd, which will be dried, cut up, and then used as a pottery-shaping tool.

made in any other way, potters use vertical-half molding mainly because they can draw unskilled members of their family into the production process and can fabricate uniform vessels.

Uniformity of vessels, however, is not important for the "nesting" of vessels for efficient transport. Rather, uniformity is important because the market for the potters' product demands it. Only certain kinds of uniform vessels (plates and bowls) can be nested with efficiency of space, as anyone knows from putting household dishes in the cupboard. Uniformity thus contributes to nesting only for shallow vessels in which the mouth diameter equals the greatest diameter. Plates and bowls are not made with molds in Ticul, and the only other mold-made vessels beside figurines cannot be nested. For these shapes, however, greater variability of size and shape, rather than uniformity, are more desirable for nesting.

Furthermore, the nesting and uniformity of vessels is not necessarily related to efficient packing of ceramic vessels. Any vessel can be packed efficiently. In Ticul, breakage of vessels during transport is more related to improper packing than the lack of nesting, and vessels can be carefully packed for transport without nesting by using a rack carried on the back (see Thompson 1958:10).

Finally, efficiency of transport is less a function of nesting than a function of the absolute weight that humans can carry. This weight probably never exceeds 100 kg and more likely occurs in the range of 50–75 kg. The number of vessels for a single carrier can often be produced quickly by a potter, and if packing efficiency is a criteria, then nesting would appear to favor vessel variability rather than uniformity except for a very restricted class of vessels (plates and bowls). Even if nesting were important for pottery transport, would nesting be important to the consumer? Will nested vessels sell? For the consumer, nesting is only important for storage of unused vessels such as serving vessels. It would not be important for vessels such as water vessels and cooking pottery which are used constantly. If nesting was a criteria for vessel acquisition, then greater variability in vessel size would be favored except for plates and bowls. Finally, nesting would not be an important criteria for the merchant or the consumer for one of the most desirable shapes made by molding: figurines.

Vertical-half molding also has significant implications for understanding the implications of skill. Costin and Hagstrum (1995: 623) suggest that skill is related to "regularity and consistency in technique, with fewer errors in manufacturing rejects" and is the "mastery of technologically and artistically complex production sequences." In addition,

> . . . skill is expected to be positively correlated with the intensity of production, because artisans who spend more time at their craft accomplish their tasks with increasing deftness through repetition and experience. (Costin and Hagstrum 1995: 630)

Apart from problems already recognized by Costin (Costin 1991), Costin and Hagstrum (1995), and Stark (1995), there are several problems with using the notion of skill in ex-

planations and inferences about production organization. First, skill may have no material correlate. Skill has both cognitive and motor habit components and neither may be reflected in the material record. Traditional pottery-making skills in Ticul are not clearly reflected in the product of those skills. Traditional potters in Ticul come from old pottery-making families that have passed their knowledge and skills down for generations. Potters in those families learn how to select appropriate clays, how to select and prepare the raw materials for temper, and how to mix clay and temper to create a usable paste. These skills require knowledge of the ethnogeology, natural raw material variability and behavioral syntax of temper preparation (see D. Arnold 1971). For forming, production requires knowledge of vessel shapes, stages of their fabrication (Arnold and Nieves 1992), the measurements of each stage (Arnold and Nieves 1992), the muscular patterns required to combine the cognitive knowledge of shape and its measurements, and the length of drying time for each stage.

The construction of a kiln is also a skilled task. Kilns are built from limestone rocks and the heat in the kiln can turn the calcite in the limestone to lime by driving off the carbon dioxide. This chemical reaction reduces rocks to powder. The "new" specialized potter with minimum skills and who has no knowledge of how to build and maintain a kiln will be faced with one which collapses from the heat decomposing the limestone rocks and from the intense rains disintegrating the mud mortar on the exterior.

Firing requires knowledge of how long to dry and fire the vessels to avoid damaging them. Vessels cannot be fired too soon after fabrication because they will break from the physically held water in the vessel walls turning to steam. Firing also requires knowledge of different woods, how to stack the vessels in the kiln, and the different stages of the firing process. Different woods have different burning characteristics. Wood that burns quickly with a high flame must be split, placed behind the pottery when the kiln is loaded, and then used exclusively during the last stage of firing. Other woods that burn slowly or burn with a smoky flame should only be used during the lengthy warming period, the first stage of the process. Firing also requires a unique motor skill for throwing wood into the kiln which consists of a wrist motion that enables the potter to position the wood without striking (and damaging) the pottery. Firing also requires understanding the physical changes of the pottery during firing. This knowledge requires positioning the pottery to allow for shrinkage and knowing when it has been appropriately fired. Finally, the potter should know how to compensate for rainfall during firing in order to minimize damage to his vessels.

More than 50 years ago, every adult potter in Ticul possessed all of this knowledge and related skills, but these they were not clearly reflected in the potters' product. Beginning in the 1940s, several changes have occurred that have affected the relationship of skill, production organization, and the finished product. The roots of some of these changes occurred immediately before Raymond Thompson studied pottery making in Ticul in 1951 (Thompson 1958). At that time, however, there was little indication of the great changes that have since transformed the organization of the potters' craft in Ticul. Even with these changes, however, the presence or absence of the producers' knowledge and skills is not clearly reflected in the pottery.

Second, increased intensity and scale in Ticul during the last 30 years is negatively correlated with skill. The effect of production evolution between 1965 and 1994 has been to reduce the skill of the average potter and has occurred largely through the segmentation of the production tasks. By 1984, raw material procurement was in the hands of six specialists who mined clay, mined and prepared temper, and sold these materials to potters. Painting had become more elaborate with workshops where painters were specialists, but were not potters. Many workshops produced copies of Classic Maya polychrome vessels that required a totally different set of paints, design organization, and behavioral syntax than traditional pottery. Few tradi-tional potters painted such vessels, and if they did, they learned the skill by working in one of the larger workshops. There are other styles of painting, as well, but such painting is relegated to specialist painters who devoted themselves entirely to painting, rather than fabricating pottery.

Besides raw material procurement and painting, firing specialists have begun to emerge. Firing has proven to be a difficult skill for new potters and even experienced potters may not be able to build and maintain a kiln. First, building a kiln requires substantial capital to buy raw materials and most potters have neither the raw materials nor the capital to purchase them. Second, the kiln must be maintained to avoid collapse from rainfall or from the prolonged heat on the limestone rocks used in its construction. Third, potters no longer procure their firewood from local maize farmers, but instead obtain it from specialists who bring it by truck from locations up to 50 km away. When potters were peasant agriculturalists (*milperos* or swidden maize farmers) as well as potters, they knew the trees and the burning characteristics of wood from local ecological zones. By 1984, however, most potters had never been maize farmers and did not know the different types of wood. For those potters who had been maize farmers, they no longer recognized the wood because it came from unfamiliar ecological zones far away from Ticul. As a result, potters had to modify their firing strategy and this change has resulted in an increase in the amount of wood required and greater risk of firing losses. In such situations, only the skilled potter schooled in traditional firing methods can fire effectively—even with the limitations imposed by the unknown wood. As a result, many potters sell their pottery unfired to large workshops and some of these workshops have potters who specialize in firing. In the early 1980s, for example, my principal informant specialized in firing for one of the workshops, and although he had abandoned making pottery by 1994, he still fired for other potters—one of which was a workshop owner in Mérida.

The result of these changes between 1965 and 1994 was a net reduction in the average individual potters' skill. In 1994, there were still some "old" potters who were trained in traditional methods, who worked in workshops, fired pottery, and in general, could do everything from selecting raw materials to firing pottery. Generally, potter's knowledge and skill, however, has been replaced by a more evolved production organization characterized by task segmentation and more abundant material technology such as vertical-half molds.

Vertical-half molding has developed in a context of more evolved production organization that includes increased intensity and scale of production in which the overall skill of the individual potter has been reduced. Production within the traditional household remains, but it has also evolved into a several different types of production organization such as large household workshops, extra-household workshops, workshops "attached" to tourist hotels, and many intermediate variants. The reduction in knowledge and production skills has thus not only co-occurred with the increased use of vertical-half molding, but also with the segmentation of production tasks in general. The last 50 years of the production evolution in Ticul has distributed skills across different personnel by means of the segmentation of the production steps in which some potters do not (and indeed cannot) perform tasks outside of a narrow range or specialty. As a result, the skill necessary to make a finished pot no longer resides in one individual as it once did.

For the archaeologist looking at a single ceramic vessel, the segmentation of tasks has profound implications. Without knowing anything about Ticul production, an archaeologist looking at a modern copy of a Classic Maya vase would probably say that the painted vessel reveals more skill than a traditional nonpainted pot. In reality, the reverse is true. The traditional water pot made 50 years ago was produced with a greater number and variety of skills than a modern copy of a Classic Maya polychrome because the potter obtained the raw materials, fabricated, slipped, and fired the pot himself. The painted vessel, however, is more pleasing to modern aesthetic tastes and requires a lot of skill and control to produce, but it does not necessarily require more *individual* skill than a traditional water pot. Rather, it is likely that such painted vessels are the product of at least ten different people who are specialists at each production step. Two individuals are required to dig the clay, and it is transported to Ticul by others. A different individual may have mined and prepared the temper and another may have transported it to Ticul. Still another has mixed the paste, and one or more potters may have formed the pot. It may have been fired by still another and then sold to a workshop where it was painted by others. Task segmentation thus diffuses the skill required for production across multiple individuals. Nevertheless, the *aggregate skill* required to make a copy of a Classic Maya vase may be greater than that of the water-carrying pot.

One thus cannot infer production organization from ceramic vessels using skill as a criterion. As production evolves and becomes more segmented, the skill traditionally resident in one potter becomes diffused throughout a larger population of potters, and it becomes less and less likely that any one potter will possess all of the skills necessary to make a pot. The increased use of vertical-half molding mirrors this reduction of skill that is a part of the larger picture of technological evolution in Ticul.

This is similar to what has happened in the modern industrial economy. In Ticul, one sees the beginnings of industrialization with strong traditional roots. When Elwood Haynes designed and built the first automobile in 1893 and drove it for half-mile in Kokomo, Indiana, on July 4, 1894, he probably made many of the parts himself and assembled them largely on his own. Today, across the road at the Delco electronics plant and the Chrysler transmission plant, no auto worker can make the parts for a car radio or automobile transmission alone, nor does he or she assemble it alone. With the beginning of assembly line manufacturing, the segmentation of tasks has decreased the skill of the individual worker. While some hobbyists can still build an automobile themselves, the skill of doing so in a manufacturing context is so diffused throughout the modern assembly line that no one auto worker could build an entire vehicle alone.

While this point may seem simple using the modern motor car as an example, it is also true that there is no way that we can infer from the pot itself whether the tasks used to produce it were highly segmented or resided in one potter. Just as Feinman (this volume) suggested uncoupling production intensity from production scale, I suggest that production "skill" should be uncoupled from both production intensity *and* scale or, perhaps, dropped entirely from discussions of ancient craft organization. While increased task segmentation is an indicator of more complex production organization, it remains to be seen how archaeologists can recognize production organization from the pottery itself. Probably the best way is through the excavation of the production areas. The content and organization of production spaces may tell us more about production organization than the object itself.

For those who might want to persist in using skill as a criterion, perhaps "aggregate skill" of a ceramic vessel would be a better concept to employ than simply "skill" or "an individual producer's skill." Aggregate skill would consist of the sum of all of the skills necessary for the completion of the object. Such a concept would by-pass the problem of task segmentation. Consequently, the aggregate skill of an Acheulean hand axe would be appropriately less than a modern motor car and the aggregate skill of a highly decorated Maya polychrome might be greater than that of a undecorated cooking pot. Yet, Classic Maya vases have a much simpler form than water-carrying vessels, further complicating the issue. In fact, Ticul potters say that besides small food bowls, vertical-walled vessels (such as the Classic Maya vases) are the easiest vessels to form with modified coiling on the turntable. While this proposed change in terminology from skill to aggregate skill might solve the ambiguity created by task segmentation in antiquity, the question remains concerning what aggregate skill means in social and economic terms. Furthermore, it creates a new set of problems. Recent Maya epigraphic work seems to suggest that the producers of the decoration on ancient Maya polychromes were writers and not potters. If the shape of those polychromes were only made with rudimentary skill, as I have suggested, using ancient Maya polychromes to reconstruct ancient Maya production organization using any kind of skill as a criterion may be very misleading.

With task segmentation, the notion of aggregate skill in pottery production shifts the focus away from that required by the individual producers to the technology involved in production. This approach would not only include the techniques of production, but would also include the organization of that production which was necessary in more evolved levels of production organization. The aggregate skill would thus include the actual production skill, but also that skill which was necessary to organize the production into task sequences. This latter skill is thus neither muscular nor artistic skill, but rather managerial in nature. In more evolved production with task segmentation, there must be individuals who can organize the behavioral chains of individual artisans in order to produce a pot.

Finally, standardization should also be decoupled from skill, scale, and intensity of production. In mold-made vessels, uniformity is the product of the technique and requires little skill. Even with other fabricating techniques, uniformity varies with shape, market, technique, and whether and how a vessel is measured or not measured during production (See Arnold and Nieves 1992). The decoupling of standardization from intensity and scale has been suggested rather obtusely by Arnold and Nieves (1992) who demonstrated that several complex factors affect vessel uniformity. This same point has been made once again, but more clearly in this volume by Longacre. In Ticul, uniformity of vessels comes from the demands of the market, fabrication technique, and the desire of the potter to measure vessels during production. Standardization is not simply related to increased intensity and scale. Although mold-made production in Ticul was "introduced" by a government workshop, it was only "adopted" by potters in response to market demand and then used in household production for many years before more complex production organization emerged. More recently, mold-made production has continued to be used in household production, but it has also been used in extrahousehold workshops, and in workshops attached to tourist hotels. Originally, molding was a response to producing innovative vessels that could not be produced in any other way, but more recently this advantage was combined with a desire for uniform vessels emanating from market demand. The use of molds, then, is not the effect of, nor the cause of, the increased production intensity. Pottery production has been full-time since the late 1960s. In the 1980s and 1990s, molding still occurred both in single potter households and in the workshops with large numbers of workers.

Probably the most important implication of this essay is a simple one that derives both from cultural anthropology and one of its theories, cultural materialism. Human behavior and its products are highly contextual and are linked to the other aspects of culture. These links cannot be reconstructed by archaeologists without recourse to understanding the links between the technology and the rest of culture in an ethnographic context. Deductive approaches to the past and theorizing about ceramic production in antiquity are insufficient without understanding more of the technology of the ceramic production process itself. Production organization, whether described in terms of skill, intensity, or scale, are all embedded in a technological context that must be understood before any form of production organization can be inferred. Technology does not determine production organization, but rather places both potentials and constraints upon on it. Like all aspects of culture, ceramic forming technologies are not *just* the products of sociocultural and organizational causation, but rather themselves exert causal pressure on other aspects of sociocultural phenomenon—in this case the amount of space and the amount of skill required for production. While vertical-half molding was introduced into Ticul by a government workshop, it was used by households for 30 years before the development of both social and spatial extrahousehold workshops. Even now, this molding technique remains an important fabrication technique for households. Understanding vertical-half molding within an ethnographic context reveals that it has important implications, among others, for the use, allocation, and amount of contemporary household space.

6

Rethinking Our Assumptions: Economic Specialization at the Household Scale in Ancient Ejutla, Oaxaca, Mexico

Gary M. Feinman

INTRODUCTION

For two decades, archaeological perspectives on craft specialization (e.g., Peacock 1982; Santley et al. 1989; van der Leeuw 1976, 1977) have generally categorized variability in a rather monolithic manner. These evolutionary models, utilized for prehispanic Mesoamerica and elsewhere, view craft specialization as varying along a single dimension, from small-scale household production to larger-scale factory manufacture. Yet, analytical application of these viewpoints has created major conundrums at the Mesoamerican sites of Colha and Teotihuacan, where high densities of stone tool manufacture have been noted, but nonresidential workshops or "factories" have not been found.

This paper builds on Costin's (1991) alternative, multidimensional framework for categorizing craft specialization. Archaeological findings are presented from an excavated Classic period (A.D. 200–800) house in highland Ejutla, Oaxaca, Mexico (Fig. 6.1), where a heavy volume of craft production appears to have been enacted in a domestic context. Based on the Ejutla findings and a reconsideration of other Mesoamerican contexts, the frequent occurrence of nonresidential craft workshops in ancient Mesoamerica is challenged, although the existence and importance of high-intensity craft manufacture for exchange is not. In other words, specialized craft production occurred in prehispanic Mesoamerica (and high volumes of nonagricultural goods were produced), but these activities generally took place in domestic contexts (houses).

MONOLITHIC MODELS OF CRAFT SPECIALIZATION

In 1976, when Sander van der Leeuw (1977: 70) proposed what he viewed as a first step toward "a general model of the economy of pottery," archaeological studies of craft specialization (e.g., Evans 1978; Matson 1965) were still relatively new. Drawing exclusively from ethnographic and historical descriptions (largely from the Old World), van der Leeuw (1976, 1977) proposed six "states" of pottery making that proceeded from household production to household industry to workshop industry to large-scale industries (Table 6.1).

In this synthesis, household production is defined as small-scale manufacture for one's own residential unit. Household industry is described as "part-time" production for use by the immediate group, involving entirely local materials, and requiring little labor or technological investment. The volume of production is presumed to be low. In contrast, workshop and factory production are viewed as full-time specializations in which increasing degrees of high-intensity production are employed to supply ever wider networks of consumers. Greater degrees of

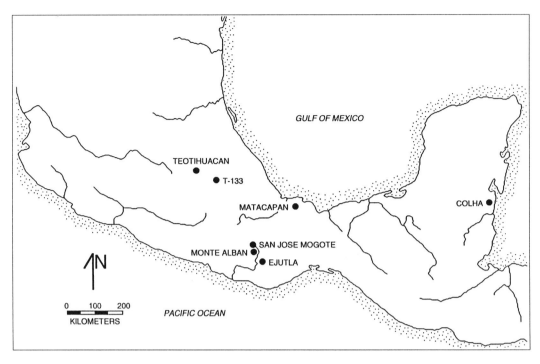

Fig. 6.1. Southern Mexico, locating places mentioned in text.

TABLE 6.1.
Monolithic Models of Craft Specialization

van der Leeuw 1977	Santley et al. 1989
Large-scale industry	Manufactory
	Nucleated Industry
Village industry	
Workshop industry	Workshop industry
Individual industry	
	Tethered specialization
Household industry	Household industry
Household production	Household production

capital investment and more distant raw materials are incorporated into the production process.

Given the basic germ of empirical validity behind van der Leeuw's eloquent model, it is not surprising that it achieved wide acceptance. In a narrower study of pottery making in the ancient Roman world, Peacock (1982: 7–11) advanced a similar evolutionary scheme that included household production, household industry, workshop, and factory production. Peacock (1982:8), in contrast to van der Leeuw, recognizes that household

producers could potentially manufacture wares for more than just their immediate group, but he also equates this domestic mode of production with part-time craft participation that generally is carried out sporadically and only as a supplement to other larger sources of household income.

More recently, Robert Santley and his colleagues (Santley et al. 1989; Santley and Kneebone 1993) have proposed a nearly identical scheme focused on six modes of production (household production, household industries, tethered specialization, workshop industries, nucleated industries, and "manufactory" production) (see Table 6.1). These modes are argued to be directly related to production output (Santley and Kneebone 1993:39), so that domestic-scale manufacture is generally presumed to be at relatively low intensities compared to workshops and "manufactories." Following van der Leeuw and Peacock, Santley and his associates (e.g., Pool 1990:73) see household industries as necessarily part-time allocations of labor that consequently only produce secondary (presumably relative to subsistence farming) sources of household income. Santley and Kneebone (1993:41) also surmise that household industries would not normally be associated with high densities of production waste or debris. Once again, the nondomestic workshop and "manufactory" modes are defined by full-time production, broader networks of exchange, and greater concentrations of debris.

In concert, these monolithic models expect general agreement between the volume of finished goods that craftworkers produce, the intensity of their work effort (part- versus full-time), the proportional weight given to craft activities in household income, the density of debris produced, the spatial extent of the distribution network for finished goods, the distances from which raw materials are procured, the size and relative elaboration of production facilities, and the scale or setting of the craft activities. Residential contexts are presumed to be associated with part-time, low- intensity, local production, while high-intensity, full-time, economically important craftwork is expected in nondomestic settings.

In the following section of this paper, general acceptance of the monolithic model (by all participants in the debate) is shown to have led to interpretive logjams in two well-known cases of prehispanic Mesoamerican craft production. Here, I review these debates, and begin to map a path out of this impasse. In considering these two cases, I temporarily move away from this volume's focus on ceramics to discuss stone tool manufacture at two important prehispanic Mesoamerican sites: Teotihuacan and Colha.

SCALE VERSUS INTENSITY: THE STONE TOOL CONUNDRUM

The presence of large and unusual quantities of lithic debris has long been recognized at the central Mexican urban center of Teotihuacan and the small lowland Maya settlement of Colha, Belize. At Teotihuacan, huge quantities of obsidian have been noted and collected from the surface of the site. Michael Spence (1967, 1981:771) has postulated the presence and location of over 100 obsidian workshops based on field observations of heavy obsidian densities, proportions of waste in the surface collections, and the presence of unfinished artifacts. Extrapolating from these data, Santley (1983:72) has stated that "the evidence for specialized workshop activity is so pervasive that it is difficult to escape the conclusion that the obsidian industry was one of the basic features, if not the most vital feature of Teotihuacan's craft economy." Santley (1983) sees obsidian production as a key factor in the emergence of the city and its hypothesized interregional importance.

These interpretations have been criticized by John Clark (1986), who questions the depositional contexts of the Teotihuacan obsidian. Clark (1986:32) argues that workshop refuse should markedly differ from household refuse in the kinds of artifacts present, their relative frequencies, and the percentage of used implements. Clark questions whether some of Spence's (1981:771) workshops are even production contexts, since these localities simply include unusual densities of obsidian mixed with other classes of artifacts that might typically be found in household trash. While Clark (1986:62–71) offers few specific alternatives concerning obsidian production at Teotihuacan, he does view most obsidian working at the site to have been tailored for local consumption, finds no evidence for a "factory-level" industry, considers there to have been many fewer workshops than previously thought, and suggests that the total number of obsidian craftworkers at the site was small. From Clark's (1986:65) perspective, the economic importance of obsidian production has been greatly exaggerated.

Current debate over chert production at Maya Colha parallels to a remarkable degree the arguments concerning obsidian working at Teotihuacan, although the claims for workshop manufacture at Colha are drawn principally from excavated, rather than surface, deposits. Based on years of research at Colha, which is located in the chert-bearing zone of northern Belize, Harry Shafer and Thomas Hester (Hester and Shafer 1994; Shafer and Hester 1983, 1986, 1991) have postulated a long history of stone tool manufacture at the site. At Colha, excavations have exposed large and dense concentrations of chert debris; the massive size and extent of these deposits is used as the prime indicator for large-scale workshop production (Hester and Shafer 1994:50). Nearly 100 concentrations of such chert waste or debitage (dated principally, but not entirely, to the Late Preclassic and Late Classic periods) were recorded as workshops (Shafer and Hester 1983:522). The abundance of certain stone tool forms (finished and unfinished) at Colha, and the presence of these same tool varieties solely as finished artifacts at other neighboring sites, provide further evidence of specialized production at Colha (Hester and Shafer 1994:50). Based on these data, the excavators conclude that the production at Colha involved "formal specialized workshops," "craft specialization on a massive scale," and "industrial-level mass production" (Shafer and Hester 1983:519, 537, 539). Nevertheless, despite recognizing the anomalous volume of stone debris unearthed at Colha, Mallory (1986) challenges the aforementioned assessment of the site. He (Mallory 1986:155) suggests that the stone debitage concentrations at Colha do not represent workshops, but could have been neighborhood dumps created by generations of separate households mostly quarrying and processing stone for their own use. In contrast to Hester and Shafer, Mallory postulates that there was little, if any, specialization in chert production at the site, that relatively few finished tools were manufactured, and that what production occurred was almost exclusively for immediate domestic needs. According to

Mallory (1986:156), all Colha households were principally involved in agriculture, only turning to stonework a few months each year during the agricultural off-season.

In part, the acceptance of key tenets of the monolithic model of craft specialization has served to cloud our current understanding of stone tool production at Teotihuacan and Colha. Those (Spence, Santley, Shafer, and Hester) who have argued for large-scale workshop manufacture at these sites have relied principally on massive debris deposits (whether surface or subsurface) to establish their case for large-scale mass production (see also Santley et al. 1989; Santley and Pool 1993). Yet, importantly, no clear nondomestic workshop or factory contexts have ever been uncovered at either site. In fact, there are preliminary indications at both sites that craftwork was indeed carried out in domestic contexts.

At Teotihuacan, the excavation of Classic period (A.D. 200–800) residential compounds has revealed the remains of production activities that clearly appear to exceed what the producing households needed for their own domestic use (e.g., Manzanilla 1993; Rattray 1988; Turner 1992:93; Widmer 1991). At the same time, Spence (1987:434) notes that many of his designated obsidian workshop areas coincide spatially with an architectural unit of some sort, usually a typical Teotihuacan residential apartment compound. Likewise, at Colha, chert debitage tends to trail off the edge of residential platforms (Roemer 1982; Shafer and Hester 1983:529). In excavated contexts, the close proximity of craft debris with contemporaneous dwellings would seem to indicate that the production activities were undertaken in residential settings (McAnany 1993:233).

In part, the problem is that the investigators at Teotihuacan and Colha have conflated two different parameters or dimensions of craft specialization: *scale* (the size and constitution of production facilities) and *intensity* (full- versus part-time production or the volume of product manufactured) (Costin 1991). Influenced by the monolithic model, they have equated the recovery of large and anomalous deposits of craft debris with non-residential "workshops," when what they actually defined are "craftwork dumps" or production and manufacturing discards (Clark 1989; Moholy-Nagy 1990). Although the volume or intensity of stone tool manufacture appears unusually high, at densities clearly signaling exchange far beyond the needs of single production or domestic units, the scale most clearly associated with these production activities is not a workshop or factory but the household.

Nevertheless, the critics of lithic specialization at these two sites (Clark, Mallory) also have been somewhat misled by the expectations of the monolithic model. At both Teotihuacan (Spence 1981:771) and Colha (Roemer 1982:77), lithic debitage was found mixed with small quantities of domestic trash. As noted above, Clark (1986:32) implies that this association indicates nonspecialized manufacture for domestic consumption. But the suggested domestic association of the deposits speaks only to the dimension of scale, not production intensity. That is, regardless of its abundance, the trash composed of heavy volumes of production waste could have been produced in a household context. In a similar vein, Mallory's inference that the Colha chert deposits are household dumps generated by accretion does not justify his further assertion of nonspecialized, part-time production at Colha (see McAnany 1993). At both Teotihuacan and Colha, what we seem to have are extremely unusual and rather massive quantities of production waste (suggestive of high-intensity manufacture), but with no clear indication that this craftwork was enacted outside domestic settings. What we have then is specialized, household-scale production that produced high volumes of craft goods at least partly for exchange.

In other words, I have proposed a new more multidimensional perspective on Teotihuacan and Colha craft specialization. This view decouples the attributes of scale and intensity, and challenges the expectations of the monolithic model of craft specialization. At both sites (Teotihuacan and Colha), the pro-

posed interpretation seems to fit the extant data better than the alternatives (household production for immediate use or nonresidential factory production). Despite the arguments presented to this point, at neither of these two sites (Teotihuacan or Colha) can we unequivocally link high-intensity, high-volume craftwork with domestic-scale contexts. At neither of these sites do we have excavated residential contexts with clear indications of high-volume obsidian (Teotihuacan) or chert (Colha) manufacture. In the remainder of this paper, I endeavor to remedy this problem through the documentation of high-intensity domestic manufacture. Our attention turns to ceramic and shell ornament production and the ancient Ejutla site to illustrate that specialized production (at high volumes) was indeed enacted at the household scale in ancient Mesoamerica.

ANCIENT EJUTLA: RESEARCH BACKGROUND
Before returning to the issue of craft specialization, I introduce the Ejutla site and the research conducted there. The Ejutla site lies in the Southern Highlands of Mexico at the southern end of the Central Valleys of Oaxaca under the modern district head town of Ejutla (see Fig. 6.1). Ejutla is situated at the center of the Ejutla Valley (largely defined by the Río Ejutla), roughly 60 km south of Oaxaca City. In 1984 and 1985, Linda Nicholas and I directed a regional survey of the Ejutla Valley (Feinman and Nicholas 1990). During this systematic survey, we mapped the prehispanic site of Ejutla, which was one of the largest sites in the region between the Terminal Formative and Late Postclassic periods (200 B.C.–A.D. 1520). At the eastern edge of the modern town and the prehispanic site, we encountered unusual densities of cut and broken marine shell in several plowed fields (Fig. 6.2). To be honest, it was this shell (and not pottery) that brought us back to excavate in this part of the Ejutla site in 1990.

During portions of four summers (1990–1993), Linda Nicholas and I directed a block excavation in this eastern sector of the Ejutla site (Fig. 6.3). The focus of this work was a 190 sq m area that was exposed

GARY M. FEINMAN

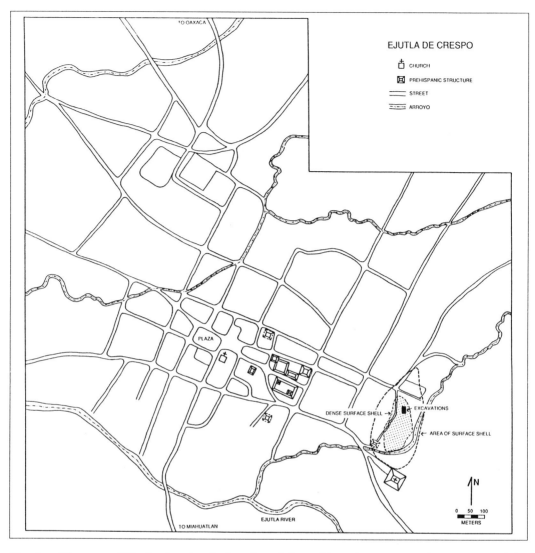

Fig. 6.2. The town of Ejutla, showing the location of the prehispanic monumental structures and the area of surface shell.

and excavated down to bedrock. The excavated area was part of a 2 ha area in which we noted and collected surface marine shell. A Classic period (A.D. 200–800) residential structure and its immediate environs were uncovered during the block excavation (Feinman and Nicholas 1993, 1995; Feinman et al. 1993), and the analysis of this material is still in a preliminary stage. We suspect that this residential structure was part of a *barrio* in which the residents of the component households worked marine shell into ornaments. Roughly 30 m south of the excavation

block we noted a second structure that was destroyed by contemporary plowing. Large quantities of shell debris, worn obsidian blades, and several cut-stone foundation blocks were noted on the surface in this area. This area likely contained a second structure that was part of this shell-working *barrio*.

The excavated structure, roughly 6-by-4 m with a small attached work area to the north, was defined by a stone foundation and a mixed earth and crushed bedrock floor. Several factors point to the domestic nature of this complex, including the discovery of a

86

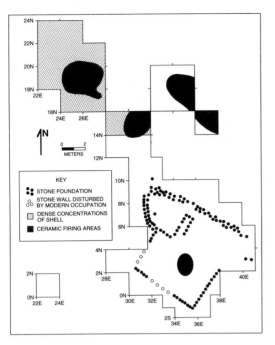

Fig. 6.3. Excavations at the Ejutla site, showing the location of the Classic period structure, dense midden, and ceramic firing features.

small subfloor tomb that included at least four individuals, the recovery of a shallow firepit and probable cooking area immediately outside the structure, and the presence of food remains and other residential trash in the middens adjacent to the house. In Classic period Oaxaca (e.g., Winter 1974, 1995), residential complexes often were associated with domestic tombs (on the order of the one found in Ejutla).

The modest contents of the tomb suggest that this household was not of especially high status. Yet the presence of the tomb, and the size and nature of the house construction (employing a stone foundation composed of roughly finished stones rather than rough cobbles) indicate that the residents of this household were not entirely disadvantaged either. Some relatively minor indications of dietary stress were evidenced on the skeletal material from the tomb. The presence of at least four individuals (three adults) in the tomb, along with the disarticulated condition of early tomb occupants (Middleton et al. 1998), indicates that the tomb (and likely the

house above it) was in use for at least a generation, if not somewhat longer.

SHELL ORNAMENT MANUFACTURE

The association of the excavated Ejutla household with the production of marine shell artifacts has already been discussed at length (Feinman and Nicholas 1993, 1995). More than 20,000 pieces of marine shell were recovered in the block excavation. Many of the pieces were cut, abraded, or in other ways modified. Broken or partially completed ornaments were relatively common, while finished artifacts were rare. The marine taxa represented, such as *Spondylus, Strombus,* and *Pinctada,* were commonly employed to fashion ornaments across prehispanic Mesoamerica. Most of the shell varieties were native to the Pacific, roughly 100 km away across high mountains. Subsequent analyses (by Linda Nicholas) of marine shell artifacts from the Classic period Valley of Oaxaca urban center of Monte Albán have revealed that many of the shell ornament forms and shell ornament taxa from that site mirror the forms and varieties noted in the Ejutla collections. Yet, while the Ejutla material is comprised mostly of broken, incomplete, or waste pieces, the Monte Albán collections include a far higher proportion of finished artifacts. Finished shell ornaments constitute almost 20 percent of the analyzed shell from Monte Albán, compared to less than 1 percent of the Ejutla assemblage.

No known site in the Central Valleys of Oaxaca equals this eastern sector of the Ejutla site in terms of the concentration of marine shell artifacts and, especially, debris. In fact, probable areas of shell craftwork have been identified at only two other valley sites, the major centers of Monte Albán and San José Mogote. Nevertheless, shell ornaments are far from rare in elite contexts at Monte Albán and elsewhere in Oaxaca, indicating a considerable volume of coastal-to-highland marine shell exchange (e.g., Kolb 1987).

In the Ejutla excavations that we directed, most of the marine shell was found in exterior midden contexts within 10 m of the residential complex. Nevertheless, two of the more finished shell ornaments recorded during the project were recovered on the floor of the house (Fig. 6.4). Some shell debris also was found in association with the structure floor, although at much lower quantities than noted in midden areas. Microartifactual flecks of shell that were derived from the heavy fraction of soil samples taken from the floor of the house also served to tie the working of marine shell to activities that took place on the floor of the domestic structure (Feinman et al. 1993). Only one of 169 chert microdrills, almost certainly used for perforating shell ornaments, was found in floor contexts. Yet, it was found on the floor of the work area (at the northern edge of the residential complex) near a flagstone pavement.

Only one tiny shell bead was found in the domestic tomb. Overall, only a tiny proportion of the entire Ejutla shell assemblage was comprised of finished or partially finished ornaments. So it seems very likely that the inhabitants of this part of the Ejutla site, and the occupants of the excavated house in particular, made shell ornaments for exchange and probable export beyond the limits of the settlement. In contrast, there is simply no empirical basis to suggest that this volume of shell ornament production (found in conjunction with so few finished pieces) was entirely intended for immediate household consumption.

CERAMIC AND FIGURINE PRODUCTION
Unexpectedly, the Ejutla excavations also yielded ample evidence for ceramic production. The initial indicator was an unusual abundance of figurines found in midden contexts. In total, 2,000 figurines were recovered, and a good number of them were broken or malformed. More than 60 ceramic molds (including 15 that definitely were for figurines) also were recorded during the project. Not surprisingly, some of the molds matched commonly noted figurine varieties (Fig. 6.5). Overall, more than 900 pottery wasters were noted. These defective pieces comprise a range of ceramic forms, and in-

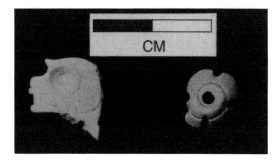

Fig. 6.4. Two finished shell artifacts recovered from the Ejutla house floor.

clude a diverse array of misfired, misformed, bubbled, and vitrified sherds (Fig. 6.6). Almost all the categories of ceramic wasters defined by Redmond (1979) were present in Ejutla. More than 160 of the wasters were figurine wasters.

Over four field seasons, we also excavated six shallow features that the prehispanic Ejutleños dug into the soft bedrock. One of these features lies under (and so clearly predates) the excavated residential structure (Fig. 6.7), but a number of the others (just north of the structure) seem contemporary with it (see Fig. 6.3). These oblong features, three of which were excavated in their entirety, are interpreted to have been used as "pit kilns" (Rye 1981) for ceramic firing (see Abascal 1976; Bordaz 1964; Heacock 1995; Sheehy 1992). All of these features face the direction of the prevailing wind, probably to improve firing performance through enhanced airflow (Krotser 1980:132). Generally, these features were associated with burned rock, charcoal, lenses of ash, and other indications of burning, as well as wasters, sherds that were overfired or fired more than once, slaglike material, and heavy densities of clay concretions (Fig. 6.8). Based on experimental and ethnographic analogies (Balkansky et al. 1997), we suspect that some of these concretions are remnants of temporary earthen roofs that were placed over the firing pits (e.g., Stark 1985:176). Roofs were needed to produce the reduced gray ware ceramic vessels (particularly certain bowl forms) that we recovered.

Fig. 6.5. Ceramic figurines and a figurine mold recovered at the Ejutla site.

Fig. 6.6. Kiln waster from a large vessel recovered at the Ejutla site.

At the base of one of these pits, we encountered large broken sherds, including upside down jars, along with cobbles that all may have been used as spacers (to separate vessels) during firing (Fig. 6.9). This kiln furniture was interspersed at the base of the pit with a thick layer of ash mixed with bits of charcoal, reflecting an incomplete burn (Russell 1994) (Fig. 6.10). In most cases, after its final use for firing, the pit kilns served as refuse depositories. The lower levels of these dumps, and the deposits surrounding the firing features, often included a number of complete, unused vessels that were flawed or broken immediately prior to deposition. These nearly pristine discards were similar in paste and form to the most prevalent classes of wasters (and certain highly abundant forms) in the Ejutla sample. Although the

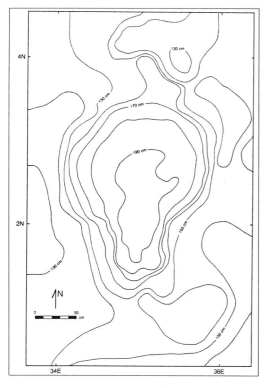

Fig. 6.7. Contour drawing of the firing feature uncovered below the house floor at the Ejutla site. Contour intervals of 10 cm show depth below the surface.

Ejutla potters made a wide range of forms, figurines, tortilla griddles *(comales)*, and incense burners *(sahumadores)* were a few of their obvious mainstays.

The abundance of ceramic wasters in our excavations, in conjunction with the presence of figurine molds, clay concretions, and the excavated pit kilns, securely point to pottery production. The determination of the intensity of prehispanic pottery manufacture is more difficult. However, in our modestly sized excavation block, we did recover a rather astounding quantity of ceramic artifacts. We recorded and analyzed more than 210,000 pottery fragments, which had a combined weight exceeding 3,500 kg.

The form and paste of ceramic artifacts above, below, and associated directly with the floor of the structure enable us to link the Ejutla house with the immediately adjacent midden and firing areas. Preliminary petrographic and elemental (ICP) analyses (by Andrea Carpenter) of raw clays taken from the current site surface itself (and from a finer clay bed in a nearby *barranca*) are qualitatively (mineralogically and elementally) similar to the pastes of Ejutla figurines and other

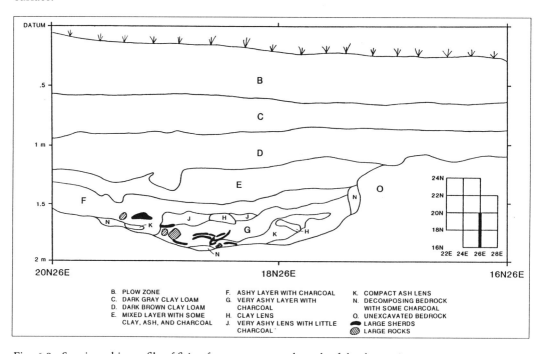

B. PLOW ZONE
C. DARK GRAY CLAY LOAM
D. DARK BROWN CLAY LOAM
E. MIXED LAYER WITH SOME CLAY, ASH, AND CHARCOAL

F. ASHY LAYER WITH CHARCOAL
G. VERY ASHY LAYER WITH CHARCOAL
H. CLAY LENS
J. VERY ASHY LENS WITH LITTLE CHARCOAL

K. COMPACT ASH LENS
N. DECOMPOSING BEDROCK WITH SOME CHARCOAL
O. UNEXCAVATED BEDROCK
LARGE SHERDS
LARGE ROCKS

Fig. 6.8. Stratigraphic profile of firing feature uncovered north of the domestic structure.

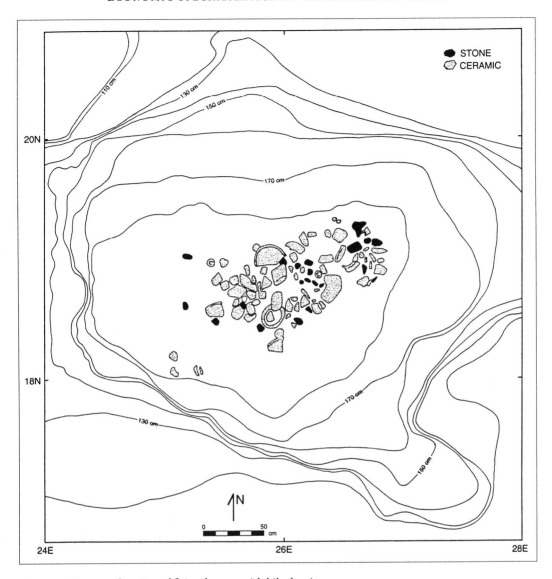

Fig. 6.9. Contour drawing of firing feature with kiln furniture.

vessels. Compositionally, a fired clay concretion found during excavation also was similar to the raw clays. Interestingly, in contrast to the figurines, for which we find lots of large inclusions in the paste, some locally produced Ejutla pottery bowls appear to have been made with processed clays that were significantly finer than the available raw clays. Carpenter has been able to reproduce these finer pastes by beating and then levigating the raw Ejutla clays.

Spatial proximity between the domestic complex, the firing features, and the midden areas (loaded with ceramic manufacturing debris), as well as artifactual associations across these features, link the Ejutla household with ceramic manufacturing. This connection is supported by the compositional similarities between readily available clay and the excavated by-products of ceramic production. Yet, could this domestic production have been entirely for household use? Although evidence against this proposition is not as clear-cut as it is for a relatively rare and exotic good (shell), I still think not. As with the shell, a high proportion of the figurines

Fig. 6.10. Debris at base of excavated firing feature.

Fig. 6.11. Figurine with cotton armor recovered at the Ejutla site.

Fig. 6.12. Figurines recovered at the Ejutla site, including one with cotton armor.

we encountered were broken, flawed, or unfinished. These unfinished pieces were in addition to the hundreds of more obvious figurine wasters. Unless the Ejutla potters were incredibly unsuccessful and had an incredibly high failure rate, the quantity of well-made, finished goods should have significantly surpassed what we did recover.

Here it should be considered that we neither were able to excavate the entire area encircling the house (which almost certainly included more midden deposits), nor do we have any idea how much production waste was transported via natural or cultural processes to distant areas away from the house. Nevertheless, from the perspective of what we did recover, it seems unlikely that any single household would have used (even over a decade or two) anything approaching the volume of figurines (or for that matter *sahumadores* or *comales*) that were probably made in this domestic context. For example, certain general varieties of figurines were noted over and over again in our sample, reflecting the use of molds. A common figurine variety wears cotton armor (Figs. 6.11–6.13), while another type sports a triangular tunic and beaded necklace (Figs. 6.14–6.15). Would a single domestic unit require so many similar figurines?

Nearly identical figurine forms also were noted in surface collections made at several sites within 10 km of the Ejutla site during the earlier Ejutla settlement pattern survey (Fig. 6.16). One such figurine also was shown

to be almost compositionally identical to similar figurines found at the Ejutla site. In addition, a figurine, attributed no more specifically than to Ejutla in *Urnas de Oaxaca* (Caso and Bernal 1952, fig. 453c), is a near match for the most complete mold that we found in our excavations almost forty years later (see mold in Fig. 6.5). Furthermore, near the base of one excavated firing feature, sherds from at least 9 to 11 different tortilla griddles were found in the same exca-

Fig. 6.13. Figurines recovered at the Ejutla site, including one with cotton armor.

vation level of one 2-sq-m unit. As with the figurines, the output from this particular production context was unlikely to have been for immediate household needs alone. If the Ejutla potters were only supplying their immediate needs, I doubt they would have concentrated so heavily on figurines, tortilla griddles, or incense burners, as those are not the forms that dominate a household's ceramic inventory.

THE SCALE AND INTENSITY OF EJUTLA CRAFTWORK

To this point, I have described domestic-scale production in which shell ornaments and a range of ceramic forms likely were made for exchange. In the excavated middens, craft debris often was found with domestic trash, such as food remains and sherds from charred cooking jars. Such remains tie the craft debris to a domestic context in which they were found. The location of the craft middens adjacent to the excavated structure also conforms with ethnoarchaeological

findings that garbage created by residential units generally is deposited on the house lot, but in areas that do not interrupt other household activities (Hayden and Cannon 1983).

At the same time, finished products in both materials (shell and ceramic) appear to have been traded beyond the limits of the Ejutla site (for which we estimate a Classic period occupation of roughly 1,500–2,000 people). Given the relative uniqueness of the Ejutla shell concentration for highland Oaxaca, shell artifacts likely were exchanged more widely than the ceramic goods. Both crafts entailed the knowledge and application of specialized technologies, including the firepits and molds for pottery, and hollow tubular (cane) drills and chert microdrills for the shell. Analysis of the exterior midden deposits has revealed that the chert microdrills were apparently finished close to the time when shell ornament manufacture was carried out, since the reduction debris from both tasks was almost always depositionally

Fig. 6.14. Figurine with triangular tunic and beaded collar recovered at the Ejutla site.

duction appears to have been of lesser importance and lower intensity than the other crafts. Nevertheless, the same hollow tubular drill technology was employed in processing both shell and onyx. The diameter of the majority of the onyx drill plugs matched that of many flat shell disks. Use of these "intersecting technologies" (Earle 1994:455; Hagstrum 1992) further supports the inference that this Ejutla household was involved in several craft activities or "multicrafting." This finding contradicts the oft-held Mesoamerican notion that each household or community of specialists focused on a single craft.

To this point, I have considered the intensity of production by this Classic period household from the perspective of product volume and applied technologies. Another aspect of intensity (Costin 1991:5–18), measuring the extent and degree of labor effort (part-time versus full-time), has been avoided. In large part, I have sidestepped this aspect of manufacturing intensity because I see few avenues for the precise archaeological examination of this often-discussed (but little examined) issue. Yet, if we are to clarify our models of ancient Mesoamerican craft specialization and amend our more general models of craft production, then a brief speculative foray into this question of labor commitment seems worthwhile. Perhaps this consideration might spark more empirically grounded examinations.

The occupants of the Ejutla household were demonstrably involved in a range of craft activities. Microartifactual analyses of the earthen floor (as well as shell and lithic artifacts) connect shell and stone work to the excavated house, while ceramic artifacts do the same. Although stratigraphic analyses of midden densities may signal an increase in the relative importance of shell working during the course of the occupational sequence, there is every indication that more than one activity co-occurred to some degree during the occupation of the structure.

Based on the artifactual and feature record, the inhabitants of the Ejutla structure worked shell in a variety of ways, including sawing, string-cutting, drilling, incising,

mixed. The chert for the microdrills was quarried from a source roughly 3 km from the Ejutla house; however, we do not know whether it was procured directly or through exchange with the occupants of a small contemporaneous settlement situated closer to the stone source.

Microartifactual analysis (by William Middleton) also has revealed tiny chert flakes as well as microscopic indicators of lapidary work on the structure floor. Rectangular onyx plaques and cylindrical drill cores, greenstone chunks and flakes, and flakes and chunks of nonlocal stones also were recovered in the excavations, principally in the exterior midden. The volume of these stone materials was much lower than the quantities of shell and pottery debris, and no fully finished stone ornaments were recovered. Consequently, lapidary manufacture and craft pro-

Fig. 6.15. Figurines recovered at the Ejutla site, including two with triangular tunic and beaded collar.

abrading, and polishing. The nature of the debris recovered suggests that shell was processed from raw, whole shell to finished ornaments. For the commonly used taxa, all parts of the shell could be accounted for either in ornament forms or waste. The Ejutla inhabitants also fashioned the chert drills (and possibly the cane drills) that they then used to perforate shell ornaments (e.g., beads and pendants). I presume that the raw shell arrived in Ejutla through trade; if not, direct procurement from the Pacific Coast would have been a major time-consuming enterprise.

Ceramic production likely began with the procurement of raw clay from the immediate vicinity. Subsequent efforts were required to process the clay and form the vessels. Numerous fired clay coils, and even a few fired globs of clay with finger impressions, were found during midden and structure excavations. Such materials imply that household members were involved with more than just firing vessels in the adjacent pit kilns. Of course,

the Ejutla occupants also constructed the firing features and fired the ceramic objects that they formed (and probably modestly decorated). Lapidary crafting with various stone materials also involved some household labor effort. A few unfinished bone ornaments also were recovered. Exotic gemstones may have been sufficiently rare and valuable that they were not discarded as readily as were the clay and shell artifacts. If that were the case, it may be possible that we are underestimating the relative importance of lapidary crafting in this context.

We also have artifacts suggesting that cooking and some spinning were undertaken by this household. Bone needles and spindle whorls were recovered from across the excavations, although some ceramic spindle whorls (of which we ve more than 100 in total) appear to have been the product of manufacture rather th n use (in spinning fiber). We suspect that a umber of the recovered whorls were made by the members of this household, since some lack any wear

Fig. 6.16. Figurines from regional survey collections, including one with cotton armor and another with triangular tunic and beaded collar.

from use, while others were whorl wasters. Nevertheless, a substantial number of the whorls and all of the bone needles (12) that were found were well worn.

The fundamental question then is how much involvement did the people in this household have in noncraft activities, primarily agriculture? Since we lack any agricultural features adjacent to the excavated house, this query is next to impossible to address in a direct manner. The Ejutla excavations did yield a total of 18 fragments from polished axes, including one small piece associated with the house floor. Yet polished axes could have had diverse functions, only some of which are directly related to farming. For example, pottery manufacture certainly necessitated the procurement of wood for firing, which likely required an ax. No other artifacts clearly indicative of agricultural work (as opposed to agricultural consumption), such as stone hoes, were found. Nevertheless, it is not evident which other artifacts

associated with agricultural labor one might expect to encounter in a house context. The 18 ax fragments would seem to be a relatively small number compared to the 32 onyx drill cores, 77 metate or grinding stone fragments, and 169 chert drills that we recovered during the Ejutla excavations, but there is no clear way to quantify such differences into proportional labor effort.

If we look at it another way, much of the ceramic work in Ejutla could have been effectively timed to be carried out in the dry season, leaving the wet season for agricultural work. Yet, much of the worked shell was string cut, requiring water and sand for use in abrasion. Processing the shell, therefore, might have been easier in the rainy season when water was more abundant. Today, water can get rather scarce during the dry season in Ejutla. However, shell working, like potting, potentially could have been undertaken in the drier months. On the other hand, it is not clear whether all of the craft activities (described above) could have been ably managed by a single household in the dry season alone. In sum, there is nothing definitive to rule out agriculture as part of this household's annual time budget, but it certainly may not have been the major component in its yearly labor allocation.

DISCUSSION AND IMPLICATIONS

As at Teotihuacan and Colha, the Ejutla findings would appear to document relatively high-intensity craft manufacture (for exchange) that was enacted at the domestic scale. In contrast to the expectations of the monolithic model, household-scale craft production was not necessarily a secondary activity supplemental to the primary economic pursuit of agriculture. The residues of craftwork were diverse, more abundant than any indicators of agricultural work. Likewise, in opposition to the tenets of the monolithic model, the Ejutla craftworkers did not produce exclusively for themselves or their close neighbors. Finished shell objects may have been traded to places as distant as Monte Albán. They also did not rely solely on local resources. In addition, the ancient Ejutleños created rather astounding quantities of debris, committed a significant time investment, and worked with various specialized and labor-intensive technologies. In sum, the nature of household craft production in Ejutla bears little similarity to the expectations for such manufacture outlined by the monolithic model.

Although the Ejutla findings do not conform to the monolithic model of craft specialization, they do correspond closely with previous empirical findings regarding the general character of craft manufacture in prehispanic Mesoamerica. As at Teotihuacan and Colha, most Mesoamerican craftwork can be linked to production at the household level (e.g., Pool 1990:111; Stark 1985). Mesoamerican archaeologists have frequently described indications of high intensity and finely skilled craft specialization, and often these findings are directly associated with residential structures or other domestic remains (e.g., Becker 1973; Charlton et al. 1993; Rattray 1990).

Despite several tentative propositions (e.g., Abascal 1976; Redmond 1979; Santley et al. 1989), true workshops or factories (large-scale manufacturing contexts outside of residential settings) have yet to be conclusively reported for prehispanic Mesoamerica. All of the familiar claims for nonhousehold production in Mesoamerica are based principally on indicators of high intensity (production in volume) rather than independent measures of scale itself. In each case, these claims rely on surface collections (Redmond 1979), apparent concentrations of firing features (Abascal 1976; Redmond 1979; Santley et al. 1989), or on surface collections in association with small test excavations (Arnold et al. 1993; Pool 1990; Santley et al. 1989). For prehispanic Mesoamerica, we still lack any evidence for workshop structures or fabrication areas that were not directly associated with domestic quarters (where people slept or prepared food). Specific structures that were associated with production tasks (e.g., fabricating and drying pottery), but clearly isolated from domestic activities, have not been found. When Peacock (1982:42–46) re-

ferred to "manufactories," his reference is to the concentration of supervised specialists, who enacted their craft, at least somewhat removed from domestic settings.

Although surface collections often can inform us about the provenience and intensity of craft activities (e.g., Feinman 1980), they cannot reveal much regarding the scale of production. As we have seen at Teotihuacan, Colha, and Ejutla, high densities of craft waste can be generated by domestic producers. Likewise, the excavated Ejutla house was associated with six firing features (and we may not have found the total number because of our excavation limits). Concentrations of firing features, therefore, are neither evidence for nor against domestic-scale production; the key question is what was immediately adjacent to those features (nondomestic work areas or residences). Neither Abascal (1976) at the T-133 site in Puebla nor Santley and his associates (Arnold et al. 1993; Pool 1990; Pool and Santley 1992; Santley et al. 1989) at Matacapan, Veracruz, have excavated a large enough area to tell us the specific contexts in which their recovered firing features were situated. This is the exact problem that Peacock (1982:165–166) bemoaned for Europe almost two decades ago. The nature of production sites can only be identified if one excavates and defines the context of a large enough block to encompass much more than a firing feature or two.

At Comoapan, Matacapan, where dense ceramic production waste and numerous firing features were noted, only one excavation block larger than a 3-m pit was unearthed (Pool 1990). Perhaps it is revealing that this somewhat larger excavation unit (dug mostly to define kilns and an associated ceramic waster dump) also noted a drain and a large metate, two things often found in Mesoamerican domestic contexts (Pool 1990:229–230, 358). Obsidian blades, also not explicitly related to the ceramic production process, were recovered during these excavations as well (Pool 1990:230, 247). Consequently, at this time, and because of the small extent of the excavations, high-intensity ceramic production cannot be definitively isolated from a domestic setting at Comoapan.

The picture from sixteenth-century central Mexican documents is rather comparable. For example, in the *Codex Mendoza* (Berdan and Anawalt 1992), the descriptions of craft activities and specialists depict the dissemination of craft skills from mother to daughter and father to son, and this training and instruction seems to have occurred in domestic contexts. Likewise, the *Florentine Codex* (Sahagún 1950–1963) illustrates craftwork in detail, but it appears to have been carried out either in domestic or "attached" palace settings with only a small number of participating specialists. As in the archaeological record, we lack any definitive evidence for nondomestic workshops of significant scale. Even in much of rural Mesoamerica today, full-time specialists, producing large volumes of craft goods for outside consumption and markets, often work in domestic settings, not factories (e.g., Hendry 1992; Papousek 1981, although dozens of examples could be cited). Consequently, for prehispanic Mesoamerica, the broadly assumed isomorphism between scale and intensity that is central to the monolithic model would seem to find little support. To understand ancient Mesoamerican craft specialization and the nature of the region's prehispanic economy, extant assumptions concerning these different parameters of craft specialization (scale and intensity) should be separated and distinguished.

This is not meant to infer that nondomestic workshops will never be securely defined for ancient Mesoamerica. In fact, I fully expect that they will be found in a few special settings. But to define them conclusively will require the opening of large excavation blocks. And I expect that even when we have exposed more such excavation blocks, the number of nonresidential workshops will be rare in prehispanic Mesoamerica. Alternatively, what this also means is that when we find high volumes of craft manufacturing debris in domestic contexts, we cannot immediately presume that it only represents the residues of a part-time industry or low-intensity production. In ancient and modern Mesoamerica, intensive craftwork can and did occur in domestic settings.

Finally, if the monolithic model of craft specialization does not adequately characterize ancient Mesoamerica, then it is fair to question its applicability and utility elsewhere. Indisputable indications for nondomestic production contexts, such as workshops and factories, are relatively rare in most of the other regions that were the settings for ancient states and empires. Since high-intensity manufacturing and production for exchange can no longer be used as a reliable indicator for large-scale production contexts or true workshops, then now is a good time to reevaluate and look more closely at the weight and strength of the evidence for specialized production (along multiple dimensions) in these other world regions as well. Although I fully expect other global areas to differ markedly from ancient Mesoamerica in the patterns of manufacture and distribution, it will be important to know more precisely how the economies of those regions differ and to consider the reasons why. Only when we begin to assemble these data can we hope to understand the nature and extent of diversity in ancient systems of economic production and exchange.

7

Ceramics and the Social Contexts of Food Consumption in the Northern Southwest

Barbara J. Mills

INTRODUCTION

One only has to walk through the aisles of a major Southwestern museum to appreciate the variation in ceramic vessels from the American Southwest. The casual observer might first notice the beauty of the painted decoration, the variety in colors of slipped surfaces, or the diversity of vessel forms. A closer look might result in the observation that one attribute of vessel form, vessel size, also varies widely in what constitutes well over a millennium of ceramic production.

Several researchers have noted that there are trends toward increasing vessel sizes through time in the American Southwest (e.g., Blinman 1988a; Crown 1994; Graves 1996; Graves and Eckert 1998; Mills 1989, 1993, 1995a; Snow 1982; Spielmann 1998; Turner and Lofgren 1966). This pattern crosscuts wares, vessel forms, and traditionally defined regions. The trend is not a gradual one and not all sites of a single time period or location show exactly the same pattern. However, the trend transcends these local and temporal discontinuities and deserves closer attention.

There are several alternative interpretations for variation and change in vessel size: differences in the foods cooked and the methods of cooking; household size; household wealth or status; and the incidence and scale of suprahousehold feasting. Each of these interpretations has ethnoarchaeological and archaeological support, and each has been applied to the middle-range societies of the American Southwest. The alternatives also reflect changing emphases of archaeological interpretation from ecological and functional arguments to those more grounded in the social and political dynamics of past societies.

Rather than focusing on only one area of interpretation over another, such as subsistence or the incidence of feasting, I suggest that these seemingly disparate conclusions are often interrelated. When they are considered together, these alternatives become the basis for a more holistic view of past societies in the Southwest (see also Plog 1995). Because different factors may not have equal influence on the outcomes, the relative strength of one interpretation over another will need to be evaluated on a contextual basis bolstered by independent lines of data.

The broader goal of this paper is to better understand changes in food consumption patterns using ceramic vessels. That is, how do ceramic vessels vary through time and space because of differences or changes in the kinds of foods consumed, the ways that those foods are prepared and served, and the social scale of those who participate in both preparation and consumption activities? My more specific goal is to understand these changes among prehistoric Pueblo communities dating between ca. A.D. 1000 and 1300 in the northern Southwest.

I focus particularly on long-term trends in vessel sizes from the Mesa Verde and Tusayan

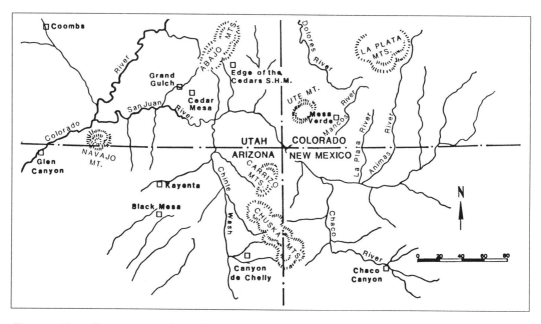

Fig. 7.1. Four Corners area of northern Southwest showing major archaeological areas discussed in text.

areas of the Four Corners area. To do so requires a closer look at those factors of food preparation and consumption that contribute to variation in ceramic vessel size. I then discuss the analysis of whole vessel sizes, both across the two areas and through time. The Tusayan and Mesa Verde areas (Fig. 7.1) contrast with each other in the details of the trend, and I discuss these differences vis-a-vis current models for the evolution of relations between production and distribution in the northern Southwest. I conclude that although households were the unit of consumption, there is significant variation across the two areas in the size of commensal units that likely reflects differences in household composition and degree of suprahousehold sharing.

VESSEL SIZE AND CUISINE

Cuisine is a form of technological style. Recipes, the timing of meals, the order of courses, and table manners are passed down through the domestic group by observation and participation. This mode of transmission tends to favor conservatism in these activities. Nonetheless, conservatism in foodways

can be overrated and movement of people and their crops, technological innovations, class differences, and demands on labor can all have far-reaching effects (Goody 1982: 150–153). Thus, changes in the types and capacities of food containers should, at least in part, be important indicators of changes in the foods themselves, the transmission of knowledge about foods, and the social contexts of food preparation and serving.

Although the specific uses may be widely varied, ceramic containers are first and foremost vessels for storing, transporting, preparing, and serving food and water. One of the major advantages of ceramics as a technology is that they improve processing of foods. The introduction of new foods or intensification of food consumption already in the diet plays an important part in many theories about the introduction of ceramics (e.g., P. Arnold, chapter 10; Barnett and Hoopes 1995; Skibo and Blinman, chapter 11), as well for changes in vessel assemblages once ceramics are present. Changes in cuisine have more often been linked with changes in the performance characteristics of different vessels, especially their shape and composition (e.g., Braun 1983; Sassaman 1993; Schiffer and Skibo 1987). However, it follows that new ways of preparing foods and intensification in the consumption of specific foods will also affect vessel size.

For example, substantial changes in Pueblo diet were wrought by European expansion into the Southwest, changes that are amply reflected in the sizes and shapes of ceramic vessels (Mills 1995a:223; Snow 1982). Two major additions to Pueblo diet are wheat-based leavened breads and domesticated animals. The former required larger bowls with different rim treatments to accommodate rising dough and large jars to store baked bread (Snow 1982). The large body sizes of most of the domesticated animals introduced into the Pueblo diet may also be tied to increased sizes of both serving bowls and cooking pots. The preparation and serving of mutton stew is well documented from more recent historic contexts (e.g., Cushing 1920). Writing on Zuni, Stevenson (1904:368) noted that most meat consumed in the village was boiled, whereas meat consumed in camp was roasted. Ceramic bowls were and still are an important component of the serving of these stews. Large bones are left in the stew when served in communal bowls. Historically, marrow processing was an important part of Zuni table manners (Cushing 1920:527). The incorporation of large bones in the stew provided an important supplemental food source, a pattern of meat processing and consumption that can be expected given high reliance on agricultural products at any period (e.g., Blinman 1988a:193; Speth and Scott 1989).

In contrast to the well-documented example discussed above, more subtle changes will ensue with changes in the intensity of consumption of specific foods. One way to look for changes in food processing that might co-occur with changes in vessel sizes is through the analysis of other food processing equipment, such as cooking features or grinding stones.

Both Snow (1990) and Adams (1991) discuss a significant change in prehistoric Pueblo cooking technology that likely had an influence on ceramic vessel use, if not their sizes. Corn-based breads cooked on griddles, comals, and *piki* (at Hopi) or *hewe* (at Zuni) stones were an important part of historic Pueblo cuisine. The incorporation of these forms of corn preparation can be traced to the late prehistoric period in several areas of the Southwest (Adams 1991; Haury 1945; Snow 1990). Adams traces the first use of piki stones or griddles in Western Pueblo sites to about A.D. 1250–1300. Along with shoepots, Adams (1991:79–82) regards *piki* stones as part of a constellation of traits related to the introduction of the kachina cult during the same period and possibly from a similar southern source. The same change in cooking technology occurred in the Rio Grande area in the late thirteenth or early fourteenth centuries (Snow 1990), slightly later than in the Western Pueblo area.

New hearth forms and new ways of processing corn went hand-in-hand with the cooking of breads on cooking stones. In fact, the identification of these stones in the archaeological record may be only the tip of the iceberg in terms of a significant change in Pueblo cuisine during the late prehistoric period. Not only do these preparations require new ways to grind corn, but they also share an important form of corn preprocessing. Historically, whether for paper bread, corn cakes, or a number of other non-griddle based corn dishes such as hominy and corn dumpling preparations, preprocessing of the corn was accomplished by soaking it in water with lime or ash (Cushing 1920:294–306; Katz and Kaiser 1995; Ladd 1995; Stevenson 1904:361–369). Snow's (1990) interesting discussion points out the nutritional benefits of this preprocessing, long known for Mesoamerican cuisines (e.g., Katz et al. 1974). The addition of lime produces a chemical reaction that not only enhances the nutritional benefit of corn, but also changes its color. Some of these preparations were even a type of fermentation that resulted in leavened corn breads (Cushing 1920:294–295).

Soaking of corn generally involves an expansion through absorption. Whether in bowls or in jars, a change in cuisine that used soaking as a preprocessing technique suggests use of larger vessels (Tani 1994:56). Ethnographic references suggest that hominy and dumpling preparations that entail boiling may require larger vessels; there is even one recipe at Zuni that used a method of double-boiling—placing one pot within another (Cushing 1920:300). These changes in Pueblo cuisine may be one of the factors that contributed to the increases in cooking jar and serving bowl sizes recently noted for the late prehistoric Pueblos. However, as discussed below, other variables of the social context of consumption may also have played important roles.

HOUSEHOLD SIZE AND VESSEL SIZE

Eating is a social experience that may take place in groups of varying scale and composition, but on a daily basis meals usually are taken with other members of the household. In fact, definitions of the household hinge on the economic role of this social unit in activities of consumption, along with those of production and reproduction (Wilk and Netting 1984). Within group variation in household size and composition may be present depending on the stage in the developmental cycle and the kinds of economic activities participated in by the household. Cross-culturally, significant differences in household sizes may arise for a number of reasons, including patterns of production, distribution, and inheritance. Of particular significance for smallholder agriculturalists is the relationship between household size and the amount of land accessed or cultivated. A balance must be struck between the number of individuals to feed and the amount of land that household members have access to for cultivation (Netting 1993:85–87).

Turner and Lofgren's hypothesis (1966) relating vessel size to household size is now a classic one in New World archaeology. They proposed that the ratio of the volumes of individual serving bowls and cooking jars could be used to estimate differences in the number of people served at a meal. By cali-

brating their analyses at the later end to known historic Hopi family size, they were able to convert this ratio into an estimate of actual household sizes in prehistory. The long-term trend that they identified is one of increasing vessel sizes through time for the period A.D. 500 to 1900, which they convert to increases of from 4.5 to 7.0 persons per household.

Nelson (1981), using data from ethnoarchaeological research in Chiapas, challenged the Turner-Lofgren hypothesis. His analysis showed that household size was only part of the picture and that family status and wealth were also significant factors. However, more recent ethnoarchaeological research extends new support to the original Turner-Lofgren hypothesis. Tani's (1994) analyses in the Kalinga village of Dangtalan show that there is a significant relationship between household size and the mean capacity of regular-sized cooking pots. He suggests that the reason Nelson obtained different results is because of the way that food is preprocessed in the Maya area. As discussed above for the late prehistoric and historic Pueblos, the Maya also preprocess corn by soaking. The volume of the pot therefore reflects the amount of corn and water, not just the corn that was consumed. In addition, enough is preprocessed for the entire day, rather than making separate batches for individual meals. When combined, scheduling and preprocessing created an imperfect relationship between vessel volume and family size in the Maya area (Tani 1994:55–56).

Thus, meal scheduling and different processing techniques may have significant effects on differences in vessel volume, but household size remains an important variable for vessels used for food preparation or consumption. As storage vessel sizes may be measuring something other than group size, cooking vessels and serving vessels are more direct indicators of the size of the consumer group (Shapiro 1984:706). If serving vessels are being used, the way that foods are served becomes important. Identification of size modes is an important step as some serving may be in individual-sized vessels. The volume of communal serving vessels will more closely reflect the size of households (or other social units eating together) than will the volumes of individual serving bowls.

HOUSEHOLD STATUS OR WEALTH AND VESSEL SIZE

Wealth and status are not always the same thing. For example, in Pueblo society one can have a high-status position in the ritual hierarchy without showing any outward material manifestations of that position. Conversely, wealth can be measured by access to high quality, agriculturally productive land, but the owners may not be those with the highest status in the society. Nonetheless, wealth and status are interrelated in that high-status positions may require the hosting of ceremonies. Even in rotating positions, such as cargoes in post-contact Mesoamerican society, authority is reinforced by and may even be selected on the basis of the ability to host.

Ethnographic and ethnoarchaeological studies identify household status as contributing to variation in the variety of goods in the household, the presence of specific types of artifacts, and even differences in vessel size (Deal 1998; Hayden and Cannon 1984; Smith 1987; Tani 1994; Trostel 1994). As noted above, household wealth is one of the variables identified by Nelson (1981) in his multivariate analysis of Maya vessels. Trostel's (1994) findings confirm the relationship between vessel size and household wealth. In the Dangtalan sample he analyzed, meat and vegetable pots *(oppaya)* were more strongly correlated with household wealth than were rice cooking pots *(ittoyom)*, but the volume of the more expensive, imported metal cooking pots was the best predictor of household wealth.

One of the reasons that household status figured so prominently in Nelson's study was because many of these households were expected to host fiestas. Feasts in the highland Maya cases discussed by Nelson were a means of reinforcing positions of power within the community (Nelson 1981:113).

Thus, when studying patterns of food consumption, I consider family wealth and status to be part of feasting behavior rather than a separate dimension.

FEASTING AND VESSEL SIZE

Feasting is commensalism on a grand scale. By definition, food is a crucial ingredient to a feast, but the purposes of the feast can be highly varied, as can their contexts. Hayden's (1990, 1995b) model summarizes relationships between feasting and sociopolitical complexity that have become a significant focus of current research. Recent interpretations of variation in ceramics primarily have used feasting to interpret sociopolitical complexity. Although they do not explicitly use vessel sizes in their argument, Clark and Blake (1994) attribute the replacement of perishable containers with ceramic vessels in Mesoamerica to competitive feasting. Blitz (1993) presents empirical data to support the idea that larger vessels were used and discarded at Mississippian mounds than at smaller sites, supporting an interpretation of centralized feasting and storage. Brumfiel (1987) and Costin and Earle (1989) use the decline in vessels associated with ritual feasting as evidence for the take-over of peer polities by the state (Brumfiel 1994:11).

However, as Hayden's own model demonstrates, all feasting is not hosted by aggrandizers to further their own positions of authority, nor is all aggrandizing carried out in the context of feasts. Feasting has many different contexts and may be organized at the corporate or individual levels. Nonetheless feasting is an important strategy to identify in the archaeological record and its variation can be used to understand varying social contexts of consumption above the level of the household.

One important dimension of feasting is the relation between hosts and guests. These relations may be institutionalized and asymmetrical, as in ranked societies. In such cases, feasting may be competitive as hosts put on ever more impressive displays of food and other goods in an effort to maintain and recruit followers (Brown 1979; Clark and Blake 1994; Clendinnen 1991:63–68; Hayden 1995b; Preucel 1996:129–130). Feasting therefore may have a political as well as a social basis as networks reach well beyond kin. However, feasting can also have important exchange functions or be celebrations of solidarity that do not imply institutionalized positions of authority (Hayden 1995b).

Toll's (1985:369–406) review of Pueblo "gatherings" points out three important variables in feasting behavior: (1) the scale of the social group, (2) scheduling within the annual cycle, and (3) the kinds of goods involved. Small-scale ceremonies with restricted sharing may occur throughout the year, because "critical rites" such as birth and death are relatively random in their temporal distribution. However, there are periods of restricted sharing that co-occur with times of particularly low food availability (see also Ford 1972). By contrast, communitywide feasts are more closely sequenced to periods of abundance such as summer and fall. In these cases, unrestricted sharing tends to take place and there is greater participation in economic activities such as trading.

Food preparation and serving is an essential component of all Pueblo ceremonies. As White (1932:132) noted for Acoma "all important ceremonies are attended with feasting." At both Acoma and Zuni (Cushing 1920), special foods may be associated with particular ceremonies that require planning and preparation to ensure that the ingredients are at hand. Cooking may take place for several days, if not weeks, before to feed participants after rehearsals. Food preparation may play as important a role after each practice as it does in the actual ceremony. Depending on the scale of the ceremony, large labor groups may be recruited to prepare foods, including the tasks of grinding and cooking, to make sure that enough food is available. Ceramics may be used as containers for the preparation of feast foods, as a means of transporting foods to other places where they are consumed, and as service to participants and audience.

There is ethnoarchaeological and ethno-graphic support for the observation that "big ceremonies require big pots" (Pauketat and Emerson 1991:923). In the Kalinga area, nearly every household in Dangtalan and most households in Dalupa have one or more large vessels that are used for special occasions (Longacre 1985:344). In these cases, multiple households pool their resources to cook for the events, which are largely critical rites. Special cooking vessels, many of which are larger sized than usual, are used in the Maya area during ritual occasions (Deal 1998; Nelson 1981, 1991). Large fermentation vessels may hold a special place at feasts as a means of labor mobilization (e.g., DeBoer and Lathrap 1979; Pastron 1974).

Archaeologically, both the size of vessels and the amount discarded may indicate variation in consumption. Blinman (1988a, 1989) uses reconstructions of vessel sizes from sherds and the ratios of serving bowl sherds to cooking jar sherds to identify whether cooking was centralized or dispersed within the community. He reasons that the higher proportion of bowl sherds discarded in roomblocks with ritual structures are evidence that food was being carried to these roomblocks in activities of ritual consumption, but prepared elsewhere in a kind of prehistoric "potluck." Larger cooking jars are not present in the trash near large ceremonial structures. In ethnographic accounts of Pueblo feasting, different households do much of the cooking and the food brought in bowls to where dancers-initiates-society members have convened (Cushing 1920; Stevenson 1904; White 1932). Thus, Blinman's results suggest ritual feasting organized at the scale of corporate groups without resource pooling at a centralized source during the Pueblo I period in the Mesa Verde area.

The Pueblo I data from southwest Colorado contrasts with analyses of Pueblo II period assemblages from Chaco Canyon (Toll 1985, 1991; Toll and McKenna 1987). In a comparison of two sites in Chaco Canyon, the small site of 29SJ627 and the great house site of Pueblo Alto, Toll and McKenna (1987) note that there is evidence for both increasing vessel sizes and increasing numbers of jars discarded through time. In fact, the total accumulation of plain ware jars at Pueblo Alto greatly exceeds the amount that could be discarded given the number of households and the estimated occupation span of the site. Over 50 percent of all of the utility pottery was made in the Chuska areas, and Toll argues that Pueblo Alto and other sites in Chaco were the locus of periodic gatherings that drew upon populations from outside Chaco Canyon. Toll's conclusion is a linchpin in the Chaco Project's pilgrimage fair model that assigns greater ritual, rather than redistributive, significance to the cluster of great houses in Chaco Canyon (Lekson et al. 1988). However, as Toll's own review notes, these large-scale gatherings likely included events of unrestricted sharing, a form of redistribution. In addition, the fact that the pots were brought to Pueblo Alto for consumption activities suggests a scale of resource pooling quite different from the case discussed above for southwest Colorado.

Late prehistoric increases in the incidence or size of large vessels have been identified in both the Western and Eastern Pueblo areas and tied to increasing feasting behavior. Crown (1994:110) notes that there is a directional change in bowl sizes from Pinto to Tonto Polychrome bowls dating to the late thirteenth through fourteenth centuries in the Western Pueblo area, which may be tied to increased participation in ritual associated with what she defines as the Southwestern Cult. Graves (1996; Graves and Eckert 1998) and Spielmann (1998) have identified changes in Eastern Pueblo vessel sizes that they associate with an increase in feasting activity from the thirteenth through the fifteenth centuries. Graves's research is most explicit in its political basis; increases in feasting are tied to the development of social power by individuals in leadership positions within a sequential hierarchy in which leadership is more situational rather than a simultaneous hierarchy with more institutionalized hierarchies (Johnson 1989). Spielmann's analysis focuses more on ritual by suggesting that an Eastern cult was developing earlier

than cults found in the Western Pueblo area's Salado polychromes (but does not consider the fact that White Mountain Redware is found earlier in the Western Pueblo area in her discussion).

Although the data are not completely comparable, the examples from the Southwest suggest suprahousehold feasting was an important context for consumption activities. In at least the Chacoan case, this consumption was at such a large scale that it suggests communitywide feasting with unrestricted sharing (see also Stoltman, this volume). In the Pueblo I case, suprahousehold ritual feasting was present that better fits with a model of more restricted sharing at the suprahousehold level. In all cases, vessel size is intimated to be an important variable. However, there are several social dimensions of consumption that can work alone or in concert to affect vessel size. Because vessel size can be influenced by each of these different social dimensions, interpretations of vessel size require multiple lines of evidence. Subsistence change is a first consideration. In the absence of such changes, household size and suprahousehold feasting at different scales can be considered. Changes in the sizes of cooking and serving vessels can be indicators of changes in household size, with the caveat that size modes be identified and considered separately. The largest modes can be evidence for suprahousehold feasting, as can differences in the frequency and locations of discard of cooking and serving vessels.

CHANGES IN VESSEL SIZE IN
THE NORTHERN SOUTHWEST

My analysis is based on a large sample of whole vessels dating A.D. 1000 to 1300 from the Mesa Verde and Tusayan areas of the northern Southwest (Table 7.1). The Mesa Verde area encompasses southwestern Colorado, including Mesa Verde National Park, and extends into southeastern Utah. The Tusayan area includes most of northeastern Arizona, including the Kayenta, Black Mesa, and Canyon de Chelly areas (Fig. 7.1). Both of these areas have distinctive architectural patterns, site layouts, and ceramic wares.

TABLE 7.1.
Sample Sizes and Date Ranges for Wares and Types
Used in the Whole Vessel Analysis

Ware/Type	Sample Size	Date Range (A.D.)
Mesa Verde Gray Ware		
Mancos Gray	5	850 to 950
Mancos Corrugated	98	900 to 1150
Dolores Corrugated	75	1025 to 1275
Mesa Verde Corrugated	19	1125 to 1300
Mummy Lake Gray	11	950 to 1200
Tusayan Gray Ware		
Tusayan Corrugated	207	1030 to 1200+
Moenkopi Corrugated	77	1130 to 1260
Kiet Siel Gray	54	1210 to 1280–90
Mesa Verde White Ware		
Cortez Black-on-white	34	875 to 1025
Mancos Black-on-white	57	975 to 1175
McElmo Black-on-white	77	1075 to 1275
Mesa Verde Black-on-white	261	1200 to 1300
Tusayan White Ware		
Black Mesa Black-on-white	67	875 to 1100
Sosi/Dogoszhi Black-on-white	48	1040 to 1180+
Flagstaff/Tusayan Black-on-white	26	1165 to 1280–90
Tsegi Orange Ware		
Medicine Black-on-red	9	1000 to 1115
Tusayan Black-on-red	20	1050 to 1210+
Early polychromes	64	1125 to 1280–90
Late polychromes	8	1185 to 1280–90

Note: The vessels used in this analysis are from the collections of the American Museum of Natural History, Museum of Northern Arizona, Western Archaeological Center, Arizona State Museum, University of Colorado Anthropology Museum, Mesa Verde National Park, University of Utah, Brigham Young University, Edge of the Cedars Museum, Black Mesa Archaeological Project of Southern Illinois University at Carbondale, Peabody Museum of Harvard University, University of California Los Angeles, and the Smithsonian Institution. The whole vessel data base is identical to that use in Mills (1989), with the exception of the Coombs site, which is not used in the present analysis. See Mills (1989, Appendix B) for a listing of all catalog numbers and vessel classes.

The present analysis is closer to the original Turner and Lofgren (1966) study in that it uses whole vessels in museum collections, rather than being a sherd-based analysis. One of the major problems with sherd-based analyses is that sherds must be converted to some estimate of total vessels represented to compensate for the fact that large vessels produce more sherds (Egloff 1973; Orton 1993). Unfortunately, too few analyses are reported at this level, making broad comparisons across regions and through time impossible given currently available data.

Even if we had comparable data from sherd-based analyses, rim sherd diameter may not always be the best proxy measure of overall vessel size. The best attribute of vessel size is vessel volume or capacity (Whallon 1982). Single linear measures of vessel size can be used as proxies, but different linear variables may be better than others depending on overall vessel shape. In general, bowl rim diameters are good proxies of vessel size because there is usually a direct linear relationship between rim diameter and vessel volume. Height has been empirically demonstrated to be the best proxy for restricted jars from the northern Southwest (Mills 1989). In the absence of volumetric data for all of the vessels used in this analysis, I use rim diameter for bowls and height for jars.

Kaldahl (1996) conducted an analysis of a subsample of 114 of the restricted jars from the Mesa Verde area included in this paper. Using AutoCAD's three-dimensional modeling routine on whole vessel profiles, he calculated the effective volumes and constructed regression equations for predicting vessel volume from rim diameter. Separate analyses were done for each of three ceramic types of Mesa Verde Gray Ware. His comparisons of histograms of vessel height and volume by type indicate that the number of modes generally remains unchanged, but that the evenness or skewness does change. Nonetheless, using vessel volume on the subsample produced the same directional changes in vessel size discussed in this paper.

Five technologically distinct wares were made between A.D. 1000 and 1300 in the northern Four Corners area: two in the Mesa Verde area (Mesa Verde Gray and White Ware), and three in the Tusayan area (Tusayan Gray and White Ware and Tsegi Orange Ware). The forms used in this analysis are: (1) unpainted, restricted (necked) jars; and (2) decorated bowls. I assume that all unpainted, necked jars are used for cooking at some point in their use-lives. Although some of these vessels were recovered archaeologically as subfloor storage vessels, each one of these was sooted, suggested that they were originally used as cooking vessels. In addition, use alteration is present on most of the gray ware jars that fit the kind that would be expected given their use over hearths, including zones of oxidation and sooting as well as interior pitting (Skibo 1992).

COOKING POTS

Between ca. A.D. 1000 and 1300 Mesa Verde Gray Ware cooking vessels show distinctive changes through time. Box plots of vessel heights through typological time show that these changes are dramatic and directional (Fig. 7.2). The one type that does not seem to fit the pattern of increasing size through time is Mummy Lake Gray, the dating of which has been considered problematic. Along side the other Mesa Verde Gray Ware types in Figure 7.2 is one type that predates A.D. 1000, Mancos Gray. Mancos Gray is common in late Pueblo I and early Pueblo II contexts, and is dated ca. A.D. 850 to 950 or 1000 (Blinman 1988b:504). I have included it here to show that the trend of increasing jar sizes has much earlier roots with virtually no overlap of interquartile ranges once Dolores Corrugated was being made.

As all distributions of vessel sizes considered here are multimodal, the nonparametric Kolmogorov-Smirnov (K-S) two-sample test was used to see which pairwise differences in the distributions were significantly different. The K-S test results for Mesa Verde Gray Ware indicate that Mancos Gray, Mancos Corrugated, and Mummy Lake Gray are not significantly different from each other, but all three are significantly different from Dolores and Mesa Verde corrugateds. The latter two types do not differ from each other. Thus, the biggest change in the shape of the distributions appears to have occurred in the late 1000s or early 1100s, at the Pueblo II/III period transition.

By contrast, the Tusayan Gray Ware types do not show the same dramatic changes in vessel size through time (Fig. 7.3). Part of the difference in the results between these two wares may be because the temporal resolution is not as great for the Tusayan Gray Ware as it is for the Mesa Verde Gray Ware. Three types of Tusayan Gray Ware were produced between A.D. 1000 and 1300, but two of them have a potential 70-year overlap in production: Tusayan and Moenkopi corrugateds (Table 7.1). The third type, Kiet Siel Gray, is more narrowly restricted to the mid- to late thirteenth century. There is a slight increase in median size of vessels between Moenkopi Corrugated and Kiet Siel Gray, and the K-S test results indicate significant differences in the shapes of the distributions. The K-S test does not show any significant

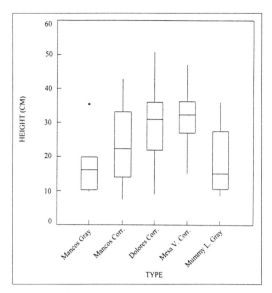

Fig. 7.2. Box plots of Mesa Verde Gray Ware cooking jar heights (cm) by ceramic type. Types are arrayed earliest to latest from left to right.

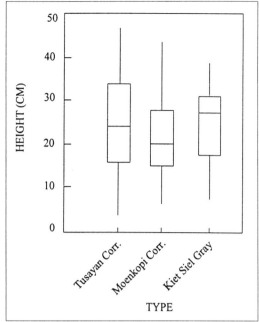

Fig. 7.3. Box plots of Tusayan Gray Ware cooking jar heights (cm) by ceramic type. Types are arrayed earliest to latest from left to right.

differences between Tusayan Corrugated and Kiet Siel Gray. A further contrast with the Mesa Verde area cooking pots, then, is that the only discernible increase in size is at least 100 years later, at about A.D. 1200 (the middle of the Pueblo III period).

SERVING BOWLS

Median sizes of Mesa Verde White Ware bowls do not show a strong directional trend through time (Fig. 7.4). However, significant K-S test results indicate that the shapes of the distributions are quite different. The pairwise tests indicate that there are significant differences in the distributions from Mancos Black-on-white to McElmo Black-on-white, and from McElmo Black-on-white to Mesa Verde Black-on-white. However, these changes are primarily because of changes in the peakedness of the small- and large-sized bowl modes.

Two size classes are present in the Mesa Verde White Ware bowl assemblage. Comparison of the coefficients of variation (CV) by size class shows distinctive decreases in variation through time (Table 7.2). Mesa Verde White Ware bowls have clear size modes, with the range of variation in sizes be-

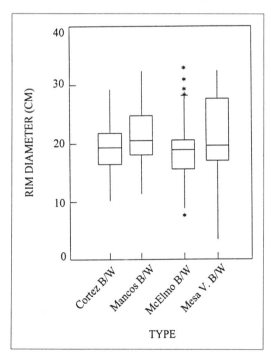

Fig. 7.4. Box plots of Mesa Verde White Ware serving bowl rim diameters (cm) by ceramic type. Types are arrayed earliest to latest from left to right.

TABLE 7.2.
Summary Statistics for Mesa Verde White Ware Bowl Rim Diameters

Functional Class/Type	N	Mean	Standard Deviation	Coefficient of Variation
Small bowls				
Mancos Black-on-white	29	19.40	2.36	0.12
McElmo Black-on-white	40	18.90	1.92	0.10
Mesa Verde Black-on-white	91	18.21	1.85	0.10
Large bowls				
Mancos Black-on-white	9	28.42	2.19	0.08
McElmo Black-on-white	10	28.11	1.94	0.07
Mesa Verde Black-on-white	84	28.09	1.69	0.06

coming more narrowly defined through time. Given arguments about standardization and production intensity (e.g., Longacre et al. 1988; see also Longacre this volume), it is reasonable that the decreasing variation represents an increase in at least one dimension of specialization. It is intriguing that these changes toward greater standardization occur with the same ceramic type (Mesa Verde Black-on-white) for which we have the most evidence of firing in kilns than anywhere else in the Southwest (Mills and Crown 1995b; Wilson and Blinman 1995). These kilns were more thermally efficient than open firing and were probably used to fire larger quantities of ceramics at one time. Based on the quantities of ceramics fired at one time, firing groups may have involved groups of potters above the level of the household (Bernardini 1997), likely women. This pattern fits with other examples of gendered specialization within aggregated communities in the prehistoric Southwest. Growing evidence points to a trend in which groups of craft producers, whether entire households or above the level of the household, became specialists in the production of different goods, raising the efficiency of craft production and opportunities for social interaction at the community level (Mills 1997).

Tusayan White Ware bowls show only slight increases in median sizes through time (Fig. 7.5). None of the distributions are significantly different from each other in the pairwise tests, even though the same bimodality is also present. Both of these wares

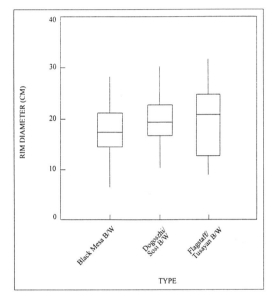

Fig. 7.5. Box plots of Tusayan White Ware serving bowl rim diameters (cm) by ceramic type. Types are arrayed earliest to latest from left to right.

contrast with the Tsegi Orange Ware bowls (Fig. 7.6). This ware shows a strong directional pattern of increasing bowl sizes through time, beginning with the two black-on-red types and continuing through the early and late Tsegi polychromes. Early polychrome types are Cameron, Citadel, and Tusayan; late polychrome types are Kayenta and Kiet Siel. Most of the early polychromes in this sample are Tusayan Polychrome. The distributions of the two black-on-red types are not different from each other, nor are there differences between the two poly-

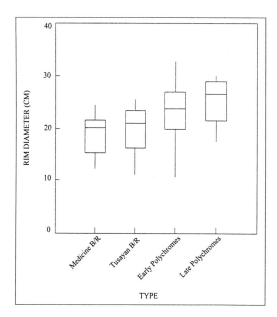

Fig. 7.6. Box plots of Tsegi Orange Ware serving bowl rim diameters (cm) by ceramic type. Types are arrayed earliest to latest from left to right.

chromes. However, all pairs of black-on-reds versus polychromes have significantly different distributions (all these and the above tests use an alpha level of 0.05). This change can be dated to about the same time as the change in Tusayan Gray Ware noted above, at ca. A.D. 1200 in the middle of the Pueblo III period.

In sum, cooking pots were made in increasingly large sizes through the period of A.D. 1000 to 1300 in the Mesa Verde area. Although the median sizes of Mesa Verde serving bowls did not change, the two size modes became more standardized. In both size and standardization, the most dramatic changes in the Mesa Verde area took place at the beginning of the Pueblo III period, or ca. A.D. 1100. By contrast, cooking jar sizes in the Tusayan area show less pronounced change through time and the only significant difference occurred relatively late in the sequence. Taken as a group, Tusayan area decorated bowl sizes increase in size through time and these increases correspond in timing with changes in cooking pot size, ca. A.D. 1200.

INTERPRETING CHANGING CERAMIC VESSEL SIZE: CUISINE, HOUSEHOLD SIZE, OR FEASTING?

Here I consider each of the three potential factors of changing vessel sizes in the northern Southwest. Fortunately, the large amount of work that has been conducted in both the Tusayan and Mesa Verde areas provides the contextual information necessary for interpretation.

CHANGES IN CUISINE

Increasing vessel sizes in the northern Southwest, especially those noted for the Mesa Verde area, could be interpreted as clear-cut evidence for a change in reliance on specific types of foods that might require boiling and serving in suitable containers. However appealing such an explanation might be, there are now many challenges to the underlying assumption of monotonic increases in agricultural reliance in the area. In fact, there is more evidence pointing towards spatial and temporal variation in agricultural productivity and use of agricultural products, especially corn (e.g., Chisholm and Matson 1994; Hard et al. 1996; Minnis 1989; Winter 1993).

For example, carbon isotopic evidence from Cedar Mesa shows the pattern of corn consumption increased dramatically between Archaic and Basketmaker II populations, but that the increase from the Basketmaker to Pueblo samples was relatively small (Chisholm and Matson 1994; Hard et al. 1996). Even more direct indications of dietary change are coprolite analyses from the Mesa Verde area. These analyses show that corn was the most ubiquitous food in the northern Southwest for both the Basketmaker and Pueblo periods, with an approximate increase in corn consumption of from 60 to 80 percent between the Basketmaker to Pueblo II periods and an apparent leveling off by the end of the Pueblo III period (Minnis 1989; Stiger 1979). In addition, Cummings's (1985) analyses of Mesa Verde area subsistence suggests that there was a decline in the ubiquity of corn pollen during the later periods of occupation of several Pueblo III period cliff dwellings, possibly from overuse of farm areas. At this time there was an increased reliance on wild plants that provided at least a seasonally available nutritional supplement to compensate for the lower productivity of the main cultigen, corn.

These analyses demonstrate several important aspects of Pueblo diet in the northern Southwest. First, that punctuated, rather than gradualistic, models apply to the adoption of maize (Lipe 1994:340). Once corn was adopted, it quickly became an essential part of the diet of the northern Southwest, but its role did not intensify on a regular basis. Second, although corn was always ranked first, other plants had different rankings (Minnis 1989), suggesting both spatial and temporal variation in the foods consumed, if not how they were prepared. And third, the final period of occupation at some sites may have seen some *decreases* in agricultural productivity and maize consumption caused by long-term use of the landscape.

Thus, the subsistence data do not show increases in the consumption of agricultural products between ca. A.D. 1000 and 1300. This is particularly evident in the Mesa Verde area, despite the fact that this is where the most dramatic increases in cooking vessel sizes are found. In addition, Snow's (1990) interesting ideas about the preprocessing of corn involve other artifacts, such as cooking stones, that are not present in the northern Southwest area at this time. The use of cooking stones and new forms of preprocessing of corn apparently occurs after the major reorganization of Puebloan groups at the end of the thirteenth century.

CHANGES IN HOUSEHOLD SIZE
Changes in the intensity of ground stone use are indicated during this period (Hard et al. 1996), suggesting changes in the structure of labor involved with food preparation. If these changes are not because of changes in actual consumption of agricultural products, then they must be indicative of changes in the number of people for whom food was being prepared. There are two lines of evidence that

support the interpretation that the size of the consumer group increased through time. One of these is in the clustering and number of ground stone features. The other is in architectural data, especially the size of roomblocks and the ratios of ritual to domestic architecture (Adams 1994).

Ortman (1998) has recently summarized data on the organization of grinding features in the northern Southwest. He notes that during the Pueblo III period in both the Tusayan and Mesa areas, grinding facilities were clustered and likely shared by a number of nuclear families organized into extended households. If the women who ground together also cooked together at least part of the time, then it is reasonable to conclude that large vessels would have been frequently used for cooking during the Pueblo III period. Unfortunately, Ortman's data do not include the late Pueblo II period (in part because fixed grinding features are largely absent), so that the time range he considers is not completely coeval with the date range of the whole vessels considered in this paper. Nonetheless, we can propose as a working hypothesis that the increasing size of cooking vessels in both the Tusayan and the Mesa Verde areas from A.D. 1000 to 1300 is at least in part related to the reorganization of labor into larger, extended households from the Pueblo II to Pueblo III periods.

CHANGES IN SUPRAHOUSEHOLD FEASTING
The data from grinding features does not account for the contrasts between the Mesa Verde and Tusayan areas in the scale or timing of changes through time. Differences between the two areas are, however, present in the relative role of integrative social units between the household and the community. As Adler (1994) discusses for southwest Colorado, by the end of the 1100s, the pattern of one to a few households living in a single roomblock with a single kiva was replaced by one of multiroomblock clusters. These multiroomblock clusters probably housed from seven to fifteen households. Along with these changes in site size and aggregation were

changes in ritual architecture. Adler's data show that during the earlier time period (A.D. 1000 to 1150), the number of kivas per roomblock ranged from one to nine, with the mode at one per roomblock. The later period (A.D. 1150 to 1300) had a range of one to twelve kivas with several modes, the largest mode being three kivas per roomblock. The changes in the number of kivas per roomblock, the number of roomblocks per site, and average roomblock sizes all suggest increased probabilities for sharing at the suprahousehold level—and a commensurate need for larger cooking vessels from the Pueblo II to Pueblo III periods.

The scale and timing of aggregation and use of ritual structures in the Mesa Verde and Tusayan areas was likely very different. Although we do not have data that are completely comparable between the two areas, Lipe (1989:63) remarks that the pattern in the Tusayan-Kayenta area was more variable than in the Mesa Verde area. Indeed, Dean (1969:38–39) notes that for the late Pueblo III Tsegi phase sites, kivas are not associated with particular roomblocks or courtyard groups, but Pueblo III sites near Navajo Mountain do show evidence for more localized ritual structures. Ortman (1998) has noted a probable decrease in the size of extended households at the end of the Pueblo III period in the Tusayan-Kayenta area along with an increase in the scale of ritual facilities. Yet, the cooking vessels from the Tusayan area show their most marked increase at this time. This suggests that in the Tusayan area, participation in social contexts of consumption above the level of the extended family compensated for decreases in consumption activities in smaller-sized extended families after ca. A.D. 1200.

The distribution of late Pueblo III bowl sizes in the Tusayan area sheds additional light on differences in the use of ceramics in different contexts of consumption. As noted earlier, two slipped and painted wares were made and used in the Tusayan area, Tusayan White Ware and Tsegi Orange Ware. Although both of these wares were made after A.D. 1000 and continued to be made until

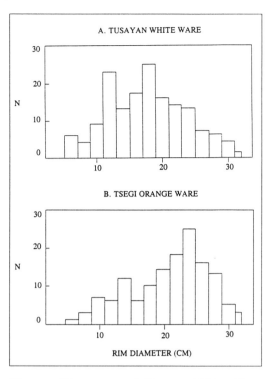

Fig. 7.7. Histograms of Tusayan White Ware (top) and Tsegi Orange Ware (bottom) bowl rim diameters.

A.D. 1300, there is an important difference in the sizes of white ware and red ware polychrome bowls that becomes more pronounced through time. Although both are painted, the Tsegi Orange Ware polychromes do not show as much evidence of a smaller, individual size bowl mode. In addition, the late polychromes are the largest bowls ever made and used in the area (Fig. 7.7).

The social contexts in which these polychrome bowls were used was probably different from the contexts of use of contemporaneous Tusayan White Ware bowls. In fact, slip color appears to have been an intentional choice in marking this distinction. Their larger size does suggest uses that exceed the level of the immediate family. Suprahousehold feasting, whether at the corporate group or community levels is indicated by these bowls. It is significant that these polychromes have exterior as well as interior designs and are among the earliest use of exterior designs on ceramics in the area. The "visual performance" value of these exterior designs (see Schiffer, this volume) would have been much different when sitting on the ground during consumption activities versus being carried outside of the household for consumption elsewhere in situations of sharing at the suprahousehold or communitywide levels. It is particularly interesting given this distinction that when exterior designs are present on Mesa Verde White Ware bowls, they are almost always on bowls of the larger size mode and occur most commonly on the latest type in the sequence—Mesa Verde Black-on-white.

CONCLUSION

This paper has investigated the potential underlying social dynamics that correspond with trends in increasing vessel sizes and has considered each of these in the interpretation of ceramics from the northern Southwest. Significant increases in the size of cooking vessels are present in the two areas, but the differences are earlier and more pronounced in the Mesa Verde area than in the Tusayan area. Changes in bowl sizes are more evident in the Tusayan area, but only when wares are considered separately. Red ware bowls, especially polychromes, are the largest serving bowls and are dramatically larger than contemporaneous white ware bowls.

A change in cuisine associated with increasing consumption of corn per person was discounted as an explanation for increasing cooking vessel sizes based on previous analyses of Pueblo diet in the northern Southwest. Instead, I have explored the social contexts of use of this vessel class. Based on independent data from ground stone and architecture, it is likely that the changes in the two areas reflect real changes in the size of the consumer group—in the case of the northern Southwest, toward larger sized, extended households with increasing participation in suprahousehold ritual feasting.

The earlier, more pronounced increases in cooking vessel sizes in the Mesa Verde area are likely because of the relatively greater scale and importance of larger, extended families as the unit of production and consumption. Although I have not compared absolute

sizes of cooking vessels to each other up to this point, it is worth noting that the absolute scale of large-sized cooking vessels in the Mesa Verde is larger than in the Tusayan area. If the relative size of the large mode of the cooking vessels in each area is indicative of the relative size of the extended family, then these households were larger in the Mesa Verde area than in the Tusayan area.

In both of the Puebloan areas considered here, the trend toward larger vessel sizes occurs along with a trend toward increasing site size and degree of aggregation. Household size, aggregation, and agricultural production are related to each other in complex, nonlinear ways. Household size is closely tied to relations of production in that increases in the number of individuals within the household is one strategy intentionally manipulated to intensify production. Aggregation implies a greater degree of agricultural intensification, but not necessarily greater consumption of agricultural products. Although larger households might be expected with aggregation and agricultural intensification (Blinman 1988a:202–203; Lightfoot 1994: 153), recent models suggest that the relationship may be more curvilinear, depending on the degree of interhousehold sharing (Adler 1994).

With cooking vessels alone, it is very difficult to separate out the effects of suprahousehold feasting from extended family consumption because of the relationship between sharing and household size under different aggregation conditions. In fact, the size of the largest extended family may actually overlap in size with the smallest unit of suprahousehold consumption. Certain crosscutting institutions may have involved feasting at a comparable demographic scale to commensalism at the social scale of the household. Nonetheless, ceramics are important material evidence for variation and change in the sizes of commensal groups in the Southwest, whether they are at the household or suprahousehold levels. Based on the analysis of whole vessels at the macroregional scale, the contributions of both household size and feasting behavior are present, but are difficult to distinguish. They are most clearly distinguishable for the serving bowls in the Tusayan-Kayenta area because of the use of different slip colors. This implies that different slip colors were used to signify different contexts of food consumption.

Independent data and sherd-based analyses of ceramics from good archaeological contexts will be necessary to further identify the relative contributions of household size and suprahousehold feasting to the patterns through time. However, the differences between the two Pueblo areas considered in this paper have suggested that changes in food consumption patterns were variable across the northern Southwest in their timing and scale—differences that indicate fundamental contrasts in social contexts.

8

Levels of Complexity: Ceramic Variability at Vijayanagara

CARLA M. SINOPOLI

INTRODUCTION

For more than a decade, the particular focus of my attempts to study pottery and people has been the archaeological site of Vijayanagara, a fourteenth- through sixteenth-century imperial capital located in south-central India (Fig. 8.1). As the capital of a vast empire, Vijayanagara is known to scholars through its numerous indigenous and foreign historical texts and its monumental architecture, including massive temples, palaces, and fortifications. The preserved architectural evidence, like the texts, presents a restricted view of Vijayanagara, filtered through elite activities, perceptions, and investments. Much of my research at Vijayanagara has focused on a more "democratic" class of remains, the earthenware ceramics used for diverse tasks by all of the inhabitants of this massive city.

Like other imperial capitals of the ancient and modern world, Vijayanagara was both large in scale and highly diverse—in social and cultural composition and in the range of activities that occurred in or around the city. Centers of empire are, in a significant sense, microcosms of the large multi-ethnic polities that they rule, and Vijayanagara was no exception. It is these issues of urban scale and social, economic, ideological, and political complexity and their impacts on domestic material culture production and consumption and on archaeological interpretation on which I focus in this paper.

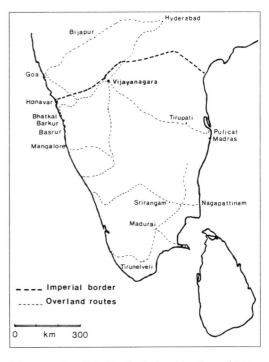

Fig. 8.1. South India depicting location of Vijayanagara and major trade routes (after Subrahmanyam 1990:81).

Discussions of ceramic production are of course, common in the archaeological literature of complex societies and urbanism, where studies of craft specialization and its relation to political complexity have been abundant in recent years (e.g., Blackman et al. 1993; Blackman and Vidale 1992; Costin 1991; Costin et al. 1989; Feinman 1985;

Stein and Blackman 1993; Vidale 1989; Wailes 1996). Studies of patterns of consumption and use (and their social interpretations) in urban contexts are somewhat scarcer, in marked contrast to their abundance in village contexts (e.g., in the prehistoric Southwestern United States, among many others areas). Where such studies have been carried out, they have tended to focus on particular elite wares (e.g., Hodge and Minc 1991; Hodge et al. 1993) and patterns of trade and exchange. As I discuss below, in Vijayanagara there were no wares that qualify as "elite wares"; instead ceramics, though products of specialist production, appear to have had relatively low social value but widespread use. In my work, I have thus focused on the full range of earthenware ceramics and their distribution in diverse areas within the Vijayanagara urban core and its metropolitan hinterland. This analysis has provided insights into Vijayanagara craft production and other aspects of the domestic economy, settlement organization, and spatial diversity. In the discussion that follows, I highlight the challenges faced in the analysis and interpretation of ceramics in a complex urban context, examine what has been learned from these analyses, and consider what questions remain to be answered.

Prior to addressing the specifics of Vijayanagara ceramics, I provide a bit of background concerning Vijayanagara as a city and as a source of archaeological materials, in order to begin to address potential sources of complexity that impact analyses and interpretations. This background is derived from a combination of historic sources and archaeological evidence, and is testimony to the wealth of evidence available for the study of Vijayanagara. Ethnographic work has also been carried out at contemporary pottery-producing workshops in the region. The modern context provides a frame of reference from which to consider Vijayanagara technologies and issues of standardization and inter-workshop variability (Sinopoli 1988; Sinopoli and Blurton 1986). These diverse sources of evidence each provide unique insights into the organization, history, and functions of the imperial capital, and though they sometimes lead in discordant directions, together they provide considerable information and perspectives from which to consider the significance and uses of material culture in Vijayanagara society. I then turn to a more focused consideration of Vijayanagara's archaeological ceramics, presenting a brief overview of the ceramic data base and analytical methods applied, before turning to a more detailed discussion of the results of the analyses. I conclude by considering what has been learned from the analysis and what still remains to be learned.

THE VIJAYANAGARA CAPITAL: HISTORIC OUTLINE

The Vijayanagara empire emerged as a major political force in south India in the mid-fourteenth century. Its capital (Sanskrit for "city of victory") was founded on the southern banks of the Tungabhadra River in an area that had previously been sparsely occupied. Pre-imperial settlement in the region focused on an area of temples on the south bank of the river, and the town of Anegundi to the north. Together, these settlements probably accounted for no more than a few thousand inhabitants. Within four to five decades after the founding of the empire and its capital, Vijayanagara had grown dramatically, to an estimated population of 100,000. By the early 1400s, the walls of the royal center and of the 12-sq-km urban core had been constructed (Fig.8.2; Michell 1992: 1–2), and the area within those walls was densely occupied.

Vijayanagara underwent a second major burst of expansion in the first half of the sixteenth century, a time of empirewide political and economic expansion. Massive investments in settlements, temple complexes, fortresses, and agricultural facilities occurred at the capital, where they are documented archaeologically and in written sources (Morrison and Lycett 1994; Sinopoli and Morrison 1995). The fortified suburban area of the capital extended over some 350 sq km; its population was well over 200,000 inhabitants.

This period of expansion was short-lived.

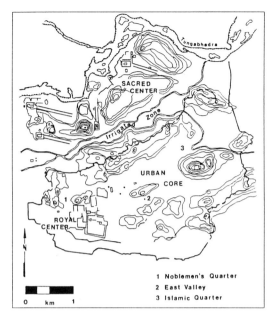

Fig. 8.2. The Vijayanagara Urban Core depicting locations of ceramic collections (from Sinopoli 1986).

In A.D. 1565, following a major military defeat and with political crises throughout the empire, the Vijayanagara capital was abandoned. Their power in decline, Vijayanagara's rulers shifted their capital south to Penukonda, and then to Chandragiri. By the late seventeenth century, the once powerful empire was no more.

From an archaeological perspective, the rapid abandonment and limited reoccupation of Vijayanagara is a great boon. Despite some continued settlement in the region and nineteenth-century modifications of the landscape by British colonial engineers (e.g., construction and modification of irrigation canals, public works, clearing and conservation of archaeological monuments), population densities in the region have only begun to approach Vijayanagara levels during the last two decades of the twentieth century. Modern areas of settlement have been focused in low-lying areas of Vijayanagara's suburban region and not in the core of the ancient capital. Thus, even today, the scale and grandeur of the imperial city are readily visible: in the site's hundreds of standing monumental structures; in the tens of thousands of

less well preserved features that provide evidence for non-elite habitations, food processing facilities, stables, and the like (e.g., foundation walls, rock-cut features, displaced sacred images, and earthen mounds); and in the millions of artifacts distributed across the site's surface. The vast majority of the latter are earthenware sherds.

SOURCES OF COMPLEXITY

In order for ceramic analysis to be able to inform on Vijayanagara economy, settlement structure, or social organization and processes, the potential impact of diverse factors relating to its scale, history, and sociopolitical and archaeological complexity must be taken into account. In this section, I consider some of these sources of complexity. This consideration benefits from the rich historical sources available for Vijayanagara period south India. While such sources are not available in many archaeological contexts, even urban ones, consideration of Vijayanagara's complexity may highlight issues relevant to studies of archaeological variability in complex societies more broadly.

VIJAYANAGARA'S URBAN COMPLEXITY

From its founding as the capital of an emergent empire, Vijayanagara was a magnet, attracting individuals and communities of migrants from throughout peninsular India. This resulted in a polyglot culturally diverse population comprised of speakers of Telugu, Kannada, and Tamil (and undoubtedly other Indian languages as well). Vijayanagara's inhabitants worshipped orthodox Hindu deities, local gods and goddesses, Jaina saints, and Allah. They labored as artisans, merchants, administrators, agriculturalists, religious practitioners, entertainers, and servants. Vijayanagara was also home to military forces numbering in the tens of thousands and, at least during portions of the year, elites and other representatives of incorporated territories and polities were required to be present to attend royal ceremonies and attest to their fealty.

As a capital, Vijayanagara was a political center. Home to the king and court, Vijayanagara was a place of coronations and royal ceremonies. And, at least during those portions of the year when the ruler was in residence, Vijayanagara was an administrative center. Even with the relatively limited bureaucracy that seems to have characterized the empire (Stein 1989), numerous accountants, scribes, and imperial officers worked and resided in buildings in the palace area.

Vijayanagara was a major economic and trading center. It lay at the end point of several major south Indian trade routes (Fig. 8.1; Subrahmanyam 1990:81). Goods flowed into the capital from throughout the empire and from overseas trade with East and Southeast Asia, the Arabian peninsula, and, by the sixteenth century, from direct trade with Europe. Demands for luxury goods were high to serve the court and imperial elite as well as emergent communities of wealthy merchants and warriors. Luxury products included elaborate textiles, precious stones and gold and silver ornaments, and to a lesser extent, East Asian ceramics (though these are comparatively rare in the Vijayanagara ceramic inventory). Other products in high demand were military goods, including weapons, horses, and elephants, as well as mercenaries (drawn from tribal populations, Islamic communities, and, later, Portuguese renegades). Demands for subsistence products and domestic goods, including foodstuffs, household goods, and implements, must also have been high. Such demands also, no doubt, encouraged the movement of numerous artisans and agriculturalists to the thriving capital. Some of these population movements may have entailed coercion; however, inscriptional sources are ambiguous, referring to communities "being settled" in particular locales (e.g., Karashima 1992; Ramaswamy 1985) but not to whether they were coerced or induced to settle in those regions. The latter seems to be the most common strategy.

Vijayanagara was a sacred center. Major temple complexes sponsored by rulers and other imperial elites became centers of pilgrimage, attracting tens of thousands of worshippers for calendrical observations and receiving a steady flow of devotees year-round. Temple complexes included dormitory facilities, markets, artisan workshops, and kitchens that prepared large quantities of food to serve pilgrims and temple employees.

If Vijayanagara's social composition and diverse functions were complex, so too was its physical form. The capital was located in an area of dramatically dissected landscape. The city was divided into large and small spatial zones by natural features (i.e., granitic outcrops) and by cultural constructions (a large irrigation canal, roads, and massive stone enclosure walls). Vijayanagara was perceived by its inhabitants as consisting of several spatially and functionally distinct communities and settlements.

The conceptual (though not physical) center of the capital was an extensive "palace" area that extended over about 2 sq km. This was a large walled area subdivided into smaller fortified compounds containing elite residences, administrative structures, markets, and temples. Contemporary archaeologists have referred to this area as Vijayanagara's "Royal Center" (Fritz 1986; Fritz et al. 1984:12).

Enclosing the royal center was a larger walled area that encompassed approximately 12 sq km. This area, referred to by archaeologists as the "Urban Core" (Fritz et al.1984: 10–12), contained residential neighborhoods and associated facilities. In traditional Indian cities, residential areas are organized by caste, occupational, and religious (and probably linguistic and geographic) groupings. That such a pattern existed at Vijayanagara is apparent in the Muslim residential zone located in the northeastern area of the urban core and in the cluster of small Jaina shrines in a valley near the center of the urban core, and is also evidenced in contemporary literary works and inscriptions (see below). The urban core also contained numerous sacred constructions, markets, roads, watch towers, and, most likely, artisan workshops.

North and west of the urban core, a large irrigation canal flowed southwest from the Tungabhadra River. Low-lying areas along the canal were planted in "wet crops," such as sugar cane, fruit trees, and rice. Further north, four large temple centers were located along the southern banks of the river. Each consisted of a large rectangular compound enclosing major and minor shrines and pavilions, and an associated bazaar street and areas of settlement. Textual sources, including inscriptions and manuscripts, refer to these temple centers as discrete communities (e.g., "Vitthalapura" or "Krishnapura" referring to the settlement *(pura)* of the deity Vitthala or Krishna, respectively). Archaeologists have referred to this area of large temple complexes and countless smaller shrines and sacred carvings as Vijayanagara's "Sacred Center" (Fritz et al.1984:9).

Beyond the core area of the capital lay a more extensive area that has been termed the Vijayanagara Metropolitan Region (Sinopoli and Morrison 1992). This area was protected both by the region's rugged topographic features and by strategically placed fortifications that spanned potential access routes into the capital. Virtually all of the 350-plus sq km area of the metropolitan region was a focus of intensive human exploitation and modification. Massive investments of resources and human labor were put into the construction of irrigation facilities (including reservoirs, terrace systems, check dams, and canals) and in the production of crops. The population of the metropolitan region resided in nucleated settlements that ranged in size from 2 to 80 ha. Hilltop forts and outposts and imposing walls defended the region and allowed the monitoring of movement into and out of the capital; large and small temples were constructed along major roads, in settlements, fields, and on hilltops.

Along with agriculturalists, artisans were also among the inhabitants of the metropolitan region. Archaeological data have provided evidence for iron and stone working in the area. Archaeological evidence for ceramic production is conspicuous in its absence, though, as discussed below, it almost certainly took place. A Vijayanagara period inscription (dated October 30, A.D. 1518) located less than a kilometer south of the urban core refers to an area called *Kummaragunte*, or "place of the potters' *(Kumbhar)* earth

(gunte)." The locale is still known by that name today (Patil and Patil 1995:124).

VIJAYANAGARA CERAMIC COMPLEXITY
Demand and Consumption.
The diverse communities and functions of the Vijayanagara capital each created very different demands for material goods in general, and ceramics in particular. Both elite and non-elite households used ceramic vessels in a variety of domestic activities, household rituals, and other functions (for example, as well linings, architectural fittings, and roof tiles). Institutions, such as temples, military barracks, and administrative offices needed vessels for food storage and preparation and for storing and serving water. Temples also required ritual vessels, though these are problematic to identify since ritual vessels are often common domestic forms whose status is a function of their use in specific contexts. In addition, in many cases ritual vessels and figurines are unfired and are deposited in water to dissolve at the completion of the ritual (Sinopoli 1996a). Vessels were also gifted by donors for use at roadside wells; in return, donors gained religious merit and social recognition (Patil and Patil 1995, inscription 423, p. 123). Ceramic fixtures and implements were used in industrial facilities, serving as tuyeres in iron furnaces and crucibles for copper smelting, and, to a limited extent, as spindle whorls (though a later historic source suggests that unfired clay lumps attached to sticks were typically used for this task; Buchanan 1807). Thus, earthenware vessels were ubiquitous across all areas and communities of Vijayanagara.

Despite their widespread use by all segments of Vijayanagara society, there were no locally produced ceramic wares or forms that can be considered elite wares or status goods. The reasons that ceramics did not serve as status markers or symbols of wealth (as they do in so many complex societies that archaeologists study), appear to lie in Hindu cultural and religious values. In particular, negative connotations of ceramics are linked to concerns with ritual purity and, more importantly, to the avoidance of impurity.

As a category of vessels, ceramics are believed to be particularly vulnerable to the absorption of impurities, and in this respect are ranked below vessels of precious metals and those of copper or bronze. This ranking of materials can be traced through sacred texts for two millennia. According to the *Dharmasastra* (a set of codes or laws for right behavior and religious practices believed to have been compiled in the first two centuries A.D., Thapar 1966:121), earthenware vessels used to hold or serve cooked foods absorb the nature or quality of those foods and of their method of preparation, as well as the nature or quality (what Marriott has termed "substance"; Marriott and Inden 1977) of the persons who come in contact with them (Davis 1983:76). Thus, to avoid pollution members of ritually high-status groups or castes should not accept vessels containing cooked foods or water from individuals belonging to lower status castes. Once polluted, vessels can in most cases be purified, but here again this is most difficult for ceramics. The Dharmasastra informs us that polluted gold and silver vessels can be purified by simply washing them in water, while brass and copper vessels must be scoured with ashes, water, and clay, and earthenware vessels (or highly polluted metal) must be immersed in fire, and in some cases, cannot be cleansed at all and must be discarded (Kane 1973, vol. 4, 315–326). As a consequence of these prohibitions, Hindus do not typically dine off of ceramic vessels, but instead use either metal vessels or banana leaves, with the latter discarded after a single use. Dining itself is, in principle, not a public practice, but should be conducted in privacy to avoid exposure to potential ritual dangers.

The negative symbolic associations of ceramic vessels and the absence of ceramic serving forms that can function in public feasting, gifting, or display contribute to the challenges of interpreting the archaeological ceramics of Vijayanagara. Yet the close relation between ceramic forms and food practices potentially provides an avenue for examining at least one dimension of social meaning (and spatial structure)—caste and community

identity. In his ethnographic study of ceramic production and consumption in a village in Malwa, central India, Miller (1985) observed that classes of ceramic (and metal) cooking vessels were closely linked to the foods that were prepared in them and to the social groups that consumed those foods. Thus, forms used to cook meat were not used by members of vegetarian castes or communities, while forms associated with heating milk (the most perfect and pure food) were perceived as having a higher status through their links to purer activities and consumers. The different cooking forms studied by Miller are distinguishable by attributes of vessel morphology, in particular, the presence or absence of shoulder carinations and diameter and diameter-height ratios (i.e., the degree of openness and vessel volume). Rim form, a characteristic commonly studied by archaeologists, does not appear to play any role in this kind of differentiation.

Further, vessel meanings and statuses were far from stable. Miller (1985) has documented a process of stylistic emulation, whereby lower-status communities adopted higher-status forms, ultimately devaluing the vessels' symbolic associations. In response, new forms were adopted by higher-status social groups in a desire to maintain distinctive material markers. Innovations in ceramic forms thus involved an interplay between specialist potters experimenting with new forms, and consumer desires for distinctive formal variants that could be linked with particular functions. Vessel forms in nonceramic materials (brass, aluminum, etc.) provide one source of formal models that the Malwa potters imitate. The imitation of metal forms in ceramics is also evident today in the products of potters working near Vijayanagara. This has affected formal attributes (in particular the appearance of double carinations, at shoulders and bases) and surface treatment (the application of a graphite or talc-based coating on the exterior surfaces of fired vessels creating a "metallic" sheen).

Since, in Malwa, consuming groups (e.g., castes) were also coresident groups, then clusters of ceramic forms could potentially provide future archaeologists studying this village with a means to identify discrete social groups within the site (admittedly, only if we can develop extremely fine control of chronologies and demonstrate localized refuse discard practices). However, the possibility of being able to apply this kind of interpretive framework to identifying units of ceramic consumption in an urban context such as Vijayanagara is complicated by the nature and organization of ceramic production and distribution, and by the scales of social interaction and degrees or scale of cultural knowledge concerning ceramic forms and their associated meanings. I address the first concerns below, and focus on issues of scale and knowledge here.

While it is possible that similar valuations may have existed at the level of local communities within the capital, given the diverse composition of the city's population it is highly unlikely that such values were shared across the city or even across large areas of the city. That is, while neighborhoods of regularly interacting individuals and families may have shared symbolic frameworks for evaluating vessels (and the foodstuffs prepared in them), it is highly unlikely that such values can be extrapolated across the site as a whole. Further, in many cases, it is quite difficult to define the relevant communities archaeologically except at a very gross level, and using ceramics alone to do so runs the risk of logical circularity.

Production and Distribution.

The organization of ceramic production at Vijayanagara provides a further source of complexity affecting ranges of variability or standardization, in the materials themselves and our ability to extrapolate social meaning from them. Like ceramics produced by contemporary village and urban potters throughout India (e.g., Saraswati and Behura 1966), Vijayanagara ceramics were made using a combination of wheel-throwing and hand-building techniques. Necked vessels comprise more than 85 percent of Vijayanagara's ceramic inventory and range from relatively open forms to large narrow-necked globular

Fig. 8.3. Contemporary ceramic production. The potter is using paddle and anvil to shape a large water pot. Note unshaped cylindrical vessels nearby and in rear of photograph (photo by Vijayanagara Metropolitan Survey).

forms (supporting literary and ethnographic sources on the nonuse of ceramics for serving and consumption). Their upper portions (rims, necks, and shoulders) were fully formed on the wheel, while lower portions were shaped using the paddle and anvil technique. Modern potters achieve this through throwing vessels whose rims are fully formed and whose lower portions are left as thick-walled (3–4 cm) open cylinders. After drying overnight, the cylinders are shaped using paddles and anvils to form the desired thin-walled, round-based vessel form (Fig. 8.3). Shoulder and base carinations are also shaped at this time. Production traces on Vijayanagara ceramics are identical to modern ones. A segment of a ninth-century text, the *Bhojaprabhanda,* written from a pot's perspective, further attests to this technique's long history:

> Potter digs me with his axe and makes me ride over an ass; then the wretched potter beats me mercilessly with his feet and rotates me on the wheel with a stick; he cuts me with a string; he beats me and bakes— all these I bear with patience; further the village lasses tap me with their fingers innumerably, which I can no longer bear.
> (quoted in Krishnamurthy 1979:75)

This production technology is highly labor intensive. Among the potters I've observed, the throwing stage of production (with vessels thrown from the hump) averages three minutes per vessel, while the paddle and anvil work takes 30–50 minutes per vessel, depending on vessel size. Models of specialization in the production of utilitarian goods have focused on productive efficiency and minimization of per vessel energy investment in contexts where demands are high and labor is scarce. The South Asia data provide evidence for very different principles structuring the practices and organization of production. Given historically high population densities in much of South Asia, surplus labor may be more of a problem than labor scarcities; efficiency, at least in the investment of human energies, is not necessarily sought after or desirable.

The complex production technology, found throughout South Asia, while not optimizing time or energy investment, may respond to other needs or desires. First, the paddle and anvil technique allows potters to shape desired (and more thermally effective) thin-walled and round-based vessels. Second, and perhaps more importantly, this technology appears to allow potters to work with lower quality and less thoroughly processed raw materials than they could with a fully wheel-thrown production technology. For example, it is not uncommon to find large stones or other inclusions (e.g., freshwater shells), more than a centimeter across, in vessel walls of both ethnographic and archaeological materials (which for most vessel forms average less than .5 cm in thickness). Such inclusions would almost certainly have torn the vessel (or the potter's hands) had it been fully wheel-formed.

Contemporary potters gather raw materials from reservoir or canal beds or from other easily accessible sources, and are more concerned with factors of proximity and cost rather than with material "quality." Vijayanagara potters, too, used clays "derived from sediments or eroded rocks of granitic composition available in and around the site" (Rautman 1991:152).

Also suggesting concern with minimizing resource investment, is evidence that firing

temperatures of Vijayanagara ceramics were quite low. Inclusions of minerals such as plagioclase and orthoclase indicating temperatures of less than 900 degrees C, and other evidence suggests temperatures were probably less than 700 degrees C (Rautman 1991: 152). Modern potters in the region fire in semipermanent facilities, defined by a horseshoe-shaped wall against which pots are piled and intermixed with fuel (Fig. 8.4). In selecting fuels, potters are again primarily concerned with minimizing costs. Agricultural byproducts (chaff, husks), dung, and brush are the main fuels used today. The resultant vessels are often very brittle, and major structural flaws are common. Use-lives are thus brief, but in return, costs of replacing vessels are low.

Thus, while "efficiency" or "optimization" of a sort may have been a concern of Vijayanagara potters, it was not oriented toward decreasing labor input per vessel nor toward improving vessel quality (through selecting better raw materials or firing at higher temperatures). Instead, potters appear to have been concerned with minimizing their investment in the raw materials of pottery production (in particular, clays and fuel), presumably linked to consumer demands for earthenware vessels (which both in modern India and the Vijayanagara period were competing with other kinds of vessel materials, i.e., precious metals, brass, and copper and, today, aluminum and plastic). The kinds of decisions we see affecting potters and consumers in this case may also be important to keep in mind when studying archaeological ceramics more generally, particularly from perspectives that focus on optimization, either of productive organization or of vessel effectiveness.

South Asia's Hindu potters belong to the *Kumbhar* (potter) caste, which is subdivided into numerous localized endogamous subcastes *(jati)* and exogamous lineages *(gotras)*. Ceramic production is organized at the level of the household workshop, with the unit of production the nuclear or extended family (see Feinman, this volume, for discussion of comparable specialist production units in

Fig. 8.4. Contemporary ceramic firing facility consisting of semicircular stone and earth wall; pots in stacked against rear wall serve to keep the stoke hole clear of debris; sherds in front are used to create smoke holes and to separate vessels stacked in oven; fuel is piled in rear (photo by Vijayanagara Metropolitan Survey).

Mesoamerica). Production tasks are organized according to sex, age, and skill. Only men can work on the potter's wheel; a mere touch by a woman is, in most cases, considered to pollute the wheel. Men also do the paddle and anvil work. Women are involved in a range of production tasks: hand-building, applying surface treatments (slips, graphite coatings, or decoration), and firing. Ethnographically documented production rates average approximately 100 vessels per workshop per week (Saraswati 1979:30; Saraswati and Behura 1966).

This scale of production seems to have held historically even in urban contexts where demand was high. In contrast to many other areas of the Old World, large-scale industrial manufacture of ceramic vessels did not develop in premodern Hindu India. Rather than the scale of production increasing in response to rises in demand, instead, the numbers of pottery-producing workshops increased. Such increases occurred through adult sons establishing independent households, through voluntary migration of potters to areas where demand was high, and in response to inducements by institutions or elites. These inducements included short- and long-term tax abatements, land grants, or other material and social privileges. This practice of altering the number of units of pottery production rather than the scale of production has held historically, even when potters were attached to or produced for large institutions (e.g., Behura 1965).

Textual sources from the Vijayanagara period, while generally mute on potters (itself important, given the many references to artisans such as weavers or metal workers), also support this picture of relatively small-scale specialist production. Where mentioned, potters appear in lists of "village servants" (along with watchmen, tanners, and blacksmiths), or in lists of "craft corporations" or caste guilds (Ramaswamy 1985:427). While for weavers and smiths, such corporate units played important roles in coordinating tax payments and temple donations, and in regulating production and organizing social protests (e.g., tax revolts and mass migrations), potters are rarely mentioned in such contexts. Ramaswamy (1985:435) has documented a very few references to potters making small cash donations to temples. In contrast, contemporary weavers and smiths often donated land and played important roles in temple administration, attesting to their relatively greater wealth and status.

The differences between these categories of artisans can be understood by considering the economic and cultural valuation and demand for the goods they produced. During the Vijayanagara period, textiles were important commodities in international and internal commerce, and elaborate textiles and garments became important symbols of sociopolitical status. Similarly, metal goods, including armaments and ornaments, were in high demand. The social status and sacred and political power of weavers and smiths increased accordingly, and there is at least some evidence to suggest the emergence of large-scale production of textiles, in workshops containing as many as 100 looms (Ramaswamy 1985). Again, there is no similar evidence suggesting any changes in the organization or scale of pottery production or in the status of potters.

Using some admittedly coarse estimates for pottery production rates and populations at Vijayanagara, we can provide a minimal estimate for the number of ceramic workshops that existed in or around the capital. Production rates are estimated using the ethnographically documented rate of 100 vessels per workshop per week. While pottery production likely diminished dramatically or did not occur at all during the summer monsoon (July–September), for present purposes I use an estimate of 50 weeks of production per year; yielding a total annual output of 5,000 pots per workshop (contemporary potters in the region appear to produce at higher rates in the two months immediately before the monsoon in order to stockpile vessels for times when production is not possible).

In estimating consumption, I employ the conservative estimate for per household needs of 30 vessels per year. This admittedly crude estimate derives from ethnographic estimates of pots per households from a number of social contexts (Arnold 1985:157; Nelson 1991) and from my observations of vessel use in contemporary South India. Actual numbers no doubt varied dramatically between households, and were probably generally much above this value, since household pots are traditionally replaced twice a year to mark calendrical ritual events, and pots are also consumed for other ritual purposes. This estimate also does not include nonhousehold use of ceramics, in temples, storehouses, or palace activities.

Nonetheless, taking these figures as a conservative baseline, each workshop could have served 166.67 households per year (5,000 vessels per workshop/30 vessels per household). As noted earlier, a cautious population estimate for Vijayanagara is 100,000 in the early 1400s and 200,000 by the early 1500s. Estimating a mean household size of five, 120 pottery workshops would have been required to meet the domestic needs of Vijayanagara's fifteenth-century population (20,000 households/166.67 household per workshop), while 240 workshops may have been present by the sixteenth century (40,000/166.67). I return to the subject of workshop location below.

SOURCES OF COMPLEXITY SUMMARIZED

In addition to demands and preferences for ceramics of the complex and vast population of ceramic consumers at Vijayanagara, the large numbers of pottery workshops provisioning them also introduced variability to the Vijayanagara ceramic industry. Interworkshop differences in raw material access, selection, and processing, and in firing practices and vessel morphology are expected to have contributed to both random and systematic variation in ceramic characteristics. Further, as a result of the comparatively low status of ceramics in Vijayanagara society and the nature of state administration of production more broadly, there is no evidence for centralized regulation or "quality control" over ceramic forms, composition, or distribution, either on the part of the state or (as far as we can document) caste organizations. Had such controls existed, we might expect high degrees of formal standardization or material uniformity even in contexts of relatively small units of household workshop production.

Yet the ubiquity of ceramics at Vijayanagara, their diverse uses, and multiple social contexts of consumption, coupled with the rich documentary sources and ethnographic parallels, provide tremendous potential for using ceramics to examine a range of issues relevant to understanding urban space, activities, and social organization. In the following sections, I summarize the ceramic analysis and some of the substantive results, before considering some of the major outstanding questions that remain to be resolved.

THE CERAMIC SAMPLE

Ceramics have been analyzed from collections made within Vijayanagara's urban core and from about 300 sites recorded in the capital's metropolitan region (approximately one-half of the 700 sites recorded by the Vijayanagara Metropolitan Survey between 1988 and 1997 have yielded ceramics; many of the sites are agricultural features or lie within modern settlements and have no archaeological ceramics associated with them).

Within the urban core, collections derive from three main areas: the "Nobleman's Quarter" (NMQ), a zone of elite residences excavated by the Karnataka Department of Archaeology and Museums; the East Valley (EV), a 1-by-.5-km residential zone containing evidence for elite and non-elite residences and a probable market place; and the city's main Islamic residential quarter (IQ), identified by the presence of a mosque and several Muslim tombs (Fig. 8.2; see Sinopoli 1986, 1993, 1996b). Collections from these three areas yielded approximately 60,000 body sherds (sorted by color and ware); 12,200 diagnostics were coded (5,938 from twelve residential compounds in NMQ; 5,678 from the EV; and 584 from the IQ). Analysis is still ongoing of ceramics collected by the Metropolitan Survey; here I limit my discussion of ceramics to a subset of 16,028 body sherds and 829 measured diagnostics from 113 sites surveyed from 1988 to 1992 (Sinopoli and Morrison, n.d.b).

It is difficult to get permission to remove artifacts from India, even for brief periods, and therefore all sherds were documented in the field using simple equipment (e.g., hand lens, vernier calipers, diameter chart, Munsell color chart, and goniometer). Since no typology existed for this material, much of my initial effort focused on developing a ceramic classification. The end result of these efforts is the first and only systematic analysis and classification of ceramics dating to the south Indian (and indeed South Asian) "medieval" period (ca. A.D. 700–1700). The absence of comparable studies from earlier or later periods has hampered the potential for establishing clear-cut chronological sequences and has prevented consideration of regional variation across the vast territory encompassed by the Vijayanagara empire.

At first glance, Vijayanagara ceramics appear tremendously uniform and classification seems a simple matter. The ceramics are mostly (more than 90 percent) dark brown or black in color; they are undecorated or have simple impressed decorations; surface treatment is minimal—most vessels were lightly smoothed or polished, but highly burnished wares are relatively scarce (< 5 percent); and they occur in a relatively restricted range of vessel forms, mostly necked vessel or jars, which comprise about 85 percent of the diagnostic sample.

Upon closer examination, however, within this broadly homogenous industry there is in fact a great deal of variability, particularly in vessel orientations and rim attributes. In order to identify patterning in such variables, I took a quantitative approach to constructing the classification. Vessels were grouped into two broad classes: unrestricted vessels (bowls) and restricted or necked vessels. For each, a range of variables was measured. These include information on inclusions (materials and percentages), color, and for some forms, categorical rim form categories. Quantitative variables measured included diameters (rim, neck, maximum, base), thickness (lip, rim, neck, body, base), height (rim, neck, height to maximum diameter, base, vessel), and angle or orientation (lip, rim, rim-exterior, body, base).

Analyses of these data examined distributions of individual variables as well as interrelations between variables, using a range of statistical techniques (more detailed information on the classification is discussed in Sinopoli 1986, 1991, 1993). Although the relatively rare bowl forms were fairly easy to define and group into broad functional classes and subclasses, the more common restricted vessel or jar forms typically exhibited continuous distributions over most attributes, with clear breaks or modes often difficult to identify. Definition of "discrete" vessel classes (based on shape, rim form, or other attributes) has thus relied on identifying statistical patterns within broad categories of similar vessels, rather than on clearly visible distinguishing features of ware, surface treatment, or vessel form.

The analytical challenge in trying to attribute culture or historical significance to these distributions and modes of ceramic variations, or to link pottery with people in the terms of this volume, lies in determining what patterns of ceramic variation result from: (1) temporal changes that occurred over the 200-plus years of Vijayanagara's occupation; (2) consumer choices in vessels associated with caste and community food preparation and consumption behaviors; (3) interworkshop differences associated with materials and techniques, learning traditions, place of origin, etc.; or (4) a combination of these and other factors. The appropriate weight to assign to each of these sources remains difficult to resolve. For example, clear-cut chronological patterning in ceramics has not yet been identified, though archaeological context does allow some sites or areas to be partitioned into early and late Vijayanagara times (and analysis of ceramics from survey data has resulted in identification of some diagnostic Vijayanagara vessel forms, though precisely when in the 200-year Vijayanagara period they date to has yet to be resolved; Sinopoli and Morrison n.d.b). Despite these limitations, much has nonetheless been learned about Vijayanagara from its ceramics.

WHAT HAS BEEN LEARNED FROM VIJAYANAGARA CERAMICS?

While difficulties in parsing the precise impact of diverse social and economic factors on Vijayanagara ceramics affect the resolution of the questions we can ask and the answers we can attain through their study, much has nonetheless been learned. In the discussion that follows, I address issues of: (1) vessel use; (2) activities and urban space at Vijayanagara; (3) site function in the metropolitan region; and (4) the scale and organization of ceramic production.

VESSEL USE

Because of its quantitative approach the classification developed for Vijayanagara ceramics was sensitive to minor variations in vessel morphology. This permitted a consideration of vessel function at a broad scale as well as the identification of finer variations within functional categories. The ceramics were divided into nine major functional or vessel-use classes, each further subdivided into sub-classes on the basis of details of vessel and rim morphology (a total of more than 70 subclasses, see Sinopoli 1986, 1993). In this discussion I limit my focus to the nine broad functional categories.

The interpretation of vessel function from complete vessels is not unproblematic and such interpretations become even more difficult when working with sherds such as comprise most of the Vijayanagara sample. Given the difficulties in obtaining permission to remove artifacts from India, techniques such as residue analysis have not been possible. Instead, I have relied on morphological and geometric characteristics, use traces (when evident), and analogies with contemporary vessel forms produced in the region, many of which have close parallels to Vijayanagara forms. "Vessel-use" categories include oil lamps, bowls or lids, small serving vessels, small and large cooking pots, small transport and serving necked vessels, medium transport and storage jars, and large storage jars (Fig. 8.5). While these broad categories were constructed to assess primary vessel use, variants within each category may be linked with interworkshop variations, social (including caste) constraints or demands of consumers, or chronological variability.

A total of 11,605 vessels could be grouped into one of the nine functional categories (other diagnostics included architectural fittings, water pipes [drains], roof tiles, game pieces, and decorated sherds). Of these, 1,386 (12.5 percent) were classed into the three unrestricted vessel or bowl categories. These include: (1) small saucer shaped vessels, used as oil lamps (n=107); (2) shallow bowls—a form diagnostic to the Vijayanagara period, and characterized by a thickened vertical rim, sharp base carination and hemispherical base (n=780), and (3) other bowls—a catch-all category for a range of other unrestricted bowl forms, exhibiting a great deal of formal variability (n=499). The low frequencies of unrestricted vessel forms in the ceramic inventory supports the interpretation that concerns with impurity inhibited dining on earthenware vessels during Vijayanagara times, supporting the diverse textual and ethnographic sources discussed earlier.

Restricted or necked vessels predominate in the Vijayanagara ceramic inventory. A total of 9,679 (87.5 percent) of the sherds were classed into one of the six restricted vessel-use classes (designated RV1–RV6). Distinctions among the classes were based on attributes of shape, size, and rim morphology. Vessels of Class RV1 (n=750) are small, relatively shallow vessels that could have been used in serving individual portions of food or beverages or for storing small quantities of substances such as spices or condiments; some may have had ritual functions as well. Class RV2 (n=4,284), the most common vessel class, consists of open, relatively shallow vessels of medium size (16–26 cm rim diameter) with low out-turning necks and steep body angles. They are typically wider than they are high. These vessels were likely used in cooking, perhaps with secondary uses as dry storage vessels. Vessels of the RV3 class (n=416) are similar in form to RV2 but larger in size, ranging from 23–45 cm in rim diameter. These are also interpreted as cooking vessels. Classes RV4–RV6 are characterized by high vertical necks and globular bodies. Vessels of class RV4 (n=522) are small in size (rim diameters range from 7–16 cm) and were probably used as water serving vessels or for transport. RV5 vessels are the second most numerous vessel class (n=3031). These range from 14–26 cm in rim diameter and are interpreted as water transport and storage vessels. RV6 vessels (n=676), ranging from 21–33 cm in rim diameter, were probably used for water storage and possibly transport.

The vessel-use categories described above are intended to assess the primary function for which vessels were best suited. It is no doubt the case that individual vessels would have been used for diverse tasks; nor need vessels always have been used in the task for which they were best suited. For example, it is not uncommon in the region today to see cooking vessels carried to village pumps to collect water despite the high rate of spillage that results from their large openings and shallow forms. Further, vessels are often subject to secondary uses once they can no longer serve their initial or primary function. At Vijayanagara sherds were common inclusions in packed earth walls and were also used as chinking in stone constructions. These caveats aside, as discussed below, the analysis of the spatial distributions of the different vessel-use classes provides insights into the organization of space within the Vijayanagara urban core and on variations in site function across the metropolitan region.

ACTIVITIES AND URBAN SPACE AT VIJAYANAGARA

Within the city core, ceramic distributions serve to highlight the complexity of urban space. While sacred texts concerning the Hindu city stress the inviolability of caste, status and occupationally restricted neighborhoods, ceramic and architectural evidence demonstrate that the actuality was significantly more complex. As discussed above, I have coded nearly 6,000 diagnostic ceramics from an area of the urban core known as the "Noblemen's Quarter"—a region of more than two dozen elite residential compounds and associated structures (Fig. 8.6; samples coded derive from 12 palace compounds excavated by the Karnataka Department of Archaeology and Museums from 1982–1986). Eight of these compounds contained evidence for large-scale burning, presumably during the sacking of the city that occurred in A.D. 1565, creating the possibility for in situ artifact remains in some compounds.

Distributions of vessel-use classes attest to a broad and diverse range of activities occurring within and between individual compounds. Some of the structures (e.g., NMQ3, NMQ12) appeared to have indeed been primarily residential in function, and contained the full range of cooking, serving, and storage forms. Others (e.g., NMQ2, NMQ4, NMQ10) were characterized by high frequencies of serving and water vessels, and a paucity of cooking vessels, suggesting that they may have served administrative or other nonresidential roles. In addition to the distributions of ceramic forms within compounds, their distributions outside of compound

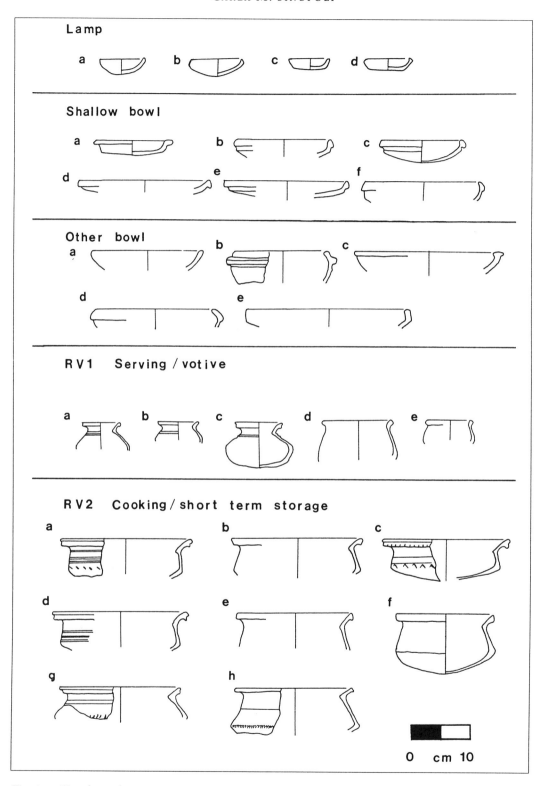

Fig. 8.5. Vessel-use classes.

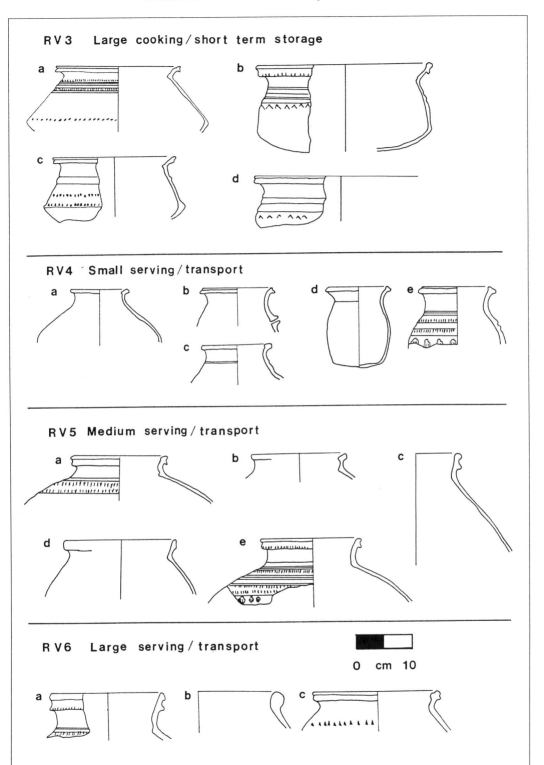

RV3 Large cooking / short term storage

a
b
c
d

RV4 Small serving / transport

a
b
c
d
e

RV5 Medium serving / transport

a
b
c
d
e

RV6 Large serving / transport

0 cm 10

a
b
c

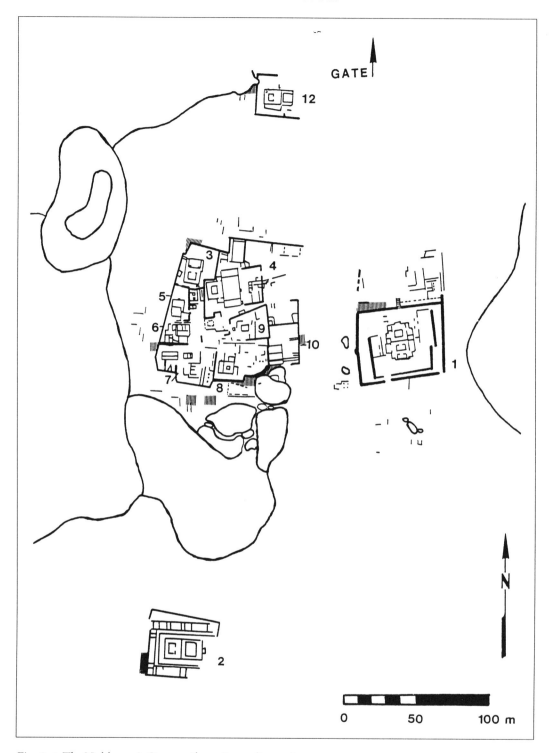

Fig. 8.6. The Noblemen's Quarter (from Sinopoli 1993).

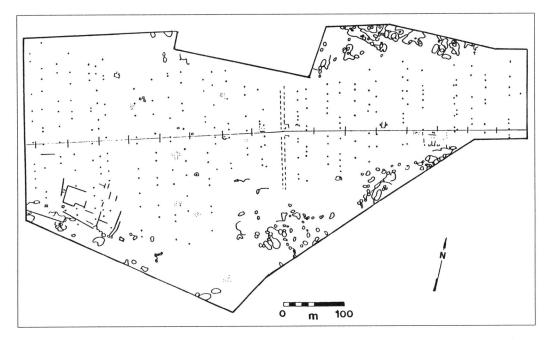

Fig. 8.7. The East Valley (solid circles indicate collection units from which diagnostic ceramics have been coded; from Sinopoli 1986).

walls provide interesting evidence on the actual complexity of settlement in this Hindu city. These ceramics are associated with subsidiary structures—often poorly constructed single-room structures with rubble wall foundations—that lie adjacent to and outside of the palaces. Ceramic samples from three such structures contain high frequencies of large transport and storage vessels and are, I suspect, associated with low-status dependents or servants who resided in this elite district.

The second area where ceramics were collected, the East Valley, is oriented roughly east-west and is bisected by the wall of the city's Royal Center, such that the western half of the valley lies within the royal center and the eastern half outside of it (Fig. 8.7). Several small Jaina shrines are located in the eastern part of the valley. An inscription associated with the gate located in the wall refers to the "Monday Gate," which is interpreted as being associated with a weekly market in that area. Overall, ceramics from the East Valley collections suggest a domestic assemblage, with a broad range of food preparation, serving, and storage vessels. The highest

diversity of vessel form variants is found closest to the gate, perhaps in keeping with the idea of a market, and some differences exist between the two halves of the valley in frequencies of vessel-use classes and their variants. In general, there are fewer large food preparation and storage vessels in the East Valley than in the NMQ, suggesting smaller units of food preparation and consumption.

The third area from which ceramics were collected lies in the northeast region of the urban core. Its interpretation as a Muslim residential area based on architecture is further supported by ceramic evidence. The area is characterized by significantly higher frequency of the two bowl categories—shallow bowls and other bowls—than in other areas of the site. They comprised more than 20 percent of diagnostic ceramics from the Islamic Quarter, approximately 11 percent of the ceramics from the NMQ, and 10 percent from the East Valley. This relates, I think, to the absence of the proscriptions against dining on earthenware that existed for Hindus in the city, among other factors.

In comparing distributions across the urban core, significant differences in vessel-use class frequencies occur among the three areas of the urban core (Table 8.1). In general, the East Valley assemblages (from both halves), with their higher frequencies of medium food preparation vessels, appeared to be more generalized domestic assemblages than either the Noblemen's Quarter or Islamic Quarter assemblages. The latter two areas contained high frequencies of storage and transport vessels, water serving vessels, and large food preparation vessels, and may have been overall more devoted to nondomestic activities than the East Valley. The higher than expected frequencies of bowl forms in the Islamic Quarter have also been noted.

SITE FUNCTION IN THE METROPOLITAN REGION

My more recent archaeological research at Vijayanagara has focused on systematic survey in the city's 350-plus sq km metropolitan region. The Vijayanagara Metropolitan Survey project, ongoing since 1988, has resulted in the identification of more than 700 archaeological sites that vary widely in function and scale (Morrison and Sinopoli 1992, 1996, n.d.a, n.d.b; Sinopoli and Morrison 1991, 1992, 1995, n.d.a, n.d.b). As noted earlier, ceramics from the first three seasons of survey, deriving from 113 of 370 recorded sites, have been analyzed. Table 8.2 compares vessel-use classes from the metropolitan region sites to those from the three areas of the urban core. Dramatic differences exist in vessel-use class frequencies among these broad areas. In particular, sites in the metropolitan region contain, overall, significantly higher than expected frequencies of other bowls and large storage vessels (RV6) than the urban core, and significantly lower than expected frequencies of medium cooking vessels (RV2) than expected.

Given the wide diversity of site types and the broader chronological range of sites in the survey region (and the admittedly much smaller sample sizes), there are several interpretations possible to account for these dramatic differences. I suspect that the higher frequency of other bowls, for example, is due in large part to the broader chronological range of the sites in the survey area (while

shallow bowls can be securely dated to the Vijayanagara period, other bowls span a much broader time and are still made in the present), and, perhaps, more pragmatic responses to ritual prohibitions against dining on earthenware in more isolated or rural areas (see discussion of VMS-591, below). The higher frequencies of large storage vessels (probably used for water storage) likely relates to differential organization of labor between the urban core and metropolitan region. The many artisans and agriculturalists engaged in strenuous labor in these areas would no doubt have played a role in needs for such vessels.

Tables 8.3 and 8.4 present information on vessel-use class distributions for 12 sites in the metropolitan region that yielded more than 25 measurable diagnostics. Although small sample sizes preclude attributing too much weight to these intersite differences in use-class distributions, the differences are striking in many cases. Combined with architectural evidence and other information relevant to interpreting site function, the ceramic data can provide useful insights into the range of activities that occurred across the metropolitan region.

As discussed earlier, within the urban core the Islamic Quarter has significantly higher than expected frequencies of shallow bowls and other bowls than NMQ or the East Valley. One site in the metropolitan region has even higher frequencies of bowls (33 percent, or 18 of 54 coded diagnostics), though in this case, the explanation seems to lie in site function rather than (or in addition to) the site's population. Recorded in the 1996 field season (and thus not included among the sites presented in Tables 8.2 and 8.3), VMS-591 is a Vijayanagara period hilltop fort located on an extremely high and rugged outcrop overlooking the city core and Tungabhadra River. The site is accessible through a narrow steep pass in the outcrop. Several large water cisterns and storage structures are found on the site, suggesting a concern with assuring secure provisions to the fort's occupants. The high frequencies of bowls at this site may similarly relate to a concern with assuring se-

TABLE 8.1.
Vessel-Use Class Distributions in the Urban Core

Area	Lamp	Shallow Bowl	Other Bowl	RV1 Small Serving	RV2 Medium Cooking	RV3 Large Cooking	RV4 Small Water Serving	RV5 Medium Transport/Storage	RV6 Large Transport/Storage	Total
NMQ[1]	52	304	144	223	1430	206	231	1193	268	4051
exp	42	293	151	284	1619	149	193	1100	221	
EVw[2]	22	155	94	186	1000	66	102	601	109	2335
exp	24	169	87	164	933	86	111	634	127	
EVe[3]	22	235	91	278	1510	88	124	838	149	3335
exp	34	241	124	234	1333	123	159	906	182	
IQ[4]	8	38	48	24	109	13	25	120	26	411
exp	4	30	15	29	264	15	20	112	22	
Total	104	732	377	711	4049	373	482	2752	552	10122

[1]Noblemen's Quarter (twelve walled residential compounds)
[2]East Valley West—western half of residential valley outside royal center, in urban core
[3]East Valley East—eastern half of residential valley, inside royal center
[4]Islamic Quarter—residential district in northeast of urban core; containing mosque and Islamic tombs
$X^2 = 278.991$, df = 24, $p < .001$ (from Sinopoli 1993:166)

TABLE 8.2.
Comparison of Vessel-Use Classes between Survey Area and Urban Core

	Lamp	Shallow Bowl	Other Bowl	RV1	RV2	RV3	RV4	RV5	RV6	Total
Metropolitan Region (Blocks O, S, T)	3 (9)	48 (66)	122 (42)	39 (63)	235 (361)	43 (35)	40 (44)	279 (255)	124 (57)	933
Urban core	104 (98)	732 (714)	377 (456)	711 (686)	4049 (3922)	373 (381)	482 (477)	2752 (2775)	552 (619)	10132
Totals	107	780	499	750	4284	416	522	3031	676	11065

Note: numbers in parentheses are expected values
$X^2 = 324.807$, df = 8, $p < .001$

TABLE 8.3.
Vessel-Use Classes by Site

Site	Site Type	Lamp	SB	OB	RV1	RV2	RV3	RV4	RV5	RV6	CT	Total
VMS-2	settlement	0	1	12	3	27	3	3	18	3	2	72
VMS-35	settlement	0	2	3	4	9	2	0	12	5	0	37
VMS-66	artifact scatter	0	0	4	0	11	1	0	13	3	0	32
VMS-78	artifact scatter/settlement	0	2	5	5	5	0	1	12	1	0	31
VMS-101	settlement	1	0	11	1	5	1	1	8	1	0	29
VMS-140	settlement	0	7	4	1	3	1	2	4	4	1	27
VMS-144	temple, in settlement area	0	5	1	3	7	2	0	6	2	0	26
VMS-169	artifact scatter/iron processing	0	0	7	3	13	3	2	5	4	0	37
VMS-179	iron processing	0	0	2	0	7	1	0	5	14	0	29
VMS-329	foundations/settlement	0	0	20	0	12	0	5	10	3	0	50
VMS-361	settlement	1	19	4	8	22	1	5	44	8	0	112
VMS-365	settlement	0	5	6	1	22	3	2	26	16	0	81
Totals		2	41	79	29	143	18	21	163	64	3	563

TABLE 8.4.
Vessel-Use Class Frequencies by Site

Site	Site Type	Lamp	SB	OB	RV1	RV2	RV3	RV4	RV5	RV6	CT
VMS-2	settlement	0	1.4	16.7	4.2	37.5	4.2	4.2	25.0	4.2	2.8
VMS-35	settlement	0	5.4	8.1	10.8	24.3	5.4	0	32.4	13.5	0
VMS-66	artifact scatter	0	0	12.5	0	34.4	3.1	0	40.6	9.4	0
VMS-78	artifact scatter/settlement	0	6.5	16.1	16.1	16.1	0	3.2	38.7	3.2	0
VMS-101	settlement	3.4	0	37.9	3.4	17.2	3.4	3.4	27.6	3.4	0
VMS-140	settlement	0	25.9	14.8	3.7	11.1	3.7	7.4	14.8	14.8	3.7
VMS-144	temple, in settlement area	0	19.2	3.8	11.5	26.9	7.7	0	23.1	7.7	0
VMS-169	artifact scatter/iron processing	0	0	18.9	8.1	35.1	8.1	5.4	13.5	10.8	0
VMS-179	iron processing	0	0	6.9	0	24.1	3.4	0	17.2	48.3	0
VMS-329	foundations/settlement	0	0	40.0	0	24.0	0	10.0	20.0	6.0	0
VMS-361	settlement	0.9	16.7	3.6	7.1	19.6	0.9	4.5	39.3	7.1	0
VMS-365	settlement	0	6.2	7.4	1.2	27.2	3.7	2.5	32.1	19.8	0
Sample Mean		0.04	7.3	14.0	5.2	25.4	3.2	3.7	29.0	11.4	0.05

cure provisions for times when access to low-lying areas (and banana leaves) was not possible. It is also possible that the site was occupied by Muslim mercenaries who comprised an important part of the Vijayanagara military, though there is at least one Hindu shrine present in the fort.

Although analysis of the metropolitan region survey data is just beginning, this preliminary consideration suggests that, as in the urban core, analyses of ceramic distributions will play an important role in enhancing our understandings of the uses of the many sites found in the survey region.

WHAT REMAINS TO BE LEARNED?

While analysis of Vijayanagara ceramics has been productive many questions remain unanswered and perhaps, unanswerable. It is certainly the case that the analysis of the nine broad vessel-use classes discussed above, while aiding in general considerations of activity distributions, does not allow consideration of the complex social dynamics and linguistic, caste, and other divisions discussed in the first part of the paper. Analyses of the finer subgroups of these nine broad classes have not yielded definitive results (Sinopoli 1986).

I have already noted the difficulties of developing a ceramic chronology for Vijayanagara. This is due in part to the absence of systematic archaeological research on artifacts associated with earlier or later periods in the region, and to the absence of stratigraphic excavations at Vijayanagara. However, it is also the case that ceramic traditions in South India appear to be quite conservative (many vessel forms from contemporary ceramic workshops in the region would blend easily into the Vijayanagara period ceramic inventory), and it may be that there was relatively little systemic ceramic change in the 200-year period that the capital was occupied. While stylistic and morphological change may have occurred at the level of individual workshop or consuming neighborhood, no clear directional changes are evident that were operative at the site or region as a whole.

Perhaps the biggest disappointment of the

archaeological work at Vijayanagara and in its hinterland has been the failure to identify any ceramic workshops, especially given the arguments presented earlier for very large numbers of household-level workshops in the region. The study of the organization of craft production from direct evidence for production was my primary goal in undertaking the Vijayanagara Metropolitan Survey project. However, production locales have in general proven difficult to identify, and only approximately 40 of the 700 documented sites have been linked with specialized craft production activities, including stone working, metallurgical activities (iron smelting and working, gold working), or lime production.

While it may well be that the remains of pottery workshops may still be identified through survey, in retrospect the invisibility of ceramic production is not all that surprising and can be attributed to two main factors (Sinopoli 1994). First, as noted earlier, production traces and firing temperatures suggest that Vijayanagara ceramic technologies were comparable to contemporary techniques in the region. Assuming that firing facilities were also similarly constructed, these would have been simple pits lined by a single horseshoe-shaped rubble wall, which would likely not preserve well. Further, the relatively low firing temperatures evidenced for the Vijayanagara ceramics (see above, Rautman 1991) yield few clearly identifiable wasters (in the form of blistered or over-fired sherds) or other surface archaeological features. Second, and perhaps more important, was the widespread use of household and industrial waste as fertilizer for agricultural fields. Such practices appear to have led to substantial redeposition of pyrotechnological waste across the metropolitan region. Archaeologically, this appears as a low density scatter of ceramics and metal slag across much of the 350-sq-km metropolitan region. While slag can clearly be linked with productive activities, this is not possible for the sherd scatter, since their presence could also result from ceramic use, breakage, and deposition.

The question remains then, where did Vijayanagara's many potters live? Evidence to answer this question is scarce. The inscription mentioning *Kummaragunte,* or place of the potters' clay, discussed earlier, provides one indication for the presence of potters outside of the walls of the urban core. An additional clue can be found in a late sixteenth-century epic poem composed by a Jaina ascetic named Srutakirti. The Kannada poem was written in A.D. 1567–1568 (two to three years after Vijayanagara was abandoned), and is a biographical sketch of a Hoysala (a late twelfth to early fourteenth-century South Indian kingdom, predecessor to Vijayanagara) Jaina female saint, named Vijayakumari. Although not explicitly referring to Vijayanagara, the author does present some vivid descriptions of the former Hoysala capital, and it is not improbable that his model for this idealized city was the recently abandoned city of Vijayanagara, certainly the most famous city in south India when the poem was written. At the very least, the poem presents a description of the layout of the ideal city. The poet describes the many streets of artisans and merchants in the heart of the city, with each specialty located in its discrete area (a theme common to many contemporary literary works). Occupational communities inhabiting these streets include: goldsmiths (who were often also moneylenders), bronze merchants, textile merchants, vendors of rice and other grains, herbal medicine merchants, sandal paste merchants, and flower merchants, as well as streets of concubines, musicians, dancers, and other artists. This pattern of occupationally restricted streets or neighborhoods is also mentioned in numerous other contemporaneous literary works.

The text continues:

The areas outside the fort wall were inhabited by the people of the lower classes such as washermen, potters, barbers, carpenters, and others.

Further away from the above sectors, there lived the untouchables, called *holeya, madiga, krura-krami,* etc.

Subjects of all the above castes, living in streets reserved for them, lived as per the established customs of the society and without giving room for any violation of them. (I, 104–106, p. 11; summarized by Kottraiah n.d.:6).

Thus, inscriptional and textual references suggest that pottery workshops were found outside but proximate to the walls of the city core, and that workshops may have clustered into neighborhoods or communities. In the absence of definitive archaeological evidence, this is all that can be said at present.

DISCUSSION

In this paper I have attempted to address the diverse cultural, social, ideological, and economic factors that impact ceramic variability in the urban context of Vijayanagara. These include the scale and cultural diversity of the Vijayanagara imperial capital, whose nearly quarter-million inhabitants derived from an area spanning much of the Indian peninsula, spoke three major South Indian languages, included practitioners of Hinduism, Jainism, and Islam, and belonged to hundreds of hereditary castes and subcastes. The particular array of factors discussed here and the kinds of evidence that can be obtained from textual sources are, of course, specific to the Vijayanagara example, a case where the low status of ceramics and the organization of production into numerous relatively small, specialized workshops creates numerous challenges to interpretation. However, they can also be taken to illustrate the complexity of analyzing and interpreting archaeological ceramics (or any other class of artifacts) from large-scale and complex urban contexts. It is perhaps not surprising, therefore, that many such attempts have been restricted in focus to particular luxury wares or to a limited range of vessel forms (e.g., Aztec decorated wares in the New World, or amphorae in the Roman world). Considering a fuller array of vessel forms in urban contexts, while not unproblematic, does nonetheless reveal much useful information, and it is to be hoped that some of the "challenges" of Vijayanagara ceramic analysis will disappear in the future as our knowledge of them increases.

9

Finely Crafted Ceramics and Distant Lands: Classic Mixtequilla

BARBARA L. STARK

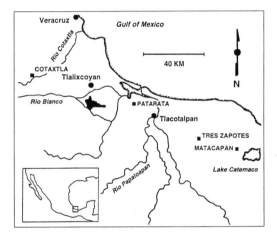

Fig. 9.1. The Lower Papaloapan Basin and the Proyecto Arqueológico La Mixtequilla (PALM) survey area (in black).

A series of principles concerning prestigious ceramics among hierarchical Mesoamerican societies guides my effort to compare two interpretive approaches. First, finely made or elaborately decorated vessels co-exist with mundane ones and may form part of a continuum of quality, skill, and labor investments in products. Second, they can play a special role in communicating social differences and sacred values. Third, they may serve as valued gifts or items of exchange over long distances even if most pottery is locally produced and distributed. Fourth, elaborate or high-value pottery may imitate prestigious styles elsewhere either in the form of close copies or stylistic "allusions" that blend in considerable local reinterpretation or innovation. There is reason to accept these principles as a background, as I discuss below.

Two interpretive approaches concerning elaborate or imported ceramics offer important insights for the active reinforcement of social hierarchies. Models concerning elaborate ceramics have been amplified with Helms's (1993) schema for understanding the cultural and social significance of fine crafts and of objects symbolizing sacred geographic and temporal distance that are used to enhance the authority of leaders. She does not address ceramics per se, but it is useful to consider the applicability of her ideas for finely crafted ceramics. I explore her ideas in comparison to an alternative focused upon cross-cutting elite differentiation among complex societies. Elite interaction associated with creating and maintaining prestige can involve importation and imitation of select objects in a different process from that described by Helms. My touchstone region is the Mixtequilla in south-central Veracruz, Mexico (Fig. 9.1), particularly in the Classic period, A.D. 300–900.

Before addressing the two interpretive approaches, which we can term the cosmological versus social interpretations of fine ceramics, I comment briefly about the general principles that guide my discussion. Ceramics are relatively easy to produce for a wide range of domestic and subsistence tasks and had no rivals in preindustrial times as abundant, practical containers, mainly for food and liquid storage, processing, and serving. Across Mesoamerica, the prevalence of suitable clays and tempers and the weight and fragility of ceramics militated against highly restricted areas of production that supplied vessels for long-distance distribution. Instead, there were numerous places of production and nearly universal access to pottery. Ceramic vessels had multiple roles in the complex backdrop of Mesoamerican societies that go beyond their subsistence functions, however. They entered into a variety of exchange networks and social communications. Their differentiated roles in social communication were possible because of the plasticity of ceramics, their decorative variety, and the diversity of manufacturing techniques and labor investment. In other words, pottery is well suited for stylistic displays. As a result, ceramics of special value or esteem were distributed interregionally in some cases. Such distinctions in value figured in expressions and reinforcement of social hierarchies in Mesoamerica, with aspects of form or decoration playing an active communication role rather than simply serving as a by-product of enculturation (Hegmon 1992).

Mesoamerican examples are instructive about highly valued pottery from the late period, when we have overlapping documentary data. In the Late Postclassic period (A.D. 1350–1521), vessels from Cholula, Puebla, "some red and some black," were preferred for the Aztec emperor's service according to historical information (Díaz 1963:226). These imports likely included Cholula polychromes, although Díaz's description is ambiguous. Prestige goods (with special social or sacred significance) and wealth items (with a high labor input and scarcity) represent two overlapping concepts of value pertinant to the Cholula vessels. Cholula polychromes constitute a good example of the prestige-wealth value of special, fancy ceramics. Cholula was a widely recognized urban center and pilgrimage destination in a valley ad-

jacent to the Basin of Mexico, the seat of Aztec authority. In addition to the rich colors, dense designs, and high burnish of the finest Cholula polychromes, they conspicuously incorporated religious and cosmological imagery. A leitmotif of Aztec imperial policy involved incorporation at the capital of idols, substances, and products from conquered provinces (Umberger and Klein 1993); the preference for Cholula ceramics partakes of this pattern.

Cholula polychromes and other decorated service wares were widely imitated or imported in the central highlands of Mexico and in parts of the Gulf lowlands, including south-central Veracruz (Curet et al. 1994; Stark 1995b); they formed part of the so-called Mixteca-Puebla ceramic sphere (Smith and Heath-Smith 1980). It is likely that greater artistic skill and labor investment distinguished vessels selected for the imperial court from the more widely circulated Cholula vessels and from regional versions, such as those in south-central Veracruz that I suspect were locally produced. Variations in form or symbolic content are possible as well. The Mixteca-Puebla style vessels and other phenomena, such as serpent motifs on Postclassic Maya ceramics (Rice 1983) and widespread Early Postclassic trade in prized Plumbate vessels (Neff and Bishop 1988; Shepard 1948) are examples of prestige-wealth values that cross-cut polities and regions. Their circulation helped identify privileged status and wealth in Mesoamerican societies.

For interpreting specially valued, elaborate ceramics, we can argue that they represent higher labor investment articles that had higher economic value warranting the added transport costs to other regions. However, we can identify a variety of high labor-investment vessels manufactured in other locations that lacked the special cachet of Cholula polychromes and received less extensive distribution and imitation. There is more to be learned from finely crafted ceramics than recognition of their greater labor investment. In addition, many nonhierarchical societies manufacture elaborately decorated vessels.

Traditionally in Mesoamerican studies, certain categories of fancy ceramics have been recognized as linked to the prestige of particular societies and their elite members, with imitation and importation or gifts to members of elevated social strata in other societies. This pattern points to a social focus for interpretation. Reents-Budet's (1994) study of finely crafted Maya polychromes provides an excellent example. Among the Classic Maya, elite "artists" attached to royal courts painted scenes on service vessels that commemorated historical personages and events or that portrayed supernaturals and rituals. Often, the painter was a member of the royal lineage. These special vessels were not only part of service ware at the courts, but also were bestowed as special gifts to royals at other centers and as funerary offerings in tombs. Social networks among elites were the conduits for the distribution, consumption, and disposal of these highly valued Maya vessels. Other polychromes lacking the quality and individualizing texts of royal-linked vessels were in wide but differential social circulation (Gonlin 1994; Hendon 1991; Reents-Budet 1994:153; Webster and Gonlin 1988). Another example of a socially focused interpretation is Flannery's (1968) model for Gulf Olmec-Oaxacan interaction in which Olmec iconography appeared on Oaxacan vessels as part of exchanges undertaken for prestige enhancement—although he has since changed his opinion concerning several particulars in this model (Flannery and Marcus 1994). In general, these examples demonstrate the peer polity interaction and symbolic entrainment discussed by Renfrew (1986).

As yet no Mesoamerican ceramic candidates have been proposed for elite-commoner interactions along the lines suggested by Pauketat and Emerson (1991) for North American Ramey Incised pots at Cahokia in Mississippian times. They suggest that these serving vessels circulated because of chiefly largesse at annual ceremonies and feasts. However, Clark and Blake (1994) interpret the forms and decorations of early Barra and Locona phase pottery on the Chiapas coast in terms of feasting and competitive leadership, which perhaps involved some elite-commoner exchanges.

A different but partly interrelated perspective on items of special value focuses more on why certain artifacts or materials become particularly significant. Helms (1993) elaborated a general model linking finely crafted objects and exotic imports to cosmological concepts in which distant lands and distant time had sacred associations. In her view, acquisition of items from afar or fine crafts produced locally (and restricted in social access) were part of the ideological underpinning of elite, especially ruler's, authority, as I elaborate below. My concern in this paper is how these two approaches—one more socially focused and the other with a cosmological and political emphasis—can be applied and the extent to which each seems compatible with Classic Mixtequilla evidence.

THE SYMBOLIC ROLE OF DISTANT PRODUCTS AND FINE CRAFTS

As mentioned, Helms (1993) explored the conceptual links among geographic distance, distant times, and supernatural or sacred realms. A crucial point in Helms's reasoning is that geographic distance is easily (if not universally) equated with distant sacred time and relatively inaccessible supernatural realms. Consequently, she offers a broad-based model of how long-distance exchange in prestige-wealth items can enhance political power and affirm rulership. According to her analysis, exotic scarce items of ritual or social significance and finely crafted items of restricted access can play crucial roles in differentiating elites, especially rulers, from commoners by linking them to primordial powers and to ritual authority. In this fashion, social hierarchies are "naturalized" because links are demonstrated with fundamental powers according to an accepted view of the cosmos. In instances of impeded access to distant exotics, local copies may be fabricated; alternatively, local highly skilled crafts produced with sacred knowledge may play an analogous role.

Helms argues that "acquisition" from afar

must be differentiated from exchanges within a sphere of common social meanings and regularized relations. For a connection to the supernatural, "acquisition" necessarily is a special act that reaches beyond the routine of ordinary life. One implication is that cosmologically significant items will be scarcer than those connected with more customary social interactions.

This distinction between acquisition and customary social and economic exchanges is difficult to apply in practice. The crux of the problem is that elites or higher-status individuals tend to develop and maintain their authority through competition and alliance with neighboring elites. Helms recognizes the roles of neighboring societies in a different way. She notes that a prestigious distant center may be a focus of acquisition or imitation. However, I suggest that a shift may occur diachronically as the distant and little-known exotic center becomes better known. Over time external elite social relations tend to forge cross-cutting behaviors and symbols of elite identification, i.e., a degree of commonality in elite culture. Thus, acquisitive interactions with an external, nonroutine world prove difficult to segregate from other cross-cutting elite activities because there is a continuing process of elite or class differentiation, especially in an area like Mesoamerica with many interacting hierarchical societies, and class-linked vessels may display sacred themes. In Mesoamerican states and empires elite social interaction increasingly reinforced class distinctions that cross-cut political boundaries (Smith 1987b; Stark 1990: 260–262).

One implication of a social interpretation is that the vessels employed in elite social negotiations and displays may become gifts that encourage client loyalty and indebtedness. The result may be a wide but differential social distribution. Imitative versions of elite wares may also be evident in wider circulation. Especially by Postclassic times in Mesoamerica, increased marketing may have made decorated ceramics much more accessible than previously. Therefore, the social model contrasts with Helms's notion of cos-

mologically significant acquisition in respect of (1) the degree of scarcity and (2) the extent of circulation of elaborate ceramics (and imitations).

Although I have indicated two points on which the social and cosmological models diverge, there is one point on which they converge. State authority and powerful elites often were able to elaborate highly valued crafts internally, with only modest and intermittent attention to outside, distant standards. Therefore, in larger, more complex polities commanding greater resources and maintaining more internal social differentiation, recourse to outside exotics may retain some importance, but internally patronized crafts may be elaborated to the point that they rival or overshadow exotics in social displays. Social and cosmological perspectives coincide in the role of local fine crafts of limited access produced by attached specialists, i.e., specialists connected to elite households or commissioned to work for important patrons. Helms underscores the frequency with which expert artisans (or "artists") are regarded as blessed with sacred powers to imbue products with appropriate symbolism and value. The scenes and inscriptions on the finest Maya vessels substantiate this perspective (Reents-Budet 1994:43–50). The products of attached specialists often exemplify "conspicuous production," encapsulating noteworthy excesses of effort and skill beyond utilitarian considerations (Clark and Parry 1990:293), and the artifacts created have a restricted social circulation and "conspicuous consumption"—in Veblen's (1953) phrase. Thus, attached artisans are an internal extension or expression of elite cultural distinctions, and they may simultaneously support a social and a cosmological interpretation.

Helms is not very restrictive about the range of societies to which her ideas apply, including mildly hierarchical situations as well as early states. She does not provide a guide to archaeological applications, which remains a challenge. How can her ideas be applied to elaborate ceramics? Can we detect a symbolic role for distant places, especially of important capitals, as a source of gifts or exotic imports? Were distant prestigious styles imitated, as suggested by Helms? If so, can we distinguish cross-cutting elite subcultures from "acquisitive" activities? Are ceramic styles, instead, interpretable in autochthonous patterns according to the historical trajectory of a particular region?

Certain aspects of the Classic Mixtequilla record suggest that ritual objects connected with outside prestigious realms were, as Helms argues, given special attention. Specifically, Teotihuacan may have played such a role in the Early Classic period (A.D. 300–600). Reciprocally, Teotihuacan displays an interest in Gulf scroll styles. In the Mixtequilla, outside poles of stylistic reference shifted as Teotihuacan waned in importance. Additionally, the infrequency of items from or directly imitating distant societies is another clue that a more cosmological or sacred association may apply. Even though valued local crafts thrived, outside styles or imports were not eclipsed if an appropriate reference polity existed. In other words, class distinctions as expressed in ceramics involved more than just differential distributions of pottery and other ceramic objects. Those differences were skewed in particular ways to incorporate references to a distant realm(s). However, outside styles provide only modest (or even tenuous) support of Helms's model in comparison to the role of an autochthonous tradition of local crafts in the Mixtequilla, especially when Late Classic (A.D. 600–900) evidence is considered. My study region shows that ceramics simultaneously expressed social distinctions and cosmological or ritual symbolism because multiple kinds of vessels (or types) were in use. Local fine crafts were more abundant than distant allusions and speak to the importance of internal processes of social differentiation and elite interaction.

THE MIXTEQUILLA AS A CASE STUDY
The Mixtequilla area in south-central Veracruz, in the western side of the lower Papaloapan basin, is the focus of a diachronic regionally oriented study that I am pursuing in the Proyecto Arqueológico La Mixtequilla (PALM). Because the Mixtequilla has not received much archaeological attention, part of my effort has concerned better defining a cultural sequence; as a consequence, I have been interested in stylistic cross-dating (Stark 1989, 1997c). These comparative data also provide a framework to consider Helms's ideas versus a more socially focused interpretation.

Archaeologists are prone to describe their studies as "preliminary" out of respect for the typically modest scale of our information compared to what once existed about ancient societies and compared to what still lies in the ground. My effort to evaluate high-value Mixtequilla ceramics can barely be described as "preliminary," considering the few controlled excavations in the region and our inability to be sure about the variability and cultural contexts of ceramics. However, I have at least an initial idea of the socially restricted, "fancier" vessels—serving bowls and vases—that characterize the assemblages over time (e.g., Stark and Hall 1993). Additionally, data from ceramic vessels can be supplemented with information from figurines and incense burners. Because of the lack of materials analyses, imitation and importation will not be distinguished in most cases. I scrutinize episodes of greater attention to or participation in "foreign" or distant styles for signs of the principles Helms explicates or for deviations from them that accord with the elite social interaction model.

PALM data derive from systematic field-by-field survey of 40 sq km during 1986–1988 (Fig. 9.2). This area encompasses the centers of Cerro de las Mesas and El Zapotal plus several other constellations of formal architecture so closely spaced that the study region may have been a "capital zone." Most of the architectural complexes date to the Classic period or continued to be used during that period, but I assume there was a sequence of construction so that not all the complexes were initially contemporaneous. A pattern of additive construction, perhaps with shifts in the principal seat of authority, is the most reasonable interpretation at pre-

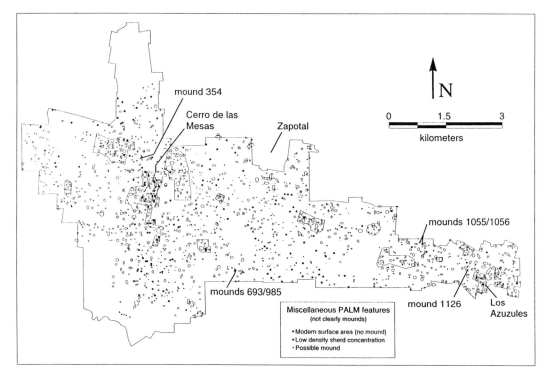

Fig. 9.2. PALM survey area showing archaeological features and centers mentioned in the text.

sent. For example, Cerro de las Mesas seems to have been particularly important in the Early Classic period, with Zapotal and Los Azuzules showing more evidence of Late Classic materials. Clearly, the Mixtequilla was a region of particular political and social importance in the Classic period.

In addition to the complexes of formal architecture, the survey area includes numerous low mounds with surface remains suggesting a residential function. Test excavations and augering confirm this interpretation at several locations (Stark 1997c). We have excavated materials from the Late Preclassic period (600–100 B.C.) at mounds 693 and 985, from the Terminal Preclassic period (100 B.C. to 300 A.D.) at mound 354, from the Early Classic period (A.D. 300–600) at mound 1126, and from the Late Classic period (A.D. 600–900) at mounds 1055 and 1056. During the Late Preclassic period, mounds 693 and 985 seem to have been part of a small village in the vicinity of Cerro de las Mesas. Later, mounds 354, 1126, 1055, and 1056 are situ-

ated close to important formal monumental architecture and likely represent relatively prosperous, stable households. In particular, mound 1055 seems to have had exceptional quantities of fine serving bowls deposited at the termination of occupation in one structure (Stark and Hall 1993).

Farther afield, east of the study zone in the mangrove swamps of the lower Papaloapan Basin, the Patarata 52 residential location lacks the full range of elaborate ceramics detected in the study zone and suggests the more ordinary materials that might be encountered in less wealthy or powerful hinterland households (Stark 1977, 1989). As I will show below, the sequence at Patarata 52 exhibits a more elaborate inventory in the first two Early Classic subphases, with a decline thereafter. During the Late Classic period, Patarata 52 was a locus of pottery manufacture with few indications of elevated social status. Patarata 52 is in an alignment that includes platform mounds and may have been part of an elongated lagoon shore or riverbank settlement. My initial reconnaissance did not detect mangrove swamp centers as sizable as those mapped in the Mixtequilla, however. The lower Cotaxtla drainage to the west appears to lack centers with the magnitude of public construction evident at Cerro de las Mesas and its vicinity (Daneels 1997b). Nor does the ceramic inventory appear to contain the same range of elaborate vessels and figurines during the Classic period (Daneels 1988).

These regional patterns are among the clues I have used to distinguish ceramics of special social value. In addition, the fineness of paste, the investment in decorating and finishing vessels, the thinness and delicacy of the sidewalls, and the scarcity of the vessels are among the considerations I applied in selecting categories for analysis. More descriptive details about Classic period ceramics and the cultural sequence are available in Stark (1977, 1989, 1997c). The pottery I consider for quantitative purposes includes negative resist (code 36), false negative (code 54), and stylistically related white-on-red bowls (code 60g), reversed false negative (code 33), textured bowls (codes 53m, 6e, 6f), incision or scraping applied to vessels with an orange slip over a white underslip, with red paint or a red interior slip (code 55, Medellín's [1960: 58] *anaranjada sobre laca esgrafiada y raspada*), Blanco White (code 44), and Tuxtla Polychrome (codes 45b, 45l). Code number-letter designations are those employed in PALM.

Below, I examine pottery from the Early and Late Classic Mixtequilla assemblages. In addition, for the Early Classic period I consider not only Mixtequilla pottery but also a scroll style that appears more commonly on molded figurine fragments than on pottery. My comparisons to scroll styles elsewhere consider stone sculpture and other materials as well in order to provide a perspective on the Mixtequilla ceramic representations.

THE CLASSIC PERIOD

EARLY CLASSIC PERIOD, A.D. 300–600

Ceramic complexes in the Early Classic period have more kinds of elaborately deco-

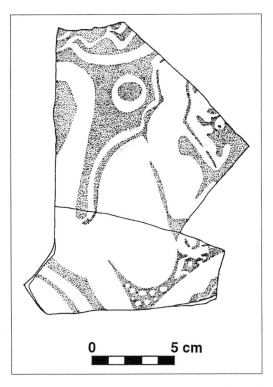

0   5 cm

Fig. 9.3. PALM negative resist, red resist-slipped, flat interior base of bowl. Monkey motif may be depicted (code 36a, mound 1126, stratigraphic unit 228).

rated serving vessels than during the Late and Terminal Preclassic periods, although we cannot yet distinguish ones that have restricted social access in a definitive way. The stylistic reference points of more elaborate vessels are complex to analyze but seem to be predominantly local to the region. For example, negative resist decoration on low-walled tripod bowls and on convex bowls was executed in a local style emphasizing spirals, dotted areas, and bold designs (Stark 1989: 12–27). The elaborate motifs appear to have been executed in a fluid, rapid manner (Fig. 9.3). Most of these vessels are perhaps of intermediate value in regard to decoration and fineness; the pastes are generally coarse at Patarata 52, while finer pastes are typical in the PALM study zone. At Patarata, a group of finer resist bowls was separated (Alvarado variant), but in the Mixtequilla this distinction could not be made reliably because of the generally finer pastes used for

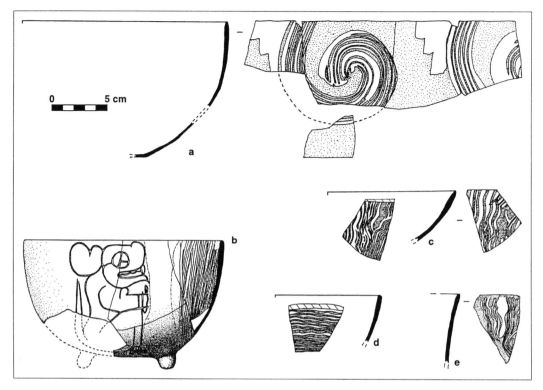

Fig. 9.4. False negative bowls; (a) code 54c, mound 1055, stratigraphic unit 322, (b) code 54f, mound 1055, stratigraphic unit 308, (c) code 54b, mound 1055, stratigraphic unit 306, (d) code 54g, mound 1055, stratigraphic unit 308, (e) code 54m, mound 1126, stratigraphic unit 235.

negative resist bowls. The paste difference may be a clue to finer quality in a locale surrounding a major center(s) versus a more modest hinterland residence. Although negative resist designs are reported for the Early Classic period from Tehuantepec and Teotihuacan (among other locales), I have not detected a close match of form and design with the Mixtequilla vessels (Stark 1989:13–19).

Perhaps toward the close of the Early Classic period, some Mixtequilla bowls are treated with a similar-appearing technique that I have called "false negative" (Figs. 9.4, 9.5). These types of vessels were not encountered at Patarata 52. False negative designs typically comprise wavy parallel lines or concentric circular lines, usually in a finer, denser pattern than the designs on negative resist vessels. A white painted area was usually partially combed away using a multiple-pronged device, followed by an overslip, usually orange but occasionally red. This technique

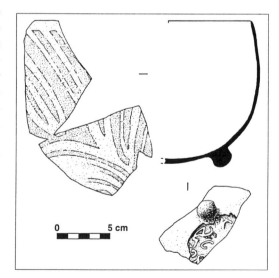

Fig. 9.5. False negative bowl (code 54m, mound 1055, stratigraphic unit 306); exterior has slanting white bands; darker stippled areas are red slipped; lighter stippled areas have white underlying a red stain.

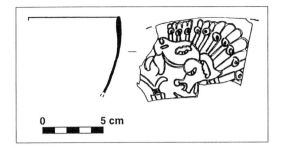

Fig. 9.6. "Laca" bowl (code 55b, mound 1055, stratigraphic unit 323); exterior polished orange over white; interior polished muddy orange slip.

appears similar to a resist slip technique in which a resistant material like wax was painted on to form a design, with the vessel then overslipped or smudged or both, resulting in a reserve design after firing. I only discovered the mechanical combing with 10-power magnification of sherds that revealed cases in which the undercoat and, rarely, the paste had been slightly scored.

More commonly to the west in central Veracruz than in the Mixtequilla, polished bowls bore red paint on an orange slip over a white underslip (but sometimes triple slipped with a thin red wash over the orange slip) or without red paint but with a red interior slip; these bowls were incised and sometimes scraped down to the white underslip to create a bichrome or polychrome effect (Fig. 9.6). These bowls are rare in the Mixtequilla and absent in collections from Patarata 52.

Textured bowls are another PALM category not represented at Patarata 52. Most of these Mixtequilla vessels were polished black with matte-stippled or matte-and-incised designs on the exterior (Fig. 9.7); others had a red or other highly polished interior slip and a delicate, basket-like textured exterior except for the polished exterior rim band (Fig. 9.8). Matte-polished designs occur at Teotihuacan but do not seem to have been applied to small convex bowls, as in the Mixtequilla, nor are the designs as elaborate (Séjourné 1966:86).

In addition to a predominantly regional tradition of elaborate vessels, some pottery partakes of extra-local styles. The Early Classic period was distinguished in part because

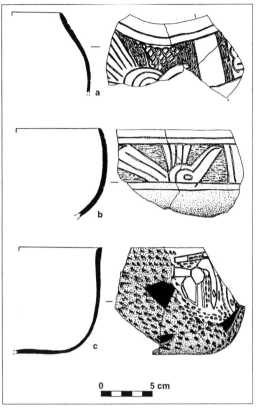

Fig. 9.7. Matte-polished and matte-stippled bowls; (a, b) code 6e, mound 1126, stratigraphic unit 228, (c) code 6f, mound 1126, stratigraphic unit 232, nonstippled areas are polished.

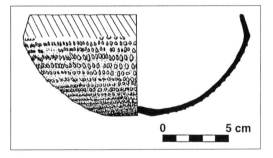

Fig. 9.8. Texture-impressed bowl (code 53m, mound 1126, stratigraphic unit 231); poished red slip on interior, carried over as exterior band.

of sporadic evidence of imitation of Teotihuacan ritual and service forms and rare, possible imports from the Teotihuacan realm. More details and illustrations concerning these ceramics are presented by Stark (1997c). The rare imports include 13 sherds of Thin Orange pottery in the PALM survey (identified by Evelyn Rattray [pers. comm. 1991]). Thin Orange appears to have been manufactured in Puebla and imported to Teotihuacan in considerable quantity over centuries (Rattray 1990). Although Rattray questions whether Teotihuacan exercised direct control over the production zone, Teotihuacan at least enjoyed highly preferential access to Thin Orange. There is no guarantee, however, that the small quantity of Thin Orange observed in the lower Papaloapan basin derives in any direct fashion from Teotihuacan. Minimally, local appreciation of Thin Orange was likely increased by high levels of Teotihuacan consumption.

Loop-foot bowls that may have served as lids or as incense burners at Teotihuacan (Cowgill et al. 1984:168) occur in small numbers at the household level in the Mixtequilla and at Patarata 52 in the first two subphases. This is a form known at Teotihuacan, but the proportions of the bowls are slightly different, with a shallower vessel typical at Teotihuacan. Likely the Mixtequilla loop-foot bowls were local copies. Additionally, four two-holed *candeleros* were encountered during the Mixtequilla fieldwork. They, too, may have been locally fabricated, but they are ritual forms important at Teotihuacan and probably should be viewed as copies.

A form closely associated with Teotihuacan is the cylinder tripod vase. The origins of this form are obscure. Cylinder tripods may first appear at Teotihuacan in the form of Lustrous Ware vessels thought to have been imported from northern Veracruz (Rattray 1979, 1992:27). Cylinder vessels without tripods appeared earlier during the Preclassic period in Olmec times (Benson and de la Fuente 1996:201–203; Coe and Diehl 1980: 165, fig. 139m). Drucker (1943, plate 19f) illustrates a black cylindrical beaker or drinking cup decorated with the Late Preclassic Minute Incision style at Cerro de las Mesas (Stark 1997b). Also at Cerro de las Mesas, a raspada-incised black cylinder vessel with unclear provenience (associated with Burial I-20 that is not otherwise discussed in the report) has a design that is probably from the Terminal Preclassic or Early Classic period (Drucker 1943, plate 19a). Daneels (1997a) argues from excavated evidence that cylinder vessels without tripods were a characteristic form in the Veracruz Protoclassic, 100 B.C. to A.D. 100. We do not know exactly when or where cylinder vessels began to be outfitted with tripod supports. Although Teotihuacan did not originate the cylinder form, cylinder tripods were embraced and elaborated with characteristic proportions, supports, and decorations associated with that city. Such vases are recognizable stylistically in distant parts of Mesoamerica as part of a range of Teotihuacan influence. At Teotihuacan they may have functioned both as service ware and as offerings placed in burials and caches (e.g., Séjourné 1959:62, 64).

Some Classic period Mixtequilla cylinder vases are taller and narrower than Teotihuacan cylinder tripod vases and are better described as "beakerlike." Also, tripod supports are typical at Teotihuacan on cylinder vessels, but do not occur so regularly on cylinder vases in the Mixtequilla. Few tripod supports in the Mixtequilla closely resemble those at Teotihuacan. Only rarely do basal moldings like those at Teotihuacan occur on Mixtequilla cylinder tripods. Tripod supports are common in the Early Classic period in the Mixtequilla, but typically they are associated with low outflaring-walled bowls, not cylinder vases. Thus, the cylinder tripod as expressed at Teotihuacan was seldom slavishly imitated in the Mixtequilla, where low tripod bowls were much more frequent. A cached plain cylinder vessel filled with seashells at Cerro de las Mesas (Drucker 1943: 10, 12; Stark and Heller 1991:9–11) suggests a ritual linked to Teotihuacan, where seashells played a prominent symbolic role (Kolb 1987). Therefore, the cylinder or cylinder tripod form may have played one or more special roles in the Mixtequilla, especially when linked to ritual practices similar to those in the highland city.

Although I have taken pains to show the very modest level of Teotihuacan stylistic impact on Early Classic Mixtequilla ceramics, an important point is that Teotihuacan ceramic styles are the only ones to which Early Classic Mixtequilla production and consumption can be shown to have responded in a variety of ways. Contemporaneous Monte Albán and the many impressive Maya centers cannot be singled out as equivalent foci of attention. It appears there was a predominantly ritual interest in the distant realm of Teotihuacan.

In a reverse pattern, styles in the Gulf lowlands influenced people in highland capitals. Two scroll styles can be identified that developed in the Early Classic Gulf lowlands out of earlier stylistic patterns in the trans-Isthmian lowlands. One of the Gulf styles is the interlace style (specifically, the variant Yoke Style A) identified by Proskouriakoff (1953, 1954) and associated with northern or north-central Veracruz (Stark 1997a). For the interlace style in northern Veracruz, key distinguishing traits include Yoke Style A interlocking scrolls, bordering lines on scrolls and other motifs, a high frequency of scroll designs combined with hominids, connecting bands, and the use of bands dominating the arrangement of scrolls. Bands guiding the composition are rarely found among other scroll styles. Less frequently, interlace designs are focused on and rotated around a pivot motif. Only one of Proskouriakoff's (1954, fig. 2, yoke 16) artifacts resembles the Patarata scroll style in its use of masses of scrolls, and the resemblance occurs in only one area of the design. Thus, there is almost no "crossover" or mixing of these styles. No Mixtequilla artifacts have been found that display the Interlace style.

The other is the Patarata scroll style, associated with south-central Veracruz (Stark 1975, 1997a). The Patarata scroll style is best documented for the lower Papaloapan Basin. In the Mixtequilla, representational forms predominate among scroll designs, with scrolls often an appurtenance of the design. A strong focus on representational forms is shared with Proskouriakoff's interlace style. In the Mixtequilla, earth monsters (saurian)

are common, and hominids are less frequent. The reverse is true of the interlace style. The Mixtequilla and Patarata also yielded small abstract scroll panels or "cartouches" with masses of plump scrolls, usually with an emphasis line, and these features are shared with Monte Albán. Both Monte Albán and south-central Veracruz frequently show a fringe motif added to scrolls.

Mixtequilla scroll motifs are usually presented in a different context than elsewhere. They occur predominantly on figurines and molded appliques and only rarely on vessel sidewalls (both pottery and one wooden bowl). Three yoke fragments observed among PALM surface materials lacked scroll compositions, but yokes, palmas, and hachas (thought to be ball game paraphernalia) are the main venues for the interlace style. Only one stela displays the Patarata scroll style: a stela from Soyoltepec in the Tuxtla Mountains has a basal scroll panel surmounted by a Teotihuacan style striding figure (von Winning 1987:22).

An evaluation of scroll styles is based on a study of 11 motifs and 12 compositional traits (Table 9.1, Fig. 9.9) (Stark 1997a). The attributes form polythetic sets in the four locales or data sets I examined, but particular constellations of traits tend to distinguish each region.

Scroll styles are evident contemporaneously in selected contexts at Monte Albán and Teotihuacan. Early in Teotihuacan's history, scroll-dominated designs appear on public buildings, monuments, and ceramics. At Teotihuacan a variety of scroll-dominated compositions in murals, on vessels, and in other media are variously described as Totonac, Tajín, or Gulf Coast in inspiration. Never abundant at Teotihuacan, they are quite different from the usual compositions there. A few objects from Teotihuacan have a close relationship to the interlace style described by Proskouriakoff (1954). The clearest examples are the La Ventilla composite stone "ballcourt marker" and a possibly comparable round carving (Aveleyra 1963). These objects are good examples of Yoke

TABLE 9.1.
Description of Traits Used in Analysis of Scroll Styles

Scroll Composition Characteristics

1. Use of 180 degree rotation(s) to produce replicate patterns
2. Diagonal panels or bands
3. Diagonal divisions of layouts using a divider band or pattern (usually applied to diagonal panels or bands)
4. Pivoting of designs around a central element
5. Placement in a horizontal register
6. Placement in a "cartouche" or small rectangular or rounded, framed space
7. Placement in a large rectangular panel on the side of vessels
8. A repetitive series of discrete scrolls, usually found in a composition with horizontal register(s)
9. A repetitive series of continuous scrolls, i.e., a continuous line links and forms them; usually found in a composition with horizontal register(s)
10. A repetitive series with regular alternation of scrolls that have contrastive placement in which one descends and the next rises
11. Composition dominated by bands to which scrolls are subordinated or attached
12. Composition dominated by a mass of scrolls

Attributes of Scrolls or Added Elements to the Composition

13. Connecting bands, as described by Proskouriakoff (1953:391); straight bands are indicated by one or two lines that link scrolls to each other or to the surrounding frame; in simplified cases, this motif is similar to "fringe" lines (see trait 18)
14. A border on scrolls or other motifs created by a line following the outer contour of the motif
15. Yoke Style A interlocking scrolls (Proskouriakoff 1953, fig. 42a, b), which are laced together curl-to-curl but rotated 180 degrees in relation to each other
16. Representative forms, i.e., with readily recognizable referents, which can be divided into (a) saurian or serpentine creatures, (b) hominid, or (c) other
17. Emphasis line(s) usually following the inner curl of the scroll (or related forms) and emphasizing its contour
18. "Fringe" lines on scrolls, i.e., small lines, usually in sets or groups placed on the scroll itself along its outer edge but sometimes crossing the width of the scroll; fringe also may be placed in a rectangular area or form bearing several lines adjacent to a scroll
19. Bead(s) (circles) added to scrolls or other motifs in a scroll composition
20. Scroll pairs placed symmetrically curl-to-curl
21. Scroll pairs placed symmetrically stem-to-stem
22. Stepped scrolls (scroll stem is bent)
23. Double-ended or "snout" scrolls, in many cases seemingly representing a stylized maxilla of a serpentine or saurian creature, as interpreted by Bernal (1949)

Style A. Two mirror backs found in the cave under the Sun Pyramid are too fragmentary to place securely in the Interlace style (Heyden 1975:133), but one is a good possibility because border lines are present.

I have not included Teotihuacan murals in my trait analysis, in part because new murals at La Ventilla are not yet published and will add to the relevant materials. However, it is worth remarking that some early murals feature scroll designs (Cabrera 1992), including interlaced scrolls. Morelos (1991:110) shows various examples of scroll-dominated murals, including one with Yoke Style A interlocking scrolls.

Teotihuacan has distinctive innovations as well as a combination of traits more frequent in other styles. Other than cases with Yoke Style A designs, designs dominated by bands are rare, and masses of scrolls are more common (as with the lower Papaloapan Basin and Monte Albán). At Teotihuacan, arrange-

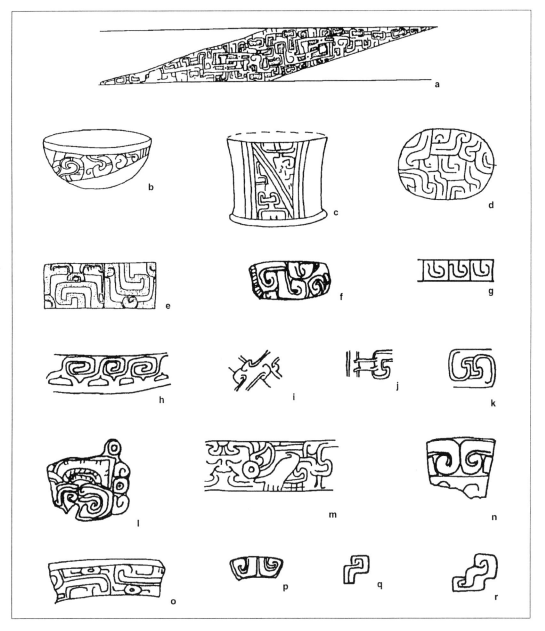

Fig. 9.9. Attributes analyzed concerning scroll designs, in numerical order when possible, with the source indicated. Each drawing is selected to illustrate some attributes clearly, but it may show others as well (in parenthesis); (a) attribute 1 (2, 12, 13, 14, 18, 19) (Berrin and Pasztory 1993, fig. 145), but I use an original drawing provided by Clare Yarborough, (b) attribute 2 (12, 13, 17, 18) (Séjourné 1966, fig. 202), (c) attributes 3 and 7 (1, 13) (Rattray 1992, plate X), (d) attribute 4 (6, 12, 17) (Bernal 1949, fig. 43), (e) attributes 5 and 10 (18, 19) (Séjourné 1966, fig. 122), (f) attributes 6, 12, and 18 (17) (Stark 1977, fig. 11b), (g) attribute 8 (5, 17) (Bernal 1949, fig. 27), (h) attribute 9 (5) (Séjourné 1966, fig. 111), (i) attribute 11 (Proskouriakoff 1953, fig. 41b), (j) attribute 13 (14) (Proskouriakoff 1953, fig. 40c), (k) attribute 14, 15 (Proskouriakoff 1953, fig. 40a), (l) attribute 16a (14, 18) (Stark 1997c, fig. 10.6j), (m) attribute 16b (13, 14, 15) (Proskouriakoff 1954, yoke 4), (n) attributes 17 and 20 (6, 12) (Stark 1977, fig. 17d), (o) attribute 19 (10, 14) (Séjourné 1959, fig. 123e), (p) attribute 21 (6, 12, 17) (Stark 1997c, fig. 8.7p), (q) attribute 22 (17) (Bernal 1949, fig. 48), (r) attribute 23 (17) (Bernal 1949, fig. 46). Drawings of (a), (c–k), and (m–r) are partial. Drawings are not to scale.

ments of masses of scrolls are more rigid or angular than elsewhere, however. Only at Teotihuacan (and Kaminaljuyú) have I located examples of 180 degree rotations to create semisymmetrical patterns. The use of a diagonal layout may represent a Teotihuacan or Monte Albán innovation. Interlocking U-shaped brackets may be a Teotihuacan innovation, probably a stylization of scroll motifs. Discrete series and running series scrolls are very abundant at Teotihuacan on pottery. In addition, scroll series often appear as borders on murals, on speech scrolls, and on cascading streams of offerings. This use of series scrolls eventually became a common subordinate aspect of Teotihuacan representational scenes, unlike scroll-dominated designs, which may be predominantly early.

At Monte Albán, scroll designs appear on pottery. Monte Albán shows a coincidence of scroll-dominated motifs and indications of Teotihuacan contacts, but without political or economic subordination to Teotihuacan. At Monte Albán during phase IIIA, A.D. 200–500, representational compositions are rare, and scroll designs usually transform any representational prototypes toward markedly abstract patterns. Bernal (1949) analyzed incised Monte Albán II–IIIA transition pottery, ca. A.D. 150–250 (dates from Spence 1992: 76), which provides the key evidence concerning scroll styles. However, Marcus and Flannery (1996:224, 230) consider these designs to be diagnostic of Monte Albán IIIA in the Early Classic period, A.D. 200–500. The chronological category of Monte Albán II–IIIA transition has been dropped in their schema. Bernal (1949) thought a saurian or serpentine form inspired the designs. In his view a double-ended "snout" scroll stands for the maxilla. If his interpretation is correct, the abstract content of many Monte Albán designs is similar to many of the more representational Mixtequilla scroll designs.

Very common at Monte Albán but scarce elsewhere are double-ended scrolls or stepped scrolls. Other local traits include designs with interlocking "L" brackets (Bernal 1949, figs. 5, 26, 28), which probably are

modifications of scroll motifs. The scroll-decorated, incised vessels draw heavily on Teotihuacan forms (e. g., cylinder tripods) and some layout traits found at Teotihuacan, such as diagonal bands, yet the scroll patterns at Monte Albán are not faithful versions of anything at Teotihuacan. Possibly they draw upon dual sources of inspiration, as there are some resemblances to the Patarata scroll style—the plump massed scrolls, cartouches, and emphasis lines.

A more detailed presentation concerning Early Classic scroll styles appears in Stark (1997a), and only a summary is presented here. Through analysis of scroll styles, two patterns are salient: the active sharing of scroll motifs among these localities or polities and the predominant tendency to reinterpret scroll styles locally. Both are signs of local craft elaboration and of cross-cutting elite social interaction rather than ultra-rare acquisitions from a distant realm or fabrication of rare local imitations due to impeded access. In the case of the few objects at Teotihuacan that are quite faithful to the Gulf interlace style (specifically, Yoke Style A), there is a possiblity of a Helmsian process, as there is in the Mixtequilla with respect to certain Teotihuacan ritual forms. However, Teotihuacan also developed local distinctive attributes in scroll motifs.

I conclude that Teotihuacan both borrowed and innovated scroll style traits, with south-central Veracruz or Monte Albán influencing the city stylistically in respect of massed scroll compositions. Even more striking is the influence of northern Veracruz, which was likely the origin zone for Yoke Style A and also the source of some imported vessels bearing scroll designs. No other exogenous style was drawn upon so frequently or prominently in Teotihuacan. In the Mixtequilla there was reciprocal interest in Teotihuacan pottery styles, especially vessels that may have had some ritual function, occasionally as faithful imitations but usually considerably transformed.

Monte Albán exhibits a local scroll style with more affinities to the Patarata scroll style than to Yoke Style A, but Monte Albán also exhibits distinctive local attributes. The scroll panels on Monte Albán vessels often appear on cylinder tripods, and the Early Classic occurrences are part of a broader pattern of elite political contacts with Teotihuacan that were commemorated in stone sculpture.

The scroll style evidence favors a mutualistic process during the Early Classic period, even though other evidence favors Teotihuacan as a stronger focus of elite emulation. In keeping with Pasztory's (1989) characterization of the Classic period, I find that each region has a clearly distinguishable "stamp" to its scroll-dominated designs. None of these regions or capitals seems to have commonly had close copies of the style associated with a different region. These multiple directions of stylistic imitation do not match Helms's model well, which would be more compatible with core-periphery assymetrical relationships in which a highly prestigious center formed a single stylistic reference point. I suspect, instead, that elite social ties and alliances that cross-cut political boundaries were responsible for some of the patterns, not necessarily always directly among these centers, but affecting people in them. Teotihuacan's attention to the interlace style and the Mixtequilla interest in selected Teotihuacan pottery and incense burners constitute possible exceptions to the social model and may conform better to Helms's model. However, these Teotihuacan-related items do not appear to be exclusive to Mixtequilla rulers or elites and it remains uncertain to what extent they circulated socially.

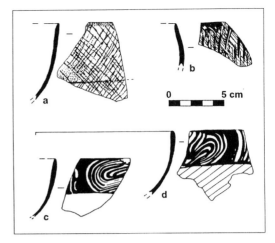

Fig. 9.10. Reversed false negative bowls; (a) code 33c, collection 1694; lower horizontal line is metallic sheen; above the line the slip is brown, below it the slip is orange; interior arrow indicates orange band; interior is brown with metallic sheen, (b) code 33c, collection 184, brown lines under orange slip, (c) code 33b, collection 1318, dark brown combed band and orange slip, (d) code 33b, collection 65.

LATE CLASSIC PERIOD, A.D. 600–900

In the Late Classic period, the decline of Teotihuacan is evident in a more diverse array of stylistic patterns in the Mixtequilla that perhaps drew upon Late Classic Maya patterns, instead of Teotihuacan, but mainly elaborated local styles for finely crafted vessels. The fact that Teotihuacan-related forms and decorations were dropped from the Mixtequilla repertoire is testimony to the selective interest in a prestigious outside center. The Teotihuacan-related traits obviously became irrelevant when Teotihuacan ceased to command international attention.

Smudge resist, resist slipping, and false negative techniques continued to be used during the Late Classic period to create a variety of elaborately decorated bowls. A new reversed false negative category employed a dark brown over-coating on a rim band that was then partly combed away to form a design (Fig. 9.10c, d); another consisted of criss-crossed lines painted or resist-applied on the exterior (Fig. 9.10a, b) (we have too few examples to determine the technological process exactly). There are additional elaborately decorated vessels from this period that had molded scenes ("Río Blanco" style vessels [von Winning 1971], not included in my quantitative assessment below).

Plumbate pottery was manufactured as early as the Late Classic period and became a widely exported, highly valued ceramic in Mesoamerica during the Early Postclassic pe-

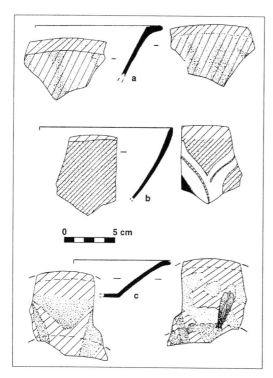

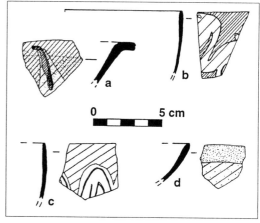

Fig. 9.12. Estrella Orange bowls. Metallic areas are stippled; (a) code 33a, collection 1821, (b) code 33a, collection 71, (c) code 33a, collection 67, (d) code 33a, collection 99.

Fig. 9.11. Estrella Orange bowls. Metallic areas are stippled; (a) code 33a, collection 1617, (b) code 33a, collection 1150, (c) code 33a, collection 938.

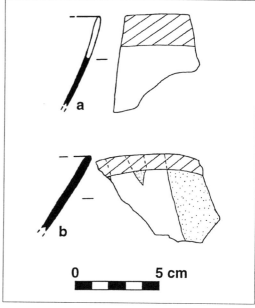

Fig. 9.13. Blanco White bowls with orange rim bands, code 44b; (a) collection 1053, (b) collection 347.

riod (Neff and Bishop 1988; Shepard 1948), although not one originating in a particularly prominent capital, so far as we know. Two body sherds of Plumbate were recovered in PALM survey, indicating that some vessels of this distinctive gray-to-orange, lustrous, metallic-appearing pottery reached the Mixtequilla; whether they date to the Late Classic or Early Postclassic period remains unknown. One Tohil Plumbate vessel (Early Postclassic period) was recovered by Drucker (1943:7) at Cerro de las Mesas, but the small PALM surface sherds cannot be assigned to San Juan (Late Classic period) versus Tohil Plumbate.

The Mixtequilla Late Classic period includes "metallic" bowls (code 25, not included in my quantitative analysis of fine bowls below). The metallic coating or slip has not been analyzed. Reents-Budet (pers. comm. 1997) has suggested alumina as a slip ingredient that might yield a metallic sheen.

Although the Mixtequilla "metallic" pottery might be an imitation of Plumbate, the paste is so coarse (and often poorly finished) that these bowls are too crude to be convincing. Instead, other bowls with a metallic overwash are better candidates: a few Mixtequilla fine paste, orange-slipped bowls had a metal-

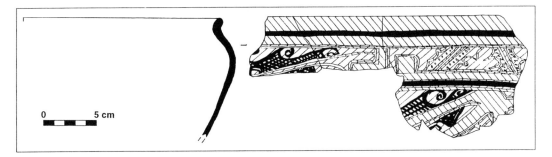

Fig. 9.14. Tuxtla Polychrome jar (code 45l, mound 1055, stratigraphic unit 308).

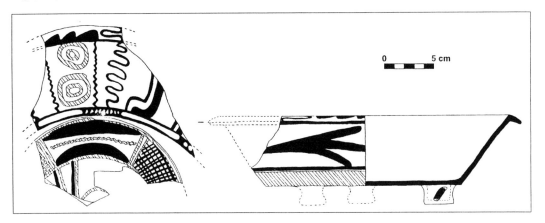

Fig. 9.15. Tuxtla Polychrome bowl (code 45b, mound 1055, stratigraphic unit 305).

lic wash over the orange slip. Because Plumbate fires orange and gray, these Mixtequilla vessels have more promise as an imitation of Plumbate. They appear quite similar to sherds of San Juan Plumbate that I observed in the Guatemalan Museo Nacional de Antropología e Historia. The presence of finer and coarser bowls with a metallic treatment could reflect a local quality gradient of imitative vessels inspired by Plumbate (or the reverse, if Plumbate production was shown to be derivative of south-central Veracruz production). In another type, Estrella Orange, vessels have a metallic overwash covering the sidewall, but they also bear a starburst negative design on the interior, which differentiates them clearly from Plumbate (Figs. 9.11, 9.12).

Additional fancy bowls from the Late Classic period include Blanco White bowls that are usually exceptionally hard and thin in the lower sidewall (Fig. 9.13). Occasionally they show an exterior white painted design creating a more opaque, subtle contrast to the white slip. Usually Blanco White bowls are differentially fired to a pinker tone at the lip, where an orange rim band was painted.

Possibly imported to the Mixtequilla from the western Tuxtlas in the Late Classic period (or else closely imitated) were Tuxtla Polychrome bowls (Figs. 9.14, 9.15). Tuxtla Polychrome may owe some of its inspiration to Classic Maya polychromes, but no detailed stylistic assessment has yet been made.

Thus, during the Late Classic period, elaborate bowls proliferated, including extremely thin-walled, hard ceramics with very fine paste. Metallic orange bowls and Tuxtla Polychrome (and some figurines, not discussed here) suggest local awareness of ceramic styles in the Maya lowlands and Pacific coast, but this outside pole of reference has a more tenuous and diffuse impact on the Mixtequilla than Teotihuacan had. Continued local elaboration of the regional tradition of dark-light decorative patterning with fluid designs characterizes the Late Classic period, along with the appearance of molded scenes on bowls that encoded detailed historical or ritual scenes (von Winning 1971). The portrayal of historic or ritual scenes on vessels is itself a point of correspondence with the Maya polychrome tradition, but a concern with display of historical events is present much earlier on Mixtequilla area stelae (Justeson and Kaufman 1993), and transfer of such representations to pottery may parallel Maya practice without indicating a derivation from the Maya area. Thus, the Late Classic evidence provides little support for viewing Mixtequilla pottery as sensitive to distant prestigious centers along the lines of Helms's cosmological interpretation. Instead, new developments within the local tradition suggest elaboration of fine crafts as a predominantly internal social process, partly replacing items that earlier were connected with an outside center stylistically (Teotihuacan).

QUANTITIES OF DECORATED BOWLS IN RELATION TO THE MODELS

Relative abundance and degree of restricted access are two diacritical features for the social versus cosmological models. All the decorated bowls are scarce but, in total, not extremely rare. Among the rim sherds at mound 1126 in the Early Classic period, all the elaborate bowl categories combined (82 among 3,646 rims) constitute 2.2 percent. At mounds 1055/1056 in the Late Classic period, these categories constitute 6.5 percent (317 among 4,833 rims). In comparison, at Patarata 52 where the less finely executed negative resist pottery predominates among decorated bowls, negative resist constitutes a peak of 12.4 percent in the Early Classic Camaron 1 subphase, dwindling to 4.3 percent in Camaron 2, and shrinking further to .4 percent in Camaron 3. In the Late Classic Limon phase, the overall frequency for two subphases combined is .1 percent, based on a single negative resist rim.

The reasons for the greater frequency of negative resist bowls in the early part of the Camaron phase at Patarata 52 compared to the Mixtequilla are unclear; different production and distribution networks may have been involved as well as the effects of the social hierarchy, with most of the Patarata bowls made from coarser paste. In any case, mounds 1126 and 1055/1056 in the Mixtequilla have a greater diversity of scarce fine bowls, particularly mounds 1055/1056. Except for the Camaron 1 and 2 subphases, the total percentage of decorated bowls at Patarata 52 is always less than at the Classic period residential excavations in the Mixtequilla, which I take to indicate that the Mixtequilla domestic excavations sampled households near a dominant center and with better access to higher-valued ceramics.

A more exacting analysis than I have attempted here would add slightly to the quantity and considerably to the variety of Mixtequilla fine bowls but would not change the values for Patarata 52. The additional categories require extra work to quantify because they are not singled out with a separate code; because of limitations of time, I do not quantify them here. For example, extremely highly burnished bowls that achieve a satiny, glassy finish on a variety of slips are rarely present in the Mixtequilla in the Early Classic period, but do not occur in Patarata collections. As another example, during the Late Classic period, carved or molded vessels are rare in the Mixtequilla and absent at Patarata 52. The mold-impressed vessels with complex "codexlike" scenes encoded esoteric knowledge of ritual and perhaps history (von Winning 1971).

Despite the modest quantities of the various decorated bowl categories, they are relatively widespread in the Mixtequilla, suggesting considerable social circulation. Some categories, such as the molded Río Blanco vessels, may prove to have very restricted access, however. On the whole, the abundance and distribution of elaborate serving vessels is more in keeping with the effects of elite social interaction than of acquisition from afar or of patronized crafts that only were used primarily in royal circles.

SUMMARY

Decorated serving bowls proliferated in the Mixtequilla during the Classic period compared to the Preclassic period. Nevertheless, they are infrequent enough to suggest restricted social access. Spatial patterning supports this inference because of the generally lesser quantities and diversity of fine decorated bowls at Patarata 52 and the lower Río Cotaxtla drainage (Daneels 1988). At present, it remains uncertain to what extent we should view the restricted access to the finest bowls as related to the social contexts in which they were used or to wealth differences among households.

During the Early and Late Classic periods alike, a local tradition predominates in respect of elaborately decorated ceramics. These vessels only occasionally are imbued with possibly sacred motifs, such as the serpent form on a negative resist bowl at Patarata 52 (Stark 1989:64), the feline in Figure 9.6, or the PALM mold-impressed vessels (Stark 1997c). Although likely restricted in access in various ways, Mixtequilla fine serving vessels are present in sufficient quantitites that most do not readily match the "acquisitive" importation or imitation discussed by Helms (1993), for which extreme scarcity is an important trait. In fact, local Mixtequilla fine ceramics seem to have had differential but wide distribution in the region, perhaps more analogous to polychromes in the Maya lowlands than to, say, imported Plumbate pottery in most parts of Mesoamerica.

Occasional imitation or importation of styles associated with distant capitals occurs during both the Early and Late Classic periods. This process is multidirectional in the case of the Early Classic period. Scroll styles show Teotihuacan attention to a Gulf interlace stylistic tradition, and, likewise, Teotihuacan enjoyed special interest or esteem for the lower Papaloapan Basin inhabitants during the Early Classic period. Mixtequilla people with access to elaborate pottery in the Early Classic period were aware of forms and decorative styles elsewhere, but only a few Teotihuacan vessels were closely imitated.

More a propos for the Classic period than cosmologically significant acquisition of ceramics from afar is elite interaction among polities combined with an internal process in which local fine crafts were controlled in an expression of internal social cleavages. As noted before, an important role for fine local crafts supports aspects of both models. I suspect that a degree of reliance upon items linked stylistically to Teotihuacan during the Early Classic period is tied to the lower frequency of PALM fine serving bowls during that time compared to the Late Classic period. Exotic allusions played a greater role when the Mixtequilla existed in the shadow of a city of extraordinary importance in Mesoamerica.

Teotihuacan's attraction to the interlace Yoke Style A from northern Veracruz might be an effort early in its history to draw upon a distant prestigious style associated with ritual (in part, the ball game) and upon special imported vessels, but it remains complex to explain because of the complicating effect of "ethnic barrios" in the city and the possibility that a Gulf lowland enclave played some role in the knowledge of and access to northern Veracruz. Thus, the early attention to the interlace style at Teotihuacan may not be an instance of the Helmsian model in a simple way.

In the Mixtequilla, the attention to Teotihuacan ritual forms during the Early Classic period constitutes the main support for Helms's perspective. However, the spatial distribution of the items linked to Teotihuacan is not particularly restrictive and does not rule out cross-cutting social processes of exchange or imitation rather than the cosmological and politically focused ties to rulers that she stressed. The bulk of the fine ceramics reflects a local fascination with light-dark patterning and transparency effects of multiple slips. The substantially autochthonous Early Classic period tradition underwent considerable elaboration during the Late Classic period. Perhaps metallic-appearing finishes were responsive to San Juan Plumbate during the Late Classic period, and perhaps an interest in a polychrome style associated with the Tuxtla Mountains was responsive to Late Classic Maya polychromes. However, autochthonous styles were paramount in the Late Classic period in the absence of a clear choice of a prestigious distant capital.

This assessment of Mixtequilla ceramics points to a better fit with an elite social interaction model than with Helms's (1993) cosmological and political model. The indications of a regional stylistic tradition suggest an important role for small-scale specialist production, perhaps by attached or controlled artisans. Local fine crafts can support either model. Stylistic references to outside sacred realms are a possible interpretation for a few ceramic and other items, but the circulation of these articles is sufficiently broad to suggest an active social process that had a differentiating but not very exclusive effect. Mesoamerican Classic period states seem to better exemplify elite interactions in a "peer polity" setting than processes of "acquisition" of cosmologically significant items from poorly known "distant" realms, at least with respect to ceramics. Other exotic or finely crafted products may provide a better fit with Helms's patterns, however, such as the importation of seashells to Teotihuacan.

10

Tecomates, Residential Mobility, and Early Formative Occupation in Coastal Lowland Mesoamerica

PHILIP J. ARNOLD III

Archaeological interest in ceramics has a long tradition in studies of Formative period Mesoamerica. In fact, convention dictates that the Formative period (1500 B.C.–A.D. 150) began with the widespread occurrence of pottery, coupled with the adoption of agriculture and a settled way of life (Coe 1994: 42; Willey and Phillips 1958:144–151). The impact of this cultural conversion is clearly visible by the end of the period—the combination of maize, sedentism, and ceramics supported large, complex Late Formative societies centered at sites like Monte Albán in Oaxaca, El Mirador in Guatemala, and Tres Zapotes in Veracruz. The onset of the Classic period is heralded, not by a major change in subsistence, settlement, or ceramics, but rather by the appearance of long-count calendrics and hieroglyphic script.

According to Hoopes (1994), the linkages among pottery, sedentism, and agriculture is a legacy of Childe's (1951) Neolithic Revolution and its subsequent application to New World contexts. New World archaeologists viewed these three traits as a cultural package that originated within one part of the Americas and diffused into other regions (Willey and Phillips 1958; cf. Ford 1969:5). Interest in the transition from Archaic to Formative period cultures, therefore, was devoted primarily to establishing the vectors along which cultural influence moved from one portion of the Americas to another.

Like their colleagues who work in other regions of the New World, Mesoamerican archaeologists are beginning to unbundle these three separate characteristics of cultural activity. It now appears that the Archaic-to-Formative period transition did not occur full blown or even at the same pace throughout Mesoamerica, but rather was configured differently in different contexts. For example, sedentism is now documented in highland Mexico well before an agrarian lifestyle appeared (e.g., Niederberger 1987). Moreover, new research suggests that pottery may have developed in Mesoamerica prior to a maize-dominated subsistence strategy (Blake et al. 1992; Clark 1994). The final linkage, between pottery and sedentism, is now under closer scrutiny (e.g., Barnett and Hoopes 1995).

This paper explores the issue of Formative period transitions from the context of the Mesoamerican coastal lowlands. Specifically, I am interested in the degree to which residential mobility continued as an adaptation from the Archaic period into the Early Formative period (1500–900 B.C.). Although residential mobility is a consistently sounded theme for the Archaic period, few archaeologists have drawn attention to the possible "overflow" of this settlement organization into the Early Formative period. To read most accounts of this transition, one would think that Mesoamerican groups became sedentary, took up agriculture, and adopted pottery as soon as they crossed the threshold from one period to the next. Apparently, few Mesoamerican archaeologists would argue with Michael Coe's (1994:38) reference to pottery as "that index fossil of fully sedentary life."

The *tecomate,* a globular, neckless jar with a restricted orifice, is perhaps the most prevalent ceramic form encountered in Early Formative lowland Mesoamerican assemblages (Fig. 10.1). Archaeologists have long been interested in the function of tecomates and have proposed a wide range of scenarios to account for the origin and ubiquity of this vessel type. Left unexplored in most cases, however, is a second important characteristic of tecomates—namely, their almost virtual disappearance from lowland Mesoamerican assemblages by the Late Formative period (400 B.C.–A.D. 150).

Models that address the appearance and widespread use of tecomates on one hand should be able to account for the absence of these vessels during subsequent periods. In this paper I propose that tecomates were a multipurpose container whose design constituted a weighted compromise responding to several performance requirements. As one component of this compromise, I suggest that tecomates were utilized within a cultural adaptation that included nonagrarian residential mobility. The disappearance of tecomates, in turn, was associated with an increased reliance on maize agriculture and the transition to a fully sedentary settlement organization.

I also argue that archaeologists lack adequate theory to evaluate how residential mobility would condition the organization of ceramic technology. By residential mobility I mean a settlement-subsistence adaptation that departs from year-round, permanent site occupation (cf. Rafferty 1985:115–116). By technology I refer to the sum total of materials, actions, and knowledge by which products are intentionally created and employed (Schiffer and Skibo 1987:595). The organization of technology implicates the selection and combination of strategies through which technology is successfully integrated within a behavioral system (Nelson 1991:57).

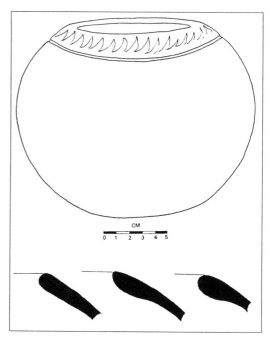

Fig. 10.1. An example of an Early Formative *tecomate,* along with *tecomate* rim profiles from La Joya, Veracruz, Mexico.

I arrange the following discussion in several sections. First, I provide archaeological data from lowland coastal Mesoamerica that strongly implicate a residentially mobile, nonagrarian use-context for tecomates. I also indicate that the disappearance of tecomates is strongly associated with a significantly different archaeological assemblage, one that clearly involves sedentism and corn agriculture.

Second, I consider the organization of ceramic technology and explore why research in this arena lags behind other fields of ceramic study. I briefly contextualize tecomates within Mesoamerican archaeology and discuss previous attempts to interpret this vessel form. Next, I consider tecomate design in terms of residential mobility, vessel function, and food preparation. I also address the issue of vessel elaboration in terms of decoration versatility and possible caching behavior. Finally, I summarize the presentation and make an appeal for improved theory devoted to the organization of ceramic technology.

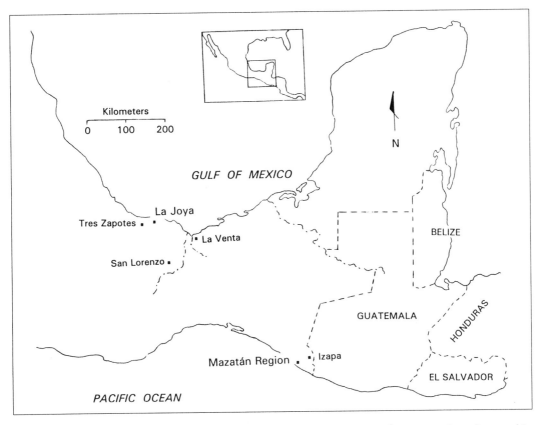

Fig. 10.2. Lowland coastal Mesoamerica, indicating Gulf Coast and Pacific Coast regions discussed in the text.

FORMATIVE PERIOD ARCHAEOLOGY IN
COASTAL LOWLAND MESOAMERICA

Most Early Formative period archaeological research in coastal lowland Mesoamerica has been undertaken at a restricted number of sites, usually with the intent to establish the temporal sequence and context of iconography on megalithic sculpture. Moreover, the dominant paradigm is that corn agriculture and sedentism were responsible for the social context within which megalithic sculpture was created and displayed (e.g., Diehl 1996). Obviously, residential mobility has not been an important research focus for Early Formative sites.

Nonetheless, a few recent studies do provide some tantalizing and suggestive evidence for Early Formative residential mobility. One such study involves the site of La Joya, located within the Tuxtla Mountains of southern Veracruz, Mexico (P. Arnold 1997;

P. Arnold et al. 1996). A second investigation was carried out within the Mazatán region of Mexico, along the Pacific Coast (Clark 1994). Both present data, albeit in differing degrees, that relate to the issue of residential mobility.

RESIDENTIAL MOBILITY AT LA JOYA

The La Joya Archaeological Project is designed to gather information on household-level settlement and subsistence activities dating to the Formative period. Specifically, the goal is to investigate the pattern of land usage and economic activities that characterized Early Formative period occupation along the Gulf lowlands (Fig. 10.2). Based on initial assessments of the La Joya surface material, the site was described as an agrarian, sedentary occupation (Santley and Arnold 1996). Nonetheless, La Joya did not exhibit the trappings of complexity that characterized previously studied Early Formative Gulf Olmec settlements.

Although situated within the Tuxtla Mountains, La Joya is considered to be part of lowland Mesoamerica by virtue of its topographic position below the 1,000 m elevation mark (e.g, Stark and Arnold 1997). The site is located along the southern side of the Catemaco River, the largest waterway that drains the western portion of the Tuxtlas. La Joya includes a sequence of occupation that begins with the Early Formative and ends with the Late Classic period. Occupation was not continuous, however; Middle Formative period (900–400 B.C.) presence is poorly represented on the site.

The available data suggest that Late Formative occupation at La Joya represents a sedentary, agrarian lifestyle. Settlement patterns from the Tuxtlas indicate the presence of a three-tiered settlement hierarchy during the Late Formative (Santley and Arnold 1996). Macrobotanical remains of corn are present and the remnants of a furrowed agricultural field were encountered in excavations. Storage pits are large (2–2.5 cubic m) and occasionally contain burials. Residential architecture includes platform mounds (also with burials) and associated pit features.

The artifact assemblage contains evidence of intensive grinding as represented by two-handed manos and footed slab metates. The chipped stone industry is dominated by obsidian prismatic blades. The Late Formative ceramic assemblage exhibits an array of vessel forms, including bowls with inward-leaning walls, cylindrical vessels, a range of plate forms, dishes, several types and sizes of jars, and a few tecomates. Vessel decoration includes "false" differential firing, fine incision on out-flaring bowl rims, and hematite-filled incision on silhouette composite bowls. Slipping is present, but surface texturing is comparatively rare.

In contrast, the Early Formative complex at La Joya suggests a considerably different adaptation. As noted above, data from surface survey indicated that Early Formative La Joya was a farming community (Santley and Arnold 1996; also Santley 1992). A program

of excavation allowed us to reevaluate this characterization.

Unlike the extensive surface distribution of material, subsurface patterns at La Joya reveal that Early Formative occupation concentrated at several "hotspots" on the landscape. In contrast to the Late Formative occupation, these earlier loci contain no evidence of mounded construction or other investment in permanent architecture. Instead, occupation is reflected in numerous compact (but not specially prepared) activity surfaces. Construction evidence includes a series of postmolds, suggesting an oval-shaped structure associated with a single, shallow exterior pit. There is no indication, however, of prepared walls, foundations, or other labor investment in the structure.

The ground stone industry from Early Formative La Joya suggests a multifunctional technology. One-handed manos are most common; many of these artifacts exhibit use-wear on one or both ends and may have also functioned as pestles. Metates have small grinding surfaces and a few pieces of stone bowls were recovered. The Early Formative obsidian industry is dominated by flakes and angular debris, implying a more generalized chipped stone technology.

Tecomates are the most common vessel form in the Early Formative ceramic assemblage at La Joya; bowls and flat-bottom dishes occur in lower proportions. Decoration on the tecomates is confined to texturing, slipping, scoring, and incising. Differential firing is introduced toward the end of the Early Formative sequence.

As important to this discussion is what Early Formative La Joya lacks relative to the later occupation. Macrobotanical corn remains are absent, as is any evidence of agricultural field features. No burials were recovered from the Early Formative deposit. Also missing are the large storage pits common in Late Formative occupations (Pool 1997). Instead, we find small, relatively shallow (70-by-40-by-30 cm) ovoid pit features. These features occasionally contain fire-cracked rock and often exhibit a fire-hardened clay band along the upper third of the pit (although prepared lips and clay bottoms are absent). Particularly noteworthy is the fact that these features invariably cluster together (they are very rare in isolation) and they often cut into one another in palimpsest fashion. These patterns suggest that areas of the landscape were reused through time, and unlike the Late Formative occupation, specific features were not used intensively (Pool 1997).

If we were to ignore the presence of pottery for the moment, there would be little reason to interpret Early Formative La Joya as a fully sedentary occupation. Rather, as currently understood, the data indicate repeated occupation by a residentially mobile group, possibly on a seasonal basis. There is no direct evidence for a sedentary or agrarian lifeway, and the nonceramic portion of the assemblage suggests a broad spectrum and flexible subsistence strategy that combined fish, fowl, and floral resources (P. Arnold 1997).

RESIDENTIAL MOBILITY IN THE MAZATÁN REGION? As noted above, Early Formative non-elite contexts are rarely the focus of research in lowland coastal Mesoamerica. Nonetheless, data recently reported by John Clark and associates (Blake et al. 1992; Clark 1994; Clark and Blake 1994) provide an interesting complement to the La Joya information. Clark's (1994) study involves the Formative Period occupation within the Mazatán region along Mexico's Pacific Coast (Fig. 10.2). Similar to the La Joya sequence, Clark's (1994) research documents a nonagrarian adaptation (dating to the Barra phase [1550–1400 B.C.]) that is followed by a corn-based subsistence economy. Noteworthy is the fact that a variety of the archaeological patterns identified at La Joya are mimicked in Clark's (1994) data. Although Clark (1994:196) believes that the Barra phase marks the beginning of "true sedentism" in his region, the marked similarities between the Mazatán region and La Joya data sets suggest that a reconsideration of the Barra phase settlement organization could be in order.

Like the pattern at Early Formative La Joya, tecomates are the overwhelming vessel type in the Barra phase assemblage (Clark 1994:184). And like Early Formative La Joya, the Barra phase ground stone industry includes one-handed manos (also used as pestles), metates with comparatively small surface areas, and in general is characterized as "unspecialized, inefficient, and light weight" (Clark 1994:236). The chipped stone industry is also dominated by obsidian chips and flakes, as opposed to prismatic blades (e.g., Lowe 1967). Carbon isotope analysis of skeletal material suggests that corn, although present, constituted a minor part of the Early Formative diet (Blake et al. 1992; Clark 1994:237).

Similar to the Early Formative Tuxtla survey data, the Barra phase survey region exhibits a two-tiered site hierarchy (Clark 1994:196). Barra phase structures are characterized by "minimal preparation and no evidence of platform construction" (Clark 1994:313). Several series of postmolds were encountered. These apparently formed oval-shaped structures but there is no evidence of wall foundations. Several "hearths" were associated with these activity areas and, like the Early Formative La Joya pattern, cluster horizontally and vertically (Clark 1994:317, fig. 83). Particularly noteworthy is Clark's (1994:32) belief that Barra phase residential occupation represents "significant continuity of basic construction techniques and styles from the Late Archaic period."

These patterns, obtained from opposite sides of the Mexican isthmus, suggest that similar processes were at work in Early Formative lowland coastal Mesoamerica. The artifact assemblages are comparable in terms of ceramics, chipped stone, and ground stone. The pattern in residential construction is consistent. The form of hearths, and their frequent grouping, is a common theme. All of these lines of evidence suggest a pattern of residential mobility rather than a fully sedentary occupation (cf. Clark 1994:196).

In contrast, the succeeding periods in both areas indicate that a decline in the proportion of tecomates is associated with radical shifts in the remaining spheres of settlement and adaptation. Within the Mazatán region, the percentage of tecomates drops from just over

80 percent in the Barra phase to just under 56 percent in the subsequent Locona phase (Clark 1994, figs. 71, 72). Importantly, it is during this Locona phase that mound construction appears, as do significant differences in the size of residential platforms and the status of their occupants (Clark 1994: 344). A four-tiered site hierarchy develops during the Locona phase (Clark 1994:197) and a "reasonable [population] estimate would be about an 800 percent increase between the end of the Barra phase and the end of the Locona phase, a 150 year span in sidereal time" (Clark 1994:213). Finally, Clark (1994:215) believes that the location of Locona phase settlement was "significantly related to agricultural activity."

In sum, both La Joya and the sites within the Mazatán region display similar patterning in their respective archaeological assemblages. During those portions of the Early Formative period when the reliance on corn is minor, when residential construction is minimal, and when settlement organization may have included a residentially mobile component, tecomates dominate the ceramic field. In contrast, when there is strong evidence for corn agriculture and a sedentary occupation, tecomate proportions decline appreciably.

This patterning suggests that tecomates as a class of pottery are sensitive to the settlement and subsistence adaptation of Early Formative lowland groups. It also suggests that tecomates may have served a wide variety of use-related activities. Finally, the data indicate that, despite conventional treatment of the Archaic-to-Formative transition in lowland coastal Mesoamerica, tecomates may not have been the product of a sedentary occupation. When interpreting the archaeological record from this juncture the simple presence of pottery should not outweigh the implications of the remaining site assemblage.

CERAMICS AND RESIDENTIAL MOBILITY: IMPLICIT RESISTANCE

Interest in the links between residential mobility and ceramic containers is not new (e.g.,

Linton 1944). Recent systematic research into this relationship has emphasized vessel transportability, especially as reflected in choices involving temper (Hunt 1991; Schiffer and Skibo 1987; Skibo et al. 1989b). Transportability, however, constitutes but one important characteristic of tools employed by residentially mobile groups. For example, research into lithic technology has established several dimensions useful for assessing the interface between residential mobility and tool design (Nelson 1991). Nonetheless, despite a growing consensus that pottery functions within contexts of residential mobility (D. Arnold 1985; Barnett and Hoopes 1995; Reid 1989; Schiffer and Skibo 1987; Simms et al. 1997), there are practically no corresponding models for the organization of ceramic technology (e.g., Nelson 1987). What other factors besides transportability might affect technological decisions? How important is versatility, or pressures for a multifunctional, as opposed to a function-specific, design? To what degree are certain activities, such as resource procurement, embedded within other tasks (e.g., DeBoer 1984)? How might caching ceramics (e.g., Graham 1994; Ozker 1982) impact decisions of vessel design? And how might design elaboration be affected by the production of pottery intended to serve as site furniture (e.g., Simms et al. 1997)?

Contributors to a recent edited volume on the origins of pottery (Barnett and Hoopes 1995) demonstrate that, time and time again, ceramics were adopted and elaborated within nonsedentary and nonagrarian contexts. In order to understand the adoption and implementation of ceramic technology, archaeologists must approach ceramic use from a broader technological perspective, one that more fully considers settlement organization and residential mobility. This approach is common for lithic technology; why has interest in the organization of ceramic technology apparently lagged?

Several possible reasons come to mind. First, archaeological models depend heavily on the extant ethnographic record, and the number of documented mobile or even semisedentary pottery-using groups is relatively small (e.g., D. Arnold 1985). The apparent tendency has been to accept this pattern as representative of ancient societies as well. Furthermore, a small sample restricts the number of potential analogues in source-side reasoning (e.g., Wylie 1985). In addition, documentation of pottery use and residential mobility is uneven, making it difficult to compare between groups and thus tease out general patterns.

As a consequence, there has been comparatively little subject-side application of these source-side models, especially in the Mesoamerican archaeological literature. In other words, there are few instances in which Mesoamerican archaeologists have suggested that a residentially mobile, pottery-using group was represented at a site. Furthermore, pottery-use among New World mobile groups is often framed in the context of a cooking technology that emphasizes stone boiling (e.g., Reid 1989; Sassaman 1993), which does not appear to characterize the early Mesoamerican pottery technology. This distinction is important, as the technological requirements of ceramic containers designed to retain heat may be very different from cooking pots designed to conduct heat (e.g., Reid 1989; Skibo and Schiffer 1995).

Traditional models of ceramics and subsistence strongly associate pottery usage with agriculture and, by extension, sedentism (Rafferty 1985:133; Willey and Phillips 1958). And while this relationship certainly occurs within contemporary and ancient contexts, there is no necessary relationship among any of these three conditions (Hoopes and Barnett 1995:4–5). These findings make it clear that the relationships between the organization of ceramic technology and settlement-subsistence activities are extremely relevant to studies of ancient societies.

TECOMATES IN FORMATIVE PERIOD COASTAL LOWLAND MESOAMERICA

Tecomates constitute the most common vessel form in Early Formative coastal lowland Mesoamerican assemblages, although other forms (dishes, bowls, and bottles) may occur in low frequencies. As noted above, tecomates have a distinctive globular shape with a restricted access to the interior. The lip of a tecomate is frequently thickened on the interior and walls become relatively thin as one moves downward past the vessel's shoulder (a "comma-shaped lip" [Ford 1969:92]). The ceramic paste of coastal lowland Mesoamerican tecomates exhibits a variety of inorganic inclusions, including quartz, feldspar, and volcanic ash. Fiber-tempered tecomates have not been reported for Early Formative coastal lowland Mesoamerican assemblages.

Tecomates occur in a wide range of sizes (less than 0.5 liters to over 20 liters) and are finished using a host of surface treatments. Along the Pacific Coast the most elaborately decorated tecomates appear first, and are followed by undecorated vessels (Clark 1994; Clark and Gosser 1995), although this sequence is not necessarily repeated in other lowland assemblages. Tecomates are also recovered in a variety of use-related states, some with obvious interior and exterior sooting while others do not appear to have been subject to post-production thermal exposure.

Archaeological discussions of tecomates customarily note the similarity between its form and the shape of bottle gourds (*Lagenaria siceraria*) and squash (*Cucurbita pepo*). These same plants are among some of the earliest domesticates in Mesoamerica and may have served originally as containers. Given the formal similarity between these items, some archaeologists suggest that the tecomate represents the ceramic extension and functional equivalent of gourds (e.g., Lowe 1971). Other researchers propose that gourds were used as molds to produce Early Formative pottery (Flannery and Marcus 1994:47).

To claim a logical sequence from gourd to tecomate does not, however, account for *why* that specific form was selected. Nor is there any necessary link between the use of a dried vegetable and the function of a ceramic container. Other "natural" objects could have been mimicked just as easily or served just as ably in pottery manufacture. The fact that the specific tecomate form was adopted, and persisted for several hundred years in some contexts, indicates that it served well its users and should provide a hint as to its function.

TECOMATES: MULTIFUNCTIONAL OR SPECIAL PURPOSE

Tecomate use is linked directly (rarely) or indirectly (frequently) to everything from ritual containers (Clark and Gosser 1995) to steaming maize tamales (Coe and Flannery 1967:81) to cooking manioc (Green and Lowe 1967; Lowe 1971). Obviously, a program of residue analysis is desperately needed. But even assuming that distinct chemical or isotope profiles were obtained, residue analysis would only indicate what a specific tecomate was used for; it would not necessarily indicate the function of tecomates as an artifact class. In fact, assumptions that tecomates served a task-specific function constitute part of the narrow approach to studies of this vessel type. Are there reasons to believe that tecomates had a specific function; i.e., were designed for only one task?

The most recent and thorough treatment of tecomates would suggest a resounding affirmative. Clark and associates (Clark 1994; Clark and Blake 1994; Clark and Gosser 1995) have considered the function of tecomates found in Early Formative deposits of the Mazatán region. Their research suggests that the tecomates of this area are the product of competitive feasting and ritual drinking among self-aggrandizers. Their Barra phase tecomates are characterized as "fancy vessels" with "exhaustive and labor intensive" exterior treatment that occur in a "limited range of forms" (Clark and Gosser 1995:215). The preponderance of tecomates in the ceramic assemblage implies a "restricted inventory" of vessels that "represents a similarly restricted set of uses and functions" (Clark and Gosser 1995:215). Clark (1994:253) found no evidence for fire-related use on basal portions of these vessels. Since the tecomates appear "not to have been appropriate for general food preparation" (Clark and Gosser 1995:215) they are in-stead interpreted as "special containers used to serve especially important liquids [atole, corn beer, chocolate] on special occasions, such as ritual drinking" (Clark and Gosser 1995:216). Finally, many of these vessels are thought to be "commissioned goods" (Clark 1994:266) produced by attached specialists.

The singular function of tecomates as ritual serving containers is thus based primarily on three assumptions. The first assumption equates the "fancy" character of an artifact with a nonutilitarian function. The second view holds that relatively high labor investment in decoration reflects a context of specialized production. The final belief is that a narrow range of forms is synonymous with a specialized function. Below I consider each assumption in turn.

The idea that "fancy" means "nonutilitarian" is perhaps the most common implicit assumption in artifact characterization. And it is certainly true that special-purpose ceramics often exhibit greater elaboration than their domestic utilitarian counterparts. But the relationship between ceramic decoration and use-context is considerably more complex than a simple "this-or-that" dichotomy. Ceramic style is regulated by a different set of principles than mechanical performance (Braun 1983:113). Consequently, decoration may be a poor measure of utilitarian purpose (see below).

Furthermore, when making statements about "fancy" versus "plain" pottery, the implication is that an assemblage contains both sets of ceramics. Otherwise, such a comparison is spurious. Noteworthy is the fact that the Barra phase assemblage discussed above *does not* appear to have many undecorated components. Besides "a small proportion of relatively coarse, buff vessels (these are extremely elaborate but are slipped only on the red rim-band and sometimes on a basal band), all Barra vessels are finely slipped and highly burnished" (Clark and Gosser 1995: 212). So common is decoration, in fact, that "an unmodified surface on a Barra sherd is unusual" (Clark and Gosser 1995:213).

The fact that almost all vessels are treated equally in terms of labor investment and degree of decoration need not suggest a specialized function. Rather, it could just as easily represent a decoration strategy whereby the degree of decoration is intended to be "appropriate" within a variety of potential use-related contexts. In other words, investment in decoration is targeted for multipurpose social contexts, rather than a special purpose social context. Such design versatility may not be expected in the sedentary settlement contexts that Clark (1994:196) envisions for the Barra phase. As noted below, however, it makes considerable sense within the context of a residentially mobile settlement strategy.

The second underlying assumption in characterizations of the Barra assemblage is that high labor investment implicates patronized craft specialization. Obviously there is an association between the product of patronized specialists and the amount of labor invested in a given artifact. Nonetheless, ceramic producers within domestic contexts may also manufacture pottery imbued with high energy investment. Among the Maghreb household potters of North Africa, for example, Balfet (1965) noted with admiration the degree of energy investment in the pottery. She states that the greatest variability in production:

> is found in the *finishing and decoration* of the pottery. . . Finishing is always carefully done, and pottery objects . . . pass again and again through the hands of the part time potter who devotes hours to polishing the slip to get a uniform smooth and brilliant finish. . . . Moreover, they show great freedom in the choice of decorative compositions. (Balfet 1965:165–166, original emphasis)

The point is not to disagree that ceramic specialists manufacture specialized pottery. Rather, it should be clear that many potters are capable of producing highly decorated ceramics. The question, therefore, is what contexts might encourage potters, whatever their "level" of production, to engage in this kind of energy investment (e.g., P. Arnold 1991b: 96–97).

Clark's (1994; Clark and Blake 1994; Clark and Gosser 1995) final assumption

centers on associating uniformity of shape with singularity of function. Nonetheless, in many cases relative design uniformity is an indicator of tool versatility, not a mark of functional specialization. A versatile artifact is "maintained in a generalized form to meet a variety of needs" (M. Nelson 1991:70). The common biface is perhaps the quintessential example of an artifact whose generalized design allows for a variety of uses. Nonetheless, the presence of a biface on an archaeological site would not be taken as direct evidence for a narrow range of activities; rather, biface design reflects a compromise response to a wide range of possible uses. An important point to remember is that a versatile tool rarely constitutes the most efficient or "optimal" design for any particular task; it is the compromise between anticipated tasks that primarily dictates tool design (Braun 1983:109; M. Nelson 1991:73; Schiffer and Skibo 1987:599).

In sum, the degree to which tecomates were special-purpose containers is questionable. Even the most thorough study of this vessel form is undermined by preconceptions of settlement organization and unwarranted assumptions about decorative elaboration. Moreover, the widespread occurrence and relative longevity of the design suggest that is was not a special purpose container. Almost all archaeologists to date evaluate the function of tecomates within the context of a sedentary, usually agrarian settlement system. In contrast, I believe that the specific characteristics of tecomates make the most sense when viewed in terms of residential mobility and the organization of ceramic technology.

TECOMATE DESIGN AND RESIDENTIAL MOBILITY
Thus far we have considered artifacts without reference to the residential context within which they perform. Archaeologists recognize that multipurpose tool kits and versatile designs are strongly influenced by the settlement and subsistence activities of a particular group. Specifically, a versatile design is anticipated when a range of use-options is required. One such context that would select for tool versatility is residential mobility.

How might the formal characteristics of tecomates fair against the requirements of this type of settlement organization?

An immediate question, of course, is to what degree residentially mobile groups make and use pottery. As noted above, there is clear evidence that ethnographic groups behaved in this fashion (D. Arnold 1985; Linton 1944; Mills 1985) and there is increasing evidence that the combination of ceramics and residential mobility was considerably more common in the past (Barnett and Hoopes 1995; Simms et al. 1997). Consequently, concerns based on this first issue can be readily allayed.

Next we should consider what characteristics pottery might display within a residentially mobile system. What are the expectations about vessel form, paste characteristics, and other traits as affected by residential mobility? Some data are available from the ethnographic record. Other insight is available from replicative and performance characteristics studies. Common sense can be used to fill in the gaps.

As Braun (1983) suggests, pots are tools and as part of tool kits are conditioned by certain performance requirements. According to Braun (1983:108) "mechanical performance characteristics" speak to the effectiveness or suitability of a container to meet specific tasks. Vessel shape or morphology is one dimension of design that reflects intended function and highlights the performance of a given pot (Hally 1986; Rice 1987; Smith 1985).

Mills (1985) considers the relationship between one aspect of vessel form, basal shape, and mobility patterns among a "fortuitous sample" of 37 North American groups selected from the Human Relations Area File (HRAF). Her findings affirm important relationships between basal shape and degrees of residential mobility. For example, Mills (1985:8–9) notes that vessels with rounded bases tend to associate with sedentary, semisedentary, and seminomadic groups, while vessels with flat bottoms and narrow bases are most strongly associated with a nomadic adaptation. Nonetheless, the wide range of

settlement patterns associated with roundedbase vessels suggests that mobility is not the only, nor perhaps the most important, factor in vessel design.

Mills (1985:9–10) considers additional factors and finds that diet and food preparation also co-vary with vessel form. Rounder vessels correlate with more intensive use of plants and seeds. Nonetheless, Mills (1985: 10) cautions that "the amount of agricultural reliance is specifically not able to be monitored by the presence of round based vessels." Instead, rounded bases reflect a greater overall *diversity of foodstuffs* in comparison to the other basal shapes.

The amount of liquid used in food preparation and overall cooking time provide additional pressures on the formal properties of a cooking pot. Extended boiling is a common method of preparing meat and vegetables (e.g., Hally 1986:268), and a cooking vessel designed to be left on a fire for a long time must mitigate the loss of moisture to evaporation. Lids are a reasonable response in this case, but a sealed vessel presents an additional problem of potentially boiling over if not carefully watched. Boiling over during vegetable cooking is problematic, since the overflow from unmonitored pots can douse the flame before the food is thoroughly cooked (e.g., Kobayashi 1994:135).

The degree to which cooking vessels are monitored in different settlement contexts has not been fully explored in the literature. Nonetheless, certain expectations can be surmised. Scheduling specific meal times is not a common practice within many nonindustrial societies (e.g., Hally 1986:270–271), nor is it common in contemporary rural areas of Mesoamerica. Instead, stews are prepared and may be left on the fire for several hours. Individuals "dip" into the pot on a need-to-eat basis. Moreover, an individual may not always be in the cooking area to monitor the meal.

Under these conditions, the design of a cooking container must respond to several different requirements. It must allow for access, either with a bowl or some type of ladle. At the same time, it must allow for some moisture to escape (minimize boiling over) while controlling the rate of liquid evaporation (minimize burning). One response might include a relatively small opening combined with high, incurving walls. This design, of course, fits tecomates nicely. As noted above, this combination of traits reflects a compromise rather than an "optimal solution" (M. Nelson 1991:61).

Temper type, especially as it affects vessel weight and transportability, has received attention in the recent literature (Skibo et al. 1989b). These studies demonstrate that, all things being equal, fiber-tempered ceramics are lighter and should be transported more easily than their counterparts tempered with inorganic additives. Furthermore, fiber-tempered ceramics can be produced more rapidly, allowing a pot to be manufactured in a single sitting. Yet, as already noted, lowland Early Formative tecomates are not fiber tempered. Is there a possible explanation for this apparent contradiction?

Despite the connection between fiber-tempered pottery and residential mobility, the nature of the link remains ambiguous. For example, Hunt (1991) analyzed a sample of 40 North American ceramic-using societies selected from the HRAF. Hunt (1991, table 2) indicates that, true to expectations, fiber-tempered cookware was only reported among seminomadic groups. However, Hunt (1991:9) then turned the question around and asked what kind of tempered cookware was actually transported by all groups. When framed in this way, the data indicate that cookware tempered with inorganics was moved as much as fiber-tempered pottery. Fiber-tempering, therefore, appears to associate more with a particular type of mobility or production timetable—it is not a necessary requirement for transporting ceramics.

Vessel decoration may also be conditioned by residential mobility. As noted in the preceding section, Clark's (1994) Barra phase assemblage contains very little undecorated ceramics. I argue that, rather than interpret this pattern as reflecting a "special purpose" function for the pottery, this strategy might represent pottery destined for a variety of use-contexts. In terms of the above discussion, decoration itself may be "versatile" rather than "specialized."

Pottery decoration operates primarily within the social sphere. Thus, the *anticipated range* of social contexts of use should condition the amount of energy invested in decoration. It follows, therefore, that pottery destined to perform within a wide range of social contexts should be embellished in anticipation of the most "decoration-demanding" context, *even if the vessel is never actually used within that context.* In other words, I suggest that, like a versatile tool design, decorative intensity also reflects compromises. In this case, however, the compromise must achieve the minimal standards for the most demanding social context. Every-day cooking with an elaborate container may seem unnecessary and even "inefficient" in production terms, but no harm is done to meal or consumer. On the other hand, using an undecorated container in an important social context may have negative political, economic, or social ramifications. In situations where vessels are versatile and ceramic forms are few, assemblages may well appear to be "over-elaborated."

The complex relationship between pottery decoration and residential mobility forms part of a recent archaeological study by Simms et al. (1997). These authors investigate the degree to which temper size, sherd thickness, and surface preparation correlate with Great Basin sites categorized in terms of residential mobility. Their hypothesis was that increasing sedentism would select for greater investment in pottery manufacture, as represented by control of temper size, thinner vessel walls, and greater surface elaboration.

Interestingly, while the first two variables correlate significantly with increasing sedentism, Simms et al. (1997:784–785) find that the proposed relationship between mobility and surface preparation "oscillates between strongly supportive and contradictory." This apparent contradiction is produced because mobile camp sites (residential and short-term) often contained ceramic assemblages exhibiting higher percentages of surface treatment than more permanent base sites (agricultural and residential). I would suggest that this "discrepancy" (Simms et al. 1997: 784) is perfectly congruent with the notion that pottery may be elaborated in anticipation of a wide range of use contexts. The "over-elaboration," therefore, reflects a decision to meet the minimum requirements of the most demanding social context that is anticipated for ceramic use.

Techniques of decoration may provide clues as to whether or not an assemblage is over-elaborated. Not all decoration is equal, and some decoration is more easily executed or may be performed by relatively "unskilled" individuals. Slipping, burnishing, polishing, and decoration through surface texturing are examples of lower-intensity embellishment. Furthermore, plastic and texturing decorations are more likely to maintain their design integrity and visibility if the pot is used to cook over an open flame.

Interestingly, these are precisely the kinds of decorations that adorn Early Formative ceramics (Fig. 10.3). Rocker stamping, punctation, scoring, scraping, slipping, and burnishing are common throughout the lowland Mesoamerican assemblages (Clark 1994: 184–186; Clark and Gosser 1995:213; Coe 1961, 1994:44; Coe and Diehl 1980; Stark 1997b). Moreover, when nonplastic decoration occurs, it is often restricted to the vessel rim, which is also that area of the vessel least likely to be adversely affected by use over an open fire. I suggest that this pattern of decoration is not fortuitous but rather can be expected when vessel forms are few and ceramics operate in multiple social contexts, including cooking and serving.

Pottery decoration also has implications for ceramics that are utilized by mobile groups but are not necessarily part of a transportable toolkit. It is quite clear that pottery can be bulky, heavy, and fragile. Among residentially mobile groups, other bulky and heavy facilities, such as ground stone implements, are frequently cached on site and become part of the site's furniture. Pottery may

Fig. 10.3. Early Formative *tecomate* sherd from La Joya, showing the use of texturing (rocker stamping). The scale is in centimeters.

also be cached, as documented among the Rarámuri (Tarahumara) by Graham (1994). The subject of cached pottery is infrequently addressed by archaeologists, but I believe that ceramic caching may have additional implications for the amount of energy invested in vessel decoration and finishing (also Simms et al. 1997:783).

Graham (1994) discusses several types of residences among the Rarámuri, all of which were abandoned for a time. Main residences may also be the locus of long-term storage activities and this storage can include food, cookware (ceramics), and other items considered valuable. These storage areas are private and information on contents is guarded (Graham 1994:42). In contrast, caching at temporary residences involves larger, heavier items (ground stone and larger pots). The remaining household assemblage is removed, as there is "no guarantee that a household will occupy the same temporary residence" when it returns to the area and "households apparently do not lay a property claim to these places" (Graham 1994:48). An important reminder for archaeologists is that caching associates with several behavioral strategies—in other words, not all caching is the same.

Unfortunately, Graham (1994) was not able to provide a description of the ceramics cached in different contexts. But it is reasonable to assume that individuals concerned with the loss or theft of vessels might take steps to reduce the possibility of this occurrence. One way to minimize the loss of pottery through theft would be to decorate pots more elaborately, thereby "tagging" them as pertaining to a particular individual or family. The fact that domestic potters may invest considerable energy in decorating vessels has been discussed. Vessel caching within particular contexts could well represent one incentive to "tag" pottery with a personal design or other form of decoration. Unlike the over-elaboration discussed above, however, "tagging" should emphasize relatively unique designs and individual expression through painting, zoning, and more labor-intensive incising and carving. Also important from the perspective of caching is the fact that ceramics within a single assemblage might reflect a diversity of decoration, based as much on the intended *storage* context as on the intended *use* context.

SUMMARY

Early Formative coastal lowland Mesoamerican assemblages in general, and tecomates in particular, reflect strategies that one would associate with a residentially mobile settlement organization. Ceramic assemblages recovered in a variety of contexts are dominated by the same basic form, implicating the presence of a versatile container, rather than a functionally specific ceramic vessel. Moreover, the emphasis on only a few vessel types within the assemblage suggests that the Early Formative ceramic toolkit was relatively transportable (e.g., M. Nelson 1991:74).

The formal properties of the tecomate also imply that it was versatile and transportable. Basal shape is consistent with ethnographic patterns that associate round bases with exploiting a variety of food resources. The small opening and inward leaning walls are reasonable within a context of prolonged cooking (common with plant products) and a pattern of unscheduled food consumption. The absence of a neck is consistent with a vessel whose contents were intended to be extracted, rather than poured (e.g., Hally 1986: 280). The combination of a rounded form, thin vessel walls, and a range of inorganic inclusions may represent a compromise between transportability, impact resistance, and heat transfer (Braun 1983; Schiffer and Skibo 1987:605–607).

The strategy for vessel decoration also appears to be designed in terms of residential mobility. Ceramics in some Early Formative contexts look to be over-elaborated, with extremely few undecorated pieces. Nonetheless, there is a pattern to the decoration, with lower-intensity embellishment such as texturing and polishing as the overwhelming favorites. These types of decoration are anticipated when multifunctional vessels are expected to perform adequately within a variety of social contexts. Ceramics that operate within a residentially mobile settlement organization would be subject to these conditions.

CONCLUSION

In reading the current literature, one is much more likely to encounter a discussion of the organization of ceramic production than a treatment of the organization of ceramic technology. In fact, a recent volume devoted to archaeological method and theory (Schiffer 1991b) provides an excellent case in point. Within that volume, front to back, one will find an extensive treatment of the organization of craft [pottery] production (Costin 1991) and an in-depth account of technological [stone tool] organization (M. Nelson 1991). The occurrence of these two chapters in the same volume is more than simple fortuity. I believe it underscores fundamental differences in how archaeologists have traditionally investigated the manufacture and use of both ceramics and stone tools.

Clearly there are differences between these technological systems. Ceramics are produced through an additive process while lithics are manufactured using subtractive techniques. Thus, lithic tools are more amenable to alterations "on-the-fly" while the functional range of pots is more likely to be "locked in" at the time of manufacture. Ceramics and lithics are also consumed and recycled differently. In other words, ceramics are considerably more than "cultural stone" (e.g., Burton and Simon 1996).

This realization, however, should not mean that the two technological systems are condemned to mutually exclusive realms of analysis. In fact, I argue that archaeologists interested in ceramics must begin making better use of the principles of technological organization originally identified in the stone tool literature. Nonetheless, there is no reason to seek perfect congruence between the concepts used to discuss pottery and those used to discuss lithics. Instead, ceramicists must begin to pen new observational language (e.g., Binford 1981) that better reflects the forces affecting the production and consumption of pottery.

In this paper I invoke the idea of residential mobility to evaluate ceramic assemblage characteristics of Early Formative coastal lowland Mesoamerica. I adopt this strategy for two reasons. First, despite the conventional wisdom, there is good reason to believe that Early Formative adaptation included residential mobility. Second, I know of no previous discussion that attempts to analyze the technological organization of pottery within such a settlement context for Mesoamerica. A need clearly exists for such analysis, and the results might be applicable to archaeological areas beyond the Mesoamerican border.

I suggest that the tecomate represents a ceramic form responding to several organizational demands. Specifically, I propose that this vessel type is designed to be versatile, a dimension that would exhibit strong pressure within a residentially mobile setting. Furthermore, I argue that the emphasis on a restricted array of vessel forms is consonant with a tool technology intended to be trans-portable. I also note that the over-elaboration that characterizes some Early Formative ceramic assemblages may result from a decoration strategy targeted toward vessel use within multiple social contexts. Elaborate decoration may also occur in response to caching behaviors and the need to identify ceramics at a later time.

Finally, this model also anticipates the decline in tecomate use. The adoption of sedentism and an agrarian lifestyle alter the conditions under which pottery is produced and used. With sedentism and agriculture come a proliferation of new vessel forms and decorations. This shift reflects changing functional and social contexts for the ceramic assemblage.

The pitfalls of this approach are many. Perhaps most apparent is the "sedentary-nonsedentary" dichotomy utilized here. Archaeologists are becoming increasingly dissatisfied with such simplistic distinctions and realize that sedentism is better seen as a continuum of behavior rather than a specific category of settlement (e.g., Kelly 1992). In addition, I have not developed a new observational language but instead have borrowed heavily from treatments of lithic technology. As archaeologists are well aware, appropriating terminology from one area to the next can generate as much confusion as it resolves.

Even with these limitations, I believe that this research direction has significant potential for understanding ceramics and ancient societies. Archaeologists can no longer ignore the implications of ceramics originating and proliferating among residentially mobile, nonagrarian groups. Furthermore, the ethnographic record provides a poor data base for investigating the relationship between mobility and ceramics. We need better documentation of how different *containers*, not just pottery, function within contexts of residential mobility. In this way we can begin to address the technological organization of ceramics and ultimately contribute to a better understanding of the fascinating relationship between pottery and people.

11

Exploring the Origins of Pottery on the Colorado Plateau

James M. Skibo and Eric Blinman

In the days of V. Gordon Childe (1951) the emergence of pottery seemed sudden and easily understood. Sedentary agriculturalists made pottery and it signaled the beginning of the Neolithic revolution worldwide. Although this is still generally true, more recent research and better dating techniques have made this once simple equation between pottery and sedentary agriculturalists much more complicated (Pavlů 1997; Rice n.d.). We now know that mobile hunter-gatherers made pottery (e.g., Aikens 1995; Bollong et al. 1993; Reid 1984; Sassaman 1993; Tuohy and Dansie 1990) and some cultivators, like those of the Lapita Culture (Green 1979), actually abandoned pottery technology. In areas such as the American Southeast pottery manufacture preceded agriculture for up to two thousand years, and in the American Southwest or the Near East agriculture was present long before the first pottery.

In this paper we first examine the origin of pottery generally, and then look more closely at one particular case—the emergence of pottery on the Colorado Plateau of the Southwestern United States. The analytical focus of this study is a sample of whole and partially reconstructed vessels from sites dating between A.D. 200 and A.D. 600. This analysis, which is the first step in a long-term study of the early pottery of this region, will focus on vessel function through an analysis of morphological characteristics and use-alteration traces. The collections of whole brown ware vessels from three sites in northeastern Arizona are dominated by globular neckless jars. From a performance perspective, it is argued that these vessels would have performed very well as storing, cooking, or processing vessels. Preliminary use-alteration analysis suggests that some of the vessels were not used over a fire while others were used in two types of cooking. Moreover, many of the vessels were used to store a substance that caused extreme interior surface attrition.

ORIGINS

The oldest ceramic objects in the world thus far are the Dolní Věstonice figurines that date to about 26,000 years ago (Vandiver et al. 1989), preceding the appearance of pottery *vessels* by over 15,000 years (see Pavlů 1997; Rice n.d., 1987:6–26, 1996a, for a general reviews of pottery origins). What concerns us here is not the initial invention of ceramic technology, but rather the innovation of ceramic containers. Most archaeologists would now agree that long before the widespread adoption of pottery, hunter-gatherers had knowledge of the basic principles of ceramics: objects can be shaped from moist clay and then be made permanent by placing the object in a fire (Brown 1989:207; Rice 1987:7). At issue is when, where, and why pottery containers make their appearance, and it is clear that there is no single answer (see P. Arnold, Chapter 10; Barnett and Hoopes 1995; Vitelli, Chapter 12).

Although there may not be one reason for the adoption of pottery containers, D. Arnold (1985) identifies a number of generalizations about pottery and people based on both ethnographic and archaeological observations. The two of most interest here are the relationship between pottery making and sedentism, and the correlation between pottery and more intensive forms of food processing.

Nonsedentary and semisedentary peoples can and do make pottery, but D. Arnold (1985:113–118) found a strong correlation between pottery making and sedentism. There are several reasons why this would occur. Pottery is less portable and more prone to breakage than other containers like baskets and skins. Although this may seem to be a logical reason for the lack of pottery among mobile peoples, in practice it may have been only a minor impediment (see also P. Arnold, Chapter 10). Some hunter-gatherers do carry their pottery vessels with them (e.g., Holmberg 1969; McGee 1971; Sapir 1923), and sedentary peoples often transport their pottery over long distances (D. Arnold 1985: 111). A more important reason behind the correlation between pottery and sedentism is that pottery making is a technology that takes some investment (D. Arnold 1985). Although clay is somewhat like McDonalds hamburgers in that you can always find some nearby, the nearest available clay may not be appropriate for particular pottery-making techniques. For example, locally available alluvial clays may be inappropriate for vessel manufacture because of excessive shrinkage. Among contemporary potters you find that once a good clay source is found it may be exploited for generations because of its known and acceptable working properties (Reina and Hill 1978). People with a mobile settlement and subsistence system may find it difficult to establish and maintain a pottery technology if they do not at least have access to the same pottery resources on a yearly basis. As Brown (1989:216) notes, at least seasonal sedentism may be required for pottery manufacture.

The final reason why sedentism is important to pottery making is because of scheduling conflicts (D. Arnold 1985:99–108; Crown and Wills 1995). Potters must be near a good clay source during a season of the year when potting is possible and when they have time, free from other tasks, to make pots. In many parts of the world, pottery can only be made during one season of the year because of climatic restrictions (e.g., too wet or too cold), so scheduling conflicts can indeed be an impediment.

The second generalization made by D. Arnold (1985:128–144) relates to pottery vessels as tools for food processing. Pottery sherds are the most ubiquitous artifact found at Neolithic or Formative villages worldwide because ceramic vessels had become an essential tool for the processing of staple cultigens, allowing high temperature processing for long periods of time. Boiling or near-boiling temperatures are essential for making many foods palatable and digestible. Cereal grain starches must be completely gelatinized for maximum digestibility, which requires sustained temperatures over 93 degrees centigrade (Reid 1990:10; Stahl 1989:181). Boiling, steaming, or simmering can also destroy potentially harmful bacteria and eliminate or reduce toxins in cultigens (D. Arnold 1985: 129–134; see also Stahl 1989:182). Moreover, cooking in pots can increase the nutritive value of meat (by extracting fat from bones) and some leafy vegetables (Reid 1990).

Compared with other cooking containers, pottery vessels permit direct heating with less constant attention. Although indirect heating of water with hot rocks (as in basket boiling) is an effective way to reach boiling or near-boiling temperatures, it requires continuous attention to avoid boil-over and to maintain those temperatures for long periods of time. When ceramic containers are used, once the relationship between the heat source and the pot is established (nestled in coals, supported over the fire, etc.) constant temperatures can be maintained by occasionally tending to the fuel. Ceramic vessels also provide sturdy processing containers for preparation techniques such as fermentation or alkaline soaking that may break down other types of containers. Clearly, ceramic containers provide many advantages as cooking and processing tools, permitting the exploitation of many new foods and the more effective processing of others (see also Crown and Wills 1995: 245–246).

Cross-cultural generalizations can provide insights into the relationship between pottery and people and shed light on ceramic vessel origins, but these data cannot be applied simply to explain pottery origins. To search for the clues to specific pottery origins we must turn to the archaeological record.

Rice (n.d.) and the chapters in Barnett and Hoopes (1995) provide a good worldwide summary of some of the earliest pottery technologies, and it is clear that there is not just one explanation for pottery origins. The striking aspect of early ceramics is the lack of correlation between pottery making and agriculture. Although pottery becomes the processing workhorse for agriculturalists, as described above, the earliest people to use pottery as a tool were hunter-gatherers. In many parts of the world it was hunter-gatherers who first employed ceramic containers to process food. Indeed the earliest known pottery vessels in the world are small cooking pots that come from Fukui Cave on Japan's southernmost island (Aikens 1995). Incipient Jomon pottery, as it is called, appears on sites with evidence of intensive marine harvesting during the Pleistocene-Holocene transition beginning about 12,400 b.p. (uncalibrated).

In North America there are many examples of hunter-gatherer pottery, mostly in the Southeastern and Northwestern United States but extending into Canada and Alaska as well. There is evidence that these pots were also used as processing tools (Reid 1990; Sassaman 1993, 1995). The majority of these vessels are low-fired open bowl or jar forms often tempered with organic matter. Although these Late Archaic vessels often have soot on the exterior suggesting that they were used over a fire (Sassaman 1993), both Reid (1990) and Sassaman (1993, 1995) make the argument that these vessels may have been used to process food by indirect moist cooking (i.e., stone boiling) as well. The highly porous thick walls and open mouth make poor heat conductors but excellent insulators, which is a performance characteristic that would be well suited to simmering foods by indirect heating. They argue that simmering temperatures, easily maintained by indirect heating, were employed by these hunter-gatherers to stew meat and obtain oils from seeds and nuts or the marrow fat from bones (Reid 1990:10; Sassaman 1995).

But processing of food cannot explain every case of early pottery. In some regions of both the Old and New World, the earliest ceramic vessels were not tools for food processing but rather were important artifacts of ritual activity. The early pottery of Colombia is highly decorated, and Oyuela-Caycedo (1995) argues that these vessels were not used for cooking. Clark and Gosser (1995:216) also suggest that early Mesoamerican pottery may not have been used for food preparation. In the Old World, Vitelli (1989, 1995, Chapter 12) also finds that early vessels of the Greek Neolithic were not used for cooking, and she suggests that these early assemblages played a symbolic or shamanistic role.

To summarize, early pottery around the world appears in three separate contexts: (1) sedentary cultivators that use the vessels to process and make digestible cereal grains, (2) seasonally sedentary hunter-gatherers who use vessels with either direct or indirect heating to extract additional nutrients from animal products or to more effectively process seeds and nuts, and (3) early cultivators or hunter-gatherers who produce and use the vessels in ritual activity. The first two contexts involve food processing and are much more widely documented than the evidence for the ritual use of pottery. The latter context will be better understood after more information is gathered on vessel use.

THEORETICAL MODELS

Several scholars have attempted to explore the origins of pottery from a theoretical perspective. We will review the models proposed by Brown (1989) and Hayden (1995a) as they may have the most relevance to the origins of pottery on the Colorado Plateau (see Rice n.d. for a thorough review of these and other models).

Brown (1989) revived interest in the origins of pottery by exploring an economic approach. His model considers that (1) pottery containers were adopted long after there was knowledge of ceramic technology, (2) pottery was introduced when people had other well-developed container options, and (3) pottery is not the only container for heating water and processing food (Brown 1989:208). Under these conditions, pottery was adopted when there was a "rising demand for watertight, fire-resistant containers . . . coupled with constraints in meeting this demand" (Brown 1989:213). In this model, groups would have to be at least seasonally sedentary to permit pottery to be a realistic container option. Pottery is adopted when other types of containers such as baskets or skins fail to meet the increasing demand brought about by new types of food processing, new forms of storage, or the emergence of food presentation as a form of social expression (Brown 1989:213). Thus pottery was not adopted because of some foreseen potential but rather because it was a container that could be made cheaply and quickly by semi-sedentary groups.

Hayden (1993, 1995a) looks at prehistory and does not see people trying to solve the practical problems of life, but rather he sees individuals involved in economically based competition. As in Brown's model, prerequisites for the emergence of pottery are technological advances and more sedentary settlement and subsistence systems. Hayden (1993) argues that as people become more sedentary and sharing of food is no longer required for survival, there is a worldwide tendency for increased economic competition along with more pronounced inequality. In this context, pottery first appears as a prestige food container made by individuals in direct competition with their neighbors.

The primary difference between the Brown and Hayden models is the role of prac-tical versus prestige technologies. Although they both are economic models, Brown suggests that the demand for pottery containers was to fulfill practical needs, whereas Hayden promotes the idea that demand for pottery was generated by economic competition. The implications are that Brown's model predicts that the earliest pottery in a region should be processing vessels, whereas Hayden's model predicts that the first pottery should be food-serving containers. As noted earlier, both situations can and do occur worldwide. Some researchers have found that the earliest pottery in a particular region was used to cook or process food (e.g., Gebauer 1995) and others have shown that the first ceramic containers, often highly ornate, were not used in food processing but, presumably, as a prestige technology (e.g., Clark and Gosser 1995:214–216; Oyuela-Caycedo 1995).

These models are not mutually exclusive. Although Brown (1989) focuses principally on practical demands as an impetus for pottery and Hayden (1995a) suggests that social or economic competition was the important factor, they each leave room in their models for the opposite to occur. Brown (1989:213) notes that one of the new container demands could be the "presentation of food as an emergent social expression." Similarly, Hayden (1995a:262) suggests that in the process of producing pottery as a prestige good, its practical benefits are quickly realized and put into use. Moreover, in some peripheral areas, "derivative practical pottery" used for cooking or storage may be the first ceramic vessels (Hayden 1995a). Clearly, there is a great deal of overlap between the two models with the main difference being the weight placed on prestige versus practical ceramic containers. It is possible that each can be used to explain the emergence of pottery in various parts of the world, but testing the models requires a level of analysis that is rarely attained. What is often lacking is a clear idea of how the earliest pottery was used (Longacre 1995; Rice n.d.). The example that follows attempts to remedy this deficiency with an analysis of the earliest pottery on the Colorado Plateau.

EMERGENCE OF ANASAZI POTTERY

Anasazi pottery is known worldwide by both collectors and archaeologists alike for the elaborate forms, all made without the benefit of the wheel, and its intricately painted designs. If you consider prehistoric North American pottery traditions from the perspective of art, Anasazi pottery is at the top. And from the perspective of the Anasazi archaeologist, no single artifact class has played a more important role. From defining culture groups and marking the passage of time, to inferring population size and social organization, Anasazi pottery is usually at center stage. But despite the attention paid to this artifact type and the important role it plays in archaeological inference, very little attention has been given to the origins of Anasazi pottery (for exceptions see Crown and Wills 1995; LeBlanc 1982).

This scant attention is not for lack of collections since much of the early ceramic material we will describe was excavated over 40 years ago. But we can identify several reasons for this lack of interest. First, it is only recently that we have better data on important issues related to pottery origins, such as the appearance of cultigens and beginnings of more sedentary settlement (Crown and Wills 1995:241). Without understanding these important co-variables, pottery emergence is not easily explained. Second, the earliest pottery on the Colorado Plateau is brown, and every introductory student in Southwestern archaeology knows that Anasazi pottery is gray, and Mogollon pottery, located just southeast in the mountain transition, is brown. Prior to more accurate dating of the brown ware sites, it was often assumed that the brown pottery was imported from the Mogollon region or represented Mogollon immigrants. Third, dates for the early brown ware pottery are consistantly prior to A.D. 600 thus placing it in the Basketmaker II period. Generations of Southwestern archaeologists were taught that there was no pottery during the Basketmaker II period. Although in the Southeastern U.S. archaeologists have come to accept that there is Archaic pottery, the time-honored Pecos Classification has indeed served as an impediment to studying the earliest Southwestern ceramics.

In the Southwest, as well as in most parts of the world, there is evidence that people were well aware of ceramic technology long before the manufacture of pottery containers (Crown and Wills 1995:244). Unfired clay figurines that date between 5600 and 5000 B.C. have been found in southeastern Utah (Coulam and Schroedl 1996) and ceramic figurines have been located in a southern Arizona pithouse village that dates to about 800 B.C. (Huckell 1990). It is safe to assume that Archaic peoples throughout the Southwest had knowledge of ceramic technology. Domesticated cultigens also precede the appearance of pottery vessels, which is analogous to the Near East and the prepottery Neolithic. Corn was introduced into a mobile hunter-gatherer subsistence system by at least 1000 B.C. (Tagg 1996), followed by an apparent transition to a more logistic settlement system with semisedentary occupation of pit structures in rock shelters and camps (Crown and Wills 1995; Matson 1991; Wills 1988). More than a millennium later, pottery appears to have been adopted on a regional scale over the course of one or two centuries, accompanied or closely followed by the architectural and material correlates of the Hohokam, Mogollon, and Anasazi (Crown and Wills 1995; LeBlanc 1982).

On the Colorado Plateau of Arizona, New Mexico, Utah, and Colorado, there is now widespread though scattered evidence that the first pottery was made sometime before A.D. 300 (see Wilson and Blinman 1993, 1994; Wilson et al. 1996). The pottery occurs in contexts that are similar in all respects to aceramic settlements of the same time. This pottery, known regionally as Los Pinos Brown, Sambrito Utility, Lupton Brown, Adamana Brown, Obelisk Utility, and Obelisk Gray, is a plain polished brown ware (Spurr and Hays-Gilpin 1996; Wilson 1989).

In most of the cases the pottery appears to be locally made (although this must be confirmed with subsequent testing), and in all cases it precedes the typical Anasazi gray and white wares. A similar stage of incipient pottery manufacture was identified by Haury (1985) to the south in the Mogollon area and in the deserts of the Hohokam homeland (Heidke et al. 1997). Although there is a good deal of regional variability, this early brown ware represents a pan-Anasazi ceramic tradition made with self-tempered alluvial or soil clays that tend to be rich in iron. All of the vessels were made using the coil and scrape technique with the possible exception of Adamana Brown, some of which may have been finished using a paddle and anvil (Mera 1934). All of the early brown wares have polished exteriors and surface color ranges from dark gray to brown (for detailed descriptions see Spurr and Hays-Gilpin 1996; Wilson and Blinman 1993; Wilson et al. 1996).

EARLY CERAMIC SITES

Early brown ware sites are currently known from three areas of the Colorado Plateau: (1) the eastern portion of the northern San Juan, which includes the Upper San Juan, Animas, La Plata, and Mancos river drainages, (2) the Prayer Rock District on the Navajo Reservation in northeastern Arizona, and (3) along the southern portion of the Colorado Plateau from the Petrified Forest to the Zuni Reservation. Other sites with this early pottery include the Little Jug site (Thompson and Thompson 1974) near the Grand Canyon, the Hay Hollow site (Martin and Rinaldo 1960), a site east of Gallup, New Mexico (Blinman and Wilson 1994), and a number of sites in Chaco Canyon (for a review of early pottery sites see Breternitz 1982; Fowler 1991; LeBlanc 1982; Morris 1927; Schroeder 1982; Wilson et al. 1996).

An early ceramic period occupation was identified in the northern San Juan area of northwestern New Mexico as part of the Navajo Reservoir archaeology project (Dittert et al. 1961; Eddy 1966). Eddy referred to the earliest pottery as Los Pinos Brown. Although the Los Pinos sites with pottery are not well dated (Eddy 1966:444–445), the pottery clearly predates the later gray wares and represents the earliest attempt at pottery manufacture in this region. Sambrito Brown, which follows Los Pinos Brown in time and is indistinguishable from this type (Wilson and Blinman 1993), provides a larger ceramic sample and comes from slightly better dated contexts (i.e., A.D. 400–700).

Sites in the Petrified National Forest may represent the best collection of pre-A.D. 300 brown ware pottery on the plateau. Excavations at the Flattop site (Wendorf 1953) and Sivu'ovi (Burton 1991) yielded a plain brown pottery type classified as Adamana Brown (Mera 1934). Recent dates from the two sites (Burton 1991:97–101) suggest that Adamana Brown may be the oldest dated pottery on the plateau.

The caves of the Prayer Rock District of the Navajo Indian Reservation provide evidence of early pottery making in the Southwest (Hays 1992; Morris 1980). The caves yielded both a classic Basketmaker III pottery assemblage and an earlier assemblage dominated by a pottery type that is called Obelisk Gray. Obelisk Gray is a polished brown ware that is similar to the brown wares described above (Wilson and Blinman 1994).

This brief review demonstrates that pottery manufacture was taking place on the Colorado Plateau after A.D. 200. There is also strong circumstantial evidence that the pottery is locally made, not "Mogollon" and thus not imported from south of the Colorado Plateau (Burton 1991:108; Eddy 1966: 384; Fowler 1991; Wendorf 1953; Wilson and Blinman 1993:16). Because similar pottery types are not made in the Mogollon region, we must be careful to distinguish ceramics of the Mogollon tradition from brown ware technology, per se (see Fowler 1991). Many alluvial clays and some geologic clays will fire to brown colors, so the similarities between Mogollon brown wares and those of the Colorado Plateau may represent a similar technology in the first attempts at pottery manufacture (see also Wilson 1989; Wilson and Blinman 1993, 1994).

THE STUDY

In the summer of 1996 the Brown Ware Project was initiated with an analysis of whole vessels and a preliminary clay resource survey from the Petrified Forest area of Arizona to the vicinity of Crownpoint, New Mexico. This is part of a multi-year project that will (1) provide a detailed technological analysis of early brown ware that focuses on how the vessels were made and used, (2) determine the manufacturing location of the vessels through petrographic and chemical analysis of the pottery and local clays, and (3) explore the performance of these vessels through replicative experiments. The objective of the larger study is to both understand why people started making pots at this place and time, and why the technology changed so rapidly to the typical Anasazi gray wares.

Initial laboratory analysis focused on collections of whole vessels curated at the Arizona State Museum and Western Archeological and Conservation Center in Tucson, and the Museum of Northern Arizona in Flagstaff. Several vessels from the Laboratory of Anthropology in Santa Fe, New Mexico, were also inspected. We will discuss two aspects of these vessels. First, we will describe the formal characteristics of this early brown ware, which comes predominately from the Prayer Rock Caves and the Petrified National Forest, drawing inferences about their intended use from the size and shape of these containers. Second, we interpret use-alteration patterns of interior carbon and exterior soot deposits, as well as attrition in an effort to understand vessel function.

The whole and partially reconstructed vessels come from three sites: Flattop, Sivu'ovi, and the Prayer Rock Caves. Sivu'ovi is located in the Petrified National Park, about 20 miles east of Holbrook, Arizona. The site is a large Basketmaker period pithouse village that was partially excavated by the National Park Service archaeologists to salvage material that was eroding off the small mesa (Burton 1991). The pottery consists of four restorable vessels and 1,072 sherds that were recovered from the surface and from two pit structures. The vast majority of the ceramics are an early brown ware referred to as Adamana Brown. Like all the other early brown wares, it is lightly polished and is tempered with fine sand that may be naturally occurring within the clay source or may be augmented by the potter (Rye 1976). The distinguishing feature of Adamana is the presence of mica inclusions in the temper (Shepard 1953).

Within sight of Sivu'ovi is Flattop, another site dominated by Adamana Brown pottery. Wendorf (1953) excavated 8 pit structures at Flattop and recovered 30 whole or restorable vessels and 2,522 sherds, with all but 84 classified as Adamana Brown. Wendorf did not obtain absolute dates, but ceramic cross-dating suggested that the site predated A.D. 500 and was contemporaneous with the earliest Mogollon ceramics (Wendorf 1950:49, 1953:51–53). For example, Adamana Brown was the most common intrusive in the Hilltop phase (tree-ring dated to A.D. 200–400) at the Bluff site (Haury 1985). Burton (1991) obtained radiocarbon dates from two Flattop houses and three houses from Sivu'ovi that confirmed Wendorf's suspicion that Adamana Brown pottery is very early. Multiple samples were obtained from outer rings of construction timbers, and calibrated dates were averaged for each structure. Burton (1991: 101) reports the dates as follows (one-sigma range): Flattop House D, A.D. 130–318; Flattop House H, A.D. 35–215; Sivu'ovi Structure 1, 86 B.C.–A.D. 131; Sivu'ovi Structure 2, A.D. 82–252; Sivu'ovi Structure 3, 406–311 B.C.

The caves in the Prayer Rock District of the Navajo Nation were excavated by Earl Morris in the 1930s, and Elizabeth Ann Morris (1980) prepared the report of the excavations and artifacts. Our analysis focuses on the Prayer Rock Caves material because it is one of the largest collections of early Basketmaker pottery. Although the majority of whole vessels come from the slightly later gray ware period, there is also a significant number of brown ware whole vessels and sherds referred to as Obelisk Gray (Morris 1980). This is a bit of a misnomer because this type is quite comparable to early brown wares found elsewhere in the Southwest (Wilson and Blinman 1993; Wilson et al. 1996).

Whole Vessel Design and Performance.
There is a total of 211 whole or partially reconstructible vessels from the Prayer Rock Caves, and 74 of those are Obelisk Gray. The remarkable aspect of the Obelisk Gray collection is that half of the vessels are globular neckless jars (Table 11.1), which in Southwestern vernacular are referred to as "seed jars" (this shape is almost identical to the Mesoamerican *tecomates* discussed by P. Arnold in Chapter 10). Three out of the four whole vessels from Sivu'ovi were also seed jars, and the most common restorable vessels from Flattop were the globular jars without a neck. The early brown ware seed jars are generally spherical in shape, although some are more elongated. They are relatively thin walled and have a restricted orifice. The exteriors, however, are what makes these seed jars and all the early brown wares unique. The exterior surfaces are typically quite irregular but they all show evidence of polishing. Sometimes the polish is only visible on the high points of the surface, whereas in other cases more time and effort was put into smoothing and polishing, resulting in relatively lustrous surfaces.

Based on these technical properties alone, one can begin to make general inferences about vessel function and performance. The globular shape of these vessels is a very strong structural design that would impart strength in both the manufacturing and use stages. Shapes approaching spherical have the most green strength and would be more likely to survive drying without cracking. This would be especially important if alluvial clays of differing shrinkage characteristics were being used within the brown ware tradition, allowing the potter to achieve successful results with either low- or high-shrinkage clay. These same spherical properties also would give the vessel a good deal of strength in use. Curved surfaces have greater structural integrity and thus can better withstand the strains imposed by both thermal shock and physical impact. Moreover, spherical

TABLE 11.1.
Obelisk Gray Vessel Forms from the Prayer Rock Caves Curated at the Arizona State Museum

Seed jars	37	(50.0%)
Necked jars	33	(44.6%)
Pitchers	2	(2.7%)
Total	74	(100.0%)

shapes are better able to distribute the weight of their contents, reducing the risk of breakage from internal loading.

The restricted orifice diameter imparts a number of techno-functional qualities. In the seed jar shapes, the strength of the pot increases as the orifice diameter decreases. The small openings are easily covered or plugged to protect the vessel's contents. Moreover, even if the vessel were left uncovered, the restricted opening would limit loss of heat during cooking, or spillage during transport or storage. But the restricted orifice also limits access to the vessel's contents. Although all of the analyzed seed jars had openings large enough to permit the entry of a hand or ladle, these openings were small enough to inhibit both access and visibility. Even with lamps for analysis it is difficult to inspect the interior of the vessels, and with a hand or implement in the opening it would have been impossible for the vessel users to see the pot's contents. Moreover, this type of opening is not well suited to pouring liquids, which would not only be difficult to control but would also slop onto the sides of the vessel.

Polishing or burnishing is usually associated with decorated wares in the Anasazi Southwest, but it is a technical property that can also greatly influence performance. One of the most important performance characteristics of polishing is its affect on water permeability (Schiffer 1988b). In low-fired earthenwares water permeability is a constant concern. Without any surface treatment to impede permeability most vessels will weep badly and greatly reduce heating effectiveness. In fact, water will not boil in some low-fired pottery without a surface treatment to at least slow down water permeability (Skibo 1992:165–168). But polishing is not often a property found in low-fired cooking pots because escaping water turns to steam and will spall the surface (Schiffer 1990; Schiffer et al. 1994b). This may be the reason for the "poor" polishing job on the early brown ware vessels. They are polished just enough to inhibit the flow of water but the surface is open enough to permit the escape of steam.

The technical properties of these seed jars, when combined, create vessels that would perform well in both cooking and storage (see also P. Arnold, Chapter 10). The two most important performance characteristics of cooking with water are thermal shock resistance and heating effectiveness. The spherical shape, thin wall, low firing temperature, and large amounts of temper create a vessel with excellent thermal shock resistance. The thin walls and high percentage of temper also provide excellent heating effectiveness. The polished exterior would also inhibit the flow of water, which is an important property related to heating effectiveness, possibly without closing the exterior surface enough to cause steam spalling. Thus from a design perspective, the seed jar forms would perform well as cooking pots. The only property of these vessels that is not well suited to cooking is the restricted access. The narrow openings would give the vessels greater strength but also make it more difficult to access the vessel's contents.

As a storage or processing vessel, the seed jar forms also would perform adequately. The spherical shape is a design well suited to storage because of its strength both in terms of holding heavy contents and in being carried while full. Moreover, its low center of gravity, despite its spherical shape, make it quite stable while resting on its base. The restricted vessel entry is also easily plugged to protect the pot's contents, but it would not be the best design for a storage pot that needs to be accessed regularly or one that requires that its liquid contents be poured out.

From purely a design perspective, the early brown ware seed jars could have adequately performed cooking, storage, transport, or food processing. These designs are multifunctional and if a person wanted a pot to perform many different functions, the early brown ware seed jars would be ideal. The globular neckless jars with the paste characteristics and surface finish of the early brown wares are the ceramic equivalent to Swiss army knives—one tool that can perform a variety of functions.

Whole Vessel Use-Alteration Traces.
The majority of analyzable seed jars are Obelisk Gray examples from the Prayer Rock Caves collection. Unfortunately, most of the vessels inspected come from burned houses, which greatly hindered my (JMS) ability to infer use from carbon deposition. A total of 26 of the 37 seed jars inspected had evidence that post-use burning significantly affected both interior and exterior carbon patterns. Only seven of the vessels survived the burning without evidence that their carbon patterns had been altered. House fires of the type at Prayer Rock Caves can either add or remove carbonized deposits. Fortunately, carbon patterns from the house burning could be easily discriminated from those created during cooking over an open fire. Of the seven pots unaffected by the house fires, two had evidence of cooking and five had no evidence that they were placed over a fire. Both cooking pots have exterior sooting patterns characteristic of being placed above the fire on rocks or some form of support. The interior of one of the vessels (ASM 14313) had a carbon pattern typical of vessels that heat food in the absence of water (Fig. 11.1). This can occur by roasting seeds or some other food, or by boiling something until all or most of the water has been removed. (Figures 11.2, 11.3 and 11.4 illustrate the expected interior carbon patterns associated with cooking in a dry and wet state.) Cooking a thick gruel would also create this pattern as would reheating previously cooked food. The other vessel (ASM 14400) has an interior carbon pattern more typical of cooking food in the presence of water (Fig. 11.5). The base has no evidence of carbon while the middle interior has a ring of carbon. When you boil with water, organic particles spatter from the water surface, adhere to the vessel wall, and car-

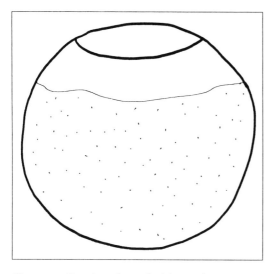

Fig. 11.1. Interior of vessel with a carbon pattern caused by heating food in the absence of water (ASM 14313).

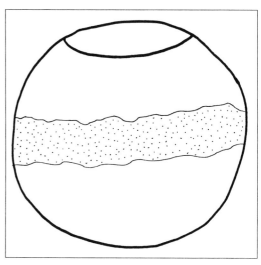

Fig. 11.2. Idealized interior carbon pattern created by boiling food (wet mode).

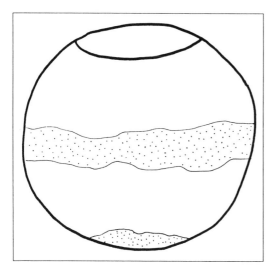

Fig. 11.3. Sometimes there is also a patch of carbon on the interior base created during wet-mode cooking.

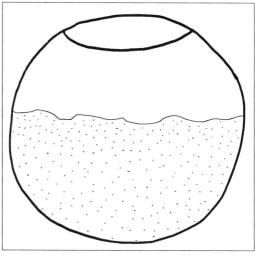

Fig. 11.4. Idealized interior carbon pattern created by heating food in the dry mode.

bonize. This vessel has a wide ring, as if this pot was used with various water levels or in cases where the water level had boiled down during use.

The three seed jars from Sivu'ovi provide the best evidence for cooking. These vessels were found in a covered storage pit and there is no evidence that they were affected by post-use burning. One of the small seed jars

(WACC 5918) demonstrates the classic carbon pattern associated with boiling food. The exterior base is slightly oxidized, which is created by having an intense fire under a pot that is raised on rocks or some type of support (Fig. 11.6). The lower third of the exterior wall has a heavy patch of soot, which gradually fades above the mid-section towards the rim. The interior of this vessel has

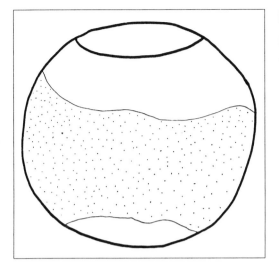

Fig. 11.5. Vessel with an interior carbon pattern characteristic of wet-mode cooking. The wider band of carbon likely resulted from variable water levels (ASM 14400).

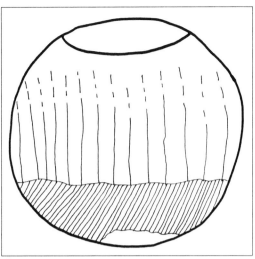

Fig. 11.6. Exterior of vessel that was used over a fire (ASM 5918).

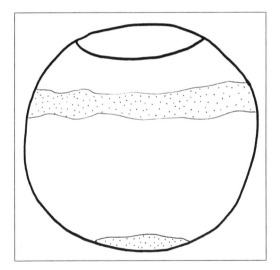

Fig. 11.7. Interior of a vessel used to heat food in the wet mode (ASM 5918).

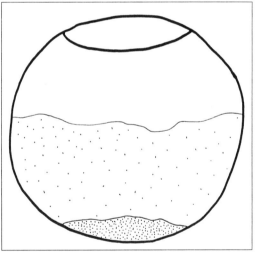

Fig. 11.8. Interior of a vessel from Sivu'ovi used to heat food in the dry mode (WACC 9155).

the band of carbon that forms in pots used to boil food (Fig. 11.7). A gray carbon patch on the interior base could have been created if most of the moisture had been removed from the vessel in the last stages of cooking.

The second vessel from Sivu'ovi (WACC 9155) also has clear evidence of use over a fire (Fig. 11.8). This vessel, however, has an interior carbonization pattern that suggests

that water was absent during at least some time during most cooking episodes. Water was either removed at the last stage of boiling or food was cooked in the pot in the absence of water.

The largest of the seed jars (WACC 9156) has a similar soot-carbon pattern. The exterior is sooted and the interior has a carbon patch below the mid-section, which is caused

TABLE 11.2.
Obelisk Gray Vessels from the Prayer Rock Caves with Heavy Interior Abrasion

ASM Vessel Number	Evidence for Cooking
14400	Yes
14369	No
14304	No
14433	No
14427	Indeterminate
14359	Indeterminate
14388	No
14391	Indeterminate
14355	Indeterminate

Note: All but vessel number 14427 are seed jars.

by heating in the absence of moisture. For food to char it must reach at least 300 degrees centigrade. This can only occur when water is removed from the vessel because food below the water line will not exceed 100 degrees centigrade.

This large seed jar also has a heavily abraded interior, which was also observed on nine of the Obelisk seed jars from the Prayer Rock Caves (see Table 11.2). Only one of these abraded Obelisk Gray pots had evidence of use over a fire, four were not used over a fire, and four were indeterminate. The source of abrasion is unknown at present but there are several possibilities. First, the abrasion could be caused by mechanical contact with a scoop or ladle. We do not think, however, that this was the case. In most of the pots with interior abrasion, all of the interior surface was removed and in other cases the abrasion patch stops abruptly and follows a relatively straight line around the vessel diameter several centimeters below the rim. Such a pattern is more likely caused by the chemical erosion of the interior surface by its liquid contents (Hally 1983:19). In low-fired pottery, contents with the opposite pH of the clay can break down the clay structure (Patrick McGovern, pers. comm.). Thus an acidic ceramic could be broken down by contents with a basic pH, such as the alkaline soaking of maize, and a ceramic with a basic pH can be eroded by acidic solutions. The latter could be caused by the fermentation of some fruits or other highly acidic food. The exact nature of this process, however, is unknown and requires further experimentation.

Implications.
The correlations between seed jar design and function suggest that the vessels could perform well as cooking, storage, or food processing vessels. The use-alteration analysis demonstrates that the users of this pottery took advantage of their vessel's multifunctionality. There is evidence that some of the vessels were used for cooking (in both the dry and wet modes) and others were not, although the exact function of the noncooking vessels is not known. The heavy interior abrasion on some vessels suggests a chemical erosion but the cause is still unknown. Organic residue analysis could shed light on what these pots contained. The use-alteration analysis also demonstrated that the vessel users cooked their food in two modes: heating with water and heating without water. The latter can be caused by either cooking dry food (roasting), reheating previously boiled foods, or by boiling something until all or most of the water has been removed. Gruel or stew cooking are cases where enough water could be removed from the contents to cause interior carbon deposits, either as part of the cooking process or by accident.

SOUTHWESTERN POTTERY ORIGINS
REVISITED
Although the data presented here are just the first step toward understanding the use of

early brown ware, we think that they are nonetheless revealing. The earliest pottery on the Colorado Plateau was made by semi-sedentary pithouse dwellers who began to rely more heavily on maize and other domesticated cultigens (Crown and Wills 1995). They used the multifunctional sturdy seed jars to boil, cook a gruel, or reheat a food in the absence of water, for storage, and probably for processing of liquid that caused the erosion of interior surfaces. Out of the 74 Obelisk Gray vessels from the Prayer Rock Caves only 2 were bowls and 2 were pitchers. One prediction of the Hayden (1995a) model is that the earliest pottery should be dominated by forms used for serving. This expectation is not met at this site because only 6 percent of the Obelisk Gray vessels were designed for serving. The data presented here agree with the characterization by Crown and Wills (1995) of the context for the adoption of pottery on the Colorado Plateau.

What appears to be happening on the plateau is that the adoption of pottery is a family-by-family decision. The evidence for the brown ware pottery, though widespread, is very scattered. It is likely that between A.D. 200 and A.D. 400 there were families that made and used pottery living next to people who did not adopt this technology. The range of early brown ware technological variability also suggests that individuals may have been copying a design (i.e., a seed jar form with sand temper and a roughly polished exterior) but attempting to make it with local resources. Each new potter had to struggle to replicate this design with their own unique local resources.

We do not yet have any direct evidence to infer what was cooked or processed in these pots. Although corn can be processed in new ways with cooking pots, you certainly can effectively prepare corn without ceramic pots as had been done for centuries. But as Crown and Wills (1995) point out, new varieties of maize are also appearing at this time that may have prompted different ways of processing in vessels. Thus the adoption of pottery could more easily be explained using Brown's model in which people had a greater demand for vessels to store food, soak maize, or store water, but they could not meet the demand with baskets, skins, or some other nonpottery container. Brown's model, however, implies that vessels were not adopted to solve a particular processing problem. Although I am in general agreement with this, I believe that we do not yet have enough evidence for the Southwest to suggest that pots were not adopted to solve a particular processing need—the boiling of beans.

Beans are the second important cultigen in the great corn, beans, and squash combination that came to dominate the entire Southwest as well as Central and South America. Beans can be soaked and ground into a meal, but by far the most common method to cook beans worldwide is by boiling. The cooking of beans, however, can often take from 2 to 3 hours. Long-term simmering of this sort would be tedious with the pre-pottery cooking technologies. The one great advantage of ceramic pots is their ability to boil foods for long periods with little monitoring. Another advantage of boiling beans instead of some other form of processing is that it reduces the levels of oligosaccharides, the substances that cause flatulence and in some cases extreme abdominal cramping (Stahl 1989:182). Although there is a humorous side to this, it certainly may explain the fact that the most common method of bean preparation is boiling. Intestinal discomfort may in fact play a role in the adoption of pottery on the Colorado Plateau. Certainly the key to solving this riddle is to further explore how these vessels were used (Longacre 1995:279). Subsequent testing will focus on identifying the organic residues in the early brown ware pottery.

12

"Looking Up" at Early Ceramics in Greece

KAREN D. VITELLI

VANTAGE POINTS

I have been working for many years with the Neolithic pottery from excavations at Franchthi Cave and Lerna in southern Greece, material that represents roughly the first three thousand years of ceramic production in that area. I am also an experimental potter, less interested in replication of particular pots or techniques than in exploring the possibilities of the medium. My experimental work is guided by two simple rules: (1) use only materials, tools, and techniques that would have been available to prehistoric potters and, (2) when I break the first rule, e.g., by using tap water, matches, or plastic covers, I must pursue the implications of the broken rule in the prehistoric context. I make pots to learn the problems and potential of the medium, to understand where the potter can or must make choices, what those choices are, and how one goes about making them (van der Leeuw 1991:15).

The experimental work has led me to put the potters' choices at the foundation of my archaeological analyses of the Franchthi and Lerna pottery, and in so doing, to try to think as a potter and think of sherds as pieces of pots that resulted from a series of choices made by a potter. In that way I expect to be able, at least sometimes, to determine what choices the potter had, to consider why a potter made a particular choice and may have rejected another (van der Leeuw 1991:30). Through the choices reflected in their prod-

ucts, I attempt to see the potters as contributors to the shaping of their societies. My perspective, then, is that individuals play a significant role in shaping the development of society within the limits imposed by their natural environment and available technology.

Probably that is why I find Hayden's aggrandizer–competitive feasting model for the origins and development of inequality (e.g., Hayden 1990, 1995a, 1995b) attractive, because it gives human decisions a primary role, yet not entirely satisfying, because it also seems to attribute to individuals a degree of prescience and premeditated control over the outcome of their choices that I find implausible (Shennan 1989:333). I was, therefore, pleased to find Wilson's articulation of my reservation:

Social scientists see other societies through an implicit, comparative lens, their own society. When, for example, we speak quite neutrally about "precapitalist" society, we isolate out economic practice as it is found in our own society and study the other society in those terms, comparatively. Because capitalism depends on relations of production, materials of production, capital, and so forth we look for the precursors or analogues of these in what we have been pleased to acknowledge as precapitalist. But this cannot be an accurate reflection of how the society in question theorized or practiced, because for them capitalism was a future and an unknown. Their way of making a living *had to be framed in terms of the past and the present.* (Wilson 1988:x, emphasis added)

Wilson proposes to "look up and around" rather than "back and down," to take a vantage point closer to that of those being studied. Van der Leeuw has made much the same point, in almost identical language:

If [archaeologists and historians] are to realize their avowed aim of reconstructing past decision making, they will have to stop *looking back* from their present position in time, trying to recognize in the past patterns that are observed in the present. *They will have to travel back* in time and *look forward* with those whom they study. (van der Leeuw 1991:13, emphasis in original. See also Torrence and van der Leeuw 1989:8)

Individuals in Neolithic Greece and other early agricultural communities had no foreknowledge of the larger social consequences of their choices on which to base those choices. They did, however, have a past and a present, and from these their choices grew. As Ucko notes "what appears at first sight to be 'new' is often, in fact, a recombination—in new form—of what went before, or of differing numbers and combinations of elements which might have been discrete in an earlier period or in a different context" (Ucko 1989:xiii).

In what follows, I attempt to "look up" at the Neolithic in southern Greece, focusing primarily on the potters and their creations, placing their innovations in the context of their immediate past and present. While the exercise is just a beginning and the inherent limitations many, it nevertheless gives a new cast to a number of previously puzzling aspects of the ceramic data. It leads me to suggest that the first potters were a kind of shaman, their pots initially an accidental by-product of the more significant performances of their production, especially their firing. These early potters and, eventually, their pots, may well have been an element in competitive feasts, as Hayden suggests. The initial role of pots as symbolic elements in rit-

ual, however, seems likely to have affected their development for use in other contexts, in turn affecting the changing roles of potters (and no doubt others) during the course of the Neolithic. By combining the vantage points of "looking up" and "looking back" we begin to sense the ways that the unintended consequences of some prehistoric choices contributed to the unforeseen development of the kinds of social and economic organization we now recognize, with hindsight, as familiar.

EARLY NEOLITHIC CERAMIC ASSEMBLAGES IN SOUTHERN GREECE

The Neolithic in Greece is generally divided into five phases: Preceramic (ca. 7000–6500 B.C., calibrated), Early Neolithic (EN, ca. 6500–6000 B.C.), Middle Neolithic (MN, ca. 6000–5500 B.C.), Late Neolithic (LN, ca. 5500–5000 B.C.) and Final Neolithic (FN, ca. 5000–4000/3500 B.C.). My work to date has concentrated, as will the following discussion, on the first three of these, with only preliminary comment on the later two.

Lerna is a low settlement mound on the coast of the Gulf of Argos in the Peloponnese, best known for its Early Bronze Age remains. Excavations in the 1950s also produced substantial Early and Middle Neolithic material in some of the deep, relatively undisturbed trenches, and a small amount of Late and Final Neolithic material from disturbed later deposits. The Franchthi Cave, also in southern Greece, and about a Neolithic day's sail across the Gulf of Argos from Lerna (Fig. 12.1), was excavated in the late 1960s and early 1970s. Inside the cave, 11–12 m of cultural debris, of which only the uppermost meter or two are Neolithic, were removed from half a dozen trenches. Out in front of the cave, along the modern shoreline called the Paralia, exclusively Neolithic deposits add to the record of that period. Between the cave and the Paralia, all five Neolithic phases are represented in stratified deposits, with over 2 metric tons of ceramics recovered from the EN through FN deposits. The earlier deposits are Paleolithic and Mesolithic, representing some 20–30,000 years of occu-

Fig. 12.1. Franchthi Cave and Lerna: Neolithic coastal sites on opposite sides of the Gulf of Argos in southern Greece.

pation during which clay was used as a building material, e.g., in packing the cracks between fireplace rocks, but was not, apparently, manipulated into discrete objects and fired for permanence.

Although it is highly probable that all the necessary technology for producing ceramics had been available for millennia, it was apparently not fully exploited in Greece until the mid-7th millennium B.C. (calibrated). We are still debating whether the earliest Neolithic phase at Franchthi and at sites in the rest of Greece is truly "preceramic," i.e., both earlier than the rest of the Neolithic and with no ceramics at all, as is the case in the Near East; or whether the occasional sherds and figurines from potentially preceramic deposits are in situ, and represent a phase when

ceramic objects were made, but only very rarely (e.g., Perlés and Vitelli 1994:226–230; Vitelli 1993:39). If the latter, then the basic idea and rudimentary knowledge of ceramics, if not actual objects, could have come to Greece with the domesticates and developed locally. That is, in fact, a simpler scenario than the former, in which ceramics would join the Neolithic repertoire in Greece fully developed, and only many generations after the domesticates and other elements of sedentary farming life, in what we call the Early Neolithic.

Most excavations in Greece, for a variety of reasons, save and publish only a small sample of all the pottery they recover from an excavation, thus we do not know—and for relevant excavations cannot go back and establish without additional excavation—the full range of variation present in their assemblages. Franchthi is, happily, an exception to the usual sampling practice. The EN ceramics from that site show, in spite of a superficial similarity of shapes and surface finish, a considerable range of consistent variation. The pots were made, throughout the EN sequence of superimposed deposits, according to five different recipes, each calling for different sets of ingredients or raw materials. I've called each of these a "ware." Besides the differences in the raw materials, subtle but consistent differences in building and firing procedures are evident for each ware and suggest that the same individual did not create pieces in more than one ware. The work of at least five potters is, therefore, represented. All the wares were apparently manufactured locally, with the possible exception of one (see below), which represents less than 1 percent of the total EN assemblage.

At least four of the same recipes or wares are present in the selected sample at Lerna, although two of those are represented by only one or two sherds each. The other two are commonly present at Lerna, and at other southern Greek Early Neolithic sites as well. Minor stylistic differences and physicochemical analyses (Jones 1986:401) suggest the wares were produced locally at each of the sites, although potters at all the sites used essentially the same sets of recipes for both ingredients and shapes. We can document very little regional exchange in ceramics in the EN. To the extent there may have been any, it was of pieces that were very like those already produced locally, so pots were not an exotic item in the sense we usually understand, and any prestige or symbolic value they carried was encoded in a way that escapes our usual measurements.

The five EN wares at Franchthi were evenly distributed around the site, occurring in consistent relative frequencies both inside the cave and on Paralia. Given even distribution and the probability that most pots were manufactured, used, and discarded at the site, we can use the recovery figures from Franchthi to arrive at a very rough idea of the scale of production in the Early Neolithic. A total of approximately 100 kg of EN pottery was recovered, from deposits representing about 2 percent of the site. An average EN vessel weighs 1 kg. Those very rough figures suggest that production over a minimum of 400 years amounted to something like 12–13 pots per year (Vitelli 1993:210). Even if the calculations are off by several magnitudes, production in the EN was extremely low. Longacre (this volume), for example, reports that a San Nicholas potter, using a paddle and anvil technique, produces several hundred vessels *per week*. While that technique may be more efficient than the simple coiling method used most frequently by the Neolithic potters, the statistic indicates that a substantially greater volume of production was a potential option for the Neolithic potters. The irregularities in the Neolithic pots confirm that they were made by potters who worked too infrequently to develop a regular rhythm in their work, suggesting that the rough calculations of scale are not unreasonable.

Yet there were at least four potters at any given time at Franchthi who could make pots, each using a distinctive recipe for ingredients and slightly different building and firing techniques, even if for only two or three pots a year. Each potter made mostly small pots: many fit comfortably in one hand, while the larger bowls have a capacity of only 4 to 8 liters (Fig. 12.2). The shapes are simple convex bowls, the easiest shape to build, although many were provided with low ring bases and small lugs that are not essential components of basic containers, but were risky additions, in that they were prone to detach during drying and firing. All the pots were carefully scraped to produce fairly uniform surfaces, with walls rarely more than 6 mm thick. All exterior surfaces were laboriously burnished, often to a high sheen. Very occasionally, potters added decoration in an iron-rich paint (fewer than 1 percent of the total). The Early Neolithic pots were labor intensive products.

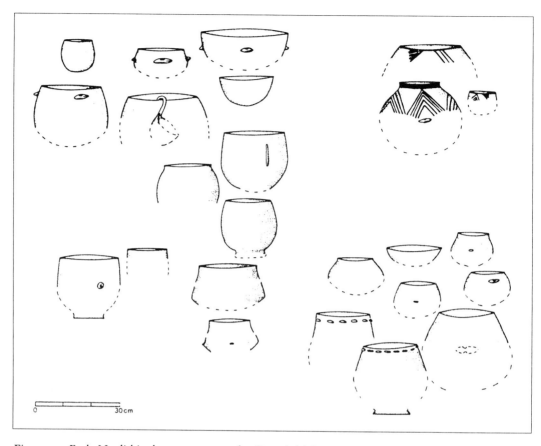

Fig. 12.2. Early Neolithic shapes represented at Franchthi Cave.

"WHY DID THEY INVENT POTTERY ANYWAY?"

In addition to the above question that Long-acre recently posed (Longacre 1995), I had long wondered, for Greece, why they invented pottery at the beginning of the Neolithic, and not earlier, or, for that matter, later? Absent a good Neolithic myth, any attempt at an answer seemed to hinge on documenting what the first pots were used for, so I set that as an early goal of my study.

Given the coincidence of early pots and early agriculture in the Aegean and many other parts of the world, and no doubt also influenced by our archaeological preoccupation with subsistence, I set out with the usual assumptions about rodent- and fire-proof storage for seeds, for the new crop surpluses, and for cooking, to document the use of Franchthi's earliest pottery as storage and cooking containers. To my surprise and ini-

tial dismay, however, I found that the numbers of pots from Early Neolithic contexts at Franchthi and their limited capacities would have been barely sufficient to store the volume of seed necessary to plant a single hectare, much less any surplus crops (Vitelli 1989:26). Nor was there evidence to support use of any of the pots on a fire, e.g., there are no signs of charring or spalling (Skibo 1992: 112), and shapes with bases are poorly designed for that function. Indeed, some evidence, e.g., of burnished surfaces with their luster undiminished by repeated exposure to fire, suggested the pots had not been so used until late in the Middle Neolithic, some 500–1,000 years after the appearance of the first pots (Vitelli 1989:24). Others have now documented a similar situation in other parts of Greece in the earlier Neolithic (Bjŝrk 1995; Gardner 1978:143), so Franchthi is not an isolated example.

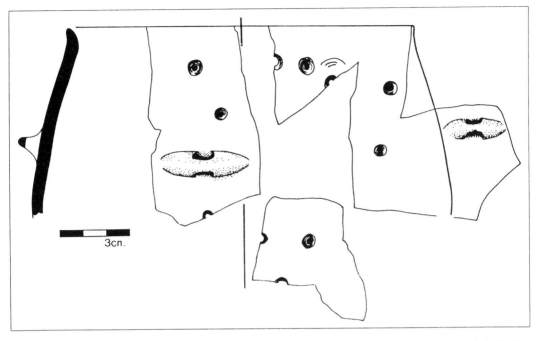

Fig. 12.3. Nonjoining fragments of an Early Neolithic pot at Franchthi with multiple holes drilled after firing to mend the broken vessel.

Probably I should not have been surprised. It is quite possible to process cereal grains without ceramics, and that was certainly done, as is, in fact, implicitly acknowledged in the term "Preceramic Neolithic." Hearths and ovens that apparently substituted for portable ceramic cooking containers have been identified at some sites (e.g., Gimbutas et al. 1989:32–68), and other means of cooking without ceramic vessels could have been available. Foster pointed out long ago that diet and taste are "tenaciously held values . . . known to inhibit cultural change" (Arnold 1985:139, referring to Foster 1962:76), and knowing that, we might expect an initial reluctance to innovations in the methods of food preparation and to the ensuing new tastes and consistencies.

Pots are too obviously useful as containers never to have been used as such, but there simply were not enough of them in the EN at Franchthi to have been used widely for that purpose. Individual pots were apparently prized enough to be mended if they broke (Fig. 12.3), but even these show no signs of use wear—in spite of the fact that all are low-fired (700 degrees C), soft, and scratch easily.

The one ware that may have reached Franchthi by exchange occurs at Franchthi only in a gray variety, in occasional sherds that occur throughout the EN sequence. The same ware at Lerna, and other sites where it occurs in much higher frequencies, occurs in oxidized yellow, red-painted, and mottled varieties as well (Vitelli 1997:24–25). The gray pieces seem to have been preferentially selected for exchange, suggesting they carried some kind of symbolic significance, although other reduced wares in the same shapes and sizes were made by the Franchthi potters, so gray and black pots in themselves were nothing novel or unavailable locally.

It was these realizations that first suggested to me that, instead of looking back from the uses to which pots were eventually put, I should try to "look up" at the origins of pottery from the perspective of people who had no experience or knowledge of pottery at all. From that vantage point my initial assumption about the relationship between food and pots makes little sense. If no one had even heard of ceramic containers in "pre-ceramic" times, they could have had no idea of the various properties of ceramic containers nor of the many advantages and efficiencies pots would eventually offer. Discovering and learning what pots were good for must have been every bit as much a part of the very beginnings of pottery as learning how to make them.

If people had to discover what ceramics were good for, then things we consider as guides to ceramic function, like thermal shock resistance and porosity, even open versus closed shapes, and the sizes of vessels could have been completely incidental to the original function and thus, if we look for such properties to elucidate initial use, we could be badly misled (see also P. Arnold, this volume). That realization put a bit of a damper on beginning my analysis of why pots were invented with trying to establish vessel function.

In "looking up" at the origins of pottery, then, I had to change my questions and direction. A more promising approach proved to be asking who would have been in a position to discover or invent pottery. Who would have had experience with the materials and processes necessary for basic ceramic manufacture, and might have been motivated or had occasion to combine them in a new way? Who would also have been in a sufficiently influential position to make the innovation acceptable, so that it was adopted by others and incorporated into general use (Prentice 1986:111).

The individuals we seek to identify must have been familiar with clay and sources of clay. They must have had experience of its properties, wet and dry. They must have known that kneading or wedging creates a more uniform and effective mixture, that additions of liquid can alter its behavior, that timing of additions and other processing is crucial, and so on (Vitelli 1995:60–61). In fact, much of the background knowledge and many of the procedures for acquiring and preparing the ingredients for pots, and for building, finishing, and firing them are very similar to those needed for the acquisition

and preparation of plant foods, an activity long attributed to the women of hunter-gatherer groups (e.g., Watson and Kennedy 1991:269). Others have also noted this relationship (Amiran 1965; Crown and Wills 1995:248). It makes sense that the two areas of production share common methods because they were practiced by the same individuals. Thus I suggest that their experience with collecting and processing plant foods put women in a good position to invent and make the first pots.

Some of the earliest pots at Franchthi are tempered with crushed calcite and limestone (Vitelli 1993:96), so the first potters already were familiar with some of the effects of non-plastics on a clay body. If it was women who had been using clay as building material and to fill cracks around hearth rocks, they would have had opportunity to observe those effects. Equally, their experience of fires would have provided opportunity to observe the effects of fire on clay used as packing—and something of that sort was crucial, for the real innovation of Neolithic potters was the *firing* of clay bodies.

Thus the answer to the first of my new questions "Who had access to the materials and processes?" seems to be "Women did." The evidence from the earliest pots at Franchthi indicates that at least four women (or five, depending on whether the fifth ware was produced locally) at any given point in the Early Neolithic at Franchthi were knowledgeable about making pots. Yet those women made only a few pots per year. If their pots were significantly useful containers or if they contributed to the social standing of their possessors—if, for example, pots were prestige containers for use at competitive feasts—the potters could have chosen to make many more of them. They could have chosen to spend less time on each pot, to combine their expertise and use a single recipe with the most readily available and most easily processed ingredients. They could have chosen less labor intensive procedures and less risky shapes. Something, then, restricted early production to only a few women and to only a few pots.

THE MAGIC OF CLAY

Raw clay is itself a rather magical substance. Dry, it may exist in a compacted, rock-hard state, or in a powdery and soft one. Add just enough water and it becomes as slippery as ice, but plastic and malleable. Apply a bit of pressure and it takes and holds a new form. Let it dry in that form and it becomes rock-like again. Add water once more, and it dissolves back to mud. These properties of clay could easily have been observed in prepottery times, and were exploited in packing the cracks between rocks sheltering a fire, and in other contexts. My students and I were once sitting outside on a beautiful early spring day, making figurines and talking about plans for a first firing. A young man from Burkina Faso came by on roller skates and nearly crashed when he saw what we were doing. Breathless and grinning, he explained that "It is just like home! We make figurines just like that in my village!" Since we were thinking about firings, we asked him how they fired the figurines in his village. "Oh we don't fire them," he said. "We just dry them and use them for decoration and make new ones the next time." That option was available to pre-historic people as well, and in temperate climates, at least, subsequent exposure to moisture (intentional or not) would have assured that no trace was left for us to find.

But add fire to the equation, and the natural material is permanently, irreversibly transformed to rocklike form. Fire must have been in prehistoric times, as it is still, a powerful symbol in its own right. Fire consumes wood, fiber, food, and flesh, giving off smoke and smells, sounds, and light. Fire even weakens rock. But combined with earth, air, and water—other ancient and powerful symbols— fire transforms the combination to something solid and permanent.

If a still-damp, newly fashioned object of clay is placed directly in a fire, it will steam and hiss and soon explode, often with a rapid series of loud cracks, possibly with flying bits and pieces. If the piece is thoroughly dry and exposed to a slow fire, one can watch the piece slowly turn black (as soot is deposited on it) and then, light again (as it heats up and

the soot burns off). The object may get hot enough to glow brightly like coals, and eventually emerge a markedly different color than when it first went in. It may be noticeably smaller, may have amorphous dark and light markings, may be intact, cracked, or in fragments—and if in fragments, some parts may have disappeared entirely. Certainly for novices, the process and the results seem, even today, unpredictable and magical. Even with modern scientific theory to explain and guide, it takes experience and luck to exert enough control to achieve predictable results. Certainly until that point is reached, the sound and light show of an open firing is potentially full of symbolism and possibilities for divining.

The first prehistoric firings of clay objects may well have been accidental, their intentional repetition as likely to have been motivated by the drama of the firing process as by the product, since it seems to me unlikely that raw beginners, with no prior experience to guide their practice could have expected to recover intact pots from their fires with any reliability. This kind of occasional practice could account for the rare sherd in a "pre-ceramic" context. It may also explain why only a few women made pots, each with a specific recipe, and only on infrequent occasions. The early potter may have been a kind of spiritual or ritual healer, or shaman, the resulting pot (when that was the result) of less consequence than the drama of its production.

EARLY POTTERS AS SHAMANS

Some women in hunter-gatherer groups were, no doubt, knowledgeable about the medicinal and mood-altering properties of some plants (e.g., Sherratt 1991:51), and were likely given special respect, or seen as imbued with supernatural powers because of the valuable contribution they made to group welfare through exercise of their specialized knowledge. They may already have been using raw clays as part of their medicine kit, for clays have, in addition to their ceramic properties, a number of medicinal properties (Abehsera 1990). They would have known the plastic properties of raw clay from experience with it as a building material, where they probably had long since learned the value of nonplastic inclusions in reducing shrinkage and weight. They may have modeled small containers for their potions from clay, using them in dry, unfired form. They may even have used clay to model hollow forms for use as drums in rituals associated with their potions. Chances are fire and smoke were already a part of their rituals. When a molded item of clay fell into a fire and exploded or changed colors, the shaman was already attuned to reading meaning into such things, and could have seized the opportunity—especially if her group was in particular need of advice and guidance at that moment. The potter-as-shaman places the discovery and initial development of pottery in the hands, not only of women, but of a few women who were positioned to take existing elements and combine them in a socially relevant new way.

Since, in Greece, that "moment" was early in the developments of the Neolithic, an unsettled time of considerable social stress, it is not hard to think of reasons that existing shamans might have needed to stretch and extend their skills, and with them, their sphere of influence. Others have pointed out the likelihood of increased social conflict in sedentary communities (e.g., Chapman 1994:136; Cullen 1985:39–40), and that ritual and ceremony are among the means available for settling and diffusing disputes and maintaining group cohesion (e.g., Johnson 1982; Kuijt 1995). If the shaman's skill in using the newly discovered drama of firing clay proved useful and effective, as it apparently did, the stature and social importance of the shaman-potter would have helped insure that the innovation was accepted by other practitioners of the supernatural arts and incorporated into traditional behavior.

If at first pots were made by shamans as part of their rituals, it would explain the restrictions on who could make pots, as well as the low level of production in the EN. With the shaman as our starting point for ceramics, we can follow, in subsequent developments during the Neolithic, some of the

surely unimagined consequences of the introduction of ceramics, including the consequences of their introduction by ritual practitioners. It is the latter, I think, that was responsible for the rather long time it took for pots to find their way to the now-familiar place in our kitchen cupboards.

Early production that focused on the process, rather than the product, would have given the potters-shamans the experience and opportunity necessary to learn that they could control the outcome, as they observed and made connections between what they did and what resulted. With more control over their performances, they produced more intact vessels—perhaps an indication that already early in the EN interest in the product was growing. With more intact vessels available in the community there were opportunities to discover ways in which pots could be useful. As the advantages of pots as durable, showy containers began to be evident, the focus of production would have changed from the process to the product itself. In fact, the pieces of one particular, long-standing Neolithic ceramic puzzle fit together rather nicely when viewed from this vantage point.

THE USE OF CALCIUM CARBONATES AS TEMPER

I mentioned above that some of the earliest pottery at Franchthi, and in fact, throughout southern Greece, makes use of crushed calcite and limestone as tempering material. Prehistoric potters around the world often chose these, or the chemically similar shell, as tempering materials even though the carbonates, if exposed to temperatures of around 800 degrees C, which are well within the range of simple open fires, tend to decompose, absorb water from the atmosphere, expand, and mar, if not actually crumble the pot soon after the original firing. For years many of us have wondered why potters would go out of their way to add a material to their clay bodies that had the potential to destroy their hard work. Modern ceramics manuals warn potters to avoid clays with carbonate inclusions (Rhodes 1957:20) for this reason. My students learn the wisdom of that advice whenever they use a nicely plastic, but fossil carbonate-rich clay that occurs all around our campus.

Recent studies have shown that, in the right combinations, calcite or shell can produce what other additives to a clay body do not, a watertight body for low-fired ceramics (Budak 1991; Green 1996). That may well explain why so many prehistoric potters sought out carbonates for temper. It does not, however, explain why it ever occurred to anyone to try that combination in the first place, and to persist until they came up with the right proportions, especially since other non-plastics such as sand were often available, required little or no preparation, and caused fewer problems in producing an intact pot.

If the first potters were, on the other hand, more interested in the process of making a pot than in the resulting product, then the very fact of the additional preparation required to find and crush the glittering calcite crystals would have contributed to the mystical or curative powers of the recipe. If the point of the ritual process was to provide direction in something like conflict resolution, then a pot that might survive the firing, but erupt with boils days later, has great mystical potential. We might imagine that the potter-shaman began using crushed calcite, as she did the other ingredients in her clay mix, for its shamanic properties (whatever they might have been). She soon realized added advantages for her ritual purposes when the pieces sometimes disintegrated. She, and the other potter-shamans working with their carbonate-free recipes, repeated their performances often enough to acquire control of the processes and produce increasing numbers of intact pots. With samples of the various shaman's pots in circulation, there would have been opportunity to notice that the pots of the carbonate-using shaman held water, while the others did not. Surely that would appear as strong magic, a testimony to the special power of some shaman-potters. No wonder the carbonate-tempered ware was the most frequently made—although in the EN at Franchthi still infrequently enough to suggest that the process was still the real focus of potting. That situation, however, sees further change in the Middle Neolithic.

THE MIDDLE NEOLITHIC POTTERS

The transition from Early to Middle Neolithic was apparently a gradual, continuous one, marked, for us, by the introduction of a new ware, or recipe. It may have been marked, for them, by a particularly stressful interval, for the development of a new recipe and its quick rise to dominance hints at an emerging sense of competition among the shaman-potters to meet a need. Before being completely displaced by the new ware, however, the five EN wares at Franchthi continued to be produced in small quantities for several more generations, so they were apparently still deemed efficacious, if in a more limited set of circumstances.

Using the same rough calculations of annual production applied above to the Early Neolithic, we may suggest that the Middle Neolithic potters produced a total of 100–200 pots per year at Franchthi (Vitelli 1993: 211 n. 10). While still within the capability of two or three potters in a few weeks of concentrated work, the numbers represent a substantial increase over levels of production in the EN. The pots themselves confirm that the potters were spending more time making pots: the surfaces are often so even and regular they show no tool marks at all, the curves so regular that large segments of rim sherds fit exactly on compass-drawn circles. The new recipe also uses calcium carbonates as temper, but they are quite uniformly distributed and much finer (well under 1 mm in maximum dimension), except in the largest vessels. For these, adjustments were made in the clay body, by adding more and larger non-plastics to better cope with the greater shrinkage of thicker walls. The walls of all the other pots are consistently quite thin (4–5 mm).

Again, it is the firing of this new ware, which defines the Middle Neolithic in southern Greece, that is most remarkable. The ware was dubbed "Urfirnis," or first glaze, by a German excavator years ago. In its developed form, in fact, Urfirnis is a hard-fired ware in which the surface slip and sometimes the fabric itself, have frequently sintered. Even more impressive than the temperatures reached is the control of atmosphere the potters achieved. The ware must have been fired in a kiln, in an at least loosely controlled three-stage process of oxidation-reduction-oxidation, similar to that used so effectively by the classical Black and Red-Figured potters of Athens nearly five millennia later (Vitelli 1997). This three-stage firing allowed the potters to produce pots with a black iron oxide-rich slip that either coated the entire surface of the vessel or, applied selectively in complex geometric patterns, formed patterns against a light colored, oxidized clay ground (Fig. 12.4). At the height of its production, this patterned Urfirnis accounts for as much as 25 percent of the assemblage. Although executed within the rather limiting rules of the decorative style, the combination of patterns and their placement make each vessel distinctive.

The innovations within the Urfirnis tradition appear gradually and in a technically logical sequence over the course of the roughly 500 years of the MN. Their occurrence in stratified deposits permits us to distinguish at least six subphases within the MN at Franchthi, demonstrating a fairly rapid rate of ceramic innovation. The MN Urfirnis potters were not mechanically reproducing the skills and the pots their predecessors had taught them to make, but were actively searching, experimenting, reaching for new and different possibilities. They took risks, and, if the examples of overfired, warped, lime-popped, and otherwise defective pieces (Vitelli 1993:77) are any guide, they often lost in the firing the pieces that they had spent much time and effort in perfecting.

Their goal was not, then, just to make *more* pots, nor even just to produce a suitable container, or an "attractive" (by whatever criteria) container, or a red or black one, or a decorated one—these they were obviously capable of doing pretty much on command. They were reaching for something more or different, showing off skills, competing. Perhaps what we see as risks that led to losses of products were acceptable because the pot

Fig. 12.4. A patterned Urfirnis pot from Franchthi Cave with the pattern in a sintered iron oxide-rich paint that fired black against the pale clay ground.

was still not the only or the main product desired. Perhaps the process, in particular the firing, was still the desired "product"—and in certain contexts, the destruction of all the time-consuming pieces that went into the firing was the desired, appropriate, or at least, an acceptable end. In "looking up" at potters who put substantial effort into producing a kiln load of pots only to have them destroyed by overzealous firing procedures we may have an origin for the ritual breaking of pots as a demonstration of power and wealth (Hayden 1995a:261).

Still, the increase in the number of pots, the high level of technical knowledge and dexterity they represent, and most persuasively, the substantial variety of new shapes (Fig. 12.5) all point to an interest in the pots themselves, as well as the process. The time spent on perfecting and embellishing the risky, angular shapes and glossy, flawless surfaces also suggests an interest in display. Some shapes, such as the many shallow bowls, and especially the large open basins on tall pedestals, also seem designed to display their contents. All the characteristics of Urfirnis, in fact, would seem to make it well suited for a role as prestige container in regional competitive feasts, where the ritual performance of shaman-potters, perhaps trying to outdo each other in the demonstration

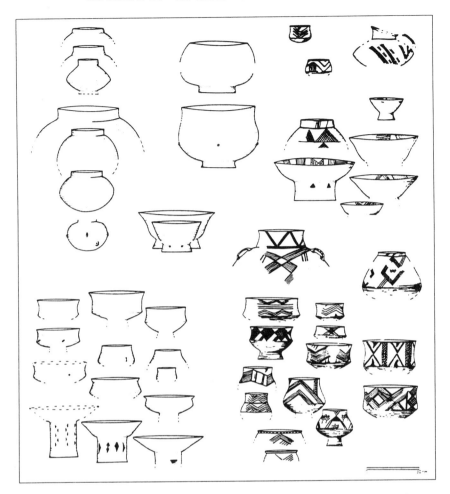

Fig. 12.5. Middle Neolithic Urfirnis shapes in monochrome and patterned varieties from Franchthi Cave.

of their powers, combined with the conspicuous display of their symbolically loaded, if not entirely exotic goods.

Another innovation of the MN potters fits neatly into a feasting model as well: the specialized cooking pot. These pots, which appear toward the end of MN, were made with a recipe that called for more and larger nonplastic inclusions than Urfirnis, and would have provided better thermal shock resistance. The shape is rounded, with no sharp angles and without a base (Fig. 12.6). The surfaces were usually smoothed, but unburnished, and were blackened, perhaps by thorough smudging in the final stage of firing. Many sherds from lower bodies have reoxidized, as one would expect if the vessels had

sat for extended periods on a flaming fire, i.e., they appear to have been specially designed for use on a fire and the evidence suggests, for the first time, that they were actually used in that context. The building and finishing techniques used for the cooking pots are sufficiently similar to those used for the contemporary Urfirnis to suggest both were made by the same individuals. Indeed, it makes sense that potters sufficiently experienced, skilled, and innovative to make Urfirnis would have the ability and the imagination to conceive of and design pots for specialized use on a fire.

They made them, however, far less frequently than they made other pots: the cooking pots make up less than 10 percent of later MN assemblages. With their small numbers,

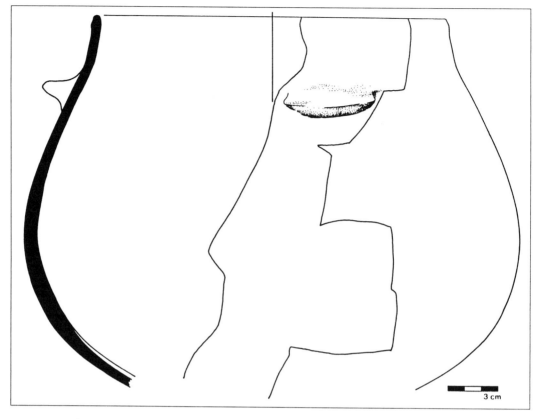

Fig. 12.6. The specially designed late Middle Neolithic cooking pot from Franchthi Cave.

and capacities of only 4 to 7 liters (Vitelli 1993:215), they would hardly have been adequate for general daily preparation of staple foods, but must have seen more limited use, such as on special feasting occasions. Even then, they could have served only for preparing something consumed in small quantities, or by only some participants. Perhaps we should, following Hayden's suggestion of the importance of delicacies in competitive feasting (Hayden 1990:36), consider whether they were used for brewing beer from some of the cultivated grain, rather than for preparing gruel (Braidwood et al. 1953; Katz and Maytag 1991; Kavanagh 1994).

THE SHAMAN-POTTER AS SPECIALIST

Hayden points out that craft specialization "emerges first among complex hunter-gatherers as part of elite prerogatives (shamans, exclusive hunters, carvers) or to provide labor-intensive craft items for elites"

(Hayden 1995a:259). The EN shaman-potters of Greece appear to qualify as craft specialists on both grounds. Their pottery-making was a restricted activity whose practice produced perceived benefits for others beyond their immediate kin.

Even without a shamanic role, the MN Urfirnis potters would qualify as craft specialists by virtue of the high level of complex technical knowledge and expertise they possessed and developed so early in the history of the medium. The evidence suggests that they were, however, also still practicing the craft as ritual specialists. Their products were labor intensive, high risk, often individualized pieces, all of which are characteristics of attached, rather than independent specialists. Costin points out that attached specialists "evolve along with social inequalities, as a means for elites and governments to supply themselves with special, high-value goods, to finance their activities, and to control the ideology and technology of power" (Costin 1991:12–13). This too would seem to place the MN Urfirnis potters firmly within the context of Hayden's model.

But if all the Urfirnis and cooking pots were produced at and for infrequent feasts and as demonstrations of a shaman's power—perhaps in the service of another's cause—they were the only pots around. There are no other wares that filled in for use between feasts, no pieces acquired through exchange with groups outside the Urfirnis sphere. The Urfirnis and cooking pot fragments are found in the same deposits and both are distributed essentially uniformly throughout all the MN sites, whether cave or open air, and with no apparent concentrations of potsherds generally, or of particular shapes or varieties, in limited specific portions of any site. A single Urfirnis vessel accompanies some burials, but the few examples we have hint at no pattern for the choice of vessel for its shape, decoration, or condition.

The presence of self-aggrandizers and their competitive feasts appears to explain many aspects of early ceramic production and consumption in southern Greece, but not all. The picture is still far from complete. Our understanding of the dynamics of Neolithic societies could surely benefit from additional and more intensive efforts at "looking up," at trying to understand how the past and present experiences of the participants led them individually and collectively to make choices that, in turn led, surely, to unintended and unimagined, as well as contrived outcomes.

THE LATER NEOLITHIC HOUSEWIFE-POTTER

Although much remains to be worked out for even the earlier Neolithic, and my close analyses of the later Neolithic ceramic assemblages are in only a preliminary stage, I would like to conclude with a broad glance up at the remainder of the Neolithic in southern Greece from the vantage point of the MN. I've argued that some women, who were already serving as a kind of spiritual leader or shaman, added ceramics to their repertoire of ritual performances early in the

Neolithic, to assist in resolving social conflicts and providing guidance through the unknown. Over the course of the EN, the shaman-potters learned to control (or manipulate) the outcome of their performances, and somewhere along the way, certainly by the Middle Neolithic, the pots that resulted from their performances became objects of importance, objects that carried prestige, power, and symbolic meaning, whether or not they carried anything else. Whether created at or for competitive feasts or some other form of gathering, a limited number of women with special ritual standing produced pots that brought something valued to their group. The groups were relatively small, the shaman-potters known to the consumers of their services and products. The close relationship between potter and pot implies that the shaman-potters shared the prestige of their products, indeed, imbued the products with their own prestige and power.

That relationship seems to change during the later Neolithic. Here, I can outline only the ceramic changes, and very briefly. The long-lived and widespread regional Urfirnis ware disappears at the end of MN and is replaced by a profusion of new styles, each apparently produced in a much more limited region, some perhaps at a single site (Demoule and Perlés 1993:392). The numbers, and presumably the scale of production, in the south seem to be much lower than in the MN. At Franchthi, Lerna, and other LN sites many sherds represent nonlocal production, and in quite a few cases seem likely to have come from well beyond the old Urfirnis region. Nonceramic evidence also documents wider and more extensive long-distance exchange in the LN than earlier (e.g., Demoule and Perlés 1993:395–396, 403). At the same time, there is a substantial increase in the amount of coarse and cooking ware present at these sites, constituting as much as 30–40 percent of the assemblage.

Fine pots acquired from far afield may suggest that the prestige of locally produced pots had declined, and that, in general, access to long-distance exchange was becoming a more important way for some to acquire power and prestige, among other things. The increase in cooking pots seems to suggest that the mystique of pottery in its ritual context had also diminished, which is not surprising since pots had become commonplace and the once-restricted knowledge of pottery making must have been accessible to more individuals. As their role in ritual declined, pots could be assigned larger roles in practical contexts. Hayden and others have noted this aspect of the "dynamics of prestige technologies" (Hayden 1995a:262–263). There is, however, another side to this dynamic, and it should have important consequences for our understanding of social developments in the later Neolithic.

When pots began to be acquired from far afield, and to be given new roles in contexts far removed from that of their production, the consumers no longer had direct or close knowledge of the potter. The prestige or value of a pot was separated from that of its once-familiar maker, and the possessor could assign to a pot any variety of meanings and functions. If the pot was acquiring different roles and significance, so was the potter. *Her* early associations with, and her control over the production of prestigious pots had enhanced her role in determining powerful social choices and in setting directions. But as her pots lost some of their social power, so, most likely, did she.

By the Final Neolithic, when our sites produce 80–100 percent coarse cooking ware, with substantial variation from piece to piece, pots appear to have become primarily a practical necessity. Many, and perhaps most women seem to have been making pottery for their own household use. Although the continued use of pots as the grave good of preference reminds us that pots never completely lost their symbolic meanings, pottery making, instead of providing access to pres-tige and power, gave women one more chore in their already burdensome collection (Crown and Wills 1995:246–247).

When we consider the changing dynamics of prestige goods, we should also pay attention to the effects of the changes on the producers of those goods. Where production was related to, or restricted by gender, changes in the value of the products probably affected not only the lives and status of the specific individuals involved in their production, but the larger social issue of gender relations as well.

Once pots had become practical necessities, acquiring the many functions we recognize from our own experience and from those documented in ethnographies, there was opportunity, and arguably, need, for the emergence of independent craft specialists motivated by basic economic needs. As that happened, the interrelationships among producer, product, and consumer would have developed along different lines, leading to new sets of planned and unplanned consequences. At that point, products and producers were working in circumstances more similar to those of our own experience, but they still provide plentiful opportunity for variation (see Feinman, this volume).

"Looking up" and attempting to consider the motivations and responses of prehistoric individuals from their perspective, rather than from our own, is difficult, for much in their lives was very different from our own and the evidence we have for those lives is very limited. Still, even a limited effort at assuming their vantage point brings out details and questions we might otherwise miss. If the Neolithic landscape becomes less neat than when we only look back with hindsight, I find it, nevertheless, more intriguing and provocative.

13

A Behavioral Theory of Meaning

MICHAEL BRIAN SCHIFFER WITH
THE ASSISTANCE OF ANDREA R. MILLER

INTRODUCTION

On a recent trip to Hopi, Arizona, my wife Annette, son Jeremy, and I visited the homes and shops of a dozen or so potters on First Mesa, seeking an anniversary gift for old friends. Dramatic changes had taken place since I first journeyed to Hopi in 1968. For example, many families now live in a low-density suburbia extending miles from Polacca, the village at the foot of First Mesa, and in their electrified homes are televisions, refrigerators, and countless other trappings of modernity. Despite the changes, potters are still at work—their wares more visible to tourists than they had been during any of our previous visits. And, in the nearby trading post at Keams Canyon, pricey pots of unsurpassed magnificence demonstrate that Hopi ceramics include *objets d'art* being produced for an international market (see Wyckoff 1990:72).

Oddly enough, I was struck not so much by the large-scale changes at Hopi but by the discourses between potters and their visitors. Without prompting, potters divulged the meanings of their painted designs to utter strangers. In one home, for example, we were invited into a large room where pottery was made and also displayed to customers. On several large cafeteria-type tables lay potting materials and tools, a book on historic Hopi pottery (Wade and McChesney 1981), and a few finished vessels. Gently grasping a small jar still warm from firing, the artisan pointed proudly to the design she had painted repeatedly around the pot; it was, she said, a "water bird." This design was apparently laden with traditional meanings that we were privileged to share. Decades ago, when we had ventured to ask Hopi potters what their designs meant, the usual answer was, "they are just designs." Why, I wondered, are these Hopi potters now so forthcoming with symbolic interpretations?

Impressed by the potter as well as the pot, we bought the jar with the "water bird" design and, upon returning home, placed it temporarily on our mantel. Also on the mantel was another Hopi pot we had bought in 1969—a small black-on-red bowl. This is my favorite Hopi vessel because its decorative motifs resemble those on prehistoric pottery from east-central Arizona where I did fieldwork long ago (Hanson and Schiffer 1975). Glancing at the bowl as I had a hundred times before, it suddenly seemed different: there on the interior were several garden-variety motifs, previously unnoticed, that now appeared to be feathers—perhaps a wing. In the space of just one day, the meaning of that bowl's decoration had changed for me.

Upon closer reflection, I found the feather interpretation perplexing. After all, the potter from whom we bought the bowl in 1969 made no mention of feathers, much less wings or birds. Did I dare assume that they had been there all along? The most comforting answer was that the potter had painted a feather symbol but declined to mention it. But what if she had simply selected that motif from a repertoire of traditional designs that had no specific meanings to her? A momentary interpretive triumph had given way to uncertainty.

Where was the meaning (or meanings) of this painted design actually situated? Was it in my present-day interaction with the pot? Was it in the painting activities of the potter? Or did it arise in our recent conversation with the maker of the "water-bird" jar? I was discovering that meaning could be a quagmire, particularly when it amounted to nothing more than a Socratic dialogue with myself.

For guidance I turned to the literatures of symbolic, structural, contextual, and interpretive archaeologies (e.g., Hodder 1987, 1989a, 1989b, 1991; Leone 1977; Leone and Potter 1988; Shanks and Tilley 1992; Tilley 1990, 1991, 1993). Although idea-rich, these programs lack methodology for rigorously handling artifact meanings in specific cases. Indeed, many postprocessualists advocate hermeneutics instead of the so-called positivist methodologies of processual and behavioral archaeologies (e.g., Shanks and Tilley 1992:103–110; Thomas 1993b; Tilley 1990, 1991). An archaeological hermeneutics properly calls on investigators to engage in critical reflection during the interpretive process and to deeply contextualize evidence, but a methodology-free hermeneutics is little more than a warrant for the empathetic engagement of analyst with object, much like the exegesis of a text or the art historian's art (e.g., Prown 1993:17). Although the most adroit interpretations rest on far more than impressions and intuition, even an interpretation informed by a host of seemingly pertinent evidence may be behaviorally problematic if it is not grounded in the concrete interactions and activities taking place during the life histories of people and artifacts (Conkey 1995). More troubling still, in humanistic disciplines where interpretive strategies prevail, scholars seem never to resolve specific issues.

Given that the study of meaning had not

been assigned a high priority by processualists and behavioralists, many postprocessualists understandably turned to humanistic frameworks focused on meaning. But, is the hermeneutic "attitude" (Gadamer 1987: 132), which privileges language and text and thus generates mainly discourses about discourses, the only way to study meaningful phenomena? I think not.

Archaeologists, I suggest, can formulate new behavioral theory and method for fashioning empirically tractable questions about meaning by considering the roles of artifacts in human communication (see also Fletcher 1996; King 1994; Richardson 1987; Thomas 1993a, 1996; Wobst 1977). In constructing an artifact-based theory of meaning, I have drawn inspiration and ideas from several disciplines, but the new theory is essentially archaeological because it takes the process of archaeological inference as the paradigm for all human communication, situating people in a material world (Thomas 1996:55, 63–65) from which they constantly obtain information to facilitate activities. Indeed, the new theory employs "activity" as the basic analytic unit (Schiffer 1992b, chapters 1 and 7). For archaeologists interested in studying meanings, the theory furnishes an alternative to hermeneutics and other humanistic approaches.

In this paper, I present a theory of communication and, employing two decorated Hopi pots, illustrate its use for framing questions and hypotheses about meaningful phenomena.

ARTIFACTS, HUMAN BEHAVIOR, AND COMMUNICATION
THE BEHAVIORAL PERSPECTIVE

As is well known, behavioral archaeologists emphasize the study of people-artifact relationships (e.g., Rathje 1977; Rathje and Schiffer 1982; Reid et al. 1975; Schiffer 1992b, 1995a; Skibo et al. 1995), even arguing that these relationships can be the starting point for building new social theory (Rathje 1979; Schiffer 1992a, 1995b; Walker et al. 1995). In promoting this perspective, behavioralists contend that artifacts participate in virtually all human activities (e.g., Rathje and Schiffer 1982:7; Schiffer 1992b:1). Few have disputed this claim in print, but students in the classroom eagerly serve up counter-examples. In addition to sex—an activity that has heavy artifact involvement, especially when it is not defined narrowly as coitus—the most commonly alleged exception is two people engaged only in conversation. I usually point out that even a conversing couple is an activity in which artifacts such as clothing, jewelry, and hairstyles take part. Moreover, people talk to each other in places—e.g., a kitchen, a patio, a hunting stand—whose artifacts also are involved in communication (Fletcher 1996; Musello 1992; Rapoport 1990; Richardson 1987).

In showing that the supposed counter-examples conform to the claim that artifacts participate in all activities, I have come to formulate an even more far-reaching assertion: virtually all human communication involves artifacts. This is so because, in order for interaction in activities to proceed, information must be obtained *and acted upon* by the activity's participants. Significantly, much of the information facilitating an activity's forward motion is acquired from artifacts (Schiffer and Skibo 1997). Thus, the theory presented below supports the evidently outrageous claim that artifacts take part in virtually all human communication.

SHORTCOMINGS IN COMMUNICATION THEORIES

Because communication theories abound in the social and behavioral sciences (Casmir 1994; Crowley 1994; Littlejohn 1991), archaeologists seemingly could adopt the most promising. Unfortunately, extant theories are deeply flawed because they take a conversing couple as *the* paradigmatic example of human communication. Four problems seem especially serious.

First, communication is modeled as a "two-body" process that transfers information from one person (the speaker or "sender") to another (the listener or "receiver"). Thus, communication involves interactions between people playing only two roles. This is a rather confining perspective, unable to accommodate common cases where people perform roles in addition to sender and receiver. And, as already noted, people in activities secure information from artifacts that also play communicative roles.

Second, in the grip of the two-body model, communication theories do not handle artifacts well. When considered at all, artifacts are treated as mediating the conversation between sender and receiver, for example, a telephone or magazine article (Fortner 1994; Gumpert and Cathcart 1990). However, as numerous archaeologists have pointed out (e.g., Binford 1962; Carr and Neitzel 1995; Conkey and Hastorf 1990; Fletcher 1996; Hodder 1982; Ingersoll and Bronitsky 1987; Leone 1977; Miller 1985, 1987; Nielsen 1995; Rathje and Schiffer 1982; Schiffer 1992b; Schiffer and Skibo 1997; Shanks and Tilley 1992; Thomas 1996; Wiessner 1984; Wobst 1977), artifacts do much more than that, playing major and minor roles in communication—even when conversation is absent. In conventional communication theories, artifacts are sometimes regarded as a separate mode or channel that links sender and receiver or as one of several nonverbal modes or codes (e.g., Burgoon 1978:144; Burgoon et al. 1996, chapter 4; Harrison and Crouch 1975:93–94; Hymes 1967:19; see also Wobst 1977:322 on the "artifact mode"), but these moves neglect artifact participation in all other communication modes (e.g., verbal, tactile, and chemical).

Third, most theories focus on the sender's actions and intent, and on how the sender can get the message across to the receiver. That the sender's role is usually privileged is not surprising since communication theorists often strive to furnish people with recipes for improving their skills in writing, public speaking, and so on. Although it is widely recognized that the receiver actively participates in communication, a satisfactory theory for archaeology must, I suggest, attach great significance to the receiver's point of view. In doing so, such a theory must shed light on how information obtained from artifacts contributes to the receiver's subsequent interaction (a response). Like the process of archaeological inference, the theory presented below is *receiver oriented.*

And fourth, although most theories acknowledge the need to consider the "context," "situation," "stage," or "setting" of communication, these factors are defined too narrowly. An archaeological theory of communication must give more than lip service, for example, to other people who are present but not conversing and to artifacts and natural phenomena in the immediate area. Indeed, factors pertaining to activity and place allow us to situate communication in its social and behavioral contexts (Burgoon et al. 1996, chapter 7; Thomas 1996).

Although problematic from an archaeological standpoint, communication theories in the social and behavioral sciences contain many useful concepts and ideas that can be exploited, along with those from archaeology, to build an artifact-based, receiver-oriented, communication theory.

BASIC DEFINITIONS
INTERACTORS AND PERFORMANCE
Human behavioral systems consist of interactors of many kinds. An interactor is any entity or phenomenon capable of taking part in interactions and activities (Schiffer and Skibo 1997). In addition to people and artifacts, interactors can include entirely natural phenomena, such as rocks, wild plants and animals, and even clouds. People, artifacts, and natural phenomena combine in various ways to form compound interactors. For example, artifacts such as body paint, hair style, jewelry, and clothing combine—that is, exhibit physical contiguity—with the individual wearing them, and thus person-plus-artifacts becomes a compound interactor.

Discrete interactions, which are the minimal units of behavior in activities, can involve any kind of matter-energy transaction—mechanical, chemical, thermal, electrical, electromagnetic, visual, acoustic—between two or more interactors (Schiffer and Skibo 1997). The contribution of one interactor to a particular interaction is its *perfor-*

mance (Schiffer and Skibo 1997). For an activity to proceed, each interactor must be capable of carrying out its interaction-specific performance(s); these capabilities are known as performance characteristics (Braun 1983; O'Brien et al. 1994; Schiffer 1996; Schiffer and Skibo 1987, 1997; Schiffer et al. 1994b).

ARTIFACTS AND ACTIVITIES
Defined here as the passage of consequential information from interactor to interactor, communication is situated in activities. The artifacts of a given activity are drawn from three artifact sets: platial, personal, and situational.

Platial artifacts reside in a "place" (Binford 1982; Gallagher 1993; Thomas 1996: 85–91)—a specific location, indoors or outdoors—and include portable artifacts stored there, semiportable artifacts (e.g., furniture), and architectural features (Rapoport 1990). More than a reservoir for potential activity artifacts, platial artifacts figure significantly in human communication. For example, platial artifact performances furnish information on a place's appropriateness for carrying out specific activities (Miller 1987:101–102).

Because people are compound interactors, the artifacts with which they are compounded—*personal artifacts*—perform in activities. Personal artifacts include: (1) artifacts that are an actual and essentially permanent part of the human body, such as tattoos, scars, and modified teeth; (2) artifacts that are an actual but temporary part of the human body, including hair style, makeup and body paint, deodorant and perfume, earrings and nose rings; and (3) artifacts that perform as if part of the human body but are very easily attached and detached, such as clothing, headgear, shoes, hair ornaments, necklaces, masks, and badges. Countless studies demonstrate that communication is greatly influenced by the silent performances of personal artifacts (for summaries and references, see Joseph 1986; Kaiser 1985; see also Barnes and Eicher 1992; Brain 1979; Craik 1994; David 1992; Polhemus 1978a, 1978b).

Situational artifacts arrive with people or turn up at a place for the conduct of an activity. Common examples include ritual para-phernalia brought from a clan house to a dance in the village plaza, a game animal carried to camp for butchering, and artifacts moving from station to station along an assembly line. Situational artifacts also take part in communication; for example, their arrival often enables the performance of a specific activity to begin.

It must be stressed that enumerations of the three artifact sets are activity-specific. As the activity occurring in a place changes, so might the personal, platial, and situational artifacts. For example, the same hair ornament could be a personal artifact while being worn in one activity and a platial artifact while being stored during another.

In making archaeological inferences, we usually sort through—and in some fashion integrate- –multiple lines of evidence (e.g., Hard et al. 1996; Rathje and Schiffer 1982, chapter 9; Schiffer 1988a). Similarly, in everyday life we often obtain information from the performances of many interactors (Burgoon et al. 1996), among which artifacts loom large. Thus, the performances of platial, personal, and situational artifacts furnish people with multiple lines of evidence for inference—for obtaining information that can affect interactions and the course of activities.

PERFORMANCE MODES, ARTIFACTS, AND EVIDENCE

People obtain information from interactors performing in five major performance modes: visual, acoustic, tactile (mechanical), thermal, and chemical. That these performance modes correspond to human senses is no accident, for any performance that can be registered through a human sense is capable of supplying evidence for inference and yielding information (Ackerman 1990). In illustrating these performance modes, I focus on people (as compound interactors); the reader can surely supply examples of artifacts and natural phenomena also performing in these modes. This discussion stresses that *artifacts play communicative roles in every performance mode.*

A person's visual performance is affected by the physical properties of his or her body—whether produced biologically or through human activities. The form and comportment of various parts of the body, as in facial features, skin color, stature and proportions, gestures, posture, gait, and arrangement in space, affect visual performance and thus can contribute to an observer's inferences (e.g., Birdwhistell 1970; Burgoon et al. 1996; Fast 1971; Hall 1966; Knapp and Hall 1992). These performances are often taken to be exemplars of "nonverbal" communication (Burgoon et al. 1996; Burling 1993; Duncan 1969; Ekman and Friesen 1969), a term that regrettably reinforces the privileged standing of verbal performance in conventional communication theories. Obviously, personal artifacts are significant determinants of visual performance (Joseph 1986; Kaiser 1985). In addition, a person's visual performance is greatly affected by activity artifacts because, in interacting with these, people exhibit particular postures (Hewes 1957), gestures (Leroi-Gourhan 1993), and facial expressions.

Acoustic performance is much more than the uttering of words and sentences. "Paralinguistic" (e.g., Trager 1958) or "vocalic" (Burgoon et al. 1996:59–67) phenomena, including coughs and cries, grunts and pants, whistles and sneezes, yawns and yells, and belches, as well as the pitch, rhythm, and loudness of speech, also contribute to acoustic performance and affect communication. Sounds made by other parts of the body, such as hand clapping and foot stomping, can as well yield information. Acoustic performance is affected by personal artifacts such as face masks, tooth modification, drugs, and tongue and lip ornaments; by situational artifacts, including musical instruments and food being chewed; and by platial artifacts, for example, a room's size, shape, and wall materials.

In the course of various activities, people touch each other in mechanical interactions known as tactile, or haptic, performance (Burgoon et al. 1996:86–88). Such performances demonstrably participate in communication (e.g., Burgoon et al. 1996; Hall

1966; Remland and Jones 1994). Needless to say, tactile performances can be affected by personal artifacts such as clothing. In addition, activity artifacts applied by one person to another, such as medical instruments and grooming utensils, perform tactilely.

The thermal performance of one person may be registered by another and participate in communication. An example is provided by a woman who, grasping her lover's hand, comments on his "cold hands and warm heart." Thermal performance is affected by personal artifacts, like clothing and body paint, as well as by platial artifacts (e.g., a hearth, a structure).

Chemical performance, which is registered by the senses of taste and smell, plays a role in the communication of most animals, including mammals (Albone 1984; Peters 1980). In human communication the role of chemical performances has been little studied, but is doubtless significant (Almagor 1990), capable of influencing inferences and affecting responses. A person's chemical performances can be affected by situational and activity artifacts, such as foods consumed; by personal artifacts like clothing, soaps, deodorants, oils, and perfumes (Van Toller and Dodd 1992); and by platial artifacts that perform chemically such as incense or that affect the concentration and movement of airborne chemicals, for example, a ceiling fan.

The previous examples demonstrate the pervasive involvement of artifacts in the five performance modes, underscoring that all modes can furnish evidence for inference. I submit that the relative importance of performance modes *in a given activity and place* is an empirical question: on the basis of which performances, in which modes, does a person make inferences, obtain information, and respond?

BUILDING A COMMUNICATION THEORY
ARCHAEOLOGICAL INFERENCE AND
COMMUNICATION

Let us begin with a brief review of archaeological inference (useful sources include Fritz 1972; Patrik 1985; Schiffer 1976, chapter 2, 1987, chapter 2; Sullivan 1978; Wylie 1985,

1992). Archaeological inference is the process of obtaining information about past interactions and interactors from present-day artifact performances. The product of this process is *an* inference—a specific claim that is warranted by relevant evidence and relevant principles. Inference is possible because traces of past interactions survive materially in artifacts found in the present. Specifically, interactions that occurred during earlier activities in an artifact's life history, which modified its formal properties, frequency, location, or associations, affect subsequent performances in laboratory activities. These latter performances yield evidence when the archaeologist applies to them specific relational statements of archaeological knowledge, particularly correlates (Schiffer 1976: 12, 17–18). Correlates enable the investigator to forge links between the performance(s) of past people and artifact performances today (for present purposes, the roles of c- and n-transforms in inference are ignored). In archaeological inference, then, interactors play three major roles: someone (or something) in the past who modified an artifact's properties, the artifact performing in laboratory activities, and the archaeologist registering that artifact's performances.

Human communication is like archaeological inference because, in order to obtain information from an interactor's performance(s), a person constructs inferences using correlate-like knowledge. To avoid confusion, I use the term *correlon* to describe the relational knowledge underlying any human communication. Correlons can range from general to highly particularistic and can be deterministic or statistical-probabilistic. Because correlons may include "nonverbal imagery" (Keller and Keller 1996:133–137) pertaining to any performance mode, verbal accounts of correlons can be highly imperfect (Keller and Keller 1996:157). The relational knowledge embodied in correlons both subsumes and presumes knowledge represented as categories, i.e., classifications. Thus, correlons permit, at the very least, inferences of identification.

Finally, because correlons consist of relational knowledge, they can be used predictively; that is, on the basis of a correlon, an interactor can make an inference about *future* interactions rather than past ones. This capability of correlons comes into play when an interactor is responding (see below).

Using archaeological inference as a springboard, I now set forth the theory's basic premises and postulates.

INTERACTOR ROLES

Like archaeological inference, human communication requires interactors to play three major roles: sender, emitter, and receiver. (1) The *sender* is an interactor whose past interactions with a second interactor imparted information to the latter. (2) That second interactor is the *emitter* (cf. Foucault 1972: 145; Wobst 1977:322), whose performances today materially embody the imparted information. (3) The *receiver,* which registers the emitter's performances and, applying correlons, constructs an inference or inferences; on the basis of the information thus obtained, the receiver responds.

The playing of major interactor roles is governed by four rules:

1. Any role can be played by any kind of interactor—person, artifact, or natural phenomenon—so long as it has the requisite performance characteristics.

2. People can play the three roles explicitly or implicitly, consciously or unconsciously, and voluntarily or involuntarily; and they are usually unaware of their own correlons (cf. Keller and Keller 1996:111–112).

3. An interactor—especially a person—can simultaneously play more than one role in an activity. For example, in the case of two people conversing, the speaker can often be regarded as playing a combined sender-emitter role.

4. Any role can be played by more than one actual interactor. This rule allows the theory to handle group performances and group responses, as in a symphony orchestra concert. Usually, many interactors—especially artifacts—simultaneously play emitter roles.

COMMUNICATION PROCESSES

The three interactor roles come together in a *communication process* (cf. Hanneman 1975:24), which is the passage of consequential information from interactor to interactor, culminating in a receiver's response. Communication processes are not self-evident but must be delineated in a specific activity by the investigator.

Any communication process consists of four sequential events:

1. *Inscription.* The sender imparts information by modifying the emitter's properties—formal, quantitative, spatial, or relational.

2. *Emission.* The emitter performs in one or more performance modes (i.e., visual, acoustic, mechanical, thermal, and chemical).

3. *Reception.* The receiver, registering the emitter's performances (along with the performances of activity and platial interactors), constructs an inference or inferences.

4. *Response.* On the basis of the information yielded by the inference(s), the receiver responds; the response is itself a performance, often in many modes.

The events of a communication process can be illustrated by the activity of painting a design on a pot in a workshop open to customers. Although many interactors are performing in this activity, including pots for sale in a large display case, the example focuses on just three: (1) the potter, (2) the pot being painted, and (3) a customer. Let us designate the customer as the receiver and the pot as the emitter of interest. From the standpoint of the customer, who observes the potter at work, the application of paint to the pot is an inscription event; that is, the interactions between a sender (the potter) and an emitter (the pot) have caused information to be inscribed on the latter. Emission—as visual performance—occurs throughout and after the painting process. Reception takes place when the customer-receiver registers the pot's visual performances and constructs an inference regarding, for example, the potter's skill as a painter. After passing judgment on the quality of the potter's work, the customer may respond with words of praise, an appropriate facial expression, and a gesture toward the pots in the display case.

Although any communication process can be broken down into a set of inscription, emission, reception, and response events, the investigator's research interests dictate the required level of detail. In the example just furnished, the level of detail supplied may suffice for explaining the customer's response. However, in studies of information transfer in craft activities (e.g., Keller and Keller 1996), the investigator might break down pot-painting into the artisan's most minute performances, such as individual brush strokes, each of which incrementally modifies the pot's decoration and, correspondingly, its visual performance. The potter in this case could be treated as both sender and receiver: each brush stroke applies paint to the pot (inscription) and thereby modifies its visual performance (emission); the potter registers the new performance and constructs an inference (reception), which furnishes the information needed for placing the next brush stroke (response). Seemingly, the theory supplies investigators with conceptual tools sufficiently flexible to define communication events at any scale needed for solving research problems.

Communication processes must be delineated, in an activity, *from the receiver's point of view.* This move may seem restrictive, but it is not: because all role-playing involves performance, the investigator can delineate a communication process in such a way as to enable *any* human performance to be treated as a receiver's response. Thus, the investigator begins analysis by focusing on a person's specific performance, seeking to explain it as the response of a receiver (see below, "On Hopi Pots and Feathers"), and delineating the communication process accordingly. I grant that proceeding in this manner is counterintuitive, since we are ordinarily inclined, as members of Western society, to focus on senders and emitters. But the theory is capable of explaining any sender and emitter

performances so long as they are framed as receiver responses in *different* communication processes.

Although an inferred inscription event may be distant in time and place from the other events in a particular communication process, the latter is always embedded in a specific activity: *the one in which the receiver takes part.* Thus, only in a receiver-anchored activity can one identify a communication process and delineate the roles played by other interactors. Because activities occur in places, activity and platial interactors figure importantly as emitters in all communication processes.

The sender imparts information by performing in interactions that modify the emitter's characteristics. These interactions leave behind traces—be they formal properties, location, frequency, or associations—that affect the emitter's subsequent performances, potentially in many modes. Employing correlons, the receiver constructs the inference(s)—explicitly or implicitly, consciously or unconsciously—from the registered performances. Correlons enable the receiver to obtain, with degrees of precision and accuracy varying from case to case, information about the sender and inscription events.

Depending on the case, receivers can construct inferences that range from very simple to very complex (Burgoon et al. 1996, chapter 9). For example, the inference may merely indicate that the other interactor is ready to play the receiver role. To wit, in a two-person conversation, the receiver might infer from the acoustic performance, facial expression, gestures, and personal artifacts of the sender-emitter that it is time to talk again. In contrast, there are many communication processes in which the receiver, such as a homicide detective, laboriously constructs a complex set of inferences about how, precisely, a victim was murdered. These inferences include many specific interactions inferred for the murderer (the sender) from the performances of multiple emitters, including the victim's body and personal artifacts, activity artifacts, and platial artifacts and natural phenomena. As these examples indicate, inferences may pertain to senders and inscription events occurring in the reference activity or in other activities, including those greatly removed from the receiver in time and place.

Even when the receiver registers mainly acoustic interactions (as in a telephone conversation), inferences are still constructed. For example, at the most basic level, the receiver fashions inferences about the sender-emitter's apparent identity and ostensible message. What is more, depending on the receiver's correlons, she can sometimes infer from voice alone the sender's age, sex, social class, region, and relative social power (Trudgill 1983)—not to mention the sincerity and truth value of the acoustic performances. Needless to say, these diverse inferences all can influence the receiver's response.

Having set forth the major premises of the theory, I now discuss each interactor role in greater detail.

THE RECEIVER

Analysis of a communication process can begin when the investigator, adopting the vantage point of someone observing an activity, designates the receiver.

In order to play the receiver role, an interactor must possess a sensory apparatus and be capable of responding. Thus, animals and some artifacts, for example, computers and smoke detectors, can serve as receivers, often having hard-wired correlons. In the case of a smoke alarm, deterministic correlons that link the chemical or visual performance of smoke to the alarm's acoustic response are literally hard-wired, embodied in specific electrical and mechanical interactions between its parts. The inference—that there is a fire—is entirely implicit in the reception event and in the smoke alarm's response. Although artifacts and animals can sometimes serve as receivers, much of the remaining discussion is tailored to cases of

more interest to archaeologists in which the receiver is a person.

The reception event can lead to three major outcomes:

1. The registered performances have no discernible affect on the receiver. In this case, there has been no communication event (Stevens 1950:689) because the information transfer has been inconsequential. This assertion clearly contrasts with humanistic approaches, which assign significance to a person's *subjective* experiences—phenomena that seem to be beyond archaeological reach.

2. Reception contributes to learning, thereby causing a biochemical change in the person's nervous system and the creation of new correlons (or the remodeling of old ones). Because the precise biochemical changes induced by a specific instance of learning are not readily discerned in humans by an outside observer (notwithstanding recent advances in brain imaging, Haberlandt 1994:63–66), the direct detection of a learning effect is highly problematic. The only accessible evidence of learning resides in a receiver's subsequent response(s). Perhaps that is why so many behaviorally oriented investigators include the response event in their studies of human and animal communication processes (e.g., Frings and Frings 1977:3; Hanneman 1975:24; Stevens 1950:689). This point brings us to the final case, from which the second is operationally indistinguishable.

3. Reception leads the receiver itself to construct correlon-based inferences, including predictions, and respond during an immediately subsequent interaction. It is useful to regard the emitter performances as having "cued" the receiver's response (see Burgoon et al. 1996:189; Miller 1985:181, 1987:101; Rathje and Schiffer 1982:63; Schiffer and Skibo 1997; Thomas 1996:59; compare to "contextual cue," e.g., Domjan 1993; Giddens 1993:110). Needless to say, the same registered performance(s) can contribute to

learning *and* cue a response (Keller and Keller 1996:17–18).

FACTORS INFLUENCING THE RESPONSES OF HUMAN RECEIVERS

Three major sets of factors affect what a human receiver registers, the inferences created, and the response.

The first set of factors is the sequence of interactions and activities that took place during a person's life history (cf. Smith 1977: 267), including his or her immediately preceding performances. It is during life-history interactions that an individual acquires many of the correlons that enable the construction of inferences and that affect responses.

Learned correlons are obtained through direct experience—for example, interactions with tools and materials in craft activities—and by indirect learning processes involving teachers, friends, family members, books, magazines, television, and so on. The acquisition of correlons through learning goes on consciously and unconsciously as well as explicitly and implicitly (Reber 1993), and much of it takes place nonverbally (Bloch 1990). Learned correlons are an important basis for many of a person's performance characteristics and thus response repertoires (Schiffer and Skibo 1997).

The second set of factors affecting responses pertains to a person's genetically constituted, biological substrate. An individual's genome is partly or wholly responsible for many performance characteristics (can the person yell loudly, sing sweetly, or jump three feet in the air?). A familiar example of a hard-wired correlon is color-"blindness" (Coren et al.1994:157–160). People afflicted with these genetic variants have impaired color reception, and this affects their responses in activities such as taking color-blindness tests or classifying pottery. Clearly, genetic variability can affect sundry performance characteristics and thus a person's responses.

The third set of factors affecting responses derives from alterations to a person's body as a result of developmental and aging processes and through life-history interactions in activ-ities. During aging, for example, regular changes take place in the senses (Coren et al. 1994:571–575), altering hard-wired corre-lons. Hearing, for one, becomes less acute with age, often with an attenuation in the reception of high frequencies. Because of such sensory differences, people vary in responses. To take the most obvious example, a person unable to hear a soft voice in face-to-face conversation may respond by interjecting "huh?" or "what?" at frequent intervals. Similarly, there are well documented age-related changes in cognitive and motor abilities that affect specific performance characteristics. In addition, accidents, illness, eating patterns, exercise, surgery, mutilation, and so on can change a person's body in ways that demonstrably alter performance characteristics, and thus the potential for generating particular responses.

TUNING

To sum up, then, a person's response as a receiver in a specific communication process is significantly affected by life-history activities and biological substrate. Because it is usually so difficult to distinguish the influences of genetics and learning on correlons and performance characteristics, and because doing so is unnecessary for the present project, all causal factors can be bundled into one overarching category called "tuning" (compare to "attuned" and "attunement"; Deacon 1997: 126; Thomas 1996:41, 45–46, 55; cf. Lieberman 1991:45; Newell 1990:27). The tuning process refers to a person's acquisition of correlons, regardless of how they were obtained. An "appropriately" tuned receiver is a person who possesses the correlons needed for constructing inferences from, and responding skillfully to, specific emissions in a given communication process. However, people who lack appropriate tuning—i.e., are less skilled—usually still respond (on skilled performance, see Keller and Keller 1996:55).

One must resist the temptation to equate tuning with enculturation or socialization. The latter concepts highlight the experiences that people *share* as members of groups in a culture or society, enabling the investigator to explain why different *groups* have dissimilar sets of correlons and response repertoires. The concept of tuning is much broader, not only because it includes the biological component, but also because it applies at the scale of the individual, explicitly recognizing a person's capacity for fashioning uncommon correlons and for generating idiosyncratic responses (see also Fletcher 1996:79; Keller and Keller 1996). Thus, the degree to which any tuning, i.e., a specific set of correlons, is shared by individuals in a behavioral system is an empirical matter. That two people "share" a correlon implies only that as receivers they would respond alike in the same communication process; no assumption is made that the correlon(s) is identically constituted.

In recognizing that tuning accommodates individual variation, it should not be forgotten that many correlons are at least partly shared, and that is what imposes a modicum of order on a behavioral system's interactions. Precisely such uniformities in tuning can allow archaeologists to fashion explanations of group-response patterns in relation to specific emitter—especially artifact—performances in a given activity (see below, "Methodological Implications").

Hierarchical Organization and Keying-In of Correlons

Another important factor contributing to patterned responses is the manner in which correlons are organized and employed. In accord with the organization of human memory and probably cognition in general (Hardcastle 1996, chapter 3; Newell 1990:7, 117), I hypothesize that a person's correlons are organized hierarchically and thus are "keyed in" sequentially by different emitter performances. (The actual mode of information processing may be serial or parallel [cf. Bloch 1990], but it is more conveniently modeled as a sequence.) At the most general level, platial interactor performances supply the person with information for inferring a place's identity (Miller 1987:101–102) such as church, bedroom, or golf course. Once the place is identified, activity-specific emissions result in

a second sorting of correlons; from the latter, a specific activity is inferred. For example, after a place has been identified as a "bedroom," additional correlons are keyed in that identify specific activities such as sleeping, making the bed, vacuuming the floor, or reading a magazine. The process eventually keys in correlons pertaining to particular interactors and interactions.

To illustrate the process of keying in correlons, let us suppose that a man—an appropriately tuned receiver—is observing a second man. The latter, playing an emitter role in this communication process, is holding his right hand aloft, rapidly moving it back and forth (cf. Goffman 1974:37). Without additional information, there is no way to know what inference(s) the receiver constructs from this gesture and what response is likely. The same emitter (with identical personal artifacts) can carry out that exact performance along the side of a road, on the beach, at the railing of a ship, or in a classroom. When the receiver registers the performances of platial interactors, however, he is able to identify the place and key in place-specific correlons. Next, on the basis of activity interactor performances, the receiver identifies the activity. To wit, is the ship arriving or departing? Is the person in the classroom a student in the midst of taking an exam or responding to a teacher's question? After the activity is identified—we can assume that the emitter is arriving on a ship—activity-specific correlons are keyed in. Even then, the receiver needs to attend to other performances of the waving person, including those of his personal artifacts along with facial expressions and other gestures. Together, these performances allow the receiver to situate the person in the activity, which in turns keys in the set of interactor-specific correlons. These permit the gesturing person to be identified with respect to contextually-relevant categories (e.g., a baggage handler, an unknown passenger, his friend John) on the basis of visual and acoustic performances (cf. Joseph 1986:71–72). These performance-based identifications allow the hand-waving performance itself to key in interaction-specific correlon(s) that enable the receiver to obtain information from the gesture, e.g., a greeting from his friend John. As this example makes clear, the keying-in process operates on (or is driven by) countless emitters performing in many modes.

It is hypothesized that, during the course of everyday activities, correlons are usually keyed in implicitly or unconsciously, with the receiver unaware of the process. However, the process can be explicit, conscious, or provoke awareness when, for example, people are confronted by novel places, activities, interactors, or interactions—or novel combinations of them (Keller and Keller 1996: 112–116).

THE EMITTER

From the vantage point of the receiver, the outside world consists of myriad emissions providing a barrage of potential evidence on which the receiver's tuning—and the keying-in of correlons—can operate. When the receiver's interactor- and interaction-specific correlons are at last keyed in, usually the performances of one emitter, a salient emitter (cf. Newell 1990:274), lead to specific inferences and cue responses; other emitters often slip into the background, having played their roles in *that* communication process by keying in the receiver's correlons.

How does a particular interactor come to emit specific performances in a given activity at a particular place? Not surprisingly, the emitter's performance(s) are influenced by the same factors that affect receiver tuning and responses—life history interactions and physical-chemical-biological substrate.

An emitter, such as an artifact, can be inscribed during any activity of its life history, from the procurement and shaping of its raw materials, to manufacture and use, to maintenance and disposal (Schiffer 1972, 1975). Thus, a specific artifact's emissions can embody information inscribed by many senders in diverse interactions and activities (Musello 1992). As we shall soon see, this potential multiplicity of senders poses problems for the two-body model of communication.

THE SENDER

The sender role is privileged in conventional communication theories, and much effort is lavished on the attempt to discern the sender's intent. In the present theory, however, the sender role cannot be privileged because it depends, ultimately, on the receiver's ability to infer the interactor responsible for a particular inscription event. Without a designated receiver, there can be no senders because the sender is a product of the receiver's inference.

This strong claim about the dependence of senders upon receivers perhaps seems bizarre when applied to two people conversing face-to-face, where at any given instant it appears possible for the participants and an outside observer to specify the sender (assuming a combined sender-emitter role). However, I emphasize that a conversing couple is but one case—a special case—of human communication. Thus, the more general claim of sender dependence, which applies to vastly more kinds of communication processes, is essential for building a communication theory useful in archaeology.

An example can illustrate the fruitfulness of the general claim. Let us assume that an archaeologist visiting my laboratory is the receiver in analytic activities; her response is to write down an inference. The object of study—the salient emitter—is a large earthenware pot of recent Cypriot manufacture having a spout and handle, which performs visually like a large pitcher. When the visiting archaeologist, who is trained in ceramic analysis (i.e., appropriately tuned with relevant correlates), examines this vessel through a hand lens, she registers various visually performing traces of previous interactions in that vessel's life history. For example, on the vessel's base she observes a heavily abraded area that contains striations generally oriented toward the spout. The archaeologist's correlates (e.g., Schiffer and Skibo 1989) permit her to infer from these striations that the pot had experienced recurrent abrasive interactions with a relatively hard, sandy surface, such as a hard-packed dirt floor. By focusing on the location and orientation of the striations, she also infers that the pot had been frequently tipped during use. Although the pot's visual performances result in straightforward inferences about inscription events, the sender can be identified only as one or more anonymous people who participated in the vessel's use activities. (Indeed, the pot had been used for several seasons on a Cypriot dig by many dozens of people.)

But suppose that instead of examining the vessel's base, the archaeologist inspects an area, below the neck, lacking abrasive traces. Here she sees small, low-density patches of striations oriented in many directions. Armed with interaction-specific correlates (Rye 1981:86), she infers that these striations were caused by the mechanical interaction between a scraping tool, probably of wood, and the vessel's leather-hard surface. She further infers that this scraping tool was wielded by the potter. In this instance the receiver is able to infer one person in the past responsible for the inscription event.

In the example of the Cypriot pot (the salient emitter), the archaeologist-receiver can construct inferences about multiple senders who inscribed the pot during various activities of its life history. Thus, the sender—or, more properly, the senders—were inferred by the receiver after she had keyed in correlates pertaining to the emitter's visual performances. This example demonstrates that senders emerge only after the receiver has built activity- and interaction-specific inferences.

As we are well aware, the inferential process can result in erroneous conclusions about specific senders and inscription events. In everyday life people make do with probable inferences, hunches and guesses, and worse. Were it not so, lack of accurate inferences would cause paralysis, rendering us unable to respond to the cues of emitters and thereby hindering the forward motion of daily activities. Because interaction proceeds during activity performance, we can be sure that the accuracy of inferences does not hinder people playing receiver roles.

A major cause of incorrect inferences is faulty correlons. Indeed, people can acquire erroneous relational knowledge through hard-wiring and life-history activities. Ethnic, class, age, and gender stereotypes are examples of flawed correlons; unfortunately, such correlons generate responses just as effectively as ones that we, as modern scientists, would regard as being correct.

That correlons can be incorrect suggests that receivers may sometimes infer senders and inscription events that lack materiality. For example, in many tribal societies, rainfall—a cloud's mechanical performance—is attributed by receivers to the action of a rain-making spirit. Similarly, a shaman-receiver might infer that a sick person's symptoms (emitter performances) result from the malevolent use of a sorcerer's powers. Clearly, as the product of a receiver's inference, senders can include spirits, witches, and other nonmaterial phenomena.

ARTIFACTS THAT PLAY SUPPORTING ROLES
Several additional concepts help the investigator to simplify, and thus study effectively, complex communication processes by calling attention to artifacts that play supporting roles. Let us return briefly to the Cypriot vessel discussed above. The archaeologist, it should be recalled, inferred that the potter had scraped the vessel's outer surface with a wooden tool. Thus, it was not the direct mechanical interaction between potter and pot that imparted the information, but the linked interactions between potter, wooden scraper, and pot. Artifacts like the wooden scraper, which facilitate inscription, are termed *sendtrons*.

Not surprisingly, an *emitron* is an artifact that enables an emitter's performances. The makeup used by mimes, for example, can be regarded as an emitron, permitting the mime's facial expressions—as visual performance—to stand out more clearly and be observed at a greater distance than those of a bare face or a face painted less flamboyantly.

Finally, we arrive at *receptrons*, artifacts that facilitate reception. Many devices used in activities of observing, measuring, and counting are receptrons, helping the receiver to register emitter performances. Thus, receptrons range from multi-million-dollar telescopes and microscopes to a 39-cent plastic ruler. Some receptrons are personal artifacts, such as the reading glasses indispensable to so many middle-aged academics.

The concepts of sendtron, emitron, and receptron allow the investigator precisely and flexibly to describe the participation of artifacts, as players of supporting roles, in complex communication processes.

METHODOLOGICAL IMPLICATIONS

The theory presented above requires that a research question about artifacts and communication be formulated in relation to specific interactors in a particular activity and place. Once the activity and place are determined, the investigator begins to delineate a communication process by indicating which interactor played the receiver role. In the next step, one specifies the interactors, including platial and situational artifacts, that performed emitter roles, and which was the salient emitter. Sender(s) and inscription events are inferred, as appropriate, depending on the inferences that an investigator imputes to the receiver. Finally, the investigator strives to explain the receiver's response as a consequence of the emissions that have been registered *and* receiver-specific factors such as tuning.

The previous statement implies that the archaeologist must model the correlons possessed by ancient people in order to account for their inferences and responses. Would the modeling of correlons inevitably take us toward a "cognitive" archaeology, concerned with the knowledge that people possessed (e.g., Keller and Keller 1996; Rathje 1979; Renfrew 1982; Renfrew and Zubrow 1994; Schiffer and Skibo 1987; Schiffer 1992b, chapter 7; Whitley 1992; Young and Bonnichsen 1984)? In the best of all possible worlds, the answer would be yes. Archaeologists would strive to obtain the correlates needed for modeling (i.e., inferring) a person's correlons, drawing upon experiments

and ethnoarchaeology, and judiciously borrowing principles from other social and behavioral sciences. But the real world of modern archaeology is far from perfect; few investigators are likely to drop what they are doing to embark on correlate-producing projects.

Given that relevant correlates will be slow in coming, can archaeologists interested in studying meaningful phenomena somehow escape the need to model correlons? The answer is yes, so long as the investigator is willing to adopt some simplifying assumptions: (1) the correlon(s) is deterministic, (2) all receivers have appropriate and identical tuning, and (3) all other features of the communication process, i.e., interactors, activity, and place, are constant. Under these conditions, the investigator assumes that unspecified (deterministic) correlons establish a one-to-one mapping between emissions and response. Thus, identical responses among a group of receivers can be explained merely by invoking the registered emissions.

These conditions, though never met perfectly, may be most closely approximated in small, relatively homogeneous societies, where major differences in tuning vary mainly by age, sex, and gender. Thus, on the basis of the simplifying assumptions, an investigator could arrive at some first-approximation explanations of stereotypical responses. Precisely this sort of simplification seems to underlie Thomas's (1996) treatment of the Neolithic in Western Europe.

In principle, this approach can be extended to more differentiated societies (sensu McGuire 1983). In handling highly differentiated societies, one could employ sociodemographic characteristics for forming smaller, more homogeneous groups whose members, because they presumably share deterministic correlons, would respond identically (Schiffer 1995b). In making this move, the investigator is treating sociodemographic characteristics as proxy measures of tuning. For example, it would be expected that all well-educated, Anglo adult males, living in a nuclear-family household in a particular neighborhood and employed in similar jobs, would, by virtue of shared but unspecified correlons, respond identically in the same communication process. Alternatively, the investigator could assume that the people playing specific social roles in a given activity possess identical, deterministic correlons, which would generate the same response.

This strategy for avoiding the reconstruction of correlons regrettably ignores the biological component of tuning, neglects individual variation in response repertoires, treats people as if they were receivers responding automatically, just like smoke alarms, and reproduces an orthodox cultural or societal determinism. Nonetheless, this strategy has an undeniable appeal to prehistorians who are loathe to model cognitive phenomena.

Although imputing deterministic correlons to a receiver on the basis of sociodemographic characteristics and social roles can permit archaeologists to handle meaningful phenomena, treating artifacts as participants in communication processes, the approach is at best a stop-gap measure. As behavioralists have argued for many years (e.g., Rathje 1979), over the long term we must work toward obtaining the relevant correlates for building a cognitive archaeology.

OF HOPI POTS AND FEATHERS

Although the theory presented above requires testing and is incomplete, for example, there is no model to explain the selection of a single response from the receiver's response repertoire, it can still help us to illustrate the treatment of artifacts in a behavioral analysis of meaningful phenomena.

Recall the two Hopi pots reposing on the mantel: one purchased in 1969 that seems to have feather motifs; and a second, bought in 1996, on which the potter had painted a "water-bird" design. These pots serve merely as examples in the following discussion, which contrasts interpretive and behavioral analyses.

The Black-On-Red Pot

The pot purchased in 1969 is ideal for illustrating an interpretive approach. Let us as-

sume that I bring the black-on-red bowl to a graduate seminar on Hopi prehistory at a large British university where, as a guest lecturer, I use the pot to provoke interpretive discourse. At the beginning of class, I indicate the "feather" motifs with an index finger and say, "These motifs could be interpreted as feathers. When I asked the potter, however, she made no mention of feather symbolism. Would anyone like to comment?" The following interpretive discussion ensues among the seminar's students.

Student 1: "During the Sikyatki Revival a century ago, when the Hopi began to produce trade pottery for Anglos on a large scale, potters copied motifs from prehistoric sherds, such as Sikyatki Polychrome (Bunzel 1929:55–57; Fewkes 1898:660; Stanislawski and Stanislawski 1978:75). These motifs have considerable appeal to Anglos (Eaton 1994), but might have no traditional meaning for modern Hopi potters who are separated by more than three centuries from their prehistoric counterparts."

Student 2: "Right! The potter probably got the feather motif on your pot from books on Hopi pottery designs that can be bought today, such as Fewkes (1973), Wade and McChesney (1981), and Patterson (1994)."

Student 3: "Even so, she might actually believe that it is a traditional Hopi symbol for feathers. She may even have intended to symbolize feathers, but refused to share that sacred knowledge with an Anglo."

Student 4: "Throughout the historic period, Hopi potters have also been quite willing to adopt motifs from other Puebloan groups (Wyckoff 1990:75–77) and even from the Spanish (Wyckoff 1990:75); this is another indication that many Hopi pottery motifs lack traditional meanings."

Student 3: "On the other hand, highly stylized birds and feather motifs *are* traditional Hopi symbols, occurring commonly on Sikyatki Polychrome from late prehistoric Hopi sites (Fewkes 1898:658, 682–698, 1919: 227–252). What is more, feathers and feather motifs decorate many Hopi religious artifacts (Fewkes 1898:689), and feathers themselves have countless ceremonial uses (Fewkes

1919:125–126). I believe it is likely that she was using feather symbolism, regardless of what she said."

Student 5: "Fewkes was very generous in his symbolic interpretations of pottery designs, many of which even he regarded as highly conventionalized (Fewkes 1898:682, 1919:127). Although the so-called feathers on this pot do resemble some feather symbols illustrated by Fewkes (1919, plates 76, 77), the motif might not be *bird* feathers because the Hopi also recognize sky-dwelling mythical beings (e.g., Fewkes 1898:691–693; Stephen, in Patterson 1994:49); the potter might have sought to symbolize one of these."

Student 6: "But the motif really does look like *bird* feathers."

Student 1: "Let us not forget that the early ethnographers, whose texts are today's sources for interpreting Hopi pottery symbolism, obtained the meanings of symbols from men, but men were not the potters. For example, Alexander Stephen's informants were chiefs and priests (Patterson 1994:20). What is more, Fewkes (1898:659) even acknowledged that 'The majority of the ancient symbols are incomprehensible to the present Hopi priests whom I have been able to consult, although they are ready to suggest many interpretations, sometimes widely divergent.' Since the revival of Sikyatki designs was only beginning when Stephen and Fewkes were at Hopi in the 1890s, the women potters at that time apparently had little to say about the symbols they were copying from prehistoric sherds; otherwise Fewkes, who was relatively explicit about his methods of 'paleography' (Fewkes 1898:657–660), would have mentioned their views. Thus, I think it is doubtful that the potter intended to symbolize feathers with this motif."

Student 3: "Let me amplify my earlier point. Only male Hopi, the priests, are privy to the most sacred and esoteric ritual knowledge, including the symbolism of altar displays. Perhaps by appropriating some of these symbols, e.g., feathers, women potters are silently yet conspicuously disputing male hegemony over the ritual realm. Thus, the de-

signs on this pot are clearly feathers, but the deeper meanings intended by the potter are highly gendered."

Finally I take a turn: "Thank you for the very illuminating discussion."

Although the classroom discourse has brought to light evidence that seemingly bears on the interpretation of the "feather" motif, no agreement was reached on the motif's meaning(s). Many students believe that the motif is a symbol whose meaning(s) can be disclosed through informed interpretation drawing on texts of Hopi ethnography and ethnoarchaeology. To decide among the varying interpretations, however, one must make a judgment about the potter's intent. Did she intend to symbolize bird feathers? Did she intend to symbolize other feathered beings? Did she intend to symbolize a woman's right to use sacred symbols? Because intent as such is behaviorally problematic, these questions appear to be unanswerable. No matter how much evidence we marshal in support of one interpretation or another, the potter's "intent" will forever remain beyond our grasp.

Questions about intent derive implicitly from the sender-focused perspective that permeates our everyday conversations. Indeed, intent is a concept that members of Western societies employ constantly in inferring motives for other peoples' performances (Ehrenhaus 1988; Giddens 1993:89–93; Goffman 1974:22). However, anthropological linguists have discovered that discussions and inferences about intent are not universal (e.g., DuBois 1993); clearly, there are other ways to model the proximate causes of human performances. In a behavioral framework, I submit, the effort to discern intent per se is unhelpful (cf. Gould 1990:235–237). Rather, in explaining an individual's given performance, for example, painting a design, purchasing a pot, the investigator must reconceptualize it, treating the performance *as a receiver's response in a communication process*. Thus, understanding a person's performance—any performance—is transformed from interminable discourse over a person's intent into our familiar problem of explaining a receiver's response. As stipulated above, all human performances can be handled in this way.

I now turn to the "water-bird" pot, which illustrates how the communication theory can be used for framing questions and hypotheses in a behavioral analysis of meaningful phenomena.

THE "WATER-BIRD" POT

In specifying a reference activity or activities for the "water-bird" pot, one appreciates that this artifact performed visually in that manner since the artisan painted the design. Thus, in activities ranging from painting, to selling, to display on the mantel, the pot's visual emission potentially is being registered and responded to by many receivers—people taking part in those activities. Thus, in a behavioral analysis, we designate the receivers in specific activities for whom the pot is an emitter—often the salient emitter. Our attention then turns to constructing hypotheses about how the pot's emissions cue the receiver's response. (The following discussions are oversimplified for illustrative purposes.)

Painting Activities.

In the painting activity, a potter can be regarded as both receiver and sender, with the visual performance of the progressing design cuing subsequent brush strokes. These responses rest on correlons she obtained through prior experience in painting pots (appropriate tuning). But there is more to it than that because what an outside observer would call her "choice" of design motifs is also affected by correlons acquired, for example, in previous selling activities (on this kind of feedback to the artisan, see Schiffer and Skibo 1997). For example, we can infer that a potter with vast sales experience is apt to possess correlons which she can use predictively to assess the likelihood that customers will respond favorably to the visual performance of specific designs (i.e., buy the pot). She may have learned that painting a "water-bird" design on small jars increases the probability of their purchase. These

design-specific correlons, part of the potter's tuning, influence her own responses to the pot's visual performance as she is painting it. Where potters work in a group, the acoustic performances of other potters as well as the visual performances of their pots also contribute to cuing the potter's responses to her own vessel's visual performance (Schiffer and Skibo 1997). Clearly, by treating the potter's brush strokes as a response in a communication process, one can offer hypotheses to explain her performances without recourse to the concept of intent.

Selling Activities.

In the selling activity, the customer and potter alternate as receivers; of special interest are the potter's acoustic performances and the customer's response, to purchase or not purchase the pot. From the standpoint of the customer-receiver, the potter is inferred to be the sender—the person who painted the design. As an emitter, the pot performs visually and tactilely; but the potter herself is also an emitter, furnishing information in diverse performance modes that help to cue the customer's response. Especially in modern times, some Hopi potters supply interpretations of design symbolism through acoustic, visual, and tactile performances.

What caused the change over the past few decades in the acoustic performance of Hopi potters during selling activities? I hypothesize that the newly found eagerness of many potters to furnish meanings for their designs stems from changes in pottery marketing activities. Decades ago, most Hopi potters disposed of their wares wholesale to museum buyers or to traders; relatively few pots were sold at retail to the occasional tourist who turned up, uninvited, at the mesas. However, in recent years the mesas themselves have become a tourist destination. Thus, some Hopi potters, while still selling wholesale, have opened retail shops in or adjacent to their homes, especially on First Mesa; these are identified prominently with signs advertising "pottery."

I hypothesize that Hopi potters, on the basis of persistent questioning from tourists, have learned (i.e., acquired a correlon) that the latter expect painted designs to have a deep symbolic significance. Further, I infer that some potters have been retuned, acquiring a correlon (which is used predictively) to the effect that a sale is more likely when the customer's expectations are met. Thus, in responding as receivers to visitor queries in their shops, Hopi potters now add acoustic performances—discussions of symbolism—to accompany the visual and tactile performances of vessels offered for sale. From these diverse performances, the customer-receiver may infer that the potter is not only skilled in her craft but is also a knowledgeable, traditional Hopi. These emissions are more likely to cue a purchase if the receiver is a tourist tuned to the trappings of apparent Indian authenticity (cf. Eaton 1994). In light of increased interaction between potters and the end-purchasers of their products, it is not surprising that artisans are now tuned to be more customer-friendly, employing verbal performances that increase the likelihood of a sale.

Display Activities.
Activities of displaying the pot may involve a host of differently tuned receivers, people who visit our home and peer at the pot on the living-room mantel along with other platial artifacts; they may infer the sender to be me, my wife, or even the potter. For example, acquaintances upon their first visit to our home might notice the variety of artifacts in the living room and respond by asking if we are collectors of ethnic art. In that case, they would infer us to be the senders who assembled these artifacts for display in our home. Other visitors might be more finely tuned. Indeed, the pot's visual performance, as the salient emitter, could cue a collector of Southwestern pottery to compliment our "lovely Hopi water-bird pot." This response is based on several inferences, including that which allows the potter (sender) to be identified as Hopi. In addition, the visitor-receiver has apparently been tuned—perhaps during interaction with Hopi potters in selling activi-

ties—to recognize the design as a "water bird," thus inferring what the potter (as sender) apparently sought to symbolize.

These examples demonstrate how the theory can help investigators to formulate questions and hypotheses about the participation of artifacts—and all other interactors—in communication processes. We are not forced to engage endlessly in interpretive discourse about a sender's intent. Instead, we can treat any performance of a person, for example, painting a design, talking about symbols, buying a pot, responding to a display, as the receiver's response in a specific communication process.

DISCUSSION AND CONCLUSION
Given that nowhere in the communication theory presented above does the term "meaning" appear, the reader might wonder how this paper could purport to present a "behavioral theory of meaning." The answer is that use of the word "meaning" in scholarly discourse merely calls attention to certain familiar communication phenomena, i.e., the passage of consequential information between interactors in an activity, that may also be studied behaviorally. Meaning, per se, is left out of the theory because information transfer is handled more rigorously by the theory's other concepts and principles.

Those reluctant to accept a meaning-less theory of meaning might insist that the theory at least define meaning behaviorally, and fortunately that is possible. Meaning is the correlate-based inference(s) constructed by the investigator (an outside observer) to account for the receiver's response in a given communication process. The theory can even supply a behavioral definition of symbol: it is the performance(s) of a salient emitter which, in a given communication process, cues the receiver's response.

Although superfluous in behavioral analysis, the concepts of meaning and symbol are sometimes still useful. For example, it is doubtful that an archaeologist could write an introductory text (e.g., Rathje and Schiffer 1982) or a book accessible to the general public (e.g., Schiffer 1991a; Schiffer et al. 1994a) without employing these terms. In principle, one could use the theory presented here to analyze a communication process, and then translate the results into meaning and symbol.

That meaning and symbol can be defined behaviorally suggests that the chasm between interpretive and behavioral approaches in archaeology may be bridgeable. By treating meaning and symbol behaviorally, one can carry out analyses of communication processes that lay a foundation for the interpretation of meaningful phenomena. Indeed, I suggest that the new theory can enable any investigator—processual, behavioral, selectionist, or postprocessual—to conceptualize and rigorously study information transfer in activities.

The artifact-based, receiver-oriented communication theory presented here is distinguished from all others in the social and behavioral sciences by the following *set* of postulates: (1) Three major interactor roles—sender, emitter, and receiver—are played in all communication processes. (2) Interactor roles can be played, in principle, by people, artifacts, and natural phenomena. (3) A communication process is delineated and studied with reference to a particular activity and a place. (4) The performances of personal, situational, and platial artifacts permeate communication processes. (5) The investigator is required to designate a receiver and, with respect to that receiver, identify the interactors playing emitter roles. (6) The receiver obtains information from emitters performing in many modes. (7) Receivers construct inferences about senders and inscription events using correlons that map to emitter performances and are keyed-in hierarchically. (8) The receiver's response is cued by emitter performance(s), including the salient emitter, and is influenced by the receiver's tuning. (9) Ideally, the explanation of a response in a specific communication process requires the investigator to model (infer) the receiver's relevant correlons. (10) Depending on how one delineates a specific communication process, any performance of any person can be treated as the receiver's response.

Not constrained by the two-body model derived from language, this theory is sufficiently flexible to handle any communication process. Moreover, with its emphasis on the myriad artifact performances that contribute to the construction of inferences and cue receiver responses, the theory demonstrates that artifacts participate in virtually all human communication.

References Cited

Abascal, R.
  1976 Los Primeros Pueblos Alfareros Pre-
         hispánicos. *Comunicaciones, Suple-
         mento, Proyecto Puebla-Tlaxcala*
         3:49–52. Fundación Alemana para
         la Investigación Científica, Puebla.

Abbott, D. R., and M. E. Walsh-Anduze
  1995 Temporal Patterns without Varia-
         tion: The Paradox of Hohokam Red
         Ware Ceramics. In *Ceramic Produc-
         tion in the American Southwest,*
         edited by B. Mills and P. Crown,
         pp. 88–114. University of Arizona
         Press, Tucson.

Abehsera, M.
  1990 *The Healing Clay.* Citadel Press,
         Carol Publishing Group, New
         York.

Ackerman, D.
  1990 *A Natural History of the Senses.*
         Random House, New York.

Adams, E. C.
  1991 *The Origin and Development of the
         Pueblo Katsina Cult.* University of
         Arizona Press, Tucson.

Adams, J. L.
  1994 *The Development of Prehistoric
         Grinding Technology in the Point of
         Pines Area, East-Central Arizona.*
         Unpublished Ph.D. dissertation,
         Department of Anthropology, Uni-
         versity of Arizona, Tucson.

Adan-Bayewitz, D.
  1995 A Lamp Mould from Sepphoris
         and the Location of Workshops for
         Lamp and Common Pottery Manu-
         facture in Northern Palestine.
         Journal of Roman Archaeology,
         Supplemental Series Number 14,
         *The Roman and Byzantine Near
         East: Some Recent Archaeological
         Research,* pp. 177–182.

Adler, M.
  1994 Population Aggregation and the
         Anasazi Social Landscape: A View
         from the Four Corners. In *The
         Ancient Southwestern Community,*
         edited by W. H. Wills and R. D.
         Leonard, pp. 85–101. University
         of New Mexico Press, Albuquerque.

Aikens, M. C.
  1995 First In the World: Jomon Pottery of
         Early Japan. In *The Emergence of
         Pottery: Technology and Innovation
         in Ancient Societies,* edited by W. K.
         Barnett and J. W. Hoopes, pp. 11–
         21. Smithsonian Institution Press,
         Washington, D.C.

Akins, N. J.
  1984 Temporal Variation in Faunal As-
         semblages from Chaco Canyon. In
         *Recent Research on Chaco Prehis-
         tory,* edited by W. J. Judge and J. D.
         Schelberg, pp. 225–240. Reports of
         the Chaco Center 8. Division of
         Cultural Research, National Park
         Service, Albuquerque.

Albone, E. S.
  1984 *Mammalian Semiochemistry: The
         Investigation of Chemical Signals
         between Mammals.* John Wiley and
         Sons, Chichester.

Almagor, U.
1990 Odors and Private Language: Observations on the Phenomenology of Scent. *Human Studies* 13:253–274.
Amiran, R.
1965 The Beginnings of Pottery-Making in the Near East. In *Ceramics and Man,* edited by F. R. Matson, pp. 240–247. Aldine, Chicago.
Anders, M., V. Chang, L. Tokuda, S. Quiroz, and I. Shimada
1994 Producción Cerámica del Horizonte Medio Temprano en Maymi, Valle de Pisco, Peru. In *Tecnología y Organización de la ón de Cerámica Prehispánica en los Andes,* edited by I. Shimada, pp. 249–267. Fondo Editorial, Pontificia Universidad Católica del Perú, Lima.
Anyon, R., and S. A. LeBlanc
1984 *The Galaz Ruin: A Prehistoric Mimbres Village in Southwestern New Mexico.* University of New Mexico Press, Albuquerque.
Arnold, D. E.
1971 Ethnomineralogy of Ticul, Yucatan Potters: Etics and Emics. *American Antiquity* 36:20–40.
1975a Ceramic Ecology in the Ayacucho Basin, Peru: Implications for Prehistory. *Current Anthropology* 16:637–640.
1975b Reply to R. Haaland and D. Browman's Comments on "Ceramic Ecology in the Ayacucho Basin, Peru: Implications for Prehistory." *Current Anthropology* 16:185–203.
1979 Comment on "On the Argument from Ceramics to History: A Challenge Based on the Evidence from Medieval Nubia" by Richard Y. Adams. *Current Anthropology* 20(4):735.
1980 Localized Exchange: An Ethnoarchaeological Perspective. In *Models and Methods in Regional Exchange,* edited by R. E. Frey, pp. 147–150. SAA Papers No. 1. Society for American Archaeology, Washington, D.C.
1981 A Model for the Identification of Non-Local Ceramic Distribution: A View from the Present. In *Production and Distribution: A Ceramic Viewpoint,* edited by H. Howard

and E. L. Morris, pp. 31–44. British Archaeological Reports, International Series 120, Oxford, England.
1985 *Ceramic Theory and Cultural Process.* Cambridge University Press, England.
1987 Maya Pottery after 20 Years: Achaeological Implications. In *Maya Ceramics: Papers from the 1985 Maya Ceramics Conference,* edited by P. M. Rice and R. J. Sharer, pp. 545–561. British Archaeological Reports International Series 345, Oxford, England.
1989 Patterns of Learning, Residence and Descent among Potters in Ticul, Yucatan, Mexico. In *Archaeological Approaches to Cultural Identity,* edited by S. J. Shennan, pp. 174–184. George Allen and Unwin, London.
1993 *Ecology of Ceramic Production in an Andean Community.* Cambridge University Press, England.
Arnold, D. E., and A. L. Nieves
1992 Factors Affecting Ceramic Standardization. In *Ceramic Production and Distribution: An Integrated Approach,* edited by G. J. Bey III and C. A. Pool, pp. 93–113. Westview Press, Boulder, Colorado.
Arnold, P. J. III
1991a Dimensional Standardization and Production Scale in Mesoamerican Ceramics. *Latin American Antiquity* 2(4):363–370.
1991b *Domestic Ceramic Production and Spatial Organization: A Mexican Case Study in Ethnoarchaeology.* Cambridge University Press, Cambridge, England.
1997 Socio-political Complexity and the Gulf Olmec: A View From the Tuxtla Mountains, Veracruz, Mexico. In *Olmec Art and Archaeology in Mesoamerica: Social Complexity in the Formative Period,* edited by J. Clark and M. Pye. National Gallery of Art, Washington, D.C. In press.
Arnold, P. J. III, V. J. McCormack, E. O. Juárez V., S. A. Wails, R. Herrera B., G. J. Fernandez S., and C. A. Skidmore
1996 *El Proyecto Arqueológico La Joya: Informe Final de Campo—Tempo-*

rada 1995. Submitted to the Instituto Nacional de Antropología e Historia, México, D.F.

Arnold, P. J. III, C. A. Pool, R. R. Kneebone, and R. S. Santley
1993 Intensive Ceramic Production and Classic-Period Political Economy in the Sierra de los Tuxtlas, Veracruz, Mexico. *Ancient Mesoamerica* 4:175–191.

Aveleyra Arroyo de Anda, L.
1963 *La Estela Teotihuacana de La Ventilla*. Museo Nacional de Antropología, Instituto Nacional de Antropología e Historia, México, D.F.

Balfet, H.
1965 Ethnographical Observations in North Africa and Archaeological Interpretation: The Pottery of the Maghreb. In *Ceramics and Man*, edited by F. R. Matson, pp. 161–177. Aldine Publishing Co., Chicago.

Balkansky, A. K., G. M. Feinman, and L. M. Nicholas
1997 Pottery Kilns of Ancient Ejutla, Oaxaca, Mexico. *Journal of Field Archaeology* 24:139–160.

Barnes, R., and J. B. Eicher
1992 (editors) *Dress and Gender: Making and Meaning in Cultural Contexts*. Berg, New York.

Barnett, W. K., and J. W. Hoopes
1995 (editors) *The Emergence of Pottery: Technological Innovation in Ancient Societies*. Smithsonian Institution Press, Washington, D.C.

Becker, M. J.
1973 Archaeological Evidence for Occupational Specialization among the Classic Maya at Tikal, Guatemala. *American Antiquity* 38:396–406.

Behura, N. K.
1965 The Potter Servants of Jagannath at Puri. *Man in India* 45:127–133.

Benco, N.
1988 Morphological Standardization: An Approach to the Study of Craft Specialization. In *A Pot for All Reasons: Ceramic Ecology Revisited*, edited by C. C. Kolb and L. M. Lackey, pp. 57–72. Temple University, Philadelphia, Pennsylvania.

Benson, E. P., and B. de la Fuente
1996 (editors) *Olmec Art of Ancient Mexico*. National Gallery of Art, Washington, D.C.

Berdan, F. F., and P. R. Anawalt
1992 (editors) *The Codex Mendoza*. University of California Press, Berkeley.

Bernal, I.
1949 La Cerámica Grabada de Monte Albán. *Anales del Instituto Nacional de Antropología e Historia*, pp. 59–77. Instituto Nacional de Antropología e Historia, México, D.F.

Bernardini, W.
1997 Kiln Firing Groups and White Ware Production in the Northern Southwest, A.D. 1100–1300. Unpublished M.A. thesis, Department of Anthropology, Arizona State University, Tempe.

Berrin, K., and E. Pasztory
1993 (editors) *Teotihuacan: Art from the City of the Gods*. Thames and Hudson, New York.

Biber, B.
1962 *Children's Drawings: From Lines to Pictures Illustrated*. Bank Street College of Education Publications, New York.

Binford, L. R.
1962 Archaeology as Anthropology. *American Antiquity* 28:217–225.
1981 *Bones: Ancient Men and Modern Myths*. Academic Press, New York.
1982 The Archaeology of Place. *Journal of Anthropological Archaeology* 1:5–31.

Birdwhistell, R. L.
1970 *Kinesics and Context*. University of Pennsylvania Press, Philadelphia.

Bishop, R. L., V. Canouts, S. P. De Atley, A. Qoyawayma, and C. W. Aikins
1988 The Formation of Ceramic Analytical Groups: Hopi Pottery Production and Exchange, A.D. 1300–1600. *Journal of Field Archaeology* 15:317–337.

Bjšrk, C.
1995 *Early Pottery in Greece: A Technological and Functional Analysis of the Evidence from Neolithic Achilleion, Thessaly*. Astroms Forlag, Jonsered.

Blackman, M. J., G. J. Stein, and P. J. Vandiver
1993 The Standardization Hypothesis and Ceramic Mass Production: Technological Compositional, and

Metric Indexes of Craft Specialization at Tell Leilan, Syria. *American Antiquity* 58:60–79.

Blackman, M. J., and M. Vidale
1992 The Production and Distribution of Stoneware Bangles at Mohenjo-Daro as Monitored by Chemical Characterization Studies. In *South Asian Archaeology 1989,* edited by R. J. Meadow, pp. 37–43. Prehistory Press, Madison, Wisconsin.

Blake, M., B. S. Chisholm, J. E. Clark, B. Voorhies, and M. W. Love
1992 Prehistoric Subsistence in the Soconusco Region. *Current Anthropology* 33:83–94.

Blanton, R. E., G. M. Feinman, S. A. Kowalewski, and P. N. Peregrine
1996 Agency, Ideology, and Power in Archaeological Theory. *Current Anthropology* 37(1):1–14.

Blinman, E.
1988a *The Interpretation of Ceramic Variability: A Case Study from the Dolores Anasazi.* Unpublished Ph.D. dissertation, Department of Anthropology, Washington State University, Pullman.
1988b Justification and Procedures for Ceramic Dating. In *Dolores Archaeological Program: Supporting Studies: Additive and Reductive Technologies,* compiled by Eric Blinman, Carl J. Phagan, and Richard H. Wilshusen, pp. 501–544. Bureau of Reclamation, Engineering and Research Center, Denver.
1989 Potluck in the Protokiva: Ceramics and Ceremonialism in Pueblo I Villages. In *The Architecture of Integration,* edited by M. Hegmon and W. D. Lipe, pp. 113–124. Crow Canyon Archaeological Center, Cortez, Colorado.

Blinman, E., and C. D. Wilson
1994 Additional Ceramic Analyses. In *Across the Colorado Plateau: Anthropological Studies for the Transwestern Pipeline Expansion Project,* vol. 14. Office of Contract Archeology and Maxwell Museum of Anthropology, University of New Mexico, Albuquerque.

Blitz, J. H.
1993 Big Pots for Big Shots: Feasting and Storage in a Mississippian Community. *American Antiquity* 58:80–96.

Bloch, M.
1990 Language, Anthropology and Cognitive Science. *Man* 26:183–198.

Bollong, C. A., J. C. Vogel, L. Jacobson, W. A. Van der Westhuizen, and C. G. Sampson
1993 Direct Dating and Identity of Fibre Temper in Pre-Contact Bushman (Basarwa) Pottery. *Journal of Archaeological Sciences* 20: 41–55.

Bordaz, J.
1964 *Pre-Columbian Ceramic Kilns at Peñitas, a Post-Classic Site in Coastal Nayarit, Mexico.* Unpublished Ph.D. dissertation, Department of Anthropology, Columbia University, New York.

Braidwood, R. J., J. D. Sauer, H. Helbaek, P. C. Mangelsdorf, H. C. Cutler, C. S. Coon, R. Linton, J. Steward, and A. L. Oppenheim.
1953 Symposium: Did Man Once Live by Beer Alone? *American Anthropologist* 55(4):515–526.

Brain, R.
1979 *The Decorated Body.* Hutchinson, London.

Brainerd, G. W.
1958 *The Archaeological Ceramics of Yucatan.* Anthropological Records, vol. 19. Berkeley and Los Angeles, California.

Braun, D.
1983 Pots as Tools. In *Archaeological Hammers and Theories,* edited by A. Keene and J. Moore, pp. 107–134. Academic Press, New York.

Breternitz, D. A.
1982 The Four Corners Anasazi Ceramic Tradition. "Southwestern Ceramics: A Comparative Review," edited by A. H. Schroeder, pp. 129–147. *The Arizona Archaeologist* 15. School of American Research, Santa Fe.

Brody, J. J.
1977 *Mimbres Painted Pottery.* School of American Research and the University of New Mexico Press, Santa Fe and Albuquerque.

Bronitsky, G.
1989 A Ceramics Manifesto. In *Pottery Technology: Ideas and Approaches,*

edited by G. Bronitsky, pp. 5–11. Westview Press, Boulder, Colorado.

Brown, D. J. J.
1979   The Structuring of Polopa Feasting and Warfare. *Man* (n.s.) 14:712–733.

Brown, J. A.
1989   The Beginnings of Pottery as an Economic Process. In *What's New? A Closer Look at the Process of Innovation,* edited by S. E. van der Leeuw and R. Torrence, pp. 203–224. Unwin Hyman, London.

Brumfiel, E. M.
1987   Consumption and Politics at Aztec Huexotla. *American Anthropologist* 89:676–686.

1994   Factional Competition and Political Development in the New World: An Introduction. In *Factional Competition and Political Development in the New World,* edited by E. M. Brumfiel and J. Fox, pp. 3–13. Cambridge University Press, England.

Brumfiel, E. M., and T. K. Earle
1987   Specialization, Exchange, and Complex Societies: An Introduction. In *Specialization, Exchange, and Complex Societies,* edited by E. M. Brumfiel and T. K. Earle, pp. 1–9. Cambridge University Press, England.

Buchanan, F.
1807   *A Journey from Madras through the Countries of Mysore, Canara, and Malabar,* 3 vols. Asiatic Society, London.

Budak, M.
1991   The Function of Shell Temper in Pottery. *The Minnesota Archaeologist* 50(2):53–59.

Bunzel, R. L.
1929   *The Pueblo Potter: A Study of Creative Imagination in Primitive Art.* Columbia University Press, New York.

Burgoon, J. K.
1978   Nonverbal Communication. In *Human Communication,* by Michael Burgoon and Michael Ruffner, pp. 129–170. Holt, Rinehart and Winston, New York.

Burgoon, J. K., D. B. Buller, and W. G. Woodall
1996   *Nonverbal Communication: the Unspoken Dialogue.* 2d edition. McGraw-Hill, New York.

Burling, R.
1993   Primate Calls, Human Language, and Nonverbal Communication. *Current Anthropology* 34:25–54.

Burton, J. F.
1991   *The Archaeology of Sivu'ovi: The Archaic to Basketmaker Transition at Petrified Forest National Park.* Publications in Anthropology No. 55. Western Archeological and Conservation Center, National Park Service, Tucson, Arizona.

Burton, J. H., and A. W. Simon
1996   A Pot Is Not a Rock: A Reply to Neff, Glascock, Bishop, and Blackman. *American Antiquity* 61:405–413.

Cabrera Castro, R.
1992   A Survey of Recently Excavated Murals at Teotihuacan. In *Art, Ideology, and the City of Teotihuacan,* edited by J. C. Berlo, pp. 113–128. Dumbarton Oaks Research Library and Collection, Washington, D.C.

Carr, C., and J. E. Neitzel
1995   (editors) *Style, Society, and Person.* Plenum, New York.

Casmir, F. L.
1994   (editor) *Building Communication Theories: A Socio/Cultural Approach.* Erlbaum, Hillsdale, New Jersey.

Caso, A., and I. Bernal
1952   *Urnas de Oaxaca.* Instituto Nacional de Antropología e Historia, México.

Chapman, J.
1994   The Origins of Farming in South East Europe. *Préhistoire Européenne* 6:133–156.

Chappel, E. D., and C. S. Coon
1942   *Principles of Anthropology.* Henry Holt and Company, New York.

Charlton, C. O., T. H. Charlton, and D. L. Nichols
1993   Aztec Household-Based Craft Production: Archaeological Evidence from the City-State of Otumba, Mexico. In *Prehispanic Domestic Units in Western Mesoamerica: Studies of Household, Compound, and Residence,* edited by R. S. Santley and K. G.

Hirth, pp. 147–171. CRC Press, Boca Raton, Florida.

Childe, V. G.
1951   *Man Makes Himself.* New American Library of World Literature, London.

Chisholm, B., and R. G. Matson
1994   Carbon and Nitrogen Isotopic Evidence on Basketmaker II Diet at Cedar Mesa, Utah. *Kiva* 60:239–256.

Clark, J. E.
1986   From Mountains to Molehills: A Critical Review of Teotihuacan's Obsidian Industry. *Research in Economic Anthropology,* supplement 2:23–74.
1989   Hacia una Definición de Talleres. In *La Obsidiana en Mesoamérica,* edited by M. Gaxiola G. and J. E. Clark, pp. 213–217. Instituto Nacional de Antropología e Historia, México.
1994   *The Development of Early Formative Rank Societies in the Soconusco, Chiapas, Mexico.* Unpublished Ph.D. dissertation, Department of Anthropology, University of Michigan, Ann Arbor.

Clark, J. E., and M. Blake
1994   The Power of Prestige: Competitive Generosity and the Emergence of Rank Societies in Lowland Mesoamerica. In *Factional Competition and Political Development in the New World,* edited by E. M. Brumfiel and J. W. Fox, p. 17–30. Cambridge University Press, England.

Clark, J. E., and D. Gosser
1995   Reinventing Mesoamerica's First Pottery. In *The Emergence of Pottery: Technology and Innovation in Ancient Societies,* edited by W. K. Barnett and J. W. Hoopes, pp. 209–221. Smithsonian Institution Press, Washington, D.C.

Clark, J. E., and W. J. Parry
1990   Craft Specialization and Cultural Complexity. In *Research in Economic Anthropology,* vol. 12, edited by B. L. Isaac, pp. 289–346. JAI Press, Inc., Greenwich, Connecticut.

Clendinnen, I.
1991   *Aztecs, An Interpretation.* Cambridge University Press, England.

Coe, M. D.
1961   *La Victoria, an Early Site on the Pacific Coast of Guatemala.* Papers of the Peabody Museum of Archaeology and Ethnology, vol. 53. Harvard University, Cambridge, Massachusetts.
1994   *Mexico: From the Olmecs to the Aztecs.* 4th edition. Thames and Hudson, London.

Coe, M. D., and R. A. Diehl
1980   *In the Land of the Olmec,* vols. 1 and 2. University of Texas Press, Austin.

Coe, M. D., and K. V. Flannery
1967   *Early Cultures and Human Ecology in South Coastal Guatemala.* Smithsonian Institution Press, Washington, D.C.

Conkey, M. W.
1995   Making Things Meaningful: Approaches to the Interpretation of the Ice Age Imagery of Europe. In *Meaning in the Visual Arts: Views from the Outside,* edited by I. Lavin, pp. 49–64. Institute for Advanced Study, Princeton, New Jersey.

Conkey, M. W., and C. Hastorf
1990   (editors) *The Uses of Style in Archaeology.* Cambridge University Press, England.

Cordell, L. S.
1991   Anna O. Shepard and Southwestern Archaeology: Ignoring a Cautious Heretic. In *The Ceramic Legacy of Anna O. Shepard,* edited by R. L. Bishop and F. W. Lange, pp.132–153. University Press of Colorado, Niwot.

Coren, S., L. M. Ward, and J. T. Enns
1994   *Sensation and Perception.* Harcourt Brace, Fort Worth, Texas.

Costin, C. L.
1991   Craft Specialization: Issues in Defining, Documenting, and Explaining the Organization of Production. In *Advances in Archaeological Method and Theory,* vol. 3, edited by M. B. Schiffer, pp. 1–56. University of Arizona Press, Tucson.

Costin, C. L., and T. Earle
1989   Status Distinction and Legitimation of Power as Reflected in Changing Patterns of Consumption in Late

Prehispanic Peru. *American Antiquity* 54:691–714.

Costin, C. L., T. Earle, B. Owen, and G. Russell
1989 The Impact of Inca Conquest on Local Technology in the Upper Mantaro Valley, Peru. In *What's New? A Closer Look at the Process of Innovation*, edited by S. E. van der Leeuw and R. Torrence, pp. 107–139. Unwin Hyman, London.

Costin, C. L., and M. B. Hagstrum
1995 Standardization, Labor Investment, Skill, and the Organization of Ceramic Production in Late Prehistoric Highland Peru. *American Antiquity* 60:619–639.

Coulam, N. J., and A. R. Schroedl
1996 Early Archaic Clay Figurines from Cowboy and Walters Caves in Southeastern Utah. *Kiva* 61:401–412.

Covarrubias, M.
1957 *Mexico South: The Isthmus of Tehuantepec*. A. A. Knopf, New York.

Cowgill, G. L., J. H. Altschul, and R. S. Sload
1984 Spatial Analysis of Teotihuacan: A Mesoamerican Metropolis. In *Intrasite Spatial Analysis in Archaeology*, edited by H. J. Hietala, pp. 154–195. Cambridge University Press, England.

Cox, M. V.
1993 *Children's Drawings of the Human Figure*. Lawrence Erlbaum Associates, Hove, England.

Craik, J.
1994 *The Face of Fashion: Cultural Studies in Fashion*. Routledge, London.

Crowley, D. J.
1994 (editor) *Communication Theory Today*. Stanford University Press, Stanford, California.

Crown, P. L.
1994 *Ceramics and Ideology: Salado Polychrome Pottery*. University of New Mexico Press, Albuquerque.
1995 The Production of the Salado Polychromes in the American Southwest. In *Ceramic Production in the American Southwest*, edited by B. J. Mills and P. L. Crown, pp. 142–166. University of Arizona Press, Tucson.

Crown, P. L., and W. H. Wills
1995 Economic Intensification and the Origins of Ceramic Containers in the American Southwest. In *The Emergence of Pottery: Technology and Innovation in Ancient Societies*, edited by W. K. Barnett and J .W. Hoopes, pp. 241–254. Smithsonian Institution Press, Washington, D.C.

Cullen, T.
1985 *A Measure of Interaction among Neolithic Communities: Design Elements of Greek Neolithic Urfirnis Pottery*. Ph.D. dissertation, Program in Classical Archaeology, Indiana University. University Microfilms, Ann Arbor.

Cummings, L. S.
1995 Agriculture and the Mesa Verde Area Anasazi Diet: Description and Nutritional Analysis. In *Soil, Water, Biology, and Belief in Prehistoric and Traditional Southwestern Agriculture*, edited by H. W. Toll, pp. 335–352. New Mexico Archaeological Council Special Publication 2, Albuquerque.

Cummins, T.
1994 La Tradición de Figurinas de la Costa Ecuatoriana: Estilo Tecnológico y el Uso de Moldes. In *Tecnología y Organización de la Producción de Cerámica Prehispánica en los Andes*, edited by I. Shimada, pp. 157–171. Fondo Editorial, Pontificia Universidad Católica del Perú, Lima.

Curet, L. A., B. L. Stark, and S. Vásquez Z.
1994 Postclassic Change in South-Central Veracruz, Mexico. *Ancient Mesoamerica* 5(1):13–32.

Cushing, F. H.
1920 *Zuni Breadstuff*. Indian Notes and Monographs vol. 8, Museum of the American Indian, Heye Foundation, New York.

Daneels, A.
1988 La Cerámica de Plaza de Toros y Colonia Ejidal. 2 vols. Informe al Instituto Nacional de Antropología e Historia, México, D.F.
1997a El Protoclásico en el Centro de Veracruz, una Perspectiva desde la Cuenca Baja del Cotaxtla. Paper presented at the IV Coloquio Pedro

Bosch-Gimpera. Instituto de Investigaciones Antropológicas, Universidad Nacional Autónoma de Mexico, Mexico City, Mexico.

1997b   Settlement History in the Lower Cotaxtla Basin, Veracruz, Mexico. In *Olmec to Aztec: Settlement Pattern Research in the Ancient Gulf Lowlands*, edited by B. L. Stark and P. J. Arnold III, pp. 206–252. University of Arizona Press, Tucson.

David, F.
1992   *Fashion, Culture, and Identity*. University of Chicago Press, Chicago.

Davis, M.
1983   *Rank and Rivalry: The Politics of Inequality in Rural West Bengal*. Cambridge University Press, England.

De Atley, S. P., and R. L. Bishop
1991   Toward an Integrated Interface for Archaeology and Archaeometry. In *The Ceramic Legacy of Anna O. Shepard*, edited by R. L. Bishop and F. W. Lange, pp. 358–380.University of Colorado Press, Niwot.

Deacon, T. W.
1997   *The Symbolic Species: The Co-Evolution of Language and the Brain*. Norton, New York.

Deal, M.
1998   *Pottery Ethnoarchaeology in the Central Maya Lowlands*. University of Utah Press, Salt Lake City.

Dean, J. S.
1969   *Chronological Analysis of Tsegi Phase Sites in Northeastern Arizona*. Papers of the Laboratory of Tree-Ring Research No. 3. University of Arizona Press, Tucson.

1992   Environmental Factors in the Evolution of the Chacoan Sociopolitical System. In *Anasazi Regional Organization and the Chaco System*, edited by D. E. Doyel, pp. 35–43. Maxwell Museum of Anthropology Anthropological Papers No. 5. Albuquerque, New Mexico.

DeBoer, W. R.
1984   The Last Pottery Show: Systems and Sense in Ceramic Studies. In *The Many Dimensions of Pottery: Ceramics in Archaeology and Anthropology*, edited by S. E. van der Leeuw and A. C. Pritchard, pp.

527–571. Institute for Pre- and Proto-history, University of Amsterdam, Amsterdam.

1990   Interaction, Imitation, and Communication as Expressed in Style: The Ucayali Experience. In *The Uses of Style in Archaeology*, edited by M. Conkey and C. Hastorf, pp. 82–104. Cambridge University Press, England.

DeBoer, W. R., and D. W. Lathrap
1979   The Making and Breaking of Shipibo-Conibo Ceramics. In *Ethnonoarchaeology: Implictions of Ethnography for Archaeology*, edited by C. Kramer, pp. 102–128. Columbia University Press, New York.

Demoule, J.-P., and C. Perlés
1993   The Greek Neolithic: A New Review. *Journal of World Prehistory* 7:355–416.

Dennis, W.
1940   *The Hopi Child*. D. Appleton-Century Company, New York.

1942   The Performance of Hopi Children on the Goodenough Draw-a-Man Test. *Journal of Comparative Psychology* 34:341–348.

Deregowski, J. B.
1980   *Illusions, Patterns and Pictures: A Cross-Cultural Perspective*. Academic Press, New York.

Díaz, B.
1963   *The Conquest of New Spain*, translated by J. M. Cohen. Penguin Books, Harmondsworth, Middlesex, England.

Diehl, R. A.
1996   The Olmec World. In *Olmec Art of Ancient Mexico*, edited by E. P. Benson, and B. de la Fuente, pp. 29–33. National Gallery of Art, Washington, D.C.

Dittert, A. E. Jr., J. J. Hestor, and F. W. Eddy
1961   *An Archaeological Survey of the Navajo Reservoir District, Northwestern New Mexico*. Monographs of the School of American Research, No. 23. Santa Fe, New Mexico.

Domjan, M.
1993   *The Principles of Learning and Behavior*. Brooks/Cole, Pacific Grove, California.

Drennan, R. D.
1984   Long-Distance Transport Costs in

Pre-Hispanic Mesoamerica. *American Anthropologist* 86:105–112.

Drucker, P.
1943 *Ceramic Stratigraphy at Cerro de las Mesas, Veracruz, Mexico.* Smithsonian Institution, Bureau of American Ethnology, Bulletin 141. Washington, D.C.

Du Bois, C.
1944 *The People of Alor: A Social-Psychological Study of an East Indian Island.* University of Minnesota Press, Minneapolis.

DuBois, J. W.
1993 Meaning Without Intention: Lessons from Divination. In *Responsibility and Evidence in Oral Discourse,* edited by J. H. Hill and J. T. Irvine, pp. 48–71. Cambridge University Press, England.

Duncan, S. Jr.
1969 Nonverbal Communication. *Psychological Bulletin* 72(2):118–137.

Earle, T. K.
1994 Wealth Finance in the Inka Empire: Evidence from the Calchaqui Valley, Argentina. *American Antiquity* 59:443–460.

Eaton, L. B.
1994 The Hopi Craftsman Exhibition: The Creation of Authenticity. *Expedition* 36(1):24–32.

Eddy, F. W.
1966 *Prehistory in the Navajo Reservoir District, Northwestern, New Mexico.* Museum of New Mexico Papers in Anthropology No. 15. Santa Fe.

Egloff, B. J.
1973 A Method for Counting Ceramic Rim Sherds. *American Antiquity* 38:351–353.

Ehrenhaus, P.
1988 Attributing Intention to Communication: Information as the Interpretation of Interaction. In *Information and Behavior,* vol. 2, edited by B. D. Ruben, pp. 248–270. Transaction Books, New Brunswick, New Jersey.

Ekman, P., and W. V. Friesen
1969 The Repertoire of Nonverbal Behavior: Categories, Origins, Usage, and Coding. *Semiotica* 1:49–98.

Evans, R.
1978 Early Craft Specialization: An Example from the Balkan Chalcolithic.

In *Social Archaeology: Beyond Subsistence and Dating,* edited by C. L. Redman, M. J. Berman, E. V. Curtin, W. T. Langhorne, Jr., N. M. Versaggi, and J. C. Wanser, pp. 113–129. Academic Press, New York.

Fast, J.
1971 *Body Language.* Pocket Books, New York.

Feinman, G. M.
1980 *The Relationship between Administrative Organization and Ceramic Production in the Valley of Oaxaca, Mexico.* Unpublished Ph.D. dissertation, Department of Anthropology, City University of New York, New York.
1985 Changes in the Organization of Ceramic Production in Prehispanic Oaxaca. In *Decoding Prehistoric Ceramics,* edited by B. A. Nelson, pp. 195–223. Southern Illinois University Press, Carbondale.
1989 Tinkering with Technology: Pitfalls and Prospects for an Anthropological Archaeology. In *Pottery Technology: Ideas and Approaches,* edited by G. Bronitsky, pp. 217–220. Westview Press, Boulder, Colorado.
1995 The Emergence of Inequality: A Focus on Strategies and Processes. In *Foundations of Social Inequality,* edited by T. D. Price and G. M. Feinman, pp. 255–279. Plenum Press, New York.

Feinman, G. M., and L. M. Nicholas
1990 At the Margins of the Monte Albán State: Settlement Patterns in the Ejutla Valley, Oaxaca, Mexico. *Latin American Antiquity* 1:216–246.
1993 Shell-Ornament Production in Ejutla: Implications for Highland-Coastal Interaction in Ancient Oaxaca. *Ancient Mesoamerica* 4:103–119.
1995 Household Craft Specialization and Shell Ornament Manufacture in Ejutla, Mexico. *Expedition* 37:14–24.

Feinman, G. M., L. M. Nicholas, and W. M. Middleton
1993 Craft Activities at the Prehispanic Ejutla Site, Oaxaca, Mexico. *Mexicon* 15:33–41.

Fewkes, J. W.

1898 *Archeological Expedition to Arizona in 1895.* Smithsonian Institution, Bureau of American Ethnology, Seventeenth Annual Report 1895–1896. Washington, D.C.

1919 *Designs on Prehistoric Hopi Pottery.* Smithsonian Institution, Bureau of American Ethnology, Thirty-Third Annual Report 1911–1912. Washington, D.C.

1973 *Designs on Prehistoric Hopi Pottery.* Dover, New York.

Flannery, K. V.

1968 The Olmec and the Valley of Oaxaca: A Model for Inter-regional Interaction in Formative Times. In *Dumbarton Oaks Conference on the Olmec, October 28th and 29th, 1967,* edited by E. P. Benson, pp. 79–110. Dumbarton Oaks Research Library and Collection, Washington, D.C.

Flannery, K. V., and J. Marcus

1994 *Early Formative Pottery of the Valley of Oaxaca, Mexico.* Memoirs of the Museum of Anthropology, University of Michigan, No. 27. Ann Arbor.

Fletcher, R.

1996 Organized Dissonance: Multiple Code Structures in the Replication of Human Culture. In *Darwinian Archaeologies,* edited by H. D. G. Maschner, pp. 61–86. Plenum Press, New York.

Ford, J. A.

1969 *A Comparison of Formative Cultures in the Americas. Diffusion or the Psychic Unity of Man.* Smithsonian Contributions to Anthropology, vol. 11. Smithsonian Institution Press, Washington, D.C.

Ford, R. I.

1972 Barter, Gift, or Violence: An Analysis of Tewa Intertribal Exchange. In *Social Exchange and Interaction,* edited by E. N. Wilmsen, pp. 21–45. Museum of Anthropology, University of Michigan, Anthropological Papers No. 46. Ann Arbor.

1983 Inter-Indian Exchange in the Southwest. In *Handbook of North American Indians,* vol. 10, *Southwest,* pp. 711–722, edited by A. Ortiz.

Smithsonian Institution, Washington, D.C.

Fortes, M.

1940 Children's Drawings among the Tallensi. *Africa* 13:293–295.

Fortner, R. S.

1994 Mediated Communication Theory. In *Building Communication Theories: A Socio/Cultural Approach,* edited by F. L. Casmir, pp. 209–240. Erlbaum, Hillsdale, New Jersey.

Foster, G. M.

1948 Some Implications of Modern Mexican Mold-Made Pottery. *Southwestern Journal of Anthropology* 4:356–70.

1955 *Contemporary Pottery Techniques in Southern and Central Mexico.* Middle American Research Institute Publication No. 2.

1962 *Traditional Cultures and the Impact of Technological Change.* Harper and Row, New York.

1965 The Sociology of Pottery: Questions and Hypotheses Arising from Contemporary Mexican Work. In *Ceramics and Man,* edited by F. R. Matson, pp. 43–61. Aldine Press, Chicago.

1967 Contemporary Pottery and Basketry. In *Handbook of Middle American Indians,* vol. 6, edited by M. Nash, pp. 103–124. University of Texas Press, Austin.

Foucault, M.

1972 *The Archaeology of Knowledge.* Harper Torchbooks, New York.

Fowler, A. P.

1991 Brown Ware and Red Ware Pottery: An Anasazi Ceramic Tradition. *Kiva* 56:123–144.

Fowler, C.

1977 *Daisy Hooee Nampeyo: The Story of an American Indian.* Dillon Press, Inc., Minneapolis, Minnesota.

Frings, H., and M. Frings

1977 *Animal Communication.* 2d edition. University of Oklahoma Press, Norman.

Fritz, J. M.

1972 Archaeological Systems for Indirect Observation of the Past. In *Contemporary Archaeology,* edited by M. P. Leone, pp. 135–157. Southern Illinois University Press, Carbondale.

1986 Vijayanagara: Authority and Meaning of a South Indian Imperial Capital. *American Anthropologist* 88:44–55.

Fritz, J. M., G. Michell, and M. S. Nagaraja Rao
1984 *The Royal Centre at Vijayanagara: Preliminary Report.* University of Melbourne, Australia.

Gadamer, H.-G.
1987 The Problem of Historical Consciousness. In *Interpretive Social Science: A Second Look,* edited by P. Rabinow and W. M. Sullivan, pp. 82–140. University of California Press, Berkeley.

Gallagher, W.
1993 *The Power of Place: How Our Surroundings Shape Our Thoughts, Emotions, and Actions.* HarperCollins, New York.

Gardner, E. J.
1978 *The Pottery Technology of the Neolithic Period in Southeastern Europe.* Ph.D. dissertation, Department of Archaeology, University of California, Los Angeles. University Microfilms, Ann Arbor.

Garrett, E. M., and H. H. Franklin
1983 Petrographic and Oxidation Analyses of NMAP Ceramics. In *Economy and Interaction along the Lower Chaco River: The Navajo Mine Archeological Program, Mining Area III, San Juan County, New Mexico,* edited by P. Hogan and J. C. Winter, pp. 311–320. Maxwell Museum of Anthropology, Albuquerque, New Mexico.

Gebauer, A. B.
1995 Pottery Production and the Introduction of Agriculture in Southern Scandinavia. In *The Emergence of Pottery: Technology and Innovation in Ancient Societies,* edited by W. K. Barnett and J. W. Hoopes, pp. 99–112. Smithsonian Institution Press, Washington, D.C.

Giddens, A.
1993 *New Rules of Sociological Method.* 2d edition. Stanford University Press, Stanford, California.

Gimbutas, M., S. Winn, and D. Shimabuku
1989 *Achilleion. A Neolithic Settlement in Thessaly, Greece, 6400–5600 B.C.*

Monumenta Archaeologica 14. Institute of Archaeology, University of California, Los Angeles.

Goffman, E.
1974 *Frame Analysis: An Essay on the Organization of Experience.* Harper and Row, New York.

Gonlin, N.
1994 Rural Household Diversity in Late Classic Copan, Honduras. In *Archaeological Views from the Countryside,* edited by G. Schwartz and S. Falconer, pp. 177–197. Smithsonian Institution Press, Washington, D.C.

Goodnow, J.
1977 *Children's Drawing.* Open Books, London.

Goody, J.
1982 *Cooking, Cuisine, and Class: A Study in Comparative Sociology.* Cambridge University Press, England.

Gosselain, O. P., and A. L. Smith
1995 The Ceramics and Society Project: An Ethnographic and Experimental Approach to Technological Choices. In *The Aim of Laboratory Analyses of Ceramics in Archaeology,* edited by A. Lindahl and O. Stilborg. *Konferenser* 34:147–160.

Gould, R. A.
1990 *Recovering the Past.* University of New Mexico Press, Albuquerque.

Graham, M.
1994 *Mobile Farmers: An Ethnoarchaeological Approach to Settlement Organization among the Rarámuri of Northwestern Mexico.* Ethnoarchaeology Series 3. International Monographs in Prehistory, Ann Arbor, Michigan.

Graves, W. M. II
1996 Social Power and Prestige Enhancement among the Protohistoric Salinas Pueblos, Rio Grande Valley, New Mexico. Unpublished M.A. thesis, Department of Anthropology, Arizona State University, Tempe.

Graves, W. M. II, and S. L. Eckert
1998 Decorated Ceramic Distributions and Ideological Developments in the Northern and Central Rio Grande Valley, New Mexico. In *Pueblo IV*

Migration and Community Reorganization, edited by K. A. Spielmann. Anthropological Research Paper, Arizona State University, Tempe. In press.

Green, D. F., and G. W. Low
1967 *Altamira and Padre Piedra, Early Preclassic Sites in Chiapas, Mexico.* Papers of the New World Archaeological Foundation No. 20. Brigham Young University, Provo, Utah.

Green, R. C.
1979 Lapita Horizon. In *The Prehistory of Polynesia*, edited by J. D. Jennings, pp. 27–60. Harvard University Press, Cambridge, Massachusetts.

Green, R. M.
1996 Calcium Carbonates as a Tempering Material in Early Prehistoric Pots. Unpublished class project, P600, Department of Anthropology, Indiana University, Bloomington.

Gumpert, G., and R. Cathcart
1990 A Theory of Mediation. In *Mediation, Information, and Communication. Information and Behavior*, vol. 3, edited by B. D. Ruben and L. A. Lievrouw, pp. 21–36. Transaction Books, New Brunswick, New Jersey.

Haberlandt, K.
1994 *Cognitive Psychology.* Allyn and Bacon, Boston.

Hagstrum, M.
1985 Measuring Prehistoric Craft Specialization: A Test Case in the American Southwest. *Journal of Field Archaeology* 12(1):65–76.
1992 Intersecting Technologies: Ceramic Tools for Inka Metallurgy. Paper presented at the 28th Annual Symposium on Archaeometry, Los Angeles.
1995 Creativity and Craft: Household Pottery Traditions in the Southwest. In *Ceramic Production in the American Southwest,* edited by B. Mills and P. Crown, pp. 281–300. University of Arizona Press, Tucson.

Hall, E. T.
1966 *The Hidden Dimension.* Doubleday, New York.

Hall, S. A.
1988 Prehistoric Vegetation and Environment at Chaco Canyon. *American Antiquity* 53:582–592.

Hally, D. J.
1983 Use Alteration of Pottery Vessel Surfaces: An Important Source of Evidence for the Identification of Vessel Function. *North American Archaeologist* 4:3–26.
1986 The Identification of Vessel Function: A Case Study from Northwest Georgia. *American Antiquity* 51:267–295.

Hanneman, G. J.
1975 The Study of Human Communication. In *Communication and Behavior,* edited by G. J. Hanneman and W. McEwen, pp. 21–49. Addison-Wesley, Reading, Massachusetts.

Hanson, J., and M. B. Schiffer
1975 The Joint Site—A Preliminary Report. In Chapters in the Prehistory of Eastern Arizona, IV. *Fieldiana: Anthropology* 65:47–91.

Hard, R. J., R. P. Mauldin, and G. R. Raymond
1996 Mano Size, Stable Carbon Isotopes Ratios, and Macrobotanical Remains as Multiple Lines of Evidence of Maize Dependence in the American Southwest. *Journal of Archaeological Method and Theory* 3:253–318.

Hardcastle, V. G.
1996 *How to Build a Theory in Cognitive Science.* State University of New York Press, Albany.

Harris, M.
1979 *Cultural Materialism: The Struggle for a Science of Culture.* Random House, New York.

Harrison, R. P., and W. W. Crouch
1975 Nonverbal Communication: Theory and Research. In *Communication and Behavior,* edited by G. J. Hanneman and W. McEwen, pp. 76–97. Addison-Wesley, Reading, Massachusetts.

Haury, E. W.
1945 *The Excavation of Los Muertos and Neighboring Ruins in the Salt River Valley, Southern Arizona.* Papers of the Peabody Museum of American Archaeology and Ethnology, 24(1). Harvard University, Cambridge, Massachusetts.

1976   *The Hohokam: Desert Farmers and Craftsmen.* University of Arizona Press, Tucson.

1985   An Early Pit House Village of the Mogollon Culture Forestdale Valley, Arizona. In *Mogollon Culture in the Forestdale Valley, East-Central Arizona,* edited by E. W. Haury, pp. 285–371. University of Arizona Press, Tucson.

Havighurst, R. J., M. K. Gunther, and I. E. Pratt

1946   Environment and the Draw-a-Man Test: The Performance of Indian Children. *Journal of Abnormal and Social Psychology* 41:50–63.

Hayden, B.

1990   Nimrods, Piscators, Pluckers, and Planters: The Emergence of Food Production. *Journal of Anthropological Archaeology* 9:31–69.

1993   *Archaeology: The Science of Once and Future Things.* W. H. Freeman, New York.

1995a   The Emergence of Prestige Technologies and Pottery. In *The Emergence of Pottery: Technology and Innovation in Ancient Societies,* edited by W. K. Barnett and J. W. Hoopes, pp. 257–264. Smithsonian Institution Press, Washington, D.C.

1995b   Pathways to Power: Principles for Creating Socioeconomic Inequalities. In *Foundations of Social Inequality,* edited by T. D. Price and G. M. Feinman, pp. 15–86. Plenum Press, New York.

Hayden, B., and A. Cannon

1983   Where the Garbage Goes: Refuse Disposal in the Maya Highlands. *Journal of Anthropological Archaeology* 2:117–163.

1984   *The Structure of Material Systems: Ethnoarchaeology in the Maya Highlands.* SAA Papers No. 3. Society for American Archaeology, Washington, D.C.

Hays, K.

1992   *Anasazi Ceramics as Text and Tool: Toward a Theory of Ceramic Design "Messaging."* Ph.D. dissertation, Department of Anthropology, University of Arizona, Tucson.

Heacock, L. A.

1995   Archaeological Investigations of Three Mesa Verde Anasazi Pit Kilns. *Kiva* 60:391–410.

Hegmon, M.

1992   Archaeological Research on Style. *Annual Review of Anthropology* 21:517–536.

Heidke, J. M., E. Miksa, and M. K. Wiley

1997   Ceramic Artifacts. In *Archaeological Investigations of Early Village Sites in the Middle Santa Cruz Valley,* edited by J. B. Mabry. Anthropological Papers No. 19. Center for Desert Archaeology, Tucson, Arizona.

Helms, M. W.

1993   *Craft and the Kingly Ideal: Art, Trade, and Power.* University of Texas Press, Austin.

Hendon, J. A.

1991   Status and Power in Classic Maya Society: An Archaeological Study. *American Anthropologist* 93:894–918.

Hendry, J. C.

1992   *Atzompa: A Pottery Producing Village of Southern Mexico in the Mid-1950's.* Vanderbilt University Publications in Anthropology No. 40. Nashville, Tennessee.

Hester, T. R., and H. J. Shafer

1994   The Ancient Maya Craft Community at Colha, Belize, and Its External Relationships. In *Archaeological Views of the Countryside: Village Communities in Early Complex Societies,* edited by G. M. Schwartz and S. E. Falconer, pp. 48–63. Smithsonian Institution Press, Washington, D.C.

Hewes, G. W.

1957   The Anthropology of Posture. *Scientific American* 196:123–132.

Heyden, D.

1975   An Interpretation of the Cave Underneath the Pyramid of the Sun in Teotihuacan, Mexico. *American Antiquity* 40(2):131–147.

Hill, J. N.

1970   *Broken K Pueblo: Prehistoric Social Organization in the American Southwest.* Anthropological Papers of the University of Arizona No. 18. University of Arizona Press, Tucson.

Hill, W. W.
 1982 *An Ethnography of Santa Clara Pueblo New Mexico,* edited and annotated by Charles H. Lange. University of New Mexico Press, Albuquerque.
Hodder, I.
 1982 *Symbols in Action.* Cambridge University Press, England.
 1987 (editor) *The Archaeology of Contextual Meanings.* Cambridge University Press, England.
 1989a (editor) *The Meaning of Things: Material Culture and Symbolic Expression.* Unwin Hyman, London.
 1989b This Is not an Article about Material Culture as Text. *Journal of Anthropological Archaeology* 8:250–269.
 1991 *Reading the Past: Current Approaches to Interpretation in Archaeology.* 2d edition. Cambridge University Press, England.
 1992 *Theory and Practice in Archaeology.* Routledge, London.
Hodge, M. G., and L. D. Minc
 1991 The Spatial Patterning of Aztec Ceramics: Implications for Understanding Prehispanic Exchange Systems. *Journal of Field Archaeology* 17:415–437.
Hodge, M. G., H. Neff, M. J. Blackman, and L. D. Minc
 1993 Black-on-Orange Ceramic Production in the Aztec Empire's Heartland. *Latin American Antiquity* 4:130–157.
Holmberg, A. R.
 1969 *Nomads of the Long Bow: The Siriono of Eastern Bolivia.* The American Museum Science Books, New York.
Hoopes, J. W.
 1994 Ford Revisited: A Critical Review of the Chronology and Relationships of the Earliest Ceramic Complexes in the New World, 6000–1500 B.C. *Journal of World Prehistory* 8:1–49.
Hoopes, J. W., and W. K. Barnett
 1995 The Shape of Early Pottery Studies. In *The Emergence of Pottery: Technology and Innovation in Ancient Societies,* edited by W. K. Barnett and J. W. Hoopes, pp. 1–7. Smith-sonian Institution Press, Washington, D.C.
Huckell, B. B.
 1990 *Late Preceramic Farmer-Foragers in Southeastern Arizona: A Cultural and Ecological Consideration of the Spread of Agriculture into the Arid Southwestern United States.* Ph.D. dissertation, Arid Lands Resource Sciences, University of Arizona, Tucson.
Hunt, N.
 1991 The Archaeological Recognition of Human Mobility through Ceramic Vessel Assemblages. Paper presented at the 31st Annual Meeting of the Northeastern Anthropological Association, Waterloo, Ontario.
Hymes, D.
 1967 The Anthropology of Communication. In *Human Communication Theory: Original Essays,* edited by F. E. X. Dance, pp. 1–39. Holt, Rinehart, and Winston, New York.
Ingersoll, D. W. Jr., and G. Bronitsky
 1987 (editors) *Mirror and Metaphor: Material and Social Constructions of Reality.* University Press of America, Lanham, Maryland.
Jett, S. C., and P. B. Moyle
 1986 The Exotic Origins of Fishes Depicted on Prehistoric Mimbres Pottery from New Mexico. *American Antiquity* 51:688–720.
John-Steiner, V.
 1975 *Learning Styles among Pueblo Children.* Final report U.S. Department of Health, Education, and Welfare National Institute of Education. College of Education, University of New Mexico, Albuquerque.
Johnson, G. A.
 1982 Organizational Structure and Scalar Stress. In *Theory and Explanation in Archaeology,* edited by A. C. Renfrew, M. J. Rowlands, and B. Segraves, pp. 389–421. Academic Press, London.
 1989 Dynamics of Southwestern Prehistory: Far Outside—Looking In. In *Dynamics of Southwestern Prehistory,* edited by L. S. Cordell and G. J. Gumerman, pp. 371–389. Smithsonian Institution Press, Washington, D.C.

Jones, R. E.
1986   *Greek and Cypriot Pottery. A Review of Scientific Studies.* Fitch Laboratory Occasional Paper 1. The British School at Athens.

Joseph, N.
1986   *Uniforms and Nonuniforms: Communicating through Clothing.* Greenwood Press, New York.

Judd, N. M.
1954   *The Material Culture of Pueblo Bonito.* Smithsonian Miscellaneous Collections, vol. 124. Washington, D.C.

Judge, W. J.
1984   New Light on Chaco Canyon. In *New Light on Chaco Canyon,* edited by D. G. Noble, pp. 1–12. School of American Research Press, Santa Fe, New Mexico.

Judge, W. J., and J. D. Schelberg
1984   (editors) *Recent Research on Chaco Prehistory.* Reports of the Chaco Center 8. Division of Cultural Research, National Park Service, Albuquerque, New Mexico.

Justeson, J. S., and T. Kaufman
1993   A Decipherment of Epi-Olmec Hieroglyphic Writing. *Science* 259:1703–1711.

Kaiser, S. B.
1985   *The Social Psychology of Clothing and Personal Adornment.* Macmillan, New York.

Kaldahl, E.
1996   A Vessel Volume Case Study of Mesa Verdean Cooking Jars. Ms. on file, Department of Anthropology, University of Arizona, Tucson.

Kane, P. V.
1973   *History of Dharmasastra (Ancient and Medieval Religious and Civil Law).* 5 vols. Bhandarkar Oriental Research Institute, Poona.

Karashima, N.
1992   *Towards a New Formation: South Indian Society Under Vijayanagara Rule.* Oxford University Press, Delhi.

Katz, S. H., M. L. Hedinger, and L. A. Valleroy
1974   Traditional Maize Processing Techniques in the New World. *Science* 184:765–773.

Katz, S. H., and K. M. Kaiser
1995   Lime Is to Corn as Yeast Is to Bread: A 100 Year Perspective on the Transition of Food Ethnography to an Evolutionary Science of Cuisine. Paper presented at the 94th Annual Meeting of the American Anthropological Association, Washington, D.C.

Katz, S. H., and F. Maytag
1991   Brewing an Ancient Beer. *Archaeology* (July):24–33.

Kavanagh, T. W.
1994   Archaeological Parameters for the Beginnings of Beer. *Brewing Techniques* (September–October):44–51.

Keller, C. M., and J. D. Keller
1996   *Cognition and Tool Use: The Blacksmith at Work.* Cambridge University Press, New York.

Kelly, R. L.
1992   Mobility/Sedentism: Concepts, Archaeological Measures, and Effects. *Annual Review of Anthropology* 21:43–66.

King, B.
1994   *The Information Continuum.* School of American Research Press, Santa Fe, New Mexico.

Kingery, W. D.
1996a   (editor) *Learning from Things: Method and Theory of Material Culture Studies.* Smithsonian Institution Press, Washington, D.C.

1996b   Introduction. In *Learning from Things: Method and Theory of Material Culture Studies,* edited by W. D. Kingery, pp. 1–15. Smithsonian Institution Press, Washington, D.C.

Knapp, M. L., and J. A. Hall
1992   *Nonverbal Communication in Human Interaction.* Harcourt Brace Jovanovich, Forth Worth, Texas.

Kobayashi, M.
1994   Use-Alteration Analysis of Kalinga Pottery: Interior Carbon Deposits of Cooking Pots. In *Kalinga Ethnoarchaeology,* edited by W. A. Longacre and J. M. Skibo, pp. 127–168. Smithsonian Institution Press, Washington, D.C.

Kolb, C. C.
1987   *Marine Shell Trade and Classic Teotihuacan, Mexico.* British Archaeological Reports International Series 364, Oxford, England.

Kottraiah, C. T. M.
  n.d. Vijayakumari Charite (Kannada Work). Composed by Srutakirti in c. A.D. 1567. English translation of select topics. Ms. in possession of author.

Kramer, C.
  1985 Ceramic Ethnoarchaeology. *Annual Review of Anthropology* 14:77–102.

Krampen, M.
  1991 *Children's Drawings: Iconic Coding of the Environment.* Plenum Press, New York.

Krishnamurthy, K.
  1979 The Pottery-Making Techniques in Early Indian Literature. *The Andhra Pradesh Journal of Archaeology* 1:73–77.

Krotser, P.
  1980 Potters in the Land of the Olmec. In *Land of the Olmec: The People of the River,* edited by M. D. Coe and R. Diehl, pp. 128–138. University of Texas Press, Austin.

Kuijt, I.
  1995 The Emergence of Social Complexity in the Levantine Neolithic: Community Identity, Ritual Practices, and Village Planning in Jericho. Paper presented at the Society for American Archaeology Meetings, May 1995, Minneapolis, Minnesota.

Kvamme, K., M. Stark, and W. A. Longacre
  1996 Alternative Procedures for Assessing Standardization in Ceramic Assemblages. *American Antiquity* 61:116–120.

Ladd, E.
  1995 Frank Hamilton Cushing at Zuni: One Hundred Years Later. Paper presented at the 94th Annual Meeting of the American Anthropological Association, Washington, D.C.

Lamphere, L.
  1979 Southwestern Ceremonialism. In *Handbook of North American Indians,* vol. 10, *Southwest,* pp. 743–763, edited by A. Ortiz. Smithsonian Institution, Washington, D.C.

LeBlanc, S. A.
  1982 The Advent of Pottery in the American Southwest. In "Southwestern

Ceramics: A Comparative Review," edited by A. Schroeder, pp. 129–148. *The Arizona Archaeologist,* vol. 15, School of American Research, Santa Fe, New Mexico.

Lekson, S. H., T. C. Windes, J. R. Stein, and W. J. Judge
  1988 The Chaco Canyon Community. *Scientific American* 256(7):100–109.

Leone, M. P.
  1977 The New Mormon Temple in Washington, D.C. In *Historical Archaeology and the Importance of Material Things,* edited by L. Ferguson, pp. 43–61. Society for Historical Archaeology, Special Publication Series, No. 2.

Leone, M. P., and P. B. Potter Jr.
  1989 (editors) *The Recovery of Meaning: Historical Archaeology in the Eastern United States.* Smithsonian Institution Press, Washington, D.C.

Leroi-Gourhan, A.
  1993 *Gesture and Speech.* MIT Press, Cambridge, Massachusetts.

Lieberman, P.
  1991 *Uniquely Human: The Evolution of Speech, Thought, and Selfless Behavior.* Harvard University Press, Cambridge, Massachusetts.

Lightfoot, K. G.
  1979 Food Redistribution Among Prehistoric Pueblo Groups. *Kiva* 44:319–339.

Lightfoot, R. R.
  1994 *The Duckfoot Site,* vol. 2, *Archaeology of the House and Household.* Occasional Paper No. 4, Crow Canyon Archaeological Center, Cortez, Colorado.

Lindauer, O.
  1988 *A Study of Vessel Form and Painted Designs to Explore Regional Interaction of the Sedentary Period Hohokam.* Ph.D. dissertation, Department of Anthropology, Arizona State University, Tempe.

Linton, R.
  1944 North American Cooking Pots. *American Antiquity* 9:369–380.

Lipe, W. D.
  1989 Social Scale of Mesa Verde Anasazi Kivas. In *The Architecture of Social Integration in Prehistoric Pueblos,*

edited by W. D. Lipe and M. Heg-
mon, pp. 53–71. Crow Canyon
Archaeological Center, Cortez,
Colorado.

1994 Comments. *Kiva* 60:337–344.

Lischka, J. J.

1975 Broken K Revisited: A Short Discussion of Factor Analysis. *American
Antiquity* 40:220–227.

Littlejohn, S. W.

1991 *Theories of Human Communication.* Wadsworth, Belmont, California.

London, G. A.

1991 Standardization and Variation in
the Work of Craft Specialists. In *Ceramic Ethnoarchaeology,* edited by
W. A. Longacre, pp. 182–204. University of Arizona Press, Tucson.

Longacre, W. A.

1970 *Archaeology as Anthropology: A
Case Study.* Anthropological Papers
of the University of Arizona No. 17.
University of Arizona Press, Tucson.

1985 Pottery Use-Life among the Kalinga,
Northern Luzon, Philippines. In *De-
coding Prehistoric Ceramics,* edited
by B. A. Nelson, pp. 334–346.
Southern Illinois University Press,
Carbondale.

1995 Why Did They Invent Pottery Any-
way? In *The Emergence of Pottery:
Technology and Innovation in Ancient Societies,* edited by W. K. Barnett and J. W. Hoopes, pp. 277–
280. Smithsonian Institution Press,
Washington, D.C.

Longacre, W. A., K. L. Kvamme, and
M. Kobayashi

1988 Southwestern Pottery Standardization: An Ethnoarchaeological View
from the Philippines. *Kiva* 53:
101–112.

Longacre, W. A., and J. M. Skibo

1994 An Introduction to Kalinga Ethnoarchaeology. In *Kalinga Ethnoarchaeology,* edited by W. A.
Longacre and J. M. Skibo, pp.
1–11. Smithsonian Institution
Press, Washington, D.C.

Loose, R. W.

1977 Petrographic Notes on Selected
Lithic and Ceramic Materials. In
*Settlement and Subsistence along

the Lower Chaco River: The CGP
Survey,* edited by C. A. Reher,
pp. 567–571. University of New
Mexico Press, Albuquerque.

Lowe, G. W.

1967 Discussion. In *Altamira and Padre
Piedra, Early Preclassic Sites in Chi-
apas, Mexico,* by D. F. Green and
G. L. Lowe, pp. 53–79. Papers of
the New World Archaeological
Foundation No. 24. Brigham Young
University, Provo, Utah.

1971 *The Civilizational Consequences of
Varying Degrees of Agricultural and
Ceramic Dependency within the
Basic Ecosystem of Mesoamerica,*
pp. 212–248. Contributions of the
University of California Archaeo-
logical Research Facility No. 11.

Mallory, J. K.

1986 "Workshops" and "Specialized Production" in the Production of Maya
Chert Tools: A Response to Shafer
and Hester. *American Antiquity*
51:152–158.

Manzanilla, L.

1993 (editor) *Anatomía de un Conjunto
Residencial Teotihuacano en Oztoya-
hualco.* Universidad Nacional
Autónoma de México, México.

Marcus, J., and K. V. Flannery

1996 *Zapotec Civilization: How Urban
Society Evolved in Mexico's Oaxaca
Valley.* Thames and Hudson, Lon-
don.

Marriott, M., and R. Inden

1977 Toward an Ethnosociology of South
Asian Caste Systems. *The New
Wind: Changing Identities in South
Asia,* edited by K. David, pp.
227–238. Mouton, The Hague.

Martin, P. S., and J. B. Rinaldo

1960 Excavations in the Upper Little Colorado Drainage, Eastern Arizona.
Fieldiana Anthropology 51(1).

Matson, F. R.

1965 (editor) *Ceramics and Man.* Viking
Fund Publications in Anthropology
No. 41. Wenner-Gren Foundation,
New York.

Matson, R. G.

1991 *The Origins of Southwestern Agriculture.* University of Arizona Press,
Tucson.

McAnany, P. A.

1993 Resources, Specialization, and Exchange in the Maya Lowlands. In *The American Southwest and Mesoamerica: Systems of Prehistoric Exchange,* edited by J. E. Ericson and T. G. Baugh, pp. 213–245. Plenum Press, New York.

McGee, W. J.

1971 *The Seri Indians of Bahia Kino and Sonora, Mexico.* Rio Grande Press, Glorieta, New Mexico.

McGuire, R. H.

1983 Breaking Down Cultural Complexity: Inequality and Heterogeneity. In *Advances in Archaeological Method and Theory,* vol. 6, edited by M. B. Schiffer, pp. 91–142. Academic Press, New York.

Medellín Zenil, A.

1960 *Cerámicas del Totonacapan, Exploraciones Arqueológicas en el Centro de Veracruz.* Instituto de Antropología, Jalapa, México.

Mera, H. P.

1934 *Observations on the Archaeology of the Petrified Forest National Monument.* New Mexico Laboratory of Anthropology Technical Series Bulletin 7. Santa Fe.

Michell, G. A.

1992 *The Vijayanagara Courtly Style.* Manohar Press, New Delhi.

Middleton, W. D., G. M. Feinman, and G. Molina Villegas

1998 Tomb Use and Reuse in Oaxaca, Mexico. *Ancient Mesoamerica.* In press.

Miller, D.

1985 *Artefacts as Categories: A Study of Ceramic Variability in Central India.* Cambridge University Press, England.

1987 *Material Culture and Mass Consumption.* Basil Blackwell, London.

Mills, B. J.

1985 "North American Cooking Pots" Reconsidered: Some Behavioral Correlates of Variation in Cooking Pot Morphology. Paper presented at the 50th Annual Meeting of the Society for American Archaeology, Denver.

1989 *Ceramics and Settlement in the Cedar Mesa Area, Southeastern Utah: A Methodological Approach.* Unpublished Ph.D. dissertation, University of New Mexico, Albuquerque.

1993 Functional Variation in the Ceramic Assemblages. In *Across the Colorado Plateau: Anthropological Studies for the Transwestern Pipeline Expansion Project,* vol. 16, *Interpretation of Ceramic Artifacts,* by Barbara J. Mills, Christine E. Goetze, and Maria Nieves Zedeño, pp. 301–346. Office of Contract Archeology and the Maxwell Museum of Anthropology, University of New Mexico, Albuquerque.

1995a The Organization of Protohistoric Zuni Ceramic Production. In *Ceramic Production in the American Southwest,* edited by B. J. Mills and P. L. Crown, pp. 200–230. University of Arizona Press, Tucson.

1995b Assessing Organizational Scale in Zuni Ceramic Production: A Comparison of Protohistoric and Historic Collections. *Museum Anthropology* 19(3):37–46.

1997 Gender, Craft Production, and Inequality in the American Southwest. Paper prepared for School of American Research Advanced Seminar, "Sex Roles and Gender Hierarchies in the American Southwest," organized by Patricia L. Crown. Santa Fe, New Mexico.

Mills, B. J., and P. L. Crown

1995a Ceramic Production in the American Southwest: An Introduction. In *Ceramic Production in the American Southwest,* edited by B. J. Mills, and P. L. Crown, pp. 1–29. University of Arizona Press, Tucson.

1995b (editors) *Ceramic Production in the American Southwest.* University of Arizona Press, Tuscon.

Minnis, P. E.

1989 Prehistoric Diet in the Northern Southwest: Macroplant Remains from Four Corners Feces. *American Antiquity* 54:543–563.

Moholy-Nagy, H.

1990 The Misidentification of Mesoamerican Lithic Workshops. *Latin American Antiquity* 1:268–279.

Morelos García, N.
1991 Adoratorios de la Calle de los Muertos: El Sistema Constructivo del Volumen. In *Teotihuacan 1980–1982: Nuevas Interpretaciones,* coordinated by Rubén Cabrera Castro, Ignacio Rodríguez García, and Noel Morelos García, pp. 93–111. Instituto Nacional de Antropología e Historia, México, D.F.

Morris, E. A.
1980 *Basketmaker Caves in the Prayer Rock District, Northeastern Arizona.* Anthropological Papers of the University of Arizona, No. 35. University of Arizona Press, Tucson.

Morris, E. H.
1927 *The Beginnings of Pottery Making in the San Juan Area: Unfired Prototypes and the Wares of the Earliest Ceramic Period.* Anthropological Papers, vol. 28, pp. 127–198. American Museum of Natural History, New York.

Morrison, K. D.
1995 *Fields of Victory: Vijayanagara and the Course of Intensification.* Contributions to the Archaeological Research Facility, University of California No. 52. Berkeley.

Morrison, K. D., and M. T. Lycett
1994 Centralized Power, Centralized Authority? Ideological Claims and Archaeological Patterns. *Asian Perspectives* 32(2):312–353.

Morrison, K. D., and C. M. Sinopoli
1992 Economic Diversity and Integration in a Pre-Colonial Indian Empire. *World Archaeology* 335–352.
1996 The Vijayanagara Metropolitan Survey: The 1990 Season. In *Vijayanagara Progress of Research,* edited by D. V. Devaraj and C. S. Patil, pp. 59–73. Department of Archaeology and Museums, Mysore.
n.d.a The Vijayanagara Metropolitan Survey: The 1994 Season. In *Vijayanagara Progress of Research,* edited by D. V. Devaraj and C. S. Patil. Department of Archaeology and Museums, Mysore. In press.
n.d.b The Vijayanagara Metropolitan Survey: The 1996 Season. In *Vijayanagara Progress of Research,* edited by

D. V. Devaraj and C. S. Patil. Department of Archaeology and Museums, Mysore. In press.

Munn, N.
1973 *Walbiri Iconography.* Cornell University Press, Ithaca, New York.

Musello, C.
1992 Objects in Process: Material Culture and Communication. *Southern Folklore* 49:37–59.

Neff, H., and R. L. Bishop
1988 Plumbate Origins and Development. *American Antiquity* 53:505–522.

Neiderberger, C.
1987 *Paléopaysages et Archéologie Pré-urbaine du Bassin de Mexico.* 2 vols. Collection Etudes Mesoaméricaines 1–11. Mexico City.

Nelson, B. A.
1981 Ethnoarchaeology and Paleodemography: A Test of Turner and Lofgren's Hypothesis. *Journal of Anthropological Research* 37:107–129.
1987 Comments on Schiffer and Skibo's "Study of Technological Change." *Current Anthropology* 28:612–613.
1991 Ceramic Frequency and Use-Life: A Highland Mayan Case in Cross-Cultural Perspective. In *Ceramic Ethnoarchaeology,* edited by W. A. Longacre, pp. 162–181. University of Arizona Press, Tucson.

Nelson, M. C.
1991 The Study of Technological Organization. In *Archaeological Method and Theory,* vol. 3, edited by M. B. Schiffer, pp. 57–100. University of Arizona Press, Tucson.

Netting, R. McC.
1993 *Smallholders, Householders: Farm Families and the Ecology of Intensive, Sustainable Agriculture.* Stanford University Press, Palo Alto, California.

Nielsen, A. E.
1995 Architectural Performance and the Reproduction of Social Power. In *Expanding Archaeology,* edited by J. M. Skibo, W. H. Walker, and A. E. Nielsen, pp. 47–66. University of Utah Press, Salt Lake City.

Newell, A.
1990 *Unified Theories of Cognition: The William James Lectures, 1987.* Har-

vard University Press, Cambridge, Massachusetts.

O'Brien, M. J., and T. D. Holland, R. H. Hoard, and G. L. Fox
1994 Evolutionary Implications of Design and Performance Characteristics of Prehistoric Pottery. *Journal of Archaeological Method and Theory* 1:259–304.

Ortman, S. G.
1998 Corn Grinding and Community Organization in the Pueblo Southwest, A.D. 1150–1550. In *Pueblo IV Migration and Community Reorganization,* edited by K. A. Spielmann. Anthropological Research Papers, Arizona State University, Tempe. In press.

Orton, C.
1993 How Many Pots Make Five? *Archaeometry* 35:169–184.

Oyuela-Caycedo, A.
1995 Rocks Versus Clay: The Evolution of Pottery Technology in the Case of San Jacinto 1, Columbia. In *The Emergence of Pottery: Technology and Innovation in Ancient Societies,* edited by W. K. Barnett and J. W. Hoopes, pp. 133–144. Smithsonian Institution Press, Washington, D.C.

Ozker, D.
1982 *An Early Woodland Community at the Schultz Site 20SA2 in the Saginaw Valley and the Nature of the Early Woodland Adaptation in the Great Lakes Region.* Museum of Anthropology Anthropological Papers No. 70, University of Michigan, Ann Arbor.

Paget, G. W.
1932 Some Drawings of Men and Women Made by Children of Certain Non-European Races. *The Journal of the Royal Anthropological Institute of Great Britain and Ireland* 62:127–144.

Papousek, D. A.
1981 *The Peasant Potters of Los Pueblos.* Van Gorcum, Assen.

Parsons, E. C.
1991 Waiyautitsa of Zuni, New Mexico. In *Pueblo Mothers and Children,* edited by B. Babcock, pp. 89–105. Ancient City Press, Santa Fe, New Mexico.

Pastron, A.
1974 Preliminary Ethnoarchaeological Investigations among the Tarahumara. In *Ethnoarchaeology,* edited by C. B. Donnan and C. W. Clewlow, pp. 93–114. Archaeological Survey Monograph 4. Institute of Archaeology, University of California, Los Angeles.

Pasztory, E.
1989 Identity and Difference: The Uses and Meanings of Ethnic Styles. In *Cultural Differentiation and Cultural Identity in the Visual Arts,* edited by S. J. Barnes and W. S. Melion, pp. 15–38. National Gallery of Art, Center for the Advanced Study in the Visual Arts, Washington, D.C.

Patil, C. S., and V. C. Patil
1995 *Inscriptions at Vijayanagara (Hampi).* Directorate of Archaeology and Museums, Mysore.

Patrik, L. E.
1985 Is There an Archaeological Record? *In Advances in Archaeological Method and Theory,* vol. 8, edited by M. B. Schiffer, pp. 27–62. Academic Press, Orlando, Florida.

Patterson, A.
1994 *Hopi Pottery Symbols.* Johnson Books, Boulder, Colorado.

Pauketat, T. R.
1989 Monitoring Mississippian Homestead Occupation Span and Economy Using Ceramic Refuse. *American Antiquity* 54:288–310.

Pauketat, T. R., and T. E. Emerson
1991 The Ideology of Authority and the Power of the Pot. *American Anthropologist* 93:919–941.

Pavlů, I.
1997 *Pottery Origins: Initial Forms, Cultural Behavior and Decorative Style.* Karolinum, Vydavatelství Univerzity Karlovy, Praha.

Peacock, D. P. S.
1982 *Pottery in the Roman World: An Ethnoarchaeological Approach.* Longman, London.

Peckham, S., and J. Wilson
1965 Chuska Valley Ceramics. Unpublished manuscript on file at the University of Colorado Museum, Boulder.

Perlés, C., and K. D. Vitelli
1994　Technologie et Fonction des Pre-
mières Productions Céramiques de
Grèce. In *Terre Cuite et Société.
La Céramique, Document Technique,
Économique, Culturel,* XIVe Ren-
contres Internationales d'Archéologie et d'Histoire d'Antibes, pp. 225–
242. Editions APCDA, Juan-les--
Pins, France.

Peters, R.
1980　*Mammalian Communication: A
Behavioral Analysis of Meaning.*
Brooks/Cole, Monterey, California.

Plog, F., and S. Upham
1989　Productive Specialization, Archaeometry, and Interpretation. In
*Pottery Technology: Ideas and Ap-
proaches,* edited by G. Bronitsky,
pp. 207–215. Westview Press, Boulder, Colorado.

Plog, S.
1980　Village Autonomy in the American
Southwest: An Evaluation of the
Evidence. In *Models and Methods
in Regional Exchange,* edited by
R. E. Fry, pp. 135–146. SAA
Papers No. 1. Society for American
Archaeology, Washington,
D.C.

1995　Equality and Hierarchy: Holistic
Approaches to Understanding
Social Dynamics in the Pueblo
Southwest. In *Foundations of
Social Inequality,* edited by T. D.
Price and G. M. Feinman, pp. 189–
206. Plenum Press, New York.

Polhemus, T.
1978a　*Fashion and Anti-Fashion: Anthropology of Clothing and Adornment.*
Thames and Hudson, London.

1978b　(editor) *The Body Reader: Social
Aspects of the Human Body.* Pan-
theon Books, New York.

Pool, C. A.
1990　*Ceramic Production, Resource Procurement, and Exchange at Matacapan, Veracruz, Mexico.* Unpublished
Ph.D. dissertation, Department of
Anthropology, Tulane University,
New Orleans, Louisiana.

1992　Integrating Ceramic Production and
Distribution. In *Ceramic Production
and Distribution: An Integrated Approach,* edited by G. J. Bey III and

C. A. Pool, pp. 275–313. Westview
Press, Boulder, Colorado.

1997　The Spatial Structure of Formative
Houselots at Bezuapan. In *Olmec to
Aztec: Settlement Patterns in the An-
cient Gulf Lowlands,* edited by B. L.
Stark and P. J. Arnold III. University
of Arizona Press, Tucson. In press.

Pool, C. A., and R. S. Santley
1992　Middle Classic Pottery Economics
in the Tuxtla Mountains, Southern
Veracruz, Mexico. In *Ceramic Production and Distribution: An Integrated Approach,* edited by G. J.
Bey III and C. A. Pool, pp. 205–234.
Westview Press, Boulder, Colorado.

Powers, R. P., W. B. Gillespie, and S. H.
Lekson
1983　*The Outlier Survey.* Reports of the
Chaco Center No. 3. Division of
Cultural Research, National Park
Service, Albuquerque, New Mexico.

Prentice, G.
1986　Origins of Plant Domestication in
the Eastern United States: Promoting the Individual in Archaeological
Theory. *Southeastern Archaeology*
5:103–119.

Preucel, R. W.
1996　Cooking Status: Hohokam Ideology,
Power, and Social Reproduction. In
*Interpreting Southwestern Diversity:
Underlying Principles and Over-
arching Patterns,* edited by P. R.
Fish and J. J. Reid, pp. 125–131.
Anthropological Research Papers
No. 48, Arizona State University,
Tempe.

Proskouriakoff, T.
1953　Scroll Patterns (Entrelaces) of Ver-
acruz. In *Huastecos, Totonacos, y
Sus Vecinos,* edited by I. Bernal and
E. Davalos Hurtado, pp. 389–401.
Revista Mexicana de Estudios
Antropologicos 8.

1954　*Varieties of Classic Central Veracruz
Sculpture.* Contributions to Ameri-
can Anthropology and History 58.
Carnegie Instition of Washington,
Washington, D.C.

Prown, J. D.
1993　The Truth of Material Culture: History or Fiction? In *History From
Things: Essays on Material Culture,*
edited by S. Lubar and W. D. King-

ery, pp. 1–19. Smithsonian Institution Press, Washington, D.C.

1996 Material/Culture: Can the Farmer and the Cowman Still Be Friends? In *Learning from Things: Method and Theory of Material Culture Studies,* edited by W. D. Kingery, pp. 19–27. Smithsonian Institution Press, Washington, D.C.

Rafferty, J. E.

1985 The Archaeological Record on Sedentariness: Recognition, Development, and Implications. In *Advances in Archaeological Method and Theory,* vol. 8, edited by M. B. Schiffer, pp. 113–156. Academic Press, New York.

Ralph D., and D. E. Arnold

1988 Socioeconomic Status, Kinship, and Innovation: The Adoption of the *Tornete* in Ticul, Yucatan. In *Ceramic Ecology Revisited, 1987: The Technology and Socio-Economics of Pottery,* edited by C. C. Kolb, pp. 145–164. British Archaeological Reports International Series 436, Oxford, England.

Ramaswamy, V.

1985 Artisans in Vijayangara Society. *Indian Economic and Social History Review* 22:417–444.

Rapoport, A.

1990 *The Meaning of the Built Environment: A Nonverbal Communication Approach.* University of Arizona Press, Tucson.

Rathje, W. L.

1975 Last Tango in Mayapán: A Tentative Trajectory of Production-Distribution Systems. In *Ancient Civilization and Trade,* edited by J. A. Sabloff and C. C. Lamberg-Karlovsky, pp. 409–448. University of New Mexico Press, Albuquerque.

1977 In Praise of Archaeology: Le Projet du Garbage. In *Historical Archaeology and the Importance of Material Things,* edited by L. Ferguson, pp. 36–42. The Society for Historical Archaeology, Special Publication Series No. 2.

1979 Modern Material Culture Studies. *In Advances in Archaeological*

Method and Theory, vol. 2, edited by M. B. Schiffer, pp. 1–37. Academic Press, New York.

Rathje, W. L., and M. B. Schiffer

1982 *Archaeology.* Harcourt Brace Jovanovich, New York.

Rattray, E. C.

1979 La Cerámica de Teotihuacan: Relaciones Externas y Cronología. *Anales de Antropología* 16:51–70. Universidad Nacional de Antropología e Historia, México, D.F.

1988 Un Taller de Cerámica Anaranjada San Martín en Teotihuacan. In *Ensayos de Alfarería Prehispánica e Histórica de Mesoamerica: Homenaje a Eduardo Noguera Auza,* edited by M. C. Serra Puche and C. Navarette, pp. 249–266. Instituto de Investigaciones Antropológicas, Universidad Nacional Autonóma de México, México.

1990 New Findings on the Origins of Thin Orange Ceramics. *Ancient Mesoamerica* 1:181–195.

1992 *The Teotihuacan Burials and Offerings: A Commentary and Inventory.* Vanderbilt University Publications in Anthropology No. 42. Nashville, Tennessee.

Rautman, A. E.

1991 A Petrographic Study of Ceramic Sherds from Vijayanagara, India. In *Vijayanagara, Progress of Research 1984–87,* edited by D. V. Devaraj and C. S. Patil, pp. 149–166. Karnataka Department of Archaeology and Museums, Mysore.

Reber, A. S.

1993 *Implicit Learning and Tacit Knowledge: An Essay on the Cognitive Unconscious.* Oxford University Press, England.

Redmond, E. M.

1979 A Terminal Formative Ceramic Workshop in the Tehuacán Valley. In *Prehistoric Social, Political, and Economic Development in the Area of the Tehuacán Valley: Some Results of the Palo Blanco Project,* edited by R. D. Drennan, pp. 111–127. Technical Reports No. 11. Museum of Anthropology, University of Michigan, Ann Arbor.

Reents-Budet, D.
1994　*Painting the Maya Universe: Royal Ceramics of the Classic Period.* Duke University Press, Durham, North Carolina.

Reid, J. J., M. B. Schiffer, and W. L. Rathje
1975　Behavioral Archaeology: Four Strategies. *American Anthropologist* 77:864–869.

Reid, K. C.
1984　Fire and Ice: New Evidence for the Production and Preservation of Late Archaic Fiber-Tempered Pottery in the Middle-Latitude Lowlands. *American Antiquity* 49:55–76.
1989　A Materials Science Perspective on Hunter-Gatherer Pottery. In *Pottery Technology: Ideas and Approaches,* edited by G. Bronitsky, pp. 167–180. Westview Press, Boulder, Colorado.
1990　Simmering Down: A Second Look at Ralph Linton's "North American Cooking Pots." In *Hunter-Gatherer Pottery in the Far West,* edited by D. R. Tuohy and A. J. Dansie, pp. 7–17. Anthropology Papers No. 23, Nevada State Museum, Carsen City.

Reina, R. E., and R. M. Hill II
1978　*The Traditional Pottery of Guatemala.* University of Texas Press, Austin.

Remland, M. S., and T. S. Jones
1994　The Influence of Vocal Intensity and Touch on Compliance Gaining. *Journal of Social Psychology* 134:89–98.

Renfrew, C.
1982　*Towards an Archaeology of Mind.* Cambridge University Press, England.
1986　Introduction: Peer Polity Interaction and Sociopolitical Change. In *Peer Polity Interaction,* edited by C. Renfrew and J. Cherry, pp. 1–18. Cambridge University Press, England.

Renfrew, C., and E. B. W. Zubrow
1994　(editors) *The Ancient Mind: Elements of a Cognitive Archaeology.* Cambridge University Press, England.

Rhodes, D.
1957　*Clay and Glazes for the Potter.* Chilton Books Company, Philadelphia, Pennsylvania.

Rice, P. M.
1981　Evolution of Specialized Pottery Production: A Trial Model. *Current Anthropology* 22:219–240.
1983　Serpents and Styles in Peten Postclassic Pottery. *American Anthropologist* 85:866–880.
1987　*Pottery Analysis: A Sourcebook.* University of Chicago Press, Chicago.
1989　Ceramic Diversity, Production, and Use. In *Quantifying Diversity in Archaeology,* edited by R. D. Leonard and G. T. Jones, pp. 109–117. Cambridge University Press, England.
1991　Specialization, Standardization, and Diversity: A Retrospective. In *The Ceramic Legacy of Anna O. Shepard,* edited by R. L. Bishop and F. W. Lange, pp. 257–279. University of Colorado Press, Niwot.
1996a　Recent Ceramic Analysis: 1. Function, Style, and Origins. *Journal of Archaeological Research* 4:133–163.
1996b　Recent Ceramic Analysis: 2. Composition, Production, and Theory. *Journal of Archaeological Research* 4:165–202.
n.d.　On the Origins of Pottery. Ms. in possession of author.

Richardson, M.
1987　A Social (Ideational-Behavioral) Interpretation of Material Culture and Its Application to Archaeology. In *Mirror and Metaphor: Material and Social Constructions of Reality,* edited by D. W. Ingersoll Jr. and G. Bronitsky, pp. 382–403. University Press of America, Lanham, Maryland.

Riley, J.
1979　Industrial Standardization in Cyrenaica during the Second and Third Centuries A.D.: The Evidence from Locally Manufactured Pottery, pp. 73–78. *Society for Libyan Studies 11th Annual Report (1979–1980).*

Roberts, F. H. H.
1927　*The Ceramic Sequence in the Chaco Canyon, New Mexico, and Its Relation to the Cultures of the San Juan.* Unpublished Ph.D. dissertation,

Harvard University, Cambridge, Massachusetts.

Roemer, E.
1982 Investigation at Four Lithic Workshops at Colha, Belize: 1981 Season. In *Archaeology at Colha, Belize: The 1981 Interim Report,* edited by T. R. Hester, H. J. Shafer, and J. D. Eaton, pp. 75–84. Center for Archaeological Research, University of Texas at San Antonio.

Rottlander, R.
1966 Is Provincial-Roman Pottery Standardized? *Archaeometry* 9:76–91.
1967 Standardization of Roman Provincial Pottery, II. *Archaeometry* 10:35–46.

Russell, G. S.
1994 Cerro Mayal, Peru: Moche Ceramic Workshop Excavated. *Backdirt* (Spring):6–7.

Russell, G., B. L. Leonard, and J. B. Rosario
1994 Producción de Cerámica a Gran Escala en el Valle de Chicama, Perú: El Taller de Cerro Mayal. In *Tecnología y Organización de la Producción de Cerámica Prehispánica en los Andes,* edited by I. Shimada, pp. 201–227. Fondo Editorial, Pontificia Universidad Católica del Perú, Lima.

Russell, R. W.
1943 The Spontaneous and Instructed Drawings of Zuni Children. *Journal of Comparative Psychology* 35:11–15.

Rye, O. S.
1976 Keeping Your Temper Under Control. *Archaeology and Physical Anthropology in Oceania* 11:106–137.
1981 *Pottery Technology: Principles and Reconstruction. Manuals on Archaeology 4.* Taraxacum, Washington, D.C.

Sahagún, B. de
1950–63 *General History of the Things of New Spain* (Florentine Codex). 12 vols. Translated by A. Anderson and C. Dibble. School of American Research, Santa Fe, New Mexico, and University of Utah, Salt Lake City.

Sahlins, M. D.
1965 On the Sociology of Primitive Exchange. In *The Relevance of Models for Social Anthropology,* edited by

M. Banton, pp. 139–236. A.S.A. Monograph 1. Tavistock Press, London.

Santley, R. S.
1983 Obsidian Trade and Teotihuacan Influence in Mesoamerica. In *Interdisciplinary Approaches to the Study of Highland-Lowland Interaction,* edited by A. Miller, pp. 69–123. Dumbarton Oaks, Washington, D.C.
1992 A Consideration of the Olmec Phenomenon in the Tuxtlas: Early Formative Settlement Pattern, Land Use, and Refuse Disposal at Matacapan, Veracruz, Mexico. In *Gardens in Prehistory: The Archaeology of Settlement Agriculture in Greater Mesoamerica,* edited by T. Killion, pp. 150–183. University of Alabama Press, Tuscaloosa.

Santley, R. S., and P. J. Arnold III
1996 Prehispanic Settlement Patterns in the Tuxtla Mountains, Southern Veracruz, Mexico. *Journal of Field Archaeology* 23:225–249.

Santley, R. S., P. J. Arnold III, and C. A. Pool
1989 The Ceramics Production System at Matacapan, Veracruz, Mexico. *Journal of Field Archaeology* 16:107–132.

Santley, R. S., and R. R. Kneebone
1993 Craft Specialization, Refuse Disposal, and the Creation of Spatial Archaeological Records in Prehispanic Mesoamerica. In *Prehispanic Domestic Units in Western Mesoamerica: Studies of Household, Compound, and Residence,* edited by R. S. Santley and K. G. Hirth, pp. 37–63. CRC Press, Boca Raton, Florida.

Santley, R. S., and C. A. Pool
1993 Prehispanic Exchange Relationships among Central Mexico, the Valley of Oaxaca, and the Gulf Coast of Mexico. In *The American Southwest and Mesoamerica: Systems of Prehistoric Exchange,* edited by J. E. Ericson and T. G. Baugh, pp. 179–211. Plenum Press, New York.

Saraswati, B.
1979 *Pottery Making and Indian Civilization.* Abhinav Publications, Delhi.

Saraswati, B., and N. K. Behura
  1966 *Pottery Techniques in Peasant India.* Memoir 13, Anthropological Survey of India, Calcutta.
Sassaman, K. E.
  1993 *Early Pottery in the Southeast: Tradition and Innovation in Cooking Technology.* University of Alabama Press, Tuscaloosa.
  1995 The Social Contradictions of Traditional and Innovative Cooking Technologies in the Prehistoric American Southeast. In *The Emergence of Pottery: Technology and Innovation in Ancient Societies,* edited by W. K. Barnett and J. W. Hoopes, pp. 223–240. Smithsonian Institution Press, Washington, D.C.
Sapir, E.
  1923 A Note on Sarcee Pottery. *American Anthropologist* 25:247–253.
Schelberg, J. D.
  1992 Hierarchical Organization as a Short-Term Buffering Strategy in Chaco Canyon. In *Anasazi Regional Organization and the Chaco System,* edited by D. E. Doyel, pp. 59–71. Maxwell Museum of Anthropology Anthropological Papers No. 5. Albuquerque, New Mexico.
Schiffer, M. B.
  1972 Archaeological Context and Systemic Context. *American Antiquity* 37:156–165.
  1975 Behavioral Chain Analysis: Activities, Organization, and the Use of Space. Chapters in the Prehistory of Eastern Arizona, IV. *Fieldiana Anthropology* 65:103–119.
  1976 *Behavioral Archeology.* Academic Press, New York.
  1987 *Formation Processes of the Archaeological Record.* University of Utah Press, Salt Lake City.
  1988a The Structure of Archaeological Theory. *American Antiquity* 53:461–485.
  1988b The Effects of Surface Treatment on Permeability and Evaporative Cooling Effectiveness of Pottery. In *Proceedings of the 26th International Archaeometry Symposium,* edited by R. M. Farquhar, R. G. V. Hancock, and L. A. Pavlish, pp. 23–29. Archaeometry Laboratory, Department of Physics, University of Toronto, Toronto.
  1989 Formation Processes of Broken K Pueblo: Some Hypotheses. In *Quantifying Diversity in Archaeology,* edited by R. D. Leonard and G. T. Jones, pp. 37–58. Cambridge University Press, England.
  1990 Technological Change in Water-Storage and Cooking Pots: Some Predictions from Experiment. In *The Changing Roles of Ceramics in Society: 26,000 B.P. to the Present,* edited by W. D. Kingery, pp. 119–136. The American Ceramic Society, Westerville, Ohio.
  1991a *The Portable Radio in American Life.* University of Arizona Press, Tucson.
  1991b (editor) *Archaeological Method and Theory,* vol. 3. University of Arizona Press, Tucson.
  1992a Archaeology and Behavioral Science: Manifesto for an Imperial Archaeology. In *Quandaries and Quests: Visions of Archaeology's Future,* edited by L. Wandsnider, pp. 225–238. Center for Archaeological Investigations, Southern Illinois University, Occasional Paper No. 20. Carbondale.
  1992b *Technological Perspectives on Behavioral Change.* University of Arizona Press, Tucson.
  1995a *Behavioral Archaeology: First Principles.* University of Utah Press, Salt Lake City.
  1995b Social Theory and History in Behavioral Archaeology. In *Expanding Archaeology,* edited by J. M. Skibo, W. H. Walker, and A. E. Nielsen, pp. 22–35. University of Utah Press, Salt Lake City.
  1996 Some Relationships between Behavioral and Evolutionary Archaeologies. *American Antiquity* 61:643–662.
Schiffer, M. B., T. C. Butts, and K. K. Grimm
  1994a *Taking Charge: The Electric Automobile in America.* Smithsonian Institution Press, Washington D.C.
Schiffer, M. B., and J. M. Skibo
  1987 Theory and Experiment in the Study of Technological Change. *Current Anthropology* 28:595–622.

1989 A Provisional Theory of Ceramic Abrasion. *American Anthropologist* 91:102–116.

1997 The Explanation of Artifact Variability. *American Antiquity* 62:27–50.

Schiffer, M. B., J. M. Skibo, T. C. Boelke, M. A. Neupert, and M. Aronson

1994b New Perspectives on Experimental Archaeology: Surface Treatments and Thermal Response of the Clay Cooking Pot. *American Antiquity* 59:197–217.

Schroeder, A. H.

1982 Historical Review of Southwestern Ceramics. "Southwestern Ceramics: A Comparative Review," edited by A. H. Schroeder, pp. 1–26. *The Arizona Archaeologist* 15. School of American Research, Santa Fe, New Mexico.

Schultz, L. G., A. O. Shepard, P. D. Blackmon, and H. C. Starkey

1971 Mixed-Layer Kaolinite-Montmorillonite from the Yucatan Peninsula, Mexico. *Clays and Clay Minerals* 19:137–150.

Sebastian, L.

1991 Sociopolitical Complexity and the Chaco System. In *Chaco and Hohokam,* edited by P. L. Crown and W. J. Judge, pp. 109–134. School of American Research Press, Santa Fe, New Mexico.

1992 Chaco Canyon and the Anasazi Southwest: Changing Views of Sociopolitical Organization. In *Anasazi Regional Organization and the Chaco System,* edited by D. E. Doyel, pp. 23–31. Maxwell Museum of Anthropology Anthropological Papers No. 5. Albuquerque, New Mexico.

Séjourné, L.

1959 *Un Palacio en la Ciudad de los Dioses (Teotihuacan).* Instituto Nacional de Antropología e Historia, México, D.F.

1966 *Arqueología de Teotihuacan, la Cerámica.* Fondo de Cultura Económica, México, D.F.

Service, E. R.

1971 *Primitive Social Organization.* Random House, New York.

Shafer, H. J., and T. R. Hester

1983 Ancient Maya Chert Workshops in Northern Belize, Central America. *American Antiquity* 48:519–543.

1986 Maya Stone-Tool Craft Specialization and Production at Colha, Belize: Reply to Mallory. *American Antiquity* 51:158–166.

1991 Lithic Craft Specialization and Product Distribution at the Maya Site of Colha, Belize. *World Archaeology* 23:79–97.

Shanks, M., and C. Tilley

1992 *Re-Constructing Archaeology: Theory and Practice.* 2d edition. Routledge, London.

Shapiro, G.

1984 Ceramic Vessels, Site Permanence, and Group Size: A Mississippian Example. *American Antiquity* 49:696–712.

Sheehy, J. J.

1992 *Ceramic Production in Ancient Teotihuacan, Mexico: A Case Study of Tlajinga 33.* Unpublished Ph.D. dissertation, Department of Anthropology, Pennsylvania State University, University Park.

Shepard, A. O.

1939 Appendix A—Technology of La Plata Pottery. In *Archaeological Studies in the La Plata District,* by Earl H. Morris, pp. 249–287. Carnegie Institution of Washington, Publication No. 519, Washington, D.C.

1948 *Plumbate: A Mesoamerican Tradeware.* Carnegie Institution of Washington, Publication No. 528, Washington, D.C.

1953 Notes on Color and Paste Composition. In *Archaeological Studies in the Petrified Forest National Monument,* by F. Wendorf, pp. 177–193. Museum of Northern Arizona Bulletin 27. Flagstaff.

1954 Letter Excerpt. In *The Material Culture of Pueblo Bonito,* by Neil M. Judd, pp. 236–238. Smithsonian Miscellaneous Collections, vol. 124. Washington, D.C.

1956 *Ceramics for the Archaeologist.* Carnegie Institution of Washington, Publication No. 609, Washington, D.C.

1958 *Yearbook*. Carnegie Institution of Washington, vol. 57, pp. 451–454. Washington, D.C.

1963 *Beginnings of Ceramic Industrialization: An Example from the Oaxaca Valley*. Notes from the Ceramic Laboratory No. 2. Carnegie Institution of Washington, Washington, D.C.

Sherratt, A.
1991 Sacred and Profane Substances: the Ritual Use of Narcotics in Later Neolithic Europe. In *Sacred and Profane. Proceedings of a Conference on Archaeology, Ritual and Religion, Oxford, 1989*, edited by P. Garwood, D. Jennings, R. Skeates and J. Toms, pp. 50–64. Monograph No. 32, Oxford University Committee for Archaeology, England.

Shennan, S.
1989 Cultural Transmission and Cultural Change. In *What's New? A Closer Look at the Process of Innovation*, edited by S. E. van der Leeuw and R. Torrence, pp. 330–346. Unwin Hyman, London.

Simms, S. R., J. R. Bright, and A. Ugan
1997 Plain-Ware Ceramics and Residential Mobility: A Case Study From the Great Basin. *Journal of Archaeological Science* 24:779–792.

Sinopoli, C. M.
1986 *Material Patterning and Social Organization: A Study of Ceramics from Vijayanagara, South India*. Ph.D. dissertation, University Microfilms, Ann Arbor.

1988 The Organization of Craft Production at Vijayanagara, South India. *American Anthropologist* 90(3):580–597.

1991 *Approaches to Archaeological Ceramics*. Plenum Press, New York.

1993 *Pots and Palaces: The Archaeological Ceramics of the Noblemen's Quarter of Vijayanagara*. American Institute of Indian Studies/Manohar Press, New Delhi.

1994 Movement and Distribution of Craft Producers and Products at the Vijayanagara Imperial Capital. Paper presented in "Trade and Contact in the Vijayanagara Empire," World Archaeology Congress, New Delhi, India.

1996a Ceramic Use and Ritual Practices in Hindi India: Historic and Archaeological Evidence. Paper presented in "Asian Ceramics: Functions and Forms," Field Museum and Asian Ceramics Research Organization, Chicago.

1996b The Archaeological Ceramics of the Islamic Quarter of Vijayanagara. In *Vijayanagara Progress of Research 1988–91*, edited by D. V. Devaraj and C. S. Patil, pp. 105–123. Directorate of Archaeology and Museums, Mysore.

Sinopoli, C. M., and T. R. Blurton
1986 Contemporary Pottery Production in Kamalapuram, South India. In *Dimensions of Indian Art: Pupul Jayakar Seventy*, edited by L. Chandra and J. Jain, pp. 439–456. Agam Kala Prakashan, Delhi.

Sinopoli, C. M., and K. D. Morrison
1991 The Vijayanagara Metropolitan Survey: The 1988 Season. In *Vijayanagara: Progress of Research, 1987–88*, edited by D. V. Devaraj and C. S. Patil, pp. 55–69. Directorate of Archaeology and Museums, Mysore.

1992 Archaeological Survey at Vijayanagara. *Research and Exploration* 8(2):237–239.

1995 Dimensions of Imperial Control: The Vijayanagara Capital. *American Anthropologist* 97:83–96.

n.d.a The Vijayanagara Metropolitan Survey: The 1992 Season. In *Vijayanagara Progress of Research 1991–92*. Directorate of Archaeology and Museums, Mysore. In press.

n.d.b *The Vijayanagara Metropolitan Survey: Preliminary Monograph, Volume 1: Blocks S, T, and O*. Museum of Anthropology Monograph Series, University of Michigan, Ann Arbor. In press.

Skibo, J. M.
1992 *Pottery Function: A Use-Alteration Perspective*. Plenum Press, New York.

Skibo, J. M., and M. B. Schiffer
1987 The Effects of Water on Processes of Ceramic Abrasion. *Journal of Archaeological Science* 14:83–96.

1995 The Clay Cooking Pot: An Explanation of Women's Technology. In *Expanding Archaeology*, edited by J. M. Skibo, W. H. Walker, and A. E. Nielsen, pp. 80–91. University of Utah Press, Salt Lake City.

Skibo, J. M., M. B. Schiffer, and N. Kowalski
1989a Ceramic Style Analysis in Archaeology and Ethnoarchaeology: Bridging the Analytical Gap. *Journal of Anthropological Archaeology* 8:388–409.

Skibo, J. M., M. B. Schiffer, and K. C. Reid
1989b Organic-Tempered Pottery: An Experimental Study. *American Antiquity* 54:122–146.

Skibo, J. M., W. H. Walker, and A. E. Nielsen
1995 (editors) *Expanding Archaeology*. University of Utah Press, Salt Lake City, Utah.

Smith, M. F., Jr.
1985 Toward and Economic Interpretation of Ceramics: Relating Vessel Size and Shape to Use. In *Decoding Prehistoric Ceramics*, edited by B. A. Nelson, pp. 254–309. Southern Illinois University Press, Carbondale.
1988 Function from Whole Vessel Shape: A Method and An Application to Anasazi Black Mesa, Arizona. *American Anthropologist* 90:912–923.
1994 Ceramic Evidence for Anasazi Subsistence and Settlement. In *Function and Technology of Anasazi Ceramics from Black Mesa, Arizona*, edited by M. F. Smith, Jr., pp. 117–130. Center for Archaeological Investigations, Occasional Paper No. 15. Southern Illinois University, Carbondale.

Smith, M. E.
1987a Household Possessions and Wealth in Agrarian States: Implications for Archaeology. *Journal of Anthropological Archaeology* 6:297–335.
1987b The Expansion of the Aztec Empire: A Case Study in the Correlation of Diachronic Archaeological and Ethnohistorical Data. *American Antiquity* 52:37–54.

Smith, M. E., and C. M. Heath-Smith
1980 Waves of Influence in Postclassic Mesoamerica? A Critique of the Mixteca-Puebla Concept. *Anthropology* 4(2):15–50.

Smith, W. J.
1977 *The Behavior of Communicating: An Ethological Approach*. Harvard University Press, Cambridge, Massachusetts.

Snow, D. H.
1982 The Rio Grande Glaze, Matte-Paint, and Plainware Tradition. In *Southwestern Ceramics: A Comparative Review*, edited by A. H. Schroeder, pp. 235–278. The Arizona Archaeologist, Arizona Archaeological Society, Phoenix.
1990 Tener Comal y Metate: Protohistoric Rio Grande Maize Use and Diet. In *Perspectives on Southwestern Prehistory*, edited by P. E. Minnis and C. E. Redman, pp. 289–300. Westview Press, Boulder, Colorado.

Spence, M. W.
1967 The Obsidian Industry of Teotihuacan. *American Antiquity* 32:507–514.
1981 Obsidian Production and the State in Teotihuacan. *American Antiquity* 46:769–788.
1987 The Scale and Structure of Obsidian Production in Teotihuacan. In *Teotihuacan: Nuevos Datos, Nuevas Síntesis, Nuevos Problemas*, edited by E. McClung de Tapia and E. C. Rattray, pp. 429–450. Universidad Nacional Autónoma de México, Mexico.
1992 Tlailotlacan, a Zapotec Enclave. In *Art, Ideology, and the City of Teotihuacan*, edited by J. C. Berlo, pp. 59–88. Dumbarton Oaks Research Library and Collection, Washington, D.C.

Speth, J. D., and S. L. Scott
1989 Horticulture and Large-Mammal Hunting: The Role of Resource Depletion and the Constraints of Time and Labor. In *Farmers as Hunters: The Implications of Sedentism*, edited by S. Kent, pp. 71–77. Cambridge University Press, England.

Spielmann, K. A.
1998 Ritual Influences on the Development of Rio Grande Glaze A Ceramics. In *Pueblo IV Migration*

Community Reorganization, edited by K. A. Spielmann. Anthropological Research Paper, Arizona State University, Tempe. In press.

Spurr, K., and K. Hays-Gilpin
1996   New Evidence for Early Basketmaker III Ceramics from the Kayenta Area. Paper presented at the 69th annual Pecos Conference, Flagstaff, Arizona.

Stahl, A. B.
1989   Plant-Food Processing: Implications for Dietary Quality. In *Foraging and Farming: The Evolution of Plant Exploitation*, edited by D. R. Harris and G. C. Hillman, pp. 171–194. Unwin Hyman, London.

Stanislawski, M. B., and B. B. Stanislawski
1978   Hopi and Hopi-Tewa Ceramic Tradition Networks. In *The Spatial Organisation of Culture*, edited by I. Hodder, pp. 61–76. Duckworth, London.

Stark, B. L.
1975   Excavaciones en los Manglares del Papaloapan y un Estilo de Volutas de Patarata. *Boletin del Instituto Nacional de Antropologia e Historia* 14:45–50.
1977   *Prehistoric Ecology at Patarata 52, Veracruz, Mexico: Adaptation to the Mangrove Swamp*. Vanderbilt University Publications in Anthropology No. 18. Nashville, Tennessee.
1985   Archaeological Identification of Pottery Production Locations: Ethnoarchaeology and Archaeological Data from Mesoamerica. In *Decoding Prehistoric Ceramics*, edited by B. A. Nelson, pp. 158–194. Southern Illinois University Press, Carbondale.
1989   *Patarata Pottery: Classic Period Ceramics of the South-central Gulf Coast, Veracruz, Mexico*. Anthropological Papers of the University of Arizona No. 51. Tucson.
1990   The Gulf Coast and the Central Highlands of Mexico: Alternative Models for Interaction. In *Research in Economic Anthropology*, vol. 12, edited by B. L. Isaac, pp. 243–285. JAI Press, Inc. Greenwich, Connecticut.
1995a   Problems in the Analysis of Standardization and Specialization in Pottery. In *Ceramic Production in the American Southwest*, edited by B. J. Mills and P. L. Crown, pp. 231–267. University of Arizona Press, Tucson.
1995b   Introducción a la Alfarería del Postclásico en la Mixtequilla, Sur-Central de Veracruz. *Arqueología* 13–14:17–36. Instituto Nacional de Antropología e Historia, Mexico, D.F.
1997a   Estilos de Volutas en el Período Clásico. In *Rutas de Intercambio en Mesoamérica*, edited by E. C. Rattray. III Coloquio Pedro Bosch-Gimpera. Universidad Nacional Autónoma de México. Mexico, D.F. In press.
1997b   Gulf Lowland Styles and Political Geography in Ancient Veracruz. In *Olmec to Aztec: Settlement Pattern Research in the Ancient Gulf Lowlands*, edited by B. L. Stark and P. J. Arnold III, pp. 278–309. University of Arizona Press, Tucson.
1997c   (editor) *Classic Period Mixtequilla, Veracruz, Mexico: Diachronic Insights from Residential Investigations*. Institute for Mesoamerican Studies, State University of New York at Albány. In press.

Stark, B. L., and P. J. Arnold III
1997   Introduction to the Archaeology of the Gulf Lowlands. In *Olmec to Aztec: Settlement Patterns in the Ancient Gulf Lowlands*, edited by B. L. Stark and P. J. Arnold III. University of Arizona Press, Tucson.

Stark, B. L., and B. A. Hall
1993   Hierarchical Social Differentiation among Late to Terminal Classic Residential Locations in La Mixtequilla, Veracruz, Mexico. In *Household, Compound, and Residence: Studies of Prehispanic Domestic Units in Western Mesoamerica*, edited by R. S. Santley and K. G. Hirth, pp. 249–273. CRC Press, Boca Raton, Florida.

Stark, B. L., and L. Heller
1991   Cerro de las Mesas Revisited: Survey in 1984–85. In *Settlement*

Archaeology of Cerro de las Mesas, Veracruz, Mexico, edited by Barbara L. Stark, pp. 1–25. Monograph 34, Institute of Archaeology, University of California, Los Angeles.

Stark, B. L., and J. T. Hepworth
1982 A Diversity Index Approach to Analysis of Standardization in Prehistoric Pottery. In *Computer Applications in Archaeology*, edited by S. Laflin, pp. 87–104. University of Birmingham, England.

Stein, B.
1989 *Vijayanagara*. Cambridge University Press, England.

Stein, G., and M. J. Blackman
1993 The Organizational Context of Specialized Craft Production in Early Mesoamerican States. *Research in Economic Anthropology* 14:29–59.

Stevens, S. S.
1950 Introduction: A Definition of Communication. *The Journal of the Acoustical Society of America* 22:689–697.

Stevenson, M. C.
1904 *The Zuni Indians: Their Mythology, Esoteric Fraternities, and Ceremonies*. Twenty-third Annual Report of the Bureau of American Ethnology, Smithsonian Institution, 1901–1902. U.S. Government Printing Office, Washington, D.C.

Steward, J. H.
1955 *Theory of Culture Change*. University of Illinois Press, Urbana.

Stiger, M. A.
1979 Mesa Verde Subsistence Patterns from Basketmaker to Pueblo III. *Kiva* 44:133–144.

Stoltman, J. B.
1989 A Quantitative Approach to the Petrographic Analysis of Ceramic Thin Sections. *American Antiquity* 54:147–160.
1991 Ceramic Petrography as Technique for Documenting Cultural Interaction: An Example from the Upper Mississippi Valley. *American Antiquity* 56:103–120.

Subrahmanyam, S.
1990 *The Political Economy of Commerce: Southern India, 1500–1650*. Cambridge University Press, England.

Sullivan, A. P.
1978 Inference and Evidence in Archaeology: A discussion of the Conceptual Problems. In *Advances in Archaeological Method and Theory*, vol. 1, edited by M. B. Schiffer, pp. 183–222. Academic Press, New York.
1988 Prehistoric Southwestern Ceramic Manufacture: The Limitations of Current Evidence. *American Antiquity* 53:23–35.

Tagg, M. D.
1996 Early Cultigens from Fresnal Shelter, Southeastern New Mexico. *American Antiquity* 61:311–324.

Tani, M.
1994 Why Should More Pots Break in Larger Households? Mechanism Underlying Population Estimates from Ceramics. In *Kalinga Ethnoarchaeology*, edited by W. A. Longacre and J. M. Skibo, pp. 51–70. Smithsonian Institution Press, Washington, D.C.

Thapar, R.
1966 *A History of India 1*. Penguin Books, Middlesex, England.

Thomas, G. V.
1995 The Role of Drawing Strategies and Skills. In *Drawing and Looking*, edited by C. Lange-Kuttner and G. V. Thomas, pp. 107–122. Harvester Wheatsheaf, New York.

Thomas, J.
1993a Discourse, Totalization and 'the Neolithic.' In *Interpretative Archaeology*, edited by C. Tilley, pp. 357–394. Berg, Providence, Rhode Island.
1993b The Hermeneutics of Megalithic Space. In *Interpretative Archaeology*, edited by C. Tilley, pp. 73–97. Berg, Providence, Rhode Island.
1996 *Time, Culture and Identity*. Routledge, London.

Thompson, R. A., and G. B. Thompson
1974 *A Preliminary Report of Excavations in the Grand Canyon National Monument, Sites: GC-670, GC-663*. Report prepared for the National Park Service, Southern Utah State College.

Thompson, R. H.
1958 *Modern Yucatecan Mayan Pottery*

Making. Memoirs of the Society for American Archaeology, No. 15.

Tilley, C.
1990   (editor) *Reading Material Culture: Structuralism, Hermeneutics, and Post-Structuralism.* Basil Blackwell, London.
1991   *Material Culture and Text: The Art of Ambiguity.* Routledge, London.
1993   (editor) *Interpretative Archaeology.* Berg, Providence, Rhode Island.

Tite, M. S.
1995   Summary of Comments of Participants at the Summing-Up Session of the Lund Workshop. In "The Aim of Laboratory Analyses of Ceramics in Archaeology," edited by A. Lindahl and O. Stilborg. *Konferenser* 34:171–172.

Toll, H. W.
1981   Ceramic Comparisons Concerning Redistribution in Chaco Canyon, New Mexico. In *Production and Distribution: A Ceramic Viewpoint,* edited by H. Howard and E. L. Morris, pp. 83–121. British Archaeological Reports International Series 120, Oxford, England.
1984   Trends in Ceramic Import and Distribution in Chaco Canyon. In *Recent Research on Chaco Prehistory,* edited by W. J. Judge and J. D. Schelberg, pp. 115–135. Reports of the Chaco Center No. 8. Division of Cultural Research, National Park Service. Albuquerque, New Mexico.
1985   *Pottery, Production, Public Architecture, and the Chaco Anasazi System.* Unpublished Ph.D. dissertation, Department of Anthropology, University of Colorado, Boulder.
1991   Material Distributions and Exchange in the Chaco System. In *Chaco and Hohokam,* edited by P. L. Crown and W. J. Judge, pp. 77–107. School of American Research Press, Santa Fe, New Mexico.

Toll, H. W., E. Blinman, and C. D. Wilson
1992   Chaco in the Context of Ceramic Regional Systems. In *Anasazi Regional Organization and the Chaco System,* edited by D. E. Doyel, pp. 147–157. Maxwell Museum of Anthropology Anthropological Papers No. 5. Albuquerque, New Mexico.

Toll, H. W., and P. J. McKenna
1987   The Ceramography of Pueblo Alto. In *Artifactual and Biological Analyses, Investigations at the Pueblo Alto Complex, Chaco Canyon, New Mexico, 1975–1979,* vol. 3, no. 1, edited by F. J. Mathien and T. C. Windes, pp. 19–230. Publications in Archeology No. 18F, National Park Service, Santa Fe, New Mexico.

Toll, H. W., T. C. Windes, and P. J. McKenna
1980   Late Ceramic Patterns in Chaco Canyon: The Pragmatics of Modeling Ceramic Exchange. In *Models and Methods in Regional Exchange,* edited by R. E. Frey, pp. 95–117. SAA Papers No. 1. Society for American Archaeology, Washington, D.C.

Torrence, R., and S. E. van der Leeuw
1989   Introduction: What's New About Innovation? In *What's New? A Closer Look at the Process of Innovation,* edited by S. E. van der Leeuw and R. Torrence, pp. 1–15. Unwin Hyman, London.

Tosi, M.
1984   The Notion of Craft Specialization and its Representation in the Archaeological Record of Early States in the Turanian Basin. In *Marxist Perspectives in Archaeology,* edited by M. Spriggs, pp. 22–52. Cambridge University Press, England.

Trager, G. L.
1958   Paralanguage: A First Approximation. *Studies in Linguistics* 13(1–2):1–12.

Trostel, B.
1994   Household Pots and Possessions: An Ethnoarchaeological Study of Material Goods and Wealth. In *Kalinga Ethnoarchaeology,* edited by W. A. Longacre and J. M. Skibo, pp. 209–224. Smithsonian Institution Press, Washington, D.C.

Trudgill, P.
1983   *Sociolinguistics: An Introduction to Language and Society.* Penguin, Harmondsworth, England.

Tuohy, D. R., and A. J. Dansie
1990   (editors) *Hunter-Gatherer Pottery of the Far West.* Anthropology Papers No. 23, Nevada State Museum, Carsen City.

Turner, C. G., and L. Lofgren
  1966 Household Size of Prehistoric Western Pueblo Indians. *Southwestern Journal of Anthropology* 22:117–132.

Turner, M. H.
  1992 Style in Lapidary Technology: Identifying the Teotihuacan Lapidary Industry. In *Art, Ideology, and the City of Teotihuacan,* edited by J. C. Berlo, pp. 89–112. Dumbarton Oaks, Washington, D.C.

Ucko, P. J.
  1989 Foreword. In *What's New? A Closer Look at the Process of Innovation,* edited by S. E. van der Leeuw and R. Torrence, pp. ix–xiv. Unwin Hyman, London.

Umberger, E., and C. F. Klein
  1993 Aztec Art and Imperial Expansion. In *Latin American Horizons,* edited by D. S. Rice, pp. 295–336. Dumbarton Oaks Research Library and Collection, Washington, D.C.

Underhill, A. P.
  1991 Pottery Production in Chiefdoms: The Longshan Period in Northern China. *World Archaeology* 23(1):12–27.

Underhill, R.
  1945 *Pueblo Crafts.* Bureau of Indian Affairs, Department of the Interior. Phoenix Press.

van der Leeuw, S. E.
  1976 *Studies in the Technology of Ancient Pottery.* Organization for the Advancement of Pure Research, Amsterdam.
  1977 Towards a Study of the Economics of Pottery Making. In *Ex Horreo,* edited by B. L. van Beek, R. W. Brandt and W. Groenman-van Waateringe, pp. 68–76. Albert Egges van Giffen Instituut voor Prae- en Protohistoire, Univeristy of Amsterdam, Amsterdam.
  1989 Risk, Perception, Innovation. In *What's New? A Closer Look at the Process of Innovation,* edited by S. E. van der Leeuw and R. Torrence, pp. 300–329. Unwin Hyman, London.
  1991 Variation, Variability, and Explanation in Pottery Studies. In *Ceramic Ethnoarchaeology,* edited by W. A. Longacre, pp. 11–39. University of Arizona Press, Tucson.

Van Toller, S., and G. H. Dodd
  1992 (editors) *Fragrance: The Psychology and Biology of Perfume.* Elsevier, London.

van Zelst, L.
  1991 Archaeometry: The Perspective of an Administrator. In *The Ceramic Legacy of Anna O. Shepard,* edited by R. L. Bishop and F. W. Lange, pp. 346–357. University of Colorado Press, Niwot.

Vandiver, P., O. Soffer, B. Klima, and J. Svoboda
  1989 The Origins of Ceramic Technology at Dolní Věstonice, Czechoslovakia. *Science* 246:1002–1008.

Veblen, T.
  1953 *The Theory of the Working of the Leisure Class: An Economic Study of Institutions.* The New American Library, New York.

Vidale, M.
  1989 Specialized Producers and Urban elites: On the Role of Craft Production in Mature Indus Urban Contexts. In *Old Problems, New Perspectives in the Archaeology of South Asia,* edited by J. M. Kenoyer, pp. 145–156. University of Wisconsin, Madison.

Vitelli, K. D.
  1989 Were Pots First Made for Foods? Doubts from Franchthi. *World Archaeology* 21:17–29.
  1993 *Franchthi Neolithic Pottery,* vol. 1, *Classification and Ceramic Phases 1 and 2.* Excavations at Franchthi Cave, Greece, Fascicle 8. Indiana University Press, Bloomington.
  1995 Pots, Potters, and the Shaping of Greek Neolithic Society. In *The Emergence of Pottery: Technology and Innovation in Ancient Societies,* edited by W. K. Barnett and J. W. Hoopes, pp. 55–63. Smithsonian Institution Press, Washington, D.C.
  1997 Inferring Firing Procedures from Sherds: Early Greek Kilns. In *Prehistory and History of Ceramic Kilns,* edited by P. M. Rice and W. D. Kingery, pp. 21–40. American Ceramics Society, Westerville, Ohio.

Vivian, G., and T. W. Mathews
1965 *Kin Kletso, A Pueblo III Community in Chaco Canyon.* Southwestern Monuments Association, Technical Series 6. Globe, Arizona.

Vivian, R. G.
1990 *The Chacoan Prehistory of the San Juan Basin.* Academic Press, Inc., San Diego, California.

von Winning, H.
1971 Relief Decorated Pottery from Central Veracruz, Mexico: Addenda. *Ethnos* 36(1–4):38–51.
1987 *La Iconografía de Teotihuacan, los Dioses y los Signos.* 2 vols. Universidad Nacional Autónoma de México, D.F.

Wade, E. L., and L. S. McChesney
1981 *Historic Hopi Ceramics: The Thomas V. Keam Collection of the Peabody Museum of Archaeology and Ethnology.* Peabody Museum Press, Harvard University, Cambridge, Massachusetts.

Wailes, B.
1996 (editor) *Craft Specialization and Social Evolution: In Memory of V. Gordon Childe.* University Museum of Archaeology and Anthropology, University of Pennsylvania, Philadelphia.

Walker, W. H.
1995 Ceremonial Trash? In *Expanding Archaeology,* edited by J. M. Skibo, W. H. Walker, and A. E. Nielsen, pp. 67–79. University of Utah Press, Salt Lake City.
1996 Ritual Deposits: Another Perspective. In *River of Change: Prehistory of the Middle Little Colorado River Valley, Arizona,* edited by C. Adams, pp. 75–91. Arizona State Museum Archaeological Series No. 185, Tucson.

Walker, W. H., and V. LaMotta
1995 Life-Histories as Units of Analysis. Paper presented at the 60th Annual Meeting of the Society for American Archaeology, Minneapolis, Minnesota.

Walker, W. H., J. M. Skibo, and A. E. Nielsen
1995 Introduction: Expanding Archaeology. In *Expanding Archaeology,* edited by J. M. Skibo, W. H. Walker,

and A. E. Nielsen, pp. 1–12. University of Utah Press, Salt Lake City.

Warren, A. H.
1967 Petrographic Analyses of Pottery and Lithics. In *An Archaeological Survey of the Chuska Valley and the Chaco Plateau, New Mexico,* by A. H. Harris, J. Schoenwetter, and A. H. Warren, pp. 104–144. Museum of New Mexico Research Records No. 4. Santa Fe.
1976 Technological Studies of the Pottery of Chaco Canyon. Unpublished manuscript on file, Division of Cultural Research, National Park Service, Albuquerque, New Mexico.

Watson, P. J., and M. C. Kennedy
1991 The Development of Horticulture in the Eastern Woodlands of North America: Women's Role. In *Engendering Archaeology. Women and Prehistory,* edited by J. M. Gero and M. W. Conkey, pp. 255–275. Basil Blackwell, Ltd., Oxford, England.

Webster, D. L., and N. Gonlin
1988 Household Remains of the Humblest Maya. *Journal of Field Archaeology* 15:169–190.

Wendorf, F.
1950 The Flattop Site in the Petrified Forest National Monument. *Plateau* 22:43–51.
1953 *Archaeological Studies in the Petrified Forest National Monument.* Museum of Northern Arizona, Bulletin 27, Flagstaff.

Whallon, R.
1982 Variables and Dimensions: The Critical Step in Quantitative Typology. In *Essays in Archaeological Typology,* edited by R. Whallon and J. A. Brown, pp. 127–161. Center for American Archaeology Press, Evanston, Illinois.

White, L. A.
1932 *The Acoma Indians.* 47th Annual Report of the Bureau of American Ethnology, Smithsonian Institution, Washington, D.C.

Whitley, D. S.
1992 Prehistory and Post-Positivist Science: A Prolegomenon to Cognitive Archaeology. *Archaeological Method and Theory* 4:57–100.

Widmer, R. J.
1991 Lapidary Craft Specialization at Teotihuacan: Implications for Community Structure at 33:S3W1 and Economic Organization in the City. *Ancient Mesoamerica* 2:131–147.

Wiessner, P.
1984 Reconsidering the Behavioral Basis for Style: A Case Study among the Kalahari San. *Journal of Anthropological Archaeology* 3:190–234.

Wilk, R. R., and R. McC. Netting
1984 Households: Changing Forms and Functions. In *Households: Comparative and Historical Studies of the Domestic Group,* edited by R. McC. Netting, R. R. Wilk, and E. J. Arnould, pp. 1–28. University of California Press, Berkeley.

Williams, H., F. J. Turner, and C. M. Gilbert
1954 *Petrography, An Introduction to the Study of Rocks in Thin Sections.* W. H. Freeman and Co., San Francisco, California.

Willey, G. R., and P. Phillips
1958 *Method and Theory in American Archaeology.* University of Chicago Press, Chicago.

Wills, W. H.
1988 *Early Prehistoric Agriculture in the American Southwest.* University of Washington Press, Seattle.

Wilson, B., and J. Ligtvoet
1992 Across Time and Cultures: Stylistic Changes in the Drawings of Dutch Children. In *Drawing Research and Development,* edited by D. Thistlewood. Longman, London.

Wilson, B., and M. Wilson
1984 Children's Drawings in Egypt: Cultural Style Acquisition as Graphic Development. *Visual Arts Research* 10:13–26.

Wilson, C. D.
1989 Sambrito "Brown" from Site LA 4169, a Description and Evaluation. *Pottery Southwest* 6:4–5.

Wilson, C. D., and E. Blinman
1993 *Upper San Juan Region Pottery Technology.* Office of Archaeological Studies, Archaeology Notes 80. Museum of New Mexico, Santa Fe.

1994 Early Anasazi Ceramics and the Basketmaker Tradition. In *Proceedings of the Anasazi Symposium 1991,* compiled by A. Hutchinson and J. E. Smith, pp. 199–211. Mesa Verde Museum Association, Mesa Verde, Colorado.

1995 Changing Specialization of White Ware Manufacture in the Northern San Juan Region. In *Ceramic Production in the American Southwest,* edited by B. J. Mills and P. L. Crown, pp. 63–87. University of Arizona Press, Tucson.

Wilson, C. D., E. Blinman, J. M. Skibo, and M. B. Schiffer
1996 The Designing of Southwestern Pottery: A Technological and Experimental Approach. In *Interpreting Southwestern Diversity: Underlying Principles and Overarching Patterns,* edited by P. R. Fish, and J. J. Reid, pp. 249–256. Arizona State University, Tempe.

Wilson, P. J.
1988 *The Domestication of the Human Species.* Yale University Press, New Haven, Connecticut.

Windes, T. C.
1977 Typology and Technology of Anasazi Ceramics. In *Settlement and Subsistence Along the Lower Chaco River: The CGP Survey,* edited by C. A. Reher, pp. 279–370. University of New Mexico Press, Albuquerque.

1984a A View of the Cibola Whiteware from Chaco Canyon. In *Regional Analysis of Prehistoric Ceramic Variation: Contemporary Studies of the Cibola Whitewares,* edited by A. P. Sullivan and J. L. Hantman, pp. 94–119. Arizona State University Anthropological Research Papers No. 31. Phoenix.

1984b A New Look at Population in Chaco Canyon. In *Recent Research on Chaco Prehistory,* edited by W. J. Judge and J. D. Schelberg, pp. 75–87. Reports of the Chaco Center No. 8. Division of Cultural Research, National Park Service. Albuquerque, New Mexico.

1985 Chaco-McElmo Black-on-White from Chaco Canyon with an Emphasis on the Pueblo del Arroyo Collection. In *Prehistory and History in the Southwest: Collected Pa-*

pers in Honor of Alden C. Hayes, edited by N. Fox, pp. 19–42. Papers of the Archaeological Society of New Mexico 11, Albuquerque.

Windes, T. C., and D. Ford
1996   The Chaco Wood Project: The Chronometric Reappraisal of Pueblo Bonito. *American Antiquity* 61:295–310.

Winter, J. C.
1993   Corn across the Southwest (with sections by Kathleen Tabaha and Karina Dawson). In *Across the Colorado Plateau: Anthropological Studies for the Transwestern Pipeline Expansion Project*, vol. 15, *Subsistence and Environment*, by Jannifer W. Gish, Julia E. Hammet, Marie E. Brown, Pamela McBride, Joseph C. Winter, Kenneth L. Brown, John J. Ponczynski, and Jeanne L. DeLanois, pp. 521–648. Office of Contract Archeology and Maxwell Museum of Anthropology, University of New Mexico, Albuquerque.

Winter, M. C.
1974   Residential Patterns at Monte Albán, Oaxaca, Mexico. *Science* 186:981–987.
1995   (editor) *Entierros Humanos de Monte Albán: Dos Estudios*. Centro INAH, Oaxaca, Mexico.

Wobst, H. M.
1977   Stylistic Behavior and Information Exchange. In *Papers for the Director: Research Essays in Honor of James B. Griffin*, edited by C. E. Cleland, pp. 317–334. Anthropo-

logical Papers No. 61, University of Michigan, Museum of Anthropology, Ann Arbor.

Wyckoff, L. L.
1990   *Designs and Factions: Politics, Religion, and Ceramics on the Hopi Third Mesa*. University of New Mexico Press, Albuquerque.

Wylie, A.
1985   The Reaction against Analogy. In *Advances in Archaeological Method and Theory*, vol. 8, edited by M. B. Schiffer, pp. 63–111. Academic Press, Orlando, Florida.
1992   The Interplay of Evidential Constraints and Political Interests: Recent Archaeological Research on Gender. *American Antiquity* 57:15–35.
1993   A Proliferation of New Archaeologies: "Beyond Objectivism and Relativism." In *Archaeological Theory: Who Sets the Agenda?*, edited by N. Yoffee and A. Sherratt, pp. 20–26. Cambridge University Press, England.

Young, D. E., and R. Bonnichsen
1984   *Understanding Stone Tools: A Cognitive Approach*. Center for the Study of Early Man, University of Maine at Orono.

Zedeño, M. N.
1994   *Sourcing Prehistoric Ceramics at Chodistaas Pueblo, Arizona: The Circulation of People and Pots in the Grasshopper Region*. Anthropological Papers of the University of Arizona No. 58. University of Arizona Press, Tucson.

Index

Contributors

Dean E. Arnold is a professor of anthropology at Wheaton College and was a recipient of the Society for American Archaeology Award for Excellence in Ceramic Research (1996). He has done extensive ethnoarchaeological research in both Central and South America, and among his publications are *Ceramic Theory and Cultural Process* (1985) and *Ecology of Ceramic Production in an Andean Community* (1993).

Philip J. Arnold III is an associate professor of anthropology at Loyola University and he has conducted ethnoarchaeological and archaeological research in Mesoamerica. His publications include *Domestic Ceramic Production and Spatial Organization: A Mexican Case Study in Ethnoarchaeology* (1991) and *Olmec to Aztec: Settlement Patterns in the Ancient Gulf Lowlands* (with B. Stark) (1997).

Eric Blinman is the assistant director of the Office of Archaeological Studies at the Museum of New Mexico, Santa Fe, and the editor of *Pottery Southwest*. He is a potter, experimental archaeologist, and much of his research is done in the Four Corners region of the Southwestern United States. His publications include "Anasazi Pottery—Evolution of a Technology," *Expedition Magazine* (1993), and "Ceramic Perspectives on Northern Anasazi Exchange," in *The American Southwest and Mesoamerica* (1993), edited by J. E. Ericson, and T. G. Baugh.

Patricia L. Crown is a professor of anthropology at the University of New Mexico and was the 1995 recipient of the Society for American Archaeology Award for Excellence in Ceramic Research. Her research focuses on the prehistoric Southwestern United States, and her most recent work is *Ceramics and Ideology: Salado Polychrome Pottery* (1994), and *Ceramic Production in the American Southwest* (with B. Mills) (1995).

Gary M. Feinman is a professor of anthropology at the University of Wisconsin-Madison. He has worked in Mesoamerica, the Southwestern United States, and north China. He is the editor of the *Journal of Archaeological Research*, *Latin American Antiquity*, and the book series Fundamental Issues In Archaeology. Among his publications are *Ancient Mesoamerica: A Comparison of Change in Three Regions*, 2d edition (with R. E. Blanton, S. A. Kowalewski, and L. M. Finsten) (1993), and "At the Margins of the Monte Alban State: Settlement Patterns in the Ejutla Valley, Oaxaca, Mexico" (with L.M. Nicholas) *Latin American Antiquity* (1990).

William A. Longacre is a professor of anthropology and Riecker Chair at the University of Arizona and he was also a recipient of the Society for American Archaeology Award for Excellence in Ceramic Research (1995). He has done work in the prehistoric Southwestern United States, but now spends most of his time doing ethnoarchaeology in the Philippines. His most recent books are *Ce-*

ramic Ethnoarchaeology (1991) and *Kalinga Ethnoarchaeology* (with J. M. Skibo) (1994).

Barbara J. Mills is an associate professor of anthropology and the director of the archaeological field school at the University of Arizona. She has done extensive field and laboratory research in the Southwestern United States. Her publications include *Ceramic Production in the American Southwest* (with P. L. Crown) (1995).

Michael Brian Schiffer is a professor of anthropology at the University of Arizona and the director of the Laboratory of Traditional Technology. His current interests are archaeological method and theory and modern material culture change. Among his publications are *Behavioral Archaeology: First Principles* (1995), and *Taking Charge: The Electric Automobile in America* (1994).

Carla M. Sinopoli is an associate professor of anthropology at the University of Michigan and Asian archaeology curator at the University of Michigan Museum of Anthropology. Much of her research has focused on the Indian city of Vijayanagara and her publications include *Approaches to Archaeological Ceramics* (1991).

James M. Skibo is an associate professor of anthropology at Illinois State University. He has done ethnoarchaeological, experimental and prehistoric research in the Philippines and North America. Among his publications are *Expanding Archaeology* (with

W. Walker and A. Nielsen) (1995), *Kalinga Ethnoarchaeology* (with W.A. Longacre) (1994), and *Pottery Function* (1992).

Barbara L. Stark is a professor of anthropology and chair of the department at Arizona State University. Her research focuses on Mesoamerica and her publications include *Patarata Pottery: Classic Period Ceramics of the South-Central Gulf Coast, Veracruz, Mexico* (1989), and *Olmec to Aztec: Settlement Pattern Research in the Ancient Gulf Lowlands* (with P. J. Arnold) (1997).

James B. Stoltman is a professor of anthropology at the University of Wisconsin-Madison. His research interests are primarily in the Midwestern and Southeastern United States, but his recent focus on petrographic analysis has expanded his area of expertise to the Southwestern United States. Among his recent publications are "A Quantitative Approach to the Petrographic Analysis of Ceramic Thin Sections," *American Antiquity* (1989) and "Ceramic Petrography as Technique for Documenting Cultural Interaction," *American Antiquity* (1991).

Karen D. Vitelli is a professor of anthropology at Indiana University. She is an accomplished potter and experimental archaeologist, and most of her research has focused on the Greek Neolithic and the excavations of Franchthi Cave. Her publications include *Franchthi Neolithic Pottery* (1993).